MORAL EDUCATION

Moral EDUCATION

A HANDBOOK

VOLUME 2
M–Z

Edited by

F. Clark Power,
Ronald J. Nuzzi,
Darcia Narvaez,
Daniel K. Lapsley, and
Thomas C. Hunt

Westport, Connecticut
London

Library of Congress Cataloging-in-Publication Data

Moral education : a handbook / edited by F. Clark Power . . . [et al.].
    v. cm.
Includes bibliographical references and index.
ISBN-13: 978–0–313–33647–8 (set : alk. paper)
ISBN-13: 978–0–313–34646–0 (v. 1 : alk. paper)
ISBN-13: 978–0–313–34648–4 (v. 2 : alk. paper)
1. Moral education—Handbooks, manuals, etc. I. Power, F. Clark.
LC268.M667 2008
370.11′4—dc22   2007033113

British Library Cataloguing in Publication Data is available.

Library of Congress Catalog Card Number: 2007033113
ISBN-13: 978–0–313–33647–8 (set)
        978–0–313–34646–0 (vol. 1)
        978–0–313–34648–4 (vol. 2)

First published in 2008

Praeger Publishers, 88 Post Road West, Westport, CT 06881
An imprint of Greenwood Publishing Group, Inc.
www.praeger.com

Printed in the United States of America

The paper used in this book complies with the
Permanent Paper Standard issued by the National
Information Standards Organization (Z39.48–1984).

10 9 8 7 6 5 4 3 2 1

Contents

List of Entries

M

Marxist Interpretation of Moral Development

The Marxist interpretation of moral development is controversial, due to the presence of different currents in Marx's thought and to the complexity of the idea of moral development. There are chiefly three Marxist interpretations of moral development, each of which tracks a distinct conception of moral development: (1) a perfectionist humanism that is most prominent in Marx's early work, (2) a critique of morality that is closely connected with Marx's "scientific socialism," and (3) a moral egalitarianism that supports Marx's critique of capitalist exploitation and vision of socialism. The cogency of these respective Marxist interpretations of moral development and their consistency with one another have been, and remain, matters of controversy and intense philosophical and scholarly debate.

Marx's earliest thought develops within the ambit of "young" or "left" Hegelianism. One of the most important works of this period is his *Economic and Philosophical Manuscripts* (1844) where he espouses a naturalistic humanism grounded in the distinctive social and productive capacities of human beings. This humanism describes an ideal of the free and harmonious development of human social and productive capacities in conditions of full equality. In opposition to this ideal, the system of private property produces forms of alienation in which people are separated and estranged from the products of their labor, their laboring activities, their fellow human beings, and the natural world. Marx somewhat speculatively envisions communism as a form of human community wherein these various separations and estrangements are transcended and the rich development of each individual is achieved in concert with the free association of all. In this humanistic outlook there is plainly a conception of moral development in the largest sense understood in terms of the full flowering of man's individual and social powers. As some interpreters have maintained, this early humanism is reminiscent of Aristotle's perfectionism. Because its locus is the realization of the specific human capacity for free social labor in conditions of equality, Marx's perfectionism differs from Aristotle's in its content, setting, and psychological basis. Yet it is structurally similar in its assumption that the highest human good consists in the full realization of distinctive human capacities within a cooperative social order.

Marx's thought shifts in the *German Ideology* (1845) and subsequent writings, where he comes to view human history through the prism of developing productive forces, modes of production, and class struggle. Marx thinks of this new perspective as properly scientific in its support of a research program into the history and political economy of capitalism, one built around the concepts of class, mode of production, economic structure, productive force, and political superstructure. He also believes that this perspective supports a distinctive revolutionary socialist politics centered on the collective agency of the emerging industrial working class. The exact nature of this "scientific socialism," the place of moral and ethical evaluation within it, and its relation to Marx's humanism are all matters of dispute. Here we find the second and third of the Marxist interpretations of moral development mentioned above. These interpretations can be fruitfully approached under the rubric of what Steven Lukes has called the "paradox of Marxism and morality." This paradox is that Marxism seems to have theoretically motivated reasons for both rejecting and embracing moral notions. First, freestanding appeals to the moral superiority of socialism (in the fashion of utopian socialism) are thought to be politically inadequate because they neglect the collective class agency by which socialism is to be achieved. Second, notions of justice and right correspond to underlying social and economic interests (rather than vice versa) and therefore are necessarily ideological and thus unsuited to revolutionary politics. Third, appeals to morality and justice are unnecessary because the future development of productive forces eliminates the material basis of social conflict and therefore renders morality and justice as traditionally conceived superfluous. These Marxist arguments in rejection of morality have been typically joined with a kind of political consequentialism. In its more positive forms this consequentialism has focused not just on the political development of the working class but also on its social and cultural development through measures such as free public schools, the elimination of child labor, the shortening of the working day, and the establishment of educational programs for workers. But in its cruder forms it has led to dubious positions on the relation of means and ends in moral reasoning and on the unimportance of "bourgeois justice and rights," positions that arguably have had disastrous real world consequences.

On the other hand, Marx does not simply seek to describe in a morally neutral voice how capitalism works, but is a forceful critic who advocates its replacement. That critique certainly includes drawing attention to capitalism's economic faults and irrationalities, but quite significantly also includes the idea that capitalism is inherently exploitative, and to that extent, it is a moral critique. There is disagreement about how this critique should be elaborated, but it is difficult to resist the idea that it rests on some notion of moral equality. In a complementary fashion, Marx's socialist advocacy stresses the importance of satisfying human needs in all their diversity, and thus relies upon a principle of need satisfaction that is similarly egalitarian in scope and content. In light of the apparent collapse of scientific socialism, some contemporary philosophers sympathetic to this latent moral egalitarianism in Marx's critique of exploitation and advocacy of socialism have sought common ground with contemporary liberal egalitarian theories of social justice. Whether such common ground can be found is a matter of controversy, about which no consensus has yet to emerge.

Further Reading: Cohen, M., Nagel, T., &d Scanlon, T. (Eds.). (1980). *Marx, justice, and history.* Princeton: Princeton University Press. Geras, N. (1993). Bringing Marx to justice: An addendum and rejoinder. *The New Left Review, 195,* 37–69. Kymlicka, W. (2002). *Contemporary political philosophy* (2nd ed.). Oxford: Oxford University Press. Lukes, S. (1985). *Marxism and morality.*

Oxford: Oxford University Press. McLellan, D. (Ed.). (2000). *Karl Marx: Selected writings* (2nd ed.). Oxford: Oxford University Press.

Paul Warren

Maslow, Abraham

Abraham Maslow was born in Brooklyn, New York, in 1908. He was the oldest of seven children born to Russian Jewish immigrants, and his parents were committed to his academic success. Maslow studied law at the City College of New York and also at Cornell. He married Bertha Goodman while still an undergraduate at the City College, and later moved to Wisconsin to study psychology at the University of Wisconsin. His interest in human developmental psychology was strengthened by his graduate research with primate behavior. After receiving his doctorate in psychology in 1934, Maslow and his wife returned to New York, where he worked on research with E.L. Thorndike at Columbia University. In 1937 Maslow accepted a faculty position at Brooklyn College, where he would remain until 1951. He subsequently moved to Brandeis University where he served on the faculty until 1969. After several years of poor health, Abraham Maslow died of a heart attack on June 8, 1970.

Abraham Maslow founded a humanistic movement in psychology in the late 1950s that placed significant value on individuality, creativity, and personal freedom as essential factors contributing to mental health and general well-being. Along with his colleagues Rollo May and Carl Rogers, Maslow created a professional organization, the Association of Humanistic Psychology, whose members shared an appreciation of the worth and dignity of all persons. This humanistic movement was referred to as the "Third Wave" in psychology because its theoretical constructs varied so greatly from Freudian psychoanalysis and Skinnerian behaviorism, which were the two dominant trends in psychology during the 1950s.

Although Maslow did acknowledge his admiration of Freudian psychoanalysis, his own view of human nature varied greatly from Freud's. Maslow thought Freud's theory was unnecessarily pessimistic with respect to our human potential for decency and kindness. He disagreed strongly with Freud's contention that we are essentially selfish beings, with little real regard for others. Freud's view of human nature portrayed human potential as a fight to keep our baser instincts in check. Maslow, by contrast, believed that we are capable of becoming "fully human" through a process of self-actualization. Maslow conceded that we do not always show our most fully human side; indeed, we often act without dignity and respect toward our fellow brothers and sisters. But Maslow believed that such reactions were due to extenuating circumstances such as stress, pain, and the lack of basic physical needs such as food and shelter. Beneath those needs lay a core of decent and good human values, which could be brought to the surface when basic needs were met.

Maslow's commitment to the full development of human potential was centrally concerned with the psychological constructs of self-actualization and self-esteem (DeCarvalho, 1991). Unlike the psychoanalysts and behaviorists who rejected the notion of free will, Maslow placed strong value on an understanding of human life as both spiritual and intuitive. He studied the lives of persons he believed best exemplified the fullest account of human potential, such as Albert Einstein, Jane Addams, Eleanor Roosevelt, and Frederick Douglas (Maslow, 1954). This methodology represented a significant shift away from Freud, who studied mentally ill and neurotic people to formulate his theory of human nature, and B. F. Skinner, who had conducted most of his studies regarding human psychology with laboratory mice. Both Freud and Skinner had observed very little difference between the motivation of humans and animals, despite their respectively varied conclusions regarding the prognosis for optimal human development. By contrast, Maslow's studies signaled a humanistic approach to developmental psychology that regarded humans and animals as vastly different with respect to motivation theory.

Maslow's most renowned work in motivational theory is his development of a hierarchy of needs and information that culminated in the most fully human construct of self-actualization (DeCarvalho, 1991). At the lowest rung of his hierarchy were the most basic physiological needs such as food, water, sex, and sleep; these needs were not distinctly human insofar as they were shared with all living creatures. Beyond the basic physiological needs were safety needs such as the need to feel secure and protected from danger, and the need to have structure and order in one's daily interactions with the community.

The third rung of Maslow's hierarchy was the need for love and a sense of belongingness; the lack of satisfaction at this level of need would inevitably result in isolation and alienation of oneself from both family and society. The need for love and belongingness could be fulfilled by a combination of close friends, strong identification with group affiliations, intimate relationships, and a supportive family. However, Maslow believed that the lack of fulfillment at this level of the hierarchy was best evidenced by major social problems he identified as contributing to the "countercultural" movement in the 1960s.

The fourth rung of Maslow's hierarchy was the need for esteem, which has also been closely aligned with Erik Erikson's need for generativity and the desire to engage in creative and useful activities. Lack of fulfillment at this level would negatively impact one's self-concept as a responsible citizen and a productive member of society. Each of these four categories of needs was essential in order to achieve the highest level of human development, which Maslow called self-actualization (Bridges, 2004). The characteristics of the self-actualized person are myriad and include a resistance to acculturation, an acceptance of self and others, and a need for privacy. According to Maslow, persons who have achieved this highest level of personal self-actualization will exhibit a greater need in their lives for the following values:

1. truth, rather than dishonesty,
2. goodness, rather than evil,
3. beauty, rather than vulgarity,
4. unity and wholeness, rather than arbitrariness,
5. aliveness, rather than the mechanization of life,
6. uniqueness, rather than uniformity,
7. perfection and necessity, rather than sloppiness and inconsistency,
8. completion, rather than incompleteness,
9. justice and order, rather than injustice and lawlessness,
10. simplicity, rather than unnecessary complexity,
11. richness, rather than impoverishment,
12. effortlessness, rather than strain,
13. playfulness, rather than humorlessness,
14. self-sufficiency, rather than dependency, and
15. meaningfulness, rather than senselessness.

In addition to his substantial work in motivation theory, Maslow conducted the first American studies on human sexuality, several years before Alfred Kinsey. He interviewed women whom he labeled as high dominance or low dominance with respect to their sexual preferences. He defined "high dominance" as the possession of strong levels of aggression and self-confidence, and he found that high dominance women were mostly attracted to men who were highly masculine and self-assured (Maslow, 1954). Low dominance women were defined as strongly maternalistic and nurturing, and were attracted to men whom they described as kind and gentle and possessing a strong love for family values. The influence of Abraham Maslow's body of work continues to be of tremendous value for humanistic psychologists today.

Further Reading: Anderson, W.T. (Ed.). (1995). *The truth about the truth.* New York: J.P. Tarcher-Putnam. Bridges, W. (2004). *Transitions: Making sense of life's changes.* New York: De Capo Press. DeCarvalho, R. (1991). *The founders of humanistic psychology.* New York: Praeger. Maslow, A.H. (1954). *Motivation and personality.* New York: Harper & Bros. Polkinghorne, D.E. (1988). *Narrative knowing and the human sciences.* Albany, NY: SUNY Press.

Monalisa M. Mullins

May, Mark A.

Mark Arthur May (born August 12, 1891; died January 2, 1977) was a pioneer in the development of psychometric techniques and instruments for the measurement and evaluation of affective qualities such as character traits. With Hugh Hartshorne, May was lead investigator in the Character Education Inquiry (CEI), which conducted the majority of its investigations in 1925 and 1926 and was at the time the largest and most expensive educational research project in history. May was brought into the project for his knowledge of statistics and measurement, but he became, as an outcome of his involvement, an acknowledged expert on character education in general and on the use of propaganda in particular.

May received his A.B. degree from Maryville College in Tennessee in 1911, his Ph.B. from the University of Chicago in 1912, an M.A. from Columbia University in 1915, a Ph.D. from Columbia in 1917, and another M.A. from Yale in 1927. May served in the Army from 1917 to 1919, where he taught military psychology. From 1919 to 1927 he taught at Syracuse University, and from 1927 until 1960 was on the faculty at Yale University, where he served from 1935 to 1960 as director of the Institute of Human Relations, which had been founded in 1928 with a major grant from Rockefeller Foundation. (See *National Cyclopedia of American Biography,* 1981, vol. 60, p. 67.)

The Character Education Inquiry, sponsored in part by the Religious Education Association and the Rockefeller-funded Institute for Social and Religious Research, had as its ambitious goal the determination of the relationship between certain forms of education and the subsequent actions of the learners, especially with regard to how social relationships (including the peer group) influence moral behavior. (See Hartshorne & May, 1928.)

In the attempt to address these questions in a systematic and scientific manner, May, Hartshorne, and their team (advised by Edward Thorndike of Teachers College, Columbia University) developed a slew of new methods of educational data collection, measurement, and statistical analysis in an attempt to find out the answer to the basic question: whether the primary determinant of character was a general character factor, the accumulation of a set of ideal traits, or the aggregation of specific behaviors.

Before the CEI had concluded its work, more than 170,000 tests were given to more than 8,000 public and 2,500 private school students over three years. These tests were analyzed using the latest statistical techniques pioneered by Charles Spearman and Karl Pearson for factor analysis, a newly developed technique for determining from a large collection of measures which measures are most important. The researchers identified three major categories of factors influencing character: intellectual factors (prediction of the effects of certain choices, vocabulary, characterizations of hypothetical choices as right, wrong, or excusable) or what is most sensible; dynamic factors (attitudes, emotions, suggestibility); and performance factors (conduct such as lying, persistence, cooperation, and persistence). Under May's leadership, the raw results of the factor analysis were corrected for reliability and attenuation and were also enhanced through predictions of what the results would have been if tests had been replicated. Hartshorne and May were not shy about reporting their success. They claimed to have completely accounted for the character of a person by identifying all of the relevant factors.

While Hartshorne and May were able to claim to have fully accounted for moral conduct, and found much consistency in how children described their beliefs about morality, the study's most striking conclusion, and the one that was most picked up on by commentators, was that the children were observed to be quite inconsistent in how they reacted to the test batteries. The specific elements of the circumstance or situation were found to be more determinative of a child's behavior than anything within the person.

In other words, generalizable character traits do not exist. One cannot make useful predictions about whether a child will be "honest" or "dishonest" in future situations—it depends entirely upon the specific circumstances involved. There is no such thing, Hartshorne and May claimed, in transfer of learning about honesty. It is meaningless to talk about a "trait" of honesty, and even less significant to try to teach "honesty" to children. This finding became known as the doctrine of "situational specificity," which was widely reported at the time and continued to be cited in educational psychology texts into the twenty-first century, although with time most commentators moved away from strict adherence to situational specificity and adopted the perspective of social learning theory that the consistency of personal traits is likely to reflect the consistency of the learning environment.

Alongside the effects of its specific conclusions, the study seemed to undermine the widespread belief among educators that they understood what is meant by the term "character." The study nurtured seeds of doubt among researchers and policy makers about whether character could be effectively taught in the public schools as they were presently constituted. In any event, the Character Education Movement, which had flourished in the 1920s and early 1930s, seemed to fade away as schools and policy makers focused on other priorities. Leming (1997), however, argues that World War II, rather than the CEI, was the major cause of this decline). Researchers in moral education increasingly began focusing on the concept of personality instead of character, a concept that seems more neutral and less culturally specific.

After the CEI, Mark A. May went on to conduct a study of the ministry as a profession (May, 1934), in which he concluded that conflicts between traditional conceptions of the ministry and the contemporary needs of individuals and congregations were creating a confusion about what ministers should do and how they should be educated. May also wrote articles and books about education in a time of war and a psychological analysis of learning from films. May retired in 1960.

Further Reading: Hartshorne, H., & May, M. (1928). *Studies in the nature of character. Vol. I: Studies in deceit.* New York: MacMillan. Hartshorne, H., & May, M., with Shuttleworth, F. K. (1930a). *Studies in the nature of character. Vol. III: Studies in the organization of character.* New York: MacMillan. Hartshorne, H., & May, M. (1930b). A summary of the work of the Character Education Inquiry, Part I. *Religious Education, 25*(7), 607–19. Hartshorne, H., & May, M. (1930c). A summary of the work of the Character Education Inquiry, Part II. *Religious Education, 25*(8), 754–62. Leming, J. S. (1997). Research and practice in character education: A historical perspective. In A. Molnar (Ed.), *The construction of children's character* (pp. 31–44). Chicago: University of Illinois Press. May, M. A. (1928, February). What science offers on character education. In *Building character: Proceedings of the Mid-West conference on character development.* Chicago: University of Chicago Press. May, M. A. (1934). *The education of American ministers* (4 vols.). New York: Institute of Social and Religious Research. *National Cyclopedia of American Biography.* (1981). Volume 60. New York: James T. White and Company.

Craig A. Cunningham

Media Literacy

"Media literacy" is defined as the ability to produce, access, interpret, understand, critically evaluate, and effectively use print and electronic resources for communication and entertainment.

Many adolescents in the United States spend more time watching television and playing video games than they spend at school or with their guardians. Adults turn to print and electronic media resources for much of their information and as primary sources of entertainment. People of all ages are exposed to hundreds of suasory messages through media in schools, in the marketplaces, in offices, in homes, and throughout the community. Mass media are ubiquitous.

While there is controversy regarding the specific effects such wide exposure to mediated messages has on particular individuals, few deny its significance in the formation of character, values, dispositional traits, and ways of knowing. The stories, sounds, information, and images conveyed through mediated forms of communication significantly affect how people "take in" and respond to the world they inhabit.

Findings by the American Psychological Association, the American Medical Association, the American Association of Pediatrics (AAP), and the United States Surgeon General's Office, among others, have led to warnings regarding the potentially harmful effects of repeated, unsupervised exposure to violence in video games, film, television programming, and other mass media. Recognizing children's particular vulnerability, these agencies urge special caution in exposing young people to potentially harmful mediated images and content (AAP).

Studies have found correlations between heavy consumption of television programming on the one hand and fear of strangers and tolerance for invasive police practices on the other. Similarly, insensitivity to others' suffering has been associated, in part, with consumption of gratuitous, undifferentiated portrayals of violence in film, video games, and television programming (Gerbner, 1986). Regular consumption of product advertisements has been shown to foster "acquisitiveness," an habituated association of success and happiness with acquisition of material goods. Programming infused with racial, ethnic, gender, and other stereotypes has been shown to reinforce prejudices and promote discriminatory practices. Further, heavy consumption of targeted advertising has been shown to influence body image and lead to poor self-esteem, as well as contribute to eating disorders in especially vulnerable teens (Kilbourne, 2000).

These risks are significant. And yet media access holds considerable promise for contributing to moral development as well. Exposure to literature, film, and other media has the potential to enlarge people's thinking, to foster development of moral imagination, compassion, and empathy, and to cultivate humane and well-informed decision making. Through literature, for example, readers gain intimate exposure to experiences of people from richly diverse backgrounds and perspectives. Film has similar potential to cultivate moral imagination and to enrich audiences' capacities to understand others' experiences and perspectives. Morally complex narratives are particularly valuable resources for postconventional moral development (Nussbaum, 1997).

Media literacy enables people to tap storytelling's constructive potential without succumbing to its hazards. The oft-cited phrase, "those who control the stories of the culture control the culture" underscores the importance of media literacy. Through stories, people acquire and share communal values. Narratives provide "terministic screens" as well through which individuals "take in" their experiences. These perceptual frameworks hold considerable sway over individual and communal decision making.

The term "videality" describes a related phenomenon. Journalistic narratives present only fragments of "reality," and each is an edited interpretation. As viewers and readers "interpret" journalistic narratives, they create a "double-editing" process. Similarly, a photo capturing the image of a young child at a moment when he/she is crying may convey a powerful message potentially unrepresentative of the child's overall state or condition. Understanding how camera angles, lighting, word, image, story selection, and other suasory tools influence audience response is key to media literacy.

Technological advances further intensify the need for media literacy. Machines capable of producing convincing "representations" of real people giving speeches they never gave offer a gripping example. Others include photoediting tools facilitating the creation of images depicting people in places they have never been, having experiences they have never had.

Issues of access and control are also critical. Internet access has enriched the diversity of information sources for many. At the same time, however, commercial media are controlled by a smaller and smaller group of transnational corporations (Bagdikian, 2004). The ubiquity, power to influence, and technical complexity of commercially driven media complicate quests to use these sources for the pursuit of knowledge, truth, wisdom, and informed decision making.

These and related factors have led to growing recognition of the important role of media literacy in moral education. Equipping young people with critical listening, reading, speaking, writing, and viewing habits enriches their ability to tap media's constructive potential and mitigate its risks. Similarly, deepening people's understanding of how images influence messages, the relationship of sound to effect, stories to value construction, and so on, enables ethical production and use of communication and entertainment resources. Development of questioning and reflective habits assists media consumers further in assessing source credibility, identifying and evaluating underlying assumptions, and critically assessing the ethical nature of specific content.

Media literacy scholars and educators have produced a variety of tools to facilitate these facets of moral education. The *Rating Ethical Content Scale,* for example, was designed to assist teachers, parents, community members, and other media consumers to recognize and evaluate the ethical content of media messages (Narvaez et al., 2004). This instructional tool is linked in particular to ethical behavior, sensitivity, judgment, and action (the "Four Process" Model). Grass-roots media literacy alliances, centers for the study and teaching of media literacy, and other programs offer related workshops and instructional resources for families and educators seeking to cultivate moral development through media literacy.

Further Reading: American Academy of Pediatrics. (2001). Media violence. *Pediatrics, 108,* 1222–1226. Bagdikian, B. (2004). *The new media monopoly.* Boston: Beacon Press. Bok, S. (1998). *Mayhem.* Reading, MA: Addison-Wesley. Christians, C., Rotzoll, K., Fackler, M., McKee, K., & Woods, R. (2005). *Media ethics: Cases and moral reasoning* (7th ed.). Boston: Pearson Press. Gerbner, G. (1986). *Television's mean world (violence profile).* Philadelphia: University of Pennsylvania. Kilbourne, J. (2000). *Can't buy my love: How advertising changes the way we think and feel.* New York: Simon and Schuster. Makau, J., & Marty, D. (2001). *Cooperative argumentation: A model for deliberative community.* Long Grove, IL: Waveland Press, Inc. Narvaez, D., Gomberg, A., & Matthews, A. (2004). *Rating ethics content—Short form.* Paper presented at Association for Moral Education Conference. Nussbaum, M. (1997). *Cultivating humanity.* Cambridge: Harvard University Press. Walsh, D. (1994). *Selling out America's children.* Minneapolis: Fairview Press.

Josina Makau

Mental and Emotional Health

Mental and emotional health is a measure of a person's psychological well-being. Individuals who are functioning at optimal levels both mentally and emotionally are said to have excellent mental and emotional health, while those who suffer with chronic stress or mental and emotional disorders are in poor mental and emotional health. Most health care professionals would agree there is a connection among the mind, body, and spirit and that illness or poor health in one area can affect other areas in negative ways. Similarly, optimum health in one area, such as in the body, can positively impact the health of the mind and spirit.

One common approach to measuring mental and emotional health is to identify mental and emotional dysfunction, or mental and emotional disorders. Both mental health and medical professionals, such as psychiatrists, family physicians, psychologists, clinical social workers, counselors, and psychiatric nurses, use a classification system found in *The Diagnostic and Statistical Manual of Mental Disorders* (*DSM-IV*) to identify and label mental and emotional disorders in their patients. The *DSM-IV* provides a common language for professionals to communicate the nature and severity of an individual's dysfunction or illness, and includes diagnostic tools such as lists of symptoms and information about severity and duration of illnesses to help professionals pinpoint the diagnosis for an individual's mental and emotional distress. Just as mental and emotional health can be measured on a continuum, mental and emotional disorders vary greatly in their severity and resultant dysfunction. The term "mental illness" can mean vastly different things, from mild problems in adjustment to stressful circumstances to the more chronic, debilitating illnesses such as major depression, bipolar disorder, and schizophrenia. There has been some controversy about diagnosing people with mental illness in the professional community, partly because of the social stigma that often accompanies the label "mentally ill."

In addition to formulating a diagnosis for an individual's mental and emotional distress or illness, many health professionals seek to optimize their patients' overall mental, emotional, and physical health by identifying strengths and areas for improvement. Professionals help individuals improve their mental and emotional health by making holistic plans for treatment that address all areas of health. Many plans for mental and emotional health improvement include exercise regimens, medication to help cope with symptoms, activities to help cope with stress, spiritual activities, good nutrition to optimize physical health, increasing self-awareness and emotional understanding, and communication tools to help improve interpersonal relationships and increase support systems. In addition, professionals work to help prevent mental and emotional dysfunction and illness in the communities by creating outreach programs in the community and in the schools that serve to educate people on how they can make changes and adopt healthy strategies to preserve their mental and emotional health and protect themselves from mental and emotional illness. Taylor (1988) finds that positive thinking, especially in the face of crisis or personal challenge, can promote mental health by increasing a person's capacity for caring about others, enhancing feelings of happiness or well-being, and promoting productivity and creativity. Many interventions used by mental health practitioners work to help people boost their mental health and well-being by teaching strategies for adopting positive thinking and changing self-destructive and negative thinking patterns.

Mental and emotional health has become an important issue in the medical community as well as in the mainstream media, in part because of the powerful benefits of mental and emotional well-being, and because of the millions of dollars poor mental and emotional health cost the U.S. health care system annually. The World Health Organization, the World Bank, and Harvard University conducted a study called the *Global Burden of Disease,* in which the adverse effects or burden of many diseases were compared. They used a measure called Disability Adjusted Life Years. The outcomes of the *Global Burden of Disease* study underscore the detrimental effects of poor mental and emotional health: mental illness makes up over 15 percent of the total burden of disease in the United States. This percentage is greater than that representing the financial and personal burden of cancer. Given the personal, financial, and social impact of poor mental and emotional health, health care professionals, lawmakers, and educators have made it a priority to explore ways to prevent and treat mental and emotional illness and improve mental and emotional health.

Further Reading: The American Psychiatric Association. (1994). *The diagnostic and statistical manual of mental disorders* (4th ed.). Washington, D.C.: Author. National Advisory Mental Health Council. (1999). *Bridging science and service: A report by the national advisory mental health council's clinical treatment and services research workgroup.* NIH Publication No. 99-4353. Taylor, S., & Brown, J. (1988). Illusion and well-being: A social psychological perspective on mental health. *Psychological Bulletin, 103*(2), 193–210.

Michelle E. Flaum

Metaethics

A four-part distinction is made by many ethical theorists among metaethics (theory about the nature of morality), normative ethics (theory about the most adequate system of moral norms or rules), applied ethics (judgments in particular cases, taking into account their contexts), and descriptive ethics (accounts of the moralities of individuals, societies, and/or cultures). In metaethics the questions include, does morality have to do primarily with evaluating actions or persons, by reference to consequences for oneself or others, or by reference to features of the action itself irrespective of consequences, or by reference to the overall kind of life the person aspires to lead?

Ethicists have recognized two types of normative ethical theories, about norms for actions and about norms for persons and lives. On some accounts of ethics as norms for action, the basic criteria for good action are constitutive, or models for good action, admitting no exceptions properly speaking, the way a rulebook stipulates how a game is to be played. Kantian ethics is an example. On other accounts, the basic criteria are representative or models of good action, the way a handbook may describe good performance by reference to the way things usually happen and what it is therefore typically good to do. J.S. Mill's utilitarianism is an example.

A theory of ethics as norms for persons resembles this second type of theory of norms for action. It begins with the observation that considerations and judgments about actions in concrete situations can be complex, and judgment or discretion may be necessary. But in contrast to the theory of norms for actions, the question is, what type of person is the best kind of judge and should have discretion in these situations? The reference is to features of such persons and to the type of life to which they aspire, rather than to features of actions. Aristotle's virtue ethics is an example.

Following this division, metaethical theories may be divided into theories that address the question, "What action should one perform?" or the question, "What type of person should one be, aspiring to what type of life?" A third category is descriptive rather than normative.

Thirteen distinct, common metaethical theories are summarized in Table 1.

Further Reading: Anscombe, E. (1958). Modern moral philosophy. *Philosophy* (Vol. 33, reprinted 1981). In E. Anscombe (Ed.), *Ethics, religion and politics.* New York: Oxford University Press, Blackwell. Korsgaard, C. (1996). *The sources of normativity.* New York: Cambridge University Press. MacIntyre, A. (1990). *Three rival versions of moral inquiry.* Notre Dame, IN: University of Notre Dame Press.

Don Collins Reed

Middle Class Morality

The actual development of the middle class began in the United Kingdom during the eighteenth century industrial revolution and initially consisted of professional and business class individuals who were distinguished from both the nobility and landed gentry, and the class of agricultural and industrial laborers (Lamont, 1992). The central values adopted by this group of individuals reflected a strong commitment to family, and their children were expected to demonstrate a heartfelt appreciation for the working sacrifices made by parents (Wolf, 1998).

In a more contemporary sense, the term "middle class" describes the group of individuals situated between the upper class and working class members of society. In the United States, the middle class comprises between 35 to 45 percent of the population (Sadovnik, Cookson, & Semel, 2001). Sometimes the middle class is further subdivided into the upper middle class and lower middle class based on distinctions in annual income and property ownership. When Wolf (1998) surveyed Americans for the level of income that would raise individuals beyond middle class status, 19 percent said $50,000 to $75,000, 17 percent claimed $75,000 to $100,000, 29 percent said $100,000 to $200,000, and 15 percent indicated more than $200,000. Recent economic analyses indicate that the

Table 1 Common Metaethical Theories

Descriptive

Cultural-Ethical Relativism	Different cultures have different standards of right and wrong, good and bad. There is no way to adjudicate between them—no morally neutral or objective standpoint from which to judge which is better or worse. They are just different.
Emotivism	What is moral for me is what feels right or good to me. Moral judgments are simply expressions of feelings of approval or disapproval.
Sociobiologism	Morality codifies the instincts. Moral codes are expressions of the consensus of humans about specific types of action of which their evolved nature has predisposed them to approve or disapprove. Morality expresses human nature; it does not merely suppress it.

Norms for Actions

Intuitionism	Every situation is complex. Rules are only generalizations of our intuitions in particular cases or types of cases. We know what is right or wrong by a kind of moral sense in particular cases, however, not by knowing some abstract set of rules. Principles bind prima facie but not absolutely. Intuition must guide us in specific cases.
Act Utilitarianism	One should always do what promotes the most happiness or pleasure or satisfaction in any particular situation, taking into account the happiness, etc., of all affected parties to the extent that they are affected.
Rule Utilitarianism	One should always act according to that system of rules that would promote the most happiness or pleasure or satisfaction for those affected if everyone or almost everyone acted according to that system of rules as well.
Care Ethics	The most important things in life are relationships. We should do what fosters and preserves relationships. We should respond especially to the needs and hurts of others.
Kantianism	Act only on those rules or maxims for action that one could consistently will to be universally followed by others as well. Do not make exceptions for oneself, and do not use people. Treat others as ends rather than as means to one's own ends.
Contractarianism/ Contractualism	Act only on those rules for action that you and others affected could agree to follow. Hold people to only those rules that they would agree to or have agreed to, either explicitly or implicitly. The basis of morality is voluntary consent.
Divine Command Theory	The rules of morality were given by God to humans. The reason they are morally binding is that God commands obedience to them. They may or may not be beneficial to humans in some sense. They may impose hardships. That does not affect their status as binding.

Norms for Persons and Lives

Cynicism, Being "Realistic"	Individuals are fundamentally selfish, and might makes right. The winners write the laws and the history books. What is "right" is determined by the party in power and is generally designed to serve their personal and group interests. The best life is one of gratification, the life of a successful tyrant.
Virtue Ethics	The best life for humans is a life of activity that exercises those specifically human capacities that humans naturally find most satisfying to exercise. When fully developed, these capacities become excellences of intelligence and character —which we call virtues.
Natural Law Theory	Humans are by nature inclined to seek certain goods. Moral rules are guides to achieving these goods. At an abstract level, considering humans as a species, the rules or laws are universal, but the best life for humans in a specific environment depends on the specific features of that environment.

percentage of middle class Americans within these classifications is shrinking with "the extremes of rich and poor growing at the expense of the middle class" (Wolf, 1998, p. 7).

The middle class, then, is a somewhat ambiguous economic classification, but the values, morals, and aspirations defining the group are somewhat more constant. Whereas poorer Americans are limited in their residential possibilities, members of the middle class enjoy annual incomes that permit some measure of choice about where and how they might live. This choice often includes living in suburban communities where family safety and the surrounding aesthetic milieu are primary considerations. The middle class members typically adopt politically conservative values, viewing themselves as the "moral class" and "ordinary people trying to live by the traditional rules of working hard, saving for the future, and being loyal to family and country" (Wolf, 1998, p. 10). The importance of moral character is fundamental to middle class morality with an emphasis on such qualities as honesty, work ethic, personal integrity, and consideration for other individuals (Lamont, 1992).

The relationship between middle class morality and religion is an important one, especially within the United States. Lamont (1992) points out, for example, that, "attitudes toward religiosity and volunteerism are directly associated with attitudes about morality" (p. 54). Max Weber (1905) describes the historic connection between the middle class work ethic and religious conviction in *The Protestant Ethic and the Spirit of Capitalism*. According to Weber, John Calvin introduced the theological ideas that deeply influenced middle class attitudes about the importance of hard work. Calvin was a sixteenth century French theologian whose concept of predestination became a mainstay of contemporary Presbyterianism.

A primary tenet of Calvinism was that certain individuals were preordained for salvation or, in other words, preselected by God to inherit eternal life. All other individuals were unavoidably damned since nothing could change their unfortunate fate determined by an unchanging God. Although it was terrestrially impossible to determine with absolute certainty whether a person was preordained for eternal life or salvation, practical life experiences, especially in the area of vocational and economic success, afforded a reliable indication of individual fate. The only evidence of salvation, then, was found in a person's life and deeds, and accomplishments in practical matters were a reliable indication of one's salvation. Individuals who were active, austere, and hardworking reassured themselves and others that they were God's chosen ones. On the other hand, individuals who displayed the qualities of idleness and indifference toward work were most certainly among the damned (Tilgher, 1930). The profound and abiding respect for hard work and the economic rewards it sometimes provides remain a defining characteristic of middle class America.

Obviously, the limitations of moral generalizations associated with any social or economic class must be appreciated when investigating proposed relationships between moral values and social classifications. However, the historic development of the so-called middle class generally indicates a set of shared values and moral commitments that support the importance of honesty, hard work, economic independence, and reflect an abiding faith in the importance of religion and family. In many ways, then, this particular set of middle class values defines the moral foundation for the American way of life.

Further Reading: Lamont, M. (1992). *Money, moral and manners.* Chicago: The University of Chicago Press. Sadovnik, A., Cookson, P. W., & Semel, S. F. (2001). *Exploring education: An introduction to the foundations of education.* Boston: Allyn and Bacon. Tilgher, A. (1930). *Homo faber: Work through the ages* (D.C. Fisher, Trans.). New York: Harcourt Brace. Weber, M. (1905). *The protestant ethic and the spirit of capitalism* (T. Parsons, Trans.). New York: Charles Scribner's Sons. Wolf, A. (1998). *One nation, after all.* New York: Viking Penguin Group.

Emery Hyslop-Margison

Milgram, Stanley

Controversy surrounds the life and research of social psychologist Stanley Milgram (1933–1984). To some, Milgram's research on obedience to authority represents the definitive contribution of social psychology to the corpus of scientific knowledge, which, beginning in 1898, empirically demonstrated the power of the situation to affect human behavior. To others, Milgram's obedience research represents all that is morally offensive and dangerous in an immature social science gone haywire—a science that, in the 1960s, relied upon the conscience of individual researchers to regulate themselves—a science that allowed Milgram to ignore the civil liberties of research participants, deceive them, and induce psychological harm under the guise of scientific discovery. In the context of moral education, there is much to learn from Stanley Milgram's biography and research.

Stanley Milgram was born to Jewish parents in the South Bronx, New York, on August 15, 1933, the same year Adolf Hitler seized control of Germany. The precocious Milgram demonstrated an early affinity for science and magic and by his late teens was deeply fascinated with the interplay between the individual psyche and larger social forces. He obtained a B.A. in political science in 1954 and received his Ph.D. from the Department of Social Relations at Harvard University in 1960. Milgram wanted to address important and socially relevant questions—such as how Hitler seized control of Germany and initiated the Holocaust—and he believed the empirical methods of social psychology could provide concrete, observable answers. Armed with his training in social psychology and an unparalleled skill in stagecraft, in the early 1960s Milgram embarked on the most controversial research line in the brief history of social science.

Milgram's 18 obedience experiments appeared in the 1974 book, *Obedience to Authority*. The studies usually consisted of three performers, including an Experimenter, a Teacher, and a Learner. The Experimenter and Learner were Milgram's accomplices and knew their lines in advance. The naïve Teachers were described as men between the ages of 20 and 50 from a variety of professional backgrounds. Upon arrival, the Teacher was informed that the experiment explored the relationship between punishment and memory. He was left unaware that the experiment was actually an elaborate ruse to test how much pain he would inflict on the Learner under the commands of the austere Experimenter.

The Teacher was seated in front of an elaborate apparatus—the Shock Machine—with an electrode leading from it to the Learner's forearm, which was bound to a desk to impede his movement. Every time the Learner made a mistake on the memory test, the Teacher's task was to administer electric shocks in increasing 15-volt increments. As the mistakes accumulated and the intensity of the shocks increased, the Teacher overheard the Learner's cries of pain through the thin wall separating them. At 150 volts, the Learner loudly withdrew his consent to participate and demanded his release. Most Teachers then turned to the Experimenter for guidance. The Experimenter firmly and impassively commanded the Teacher to continue administering shocks. At 300 volts, blood-curdling screams emitted from the Learner's lab. Beyond 330 volts, the Learner was ominously silent. The Experimenter concluded the experiment when the Teacher either (a) administered three 450-volt shocks to the Learner or (b) refused to continue. The Teacher was finally informed that the shocks were not real and that the Learner was, in fact, unharmed. After providing his reactions, the Teacher was released from the experiment.

Milgram's research led to important insights. First, he showed that physical proximity moderated levels of destructive obedience. The closer the Experimenter stood to the Teacher the more likely he was to fully comply. Conversely, the closer the Teacher sat to the Learner—such as when the Teacher was required to hold the Learner's hand on a shock plate during the memory trials—the less likely he was to fully comply. Second, the presence of an additional defector, who was ostensibly another Teacher and had defected from the experiment first, also noticeably reduced levels of obedience.

Prior to publishing the results, Milgram asked Yale psychiatric residents to predict the proportion of Teachers who would continue to 450 volts. The residents predicted that only 1 in 1000 men would deliver the strongest shock. They were wrong. According to Milgram, 2 out of 3 Teachers (65 percent) across a variety of study replications fully complied with the Experimenter's commands. More disconcerting was the observation that these Teachers were not deranged sadists. Instead, the Teachers were normal, healthy men recruited from New Haven, Connecticut, neighbors and friends who seemed capable of atrocities akin to German soldiers, including Adolf Eichmann, who were perhaps simply following orders during the Holocaust some 20 years before.

The results of the obedience experiments sent shock waves throughout academic circles and the general public, and Milgram was quickly beset by critics and supporters. Examining the same set of data, some argued that Milgram's obedience research uncovered the single greatest cause of the Holocaust, thereby demonstrating the banality of evil, while others attacked Milgram's research as unethical and irreparably damaging to the implicit trust afforded to the scientific community by the populace it served. Unfortunately, Milgram neither provided a convincing theory of why two-thirds of his Teachers fully complied with the Experimenter, nor did he adequately explain the behavior of Teachers who did defy the Experimenter. Post hoc explanations abound, including deindividuation (that is, loss of personal identity), diffusion of responsibility (that is, loss of personal responsibility), and systematic desensitization (that is, committing a series of "little evils" that, over time, inures a person to serious atrocities). In retrospect, social scientists generally contend that the Holocaust was multiply determined by an interaction between social forces, including a depressed German economy, and characteristics of German's soldiers, in particular an authoritarian personality, which initiated the ultimate example of human atrocity.

Genocides are a persistent phenomenon in human history, such as the estimated 800,000 murders in Rwanda in 1994. How will scientists continue to unravel the causes of genocide? Although Milgram compared Teacher stress levels to watching an Alfred Hitchcock movie like *Psycho,* most analysts now contend his obedience experiments would be disallowed by contemporary Institutional Review Boards (IRBs) that were created, in part, as a response to Milgram's research. The principal function of an IRB is to safeguard the rights and well-being of research participants. Beginning in 1975, social scientists in the United States were required to submit all research proposals to an IRB prior to engaging in research, which prohibits research deemed too potentially harmful to participants.

In addition to the formation of IRBs, in 1973 the American Psychological Association issued the "Ethical Principles in the Conduct of Research with Human Participants." In short, Milgram's contributions to moral education are substantial. His obedience research not only prompted the adoption of ethical safeguards for research with human participants, he convincingly demonstrated that a person of considerable moral fortitude can maintain a sense of personal responsibility and reject the commands of a malignant authority.

Further Reading: Blass, T. (2004). *The man who shocked the world: The life and legacy of Stanley Milgram.* New York: Basic Books. Milgram, S. (1974). *Obedience to authority: An experimental view.* New York: Harper & Row. Miller, A. (2005). *The social psychology of good and evil.* New York: Guilford.

Scott Wowra

Modeling

There is little doubt that the earliest form of instruction among humans involved modeling. As a species as well as individuals, our first learning experiences occur through the process of observing and imitating others. From the acquisition of language skills to the emulation of moral virtues, modeling has always been and remains a powerful way we both learn and teach. There is also little doubt that the most prominent scholar of modeling is Albert Bandura. From his early work on the role of parental modeling in adolescent aggression to his recent publication on the mechanisms of spiritual modeling, Bandura's empirical and theoretical work on modeling has been immeasurably influential in the fields of psychology and education.

In psychology, Bandura's seminal research on aggression, including his famous experiments with the Bobo doll, challenged the then dominant trial and error learning of behaviorism. Bandura's work made clear that virtually all types of learning—behavioral, cognitive, and affective—can be learned vicariously, by observing the behaviors of others and their consequences. In education, Bandura's articulation of the four mechanisms or processes that govern observational learning has proved most endurable. Virtually every educational psychology textbook, standard reading for students seeking teacher certification, prominently features modeling and describes the four processes of attention, representation, reproduction, and motivation.

Attentional processes are the first essential set of subfunctions that must be activated and directed in order for observational learning to be effective. Any given situation offers an abundance of potential behaviors or persons that could be modeled. Educators must be aware of this fact and help direct learners' attention to the behavior or person they wish to be modeled. Educators must also realize that learners' existing conceptions, their level of development (cognitive and psychosocial), and their current interests or value preferences will greatly affect what they pay attention to and how it is perceived.

The second set of subfunctions critical to effective observational learning involves cognitive representational processes. Specifically, learners cannot be affected by models or modeled behaviors if they do not create a relatively permanent representation or memory of them. While the precise mechanisms involved in retention vary according to the nature of the information, event, or person to be remembered, it is sufficient for our purposes here to say that it is an active process whereby the learner transforms and restructures the words, actions, and so on of modeled behavior into rules or propositions or schemes for producing new patterns of behaviors or ways of being for the self.

Behavioral production processes constitute the third set of mechanisms in effective modeling or observational learning. It is through these processes that the cognitive representations created in preceding subfunctions are transformed into demonstrable patterns of behavior. Bandura has referred to the perfection of skills in this subfunction as a "conception-matching process," whereby the learners' conceptions inform and guide the execution of and modification of behavioral patterns until conceptions and actions are (nearly) one and the same. This process of "practice making perfect" is often facilitated by coaches or teachers in formal settings and by parents or peers in informal settings.

It is important to note at this point that modeling is not just a process whereby the learner simply mimics modeled behavior. In many domains of activity, specific patterns of behaviors almost always need to be adjusted to fit the demands of each particular situation. Bandura refers to the process of extracting rules, values, or principles from observations in one situation and later applying them to a different situation as abstract modeling. In the moral domain, for example, comforting someone who has been hurt, resolving a conflict peacefully, and distributing scarce resources equitably are complex phenomena. Though all are rooted in moral principles (such as care and justice), there is no one right or best way to care for, negotiate with, or fairly treat others. Characteristics of the persons involved and features of the situation greatly affect which course(s) of action would be the most appropriate.

The fourth and final subfunction of observational concerns is motivational processes. As the saying goes, "we know more than we show"; we do not reproduce or perform everything we have learned from watching others. Bandura identified three types of incentive motivators: (1) direct, which the performer experiences personally; (2) vicarious, whereby one is inspired to act (or not act) because of the rewards (or adverse consequences) that others have experienced; and (3) self-produced, personal goals, standards, or values that one finds self-satisfying or inherently worthy. There are, for example, many "successful" models of stealing, lying, cheating, and so forth, but one may refrain from doing so because one believes such behavior to be wrong or immoral.

Further Reading: Bandura, A. (1986). *Social foundations of thought and action: A social cognitive theory.* Englewood, NJ: Prentice-Hall. Bandura, A. (1997). *Self-efficacy: The exercise of control.* New York: Freeman.

Jason M. Stephens

Moral Agency

By "agency" and "agentic" we refer to the characteristic of human action, whereby the actor, in the process of acting, has the immediate sense of being the source and the owner of the action. The simplest, and developmentally earliest, kind of agency is expressed in the infant's intention by which he or she directs the action to the satisfaction of his or her desire. Therefore, since in our everyday understanding of the concept moral action requires an intention that is motivated by the moral good, it seems that to add "agency" as an attribute of morality would be redundant and unnecessary.

In fact, considering the history of moral psychology, far from being redundant, it may be necessary to speak of moral agency, and also to clarify the precise meaning of agency in the context of moral functioning. The most influential theories that offered psychological explanations of moral phenomena could not accept the intervention of a free subject, but interpreted the facts of morality as proceeding impersonally from the human organism, causally determined either by internal dynamisms or by external conditioning factors. This is clearly the case of most psychoanalytic theories and of the various behavioristic or learning theories. Surprising as it may seem, something similar should be said also of Piaget's and those Piagetian theories, which rely on a strict form of structuralism. In this theoretical perspective, conscious intentions have no place in the central processes of assimilation, accommodation, and equilibration, through which moral structures are acquired and maintained. Of course, it is recognized that concrete moral judgments are a result of a conscious, intentional activity; and yet, no theoretical room is made for a subject who responsibly guides moral reasoning and its expression in moral action, and who feels accountable for the correctness of his or her judgment, actively resisting the corruptive influence of defenses and self-deception.

Recently many psychologists have been using the language of agency, while following theories that deny agency in its proper sense. On closer examination, it seems clear that they frequently confuse "agency" with "active," namely, with the capacity of an organism to spontaneously generate operations and processes from within, according to the internal properties of the organism, and not only as reactions to external stimulation. But an organism can be active also when there is no conscious self and no intentional action, for instance, in many activities of the nervous system, and in many assimilatory operations of the cognitive system. In sum, terms referring to agency and agentic processes are being frequently used in a nonagentic sense, and this could be a source of serious theoretical confusion.

Agency is expressed in a series of processes, of various complexity, appearing at different points along the developmental continuum. Some of these are will, effort, sense of mastery and control, self-control, choice, decision, persistence, sense of responsibility, and commitment. These processes articulate the unfolding and the turns of the action, from its initial intention to its completion in reaching the goal; they all depend on intention, and cannot be understood without being related to the sense of being the source and the owner of one's action. Collectively and individually, these processes have been the objects of study of Action Theory in philosophy. Several of them were also the object of a large body of research both in social psychology, following Heider's (1958) "naïve analysis of action," and in developmental psychology, following Piaget's early work (1930; 1932). As already suggested, much of this work either proceeded from premises that ignored or denied the crucial difference between physical causality and agency, or did not attend to the role of the self and the sense of ownership in agency. Recently, however, important work is being pursued on intention and intentionality, which marks a clear departure from psychology's traditional positivistic premises (e.g., Malle, Moses, & Baldwin, 2001; Russell, 1996).

Obviously, all the agentic processes listed above are central to moral functioning, a fact that is recognized in philosophy, where action theory is frequently related to ethical theory and to the area of practical reasoning. In psychology, however, with the important exception of intention and its use in judgments of blameworthiness, these processes were rarely studied explicitly for their moral significance. The role of effort, investigated in the context of school achievement, was rarely related to moral functioning. By contrast, self-control was the object of moral research, particularly in studies on resistance to temptation, but typically from perspectives that are antithetical to agency. Similarly, defensive responses, as, for instance, manifested in the attribution of blame, are most frequently understood as simply happening to people, who are seen as the helpless victims of cognitive and motivational structures. This situation is regrettable, because, on one end, the sense of action ownership that accompanies agency intuitively seems to be important for moral functioning, and, on the other, when available, studies do indicate that children and adults are sensitive to this aspect of their experience.

Further Reading: Heider, F. (1958). *The psychology of interpersonal relations.* New York: Wiley. Malle, B. F., Moses, L. J., & Baldwin, D. A. (Eds.). (2001). *Intentions and intentionality. Foundations of social cognition.* Cambridge, MA: MIT Press. Piaget, J. (1930). *The child's conception of physical causality.* London: Kegan Paul. Piaget, J. (1932). *The moral judgment of the child.* London: Kegan Paul. Russell, J. (1996). *Agency: Its role in mental development.* Hove, UK: Erlbaum.

Augusto Blasi

Moral Atmosphere/Moral Climate

The term "atmosphere" or "climate" is used in organizational change literature to refer to an organization's personality, ethos, or morale. In the moral education literature, the moral atmosphere of the school refers to its moral character. This moral character emerges from the interactions among teachers, students, administrators, and staff members, and it, in turn, influences their moral functioning.

Investigations of the moral atmosphere of schools begin with the assumption common to the organizational climate literature that climate can be assessed only through the perceptions of the organization's members. In this sense, the moral atmosphere is largely a reflection of the organization's culture. On the other hand, following the classification scheme advanced by Taguri, the term "moral atmosphere" may be used more globally to refer to schools' ecology (its building and facilities), milieu (the characteristics of the students and staff, such as their ethnicity, socioeconomic status, and educational backgrounds), and organization (the structures and processes of decision making, communication, and teaching) in addition to their culture.

This broad definition of moral atmosphere makes us aware of the many subtle ways that schools communicate moral messages. For example, if we were to step inside a high school in a poor urban neighborhood, we might have to pass through a metal detector. As we walk down the corridors, we might find security guards posted throughout the corridors and surveillance cameras throughout the building. We might also notice during passing periods that the school feels something like a busy airport as large numbers of students and teachers pass hurriedly from one classroom to another. If we were to visit a classroom in a wealthy suburban high school when students are taking a test, we might find a teacher pacing the aisles and constantly looking around the room for signs of cheating. What effect do these conditions have on students? How does it feel to be under constant surveillance or to be lost in the crowd? The ecology alone can foster trust or mistrust, connectedness or isolation.

The milieu also plays an important role in establishing the moral tone of an environment. For example, poorly prepared and unmotivated teachers lead students to feel that they are being baby-sat rather than educated. Schools that are segregated by race and social class and school tracks that are segregated by race and social class send powerful messages about equal opportunity. Schools' organizational practices are crucial in establishing the moral climate that students will experience. Arbitrary and harsh disciplinary practices, for instance, result in students believing that the rules are not fair and that teachers and administrators are simply interested in asserting their power. Top down decision making can harm the moral atmosphere by destroying the morale of teachers as well as students.

School administrators and teachers are often unaware of the moral atmosphere of their school and its influence. The moral atmosphere is often a "hidden curriculum" of values education because the value lessons that are taught may be barely visible and unintended (Jackson et al., 1993). The administrator who decides to rule with an iron fist may feel this is the only way to achieve order, just as the teacher patrolling the aisles may feel that this is the only way to stop cheating. Yet actions may speak more loudly than words. What are we communicating when we extol democracy in the civics class but run the school as an autocracy? How can we claim to be building classroom community when we do not trust students to be honest while taking a test?

Typically organizations articulate their moral ideals and aspirations in mission statements and statements of institutional purpose and vision. Although such statements may provide a basis for establishing an organization's moral atmosphere, they do not in themselves constitute a moral atmosphere. Often, as the above examples illustrate, statements of mission and vision have little influence on school ecology, milieu, organization, or culture. If schools are to build a moral atmosphere, an effort must be made at all levels to translate the mission statement into practice.

The just community approach as described by Power, Higgins, and Kohlberg (1989) provides a framework for fostering the moral climate and, in particular, for establishing a culture of justice and care. Key to establishing culture is developing shared norms that exemplify values of justice and care. For example, a school that aspires to become a community should develop a norm that members of different cliques and friendship groups should try to get along with each other. Norms can be defined in terms of either typical behavior or desirable behavior. How members act and how they believe they ought to act are both relevant to a group's moral atmosphere. The just community approach focuses on influencing students' actions not through tactics designed to produce conformity but through deliberation and agreement. Thus, in assessing the moral atmosphere of a group, it is crucial to describe not only students' behavior but also their perceptions of their duties as group members. A student who says, "I know that as a member of this school community, I should treat everyone respectfully, but I sometimes lose sight of this when I am joking around with my friends," perceives that a norm exists no matter how he/she may behave.

In emphasizing the importance of expectations for assessing the moral culture, a distinction should be made between norms that arise out of a sense of group membership and those that arise out of personal conscience. An individual member of a group who says, "I believe that I ought to treat everyone with respect," describes a personal norm, not necessarily a group norm. On the other hand, if that individual were to go on to say, "in our school, we believe we should respect everyone," we would then conclude that this individual perceives (and also represents) a shared expectation for respect. A school's moral culture, therefore, refers to a shared conscience as distinct from an aggregate of individual consciences.

Not all shared expectations are moral norms; some may simply be conventions. For example, a school may have a rule that students are to wear a uniform to school, which students feel obligated to obey as members of the school. The key to determining whether a rule is a norm that is moral or not depends on the values that members understand the norm to uphold. Moral norms have as their end respect for the dignity of others, fairness, the common good, and the relationships that bond individuals with each other and with the group as a whole. Simple conformity for its own sake may indicate the existence of a group norm, but not a moral norm. It is difficult if not impossible to determine whether a norm is moral or not without knowledge of how the individual members of a group regard the group norm. Even a rule about wearing a uniform could indicate the presence of a moral norm if the members of the group wear the uniform as a sign of their commitment to each other and the common good. In assessing moral culture, we must take into account what the norms mean for the students.

Although moral culture is but one dimension of moral atmosphere, it is the product of the other three. Students and staff (milieu) interacting through a system of structures and procedures (organization) in a physical setting (ecology) establish a culture over time. The extent to which that culture becomes moral or not depends upon their willingness to engage all dimensions of the school's moral atmosphere.

Further Reading: DeVries, R., & Zan, B. (1994). *Moral classrooms, moral children: Creating a constructivist atmosphere in early education.* New York: Teachers College Press. Host, K., Brugman, D., Tavecchio, L., & Beem, L. (1998). Students' perception of the moral atmosphere in secondary schools and the relationship between moral competence and moral atmosphere. *Journal of Moral Education, 27*(1), 47–71. Jackson, P.W., Boostrom, R.E., & Hansen, D.T. (1993). *The moral life of schools.* San Francisco: Jossey-Bass. Owens, R.G. (2004). *Organizational behavior in education: Adaptive leadership and school reform* (8th ed.). Boston: Allyn & Bacon. Power, F.C., Higgins, A., & Kohlberg, L. (1989). *Lawrence Kohlberg's approach to moral education.* New York: Columbia University Press.

F. Clark Power

Moral Bias

How is a bias against Gravenstein apples different from a bias against Irish Catholics? When is a bias a moral concern? A bias consistently, habitually contrains decision making—one is unwilling to taste Gravensteins. It becomes a moral bias when, in addition, it causes harm to others and corrupts one's integrity. In its most common contemporary use moral bias occurs, for example, when a heart medicine that has been tested only on men is prescribed for women as well; when IQ test items from one culture are used to measure the "intelligence" of people from other cultures; when hiring criteria favor one group over another (tall, clean shaven).

Types of Moral Bias

Moral bias can be explicit or implicit. Explicit moral biases are conscious prejudices and stereotypes, usually manifest in discriminatory behavior: "No Blacks or Jews allowed." Explicit moral biases are increasingly condemned as "politically incorrect" and in many countries explicitly illegal. Implicit moral biases are more subtle and less conscious than explicit moral bias. Churches may be referred to as "Black churches"; a bad day on the stock exchange is called "Black Friday." Saying that women are "more sensitive" or men are "better at math" states an explicit moral bias, whereas unconsciously assigning difficult clients to female accountants and difficult math problems to male staff reflects an implicit bias. Explicit bias is easier to detect because it can be directly linked to harm.

Sources of Moral Bias

Moral bias can derive from lack of information (the Deficit model); from the presence of negative moral emotions (the Discordance model); or from cultural norms (the Ethnocentric model).

Cognitive Deficit Model

MacKenzie (1997) argues, optimistically, that moral bias most likely arises from a deficit of information: Asians are good in math. Although Deficit bias can be found across social classes, it is statistically associated with lack of contact, limited experience, generally lower intelligence, and lower stages of moral development, but only among members of the privileged majority group. The opposite is often the case for members of minority groups or oppressed classes (see below). Here the historical victims of prejudice and discrimination may become more biased with more contact, experience, and intelligence. Deficit bias is harmful when, for example, it leads school counselors habitually and stubbornly to program children from one ethnic group (or gender) into particular classes (for example, basic math instead of algebra).

Moral Discordance Model

Discordant bias reflects a historically grounded emotional reactivity in situations of moral choice. It arises, like post-traumatic stress disorder (PTSD), as an habitual response to a moral trigger. Sometimes such hypersensitivity is adaptive—for example, when rape victims stay away from strange men, or brown-skinned youth avoid the police. But discordant bias can also operate when it is anachronistic, as in the hypervigilance of soldiers after a war. Refugees understandably have a discordant bias against those from whom they fled, and they may be biased in favor of those who took them in and protected them, for generations beyond the time when such discordant moral biases are adaptive, functional, or even logical. Discordant bias can fuel intractable intergroup violence, and can manifest a moral sensitivity not only to people, but also to particular moral issues: child abuse, the unfair distribution of water, and so on.

Negative Moral Emotions as a Source of Moral Bias

Jonathan Haidt and others have shown that people try to give reasons to justify their moral intuitions, feelings, and beliefs after they have made a judgment about a behavior ("incest is disgusting"). Blakeney and Blakeney (1993) showed that over 30 percent of Blacks and Jews used different stages of moral reasoning to solve moral problems, dependent on the group identity of the people in a dilemma situation. Pizarro and his colleagues found that American college students endorsed American soldiers killing innocent Iraqis or Iraqi soldiers killing innocent Americans based on their political preferences. In these cases, biased emotional reactions and beliefs lead to the differential application of moral norms based on group membership. Studies using fMRI technology show that rational, abstract moral decision making uses different parts of the brain than does emotional, intuitive, social-cognitive decision making. Discordance bias relies on emotionally charged memories.

Ethnocentric Bias

. Cultural norms are a third source of moral bias. While some normative bias is related to a history of mistreatment, here we speak of preservative cultural norms that define the in-group and the out-group as having equal moral worth, and also recognize special obligations to one's own group, like the moral acceptability of saving one's own child before one saves the child of a stranger. Such ethnocentric bias may not harm others directly, except in the case where there is an unfair exercise of social, economic, or physical power. Culturally binding norms may, however, become a source of interethnic bias: Muslim women's head coverings, Indians' arranged marriages, and the Christian fundamentalist stand against homosexuality all represent culturally derived and normatively sanctioned moral biases that may or may not cause harm, but which are not likely open to logical argument or potentially transformative information.

Societal and Institutional Bias

Although we are likely to think of moral bias as something one individual does with respect to another, there are also forms of institutional bias—this occurs when morally biased policies and practices govern individual behavior (for example, hiring and admissions, differential distribution of health care).

In sum, moral bias can be explicit or implicit; it can result from a deficit of information, from discordant moral emotions, or from culturally isolating norms. To the extent that moral bias is closed to disconfirming information, it constrains moral development and corrupts individual and social integrity.

Further Reading: Blakeney, C.D., & Blakeney, R.F. (1993). Pluralism and the dilemma of discordance among Blacks and Jews. In D.K. Lapsley & F.C. Power (Eds.), *The challenge of pluralism: Education, politics and values.* Notre Dame, IN: University of Notre Dame Press. Greene, J.D.,

Nystrom, L.E., Engell, A.D., Darley, J.M., & Cohen, J.D. (2004). Neural bases of cognitive conflict and control in moral judgment. *Neuron, 44,* 389–400. Kahneman, D., & Frederick, S. (2005). A model of heuristic judgment. In K.J. Holyoak & R.G. Morrison (Eds.), *The Cambridge handbook of thinking and reasoning.* New York: Cambridge University Press. MacKenzie, J. (1997). Two images of bias. *Oxford Review of Education, 23,* 487–502. Walker, V.S., & Snarey, J. (2004). *Race-ing moral formation: African-American perspectives on justice and care.* New York: Columbia University Press.

Ronnie Frankel Blakeney and Charles Blakeney

Moral Character

Character is derived from a Greek work that means "to mark," as on an engraving. One's character is an indelible mark of consistency in behavior. It implies something deeply rooted in the personality that organizes its dispositional tendencies. Although definitions of moral character abound, most accounts settle upon three core concepts: habits, traits, and virtues. Moral character, on this view, is a manifestation of certain personality traits called virtues that dispose one to habitual courses of action.

The habits required for moral character must be cultivated by habituation. For Aristotle, this was similar to the way one acquires any skill in the arts and crafts—by practice. We acquire virtues by acting virtuously. Habituation is learning by doing with regular and consistent practice, but under the watch of a virtuous tutor. The habits that emerge from Aristotelian habituation become settled dispositions to do things in certain ways, but automatically without reflective deliberation, choice, or planning. A common view, then, is that individuals of sound moral character are virtuous habitually.

Virtue (*arête*) is an excellence that disposes one to live well the life that is good for one to live. Aristotle argued famously that virtues are the mean between excess and deficiency. The virtue of courage, for example, lies between excess (reckless foolhardiness) and its deficiency (cowardice). Similarly, sexual virtue lies at the midpoint between lust (an excess of sexual desire) and its deficiency (frigidity of desire). Virtue, then, is a trained faculty of choice that aims toward temperance and moderation, that is, for the intermediate between passions, appetites, and action, as determined by reason. What constitutes the mean varies depending on the situation; hence, virtue bids us to display excellence at the right time, with the proper intensity and motive, toward the proper objects, and in the right way. Clearly, practical reasoning is important to the display of virtue. Proper training of virtues requires a critical facility. It includes learning how to discern, make distinctions, judge the particulars of the case, examine the exigencies of concrete situations, and make considered choices (sometimes automatically).

The Aristotelian concern to cultivate virtues as states of character is an approach to the moral life that is contrasted often with Kant's deontological approach to moral philosophy, and with utilitarianism. For Kant the central moral duty is to submit to the obligations of the universal moral law. In contrast, virtue ethics is concerned primarily with the qualities of agents and not with actions. It asks, "What sort of person should I become?" rather than "What should I do?" The basic moral facts for virtue ethics concern qualities of character, where judgments about agents have explanatory primacy over judgments about duty, obligation, and utility. Whereas deontology and utilitarianism are deployed as guides for decision making, Aristotelian character ethics is oriented toward *eudemonia.* Virtues are excellent qualities of character that help us flourish as persons.

Moral character is an ethical concept that has defied adequate conceptualization in psychological science. Typically the virtues of moral character are understood as personality traits that exhibit consistency across situations. An honest person, for example, is presumed to display this personality trait in all situations that require honesty. Yet modern personality theory has abandoned the notion that traits display cross-situational consistency. Instead, dispositions require contextual specification. A stable behavioral signature is responsive to environments. An aggressive child, for example, is not aggressive in every context, but only when placed in situations of certain kinds. Although this contextual approach is not incompatible with Aristotle's account of virtue, it is viewed with suspicion by traditional approaches to character education that impute situational constancy to persons of good moral character.

Another way to conceptualize moral character is in terms of the constructs of cognitive psychology. For example, Aristotelian habits might be considered dispositions of interpretation that cognitive psychologists understand as schemas, prototypes, or scripts whose accessibility and activation make possible the discriminative facility that allows one to act in ways appropriate to situations. A person of good moral character on this interpretation is one who has moral schemas chronically accessible for social information processing.

Moral character is understood also in terms of self-identity. A moral person is one for whom moral notions define what is essential, important, and central to one's self-understanding. One has a moral identity to the extent that the self is organized around moral commitments, chosen for good moral reasons. One has a moral identity when the functional dispositional virtues (such as self-control, delay of gratification, among others) are attached to moral desires. When a person constructs self-understanding around moral desires, then living out one's moral commitments does not feel like a choice; and failure to act in ways that keep faith with one's identity-defining commitments is to risk self-betrayal, a possibility that adds a motivational property to the moral personality.

Further Reading: Aristotle. (1985). *Nicomachean ethics* (T. Irwin, Trans.). Indianapolis, IN: Hackett. (Original work written 350.) Carr, D. (2003). Character and moral choice in the cultivation of virtue. *Philosophy, 78,* 219–32. Carr, D., & Steutal, J. (Eds.). (1999). *Virtue ethics and moral education*. London: Routledge. Lapsley, D.K., & Narvaez, D. (2006). Character education. In W. Damon & R. Lerner (Series Eds.) & A. Renniger & I. Siegel (Vol. Eds.), *Handbook of child psychology. Volume 4: Child psychology in practice* (6th ed., pp. 248–96). New York: Wiley. Lapsley, D.K., & Power, F.C. (Eds.). (2005). *Character psychology and character education*. Notre Dame, IN: University of Notre Dame Press.

Daniel K. Lapsley

Moral Compass

"Moral compass" is a term frequently used as a synonym for conscience and is used by individuals from a range of the traditions of moral philosophy. The analogy of the compass for treating morality as an equivalent of magnetism assumes that morality has an external source and power. Accordingly, those who use the term tend to see the ethical challenge for a moral agent is to align his or her reasoning and action with the force. This notion is typically more appealing to individuals who see the foundations of ethics (that is, metaethics) as religious or spiritual rather than constructed through human experience, actions, and reflection.

Losing one's moral compass is frequently used in explanation of morally objectionable behaviors—especially those made in an effort to understand the actions of leaders or others who are viewed either with respect or as conventional upstanding community members. Sometimes it is the person who has made bad choices who seeks an explanation through analogy. One such example is Jeb Stuart Magruder who pled guilty to felonious wrongdoing in the Watergate scandal of the Richard Nixon presidency and is reported as saying, "Somewhere between college and Watergate, I lost my moral compass." (Different versions of this quotation are attributed to Magruder, but the gist remains the same.)

The lack of a moral compass was cited by some as a factor in the torture of detainees in Abu Ghraib prison in Iraq by United States personnel. In a press conference held at the release of the investigative report of the prison, the panel—led by James Schlesinger, former U.S. Secretary of Defense—made a recommendation of preventing future such events by providing better training for U.S. guards to equip them with a "sharp moral compass."

To develop a moral compass, former U.S. Secretary of Education and leader in conservative politics in the United States, William J. Bennett—in his book titled *The Moral Compass*—recommends the study of great works of literature and an examination of the lives of moral exemplars. In 2003, when Bennett's habit of high-stakes gambling became public knowledge, some of his former supporters (who consider gambling a moral rather than a conventional matter) questioned whether another moral compass had gone missing.

Accusing someone of losing a moral compass is a powerful polemic and can be used by individuals to argue for a variety of political and ethical positions. For example, the philosopher Peter Singer uses the term "meandering moral compass" to throw into question the ethical judgment of President George W. Bush and the morality of his administration's policies or, with a focus on the last U.S. President from the opposing major party, the impeachment of William Jefferson Clinton.

Leaving the polemics behind and taking the notion of moral compass in the best possible light, unethical decisions and actions exist, so can losing one's moral way be a useful way of constructing the phenomenon? Several famous research studies have been conducted in an effort to examine how individuals make unethical choices and actions. While they use different terms, the "shock" experiments conducted by Stanley Milgram in the 1960s to see how far individuals would go in obedience to a perceived authority and the simulated prison environment created by Philip Zimbardo to investigate how human beings come to treat others in immoral ways demonstrate being without (or with a malfunctioning) moral compass.

Further Reading: Bennett, W.J. (1995). *The moral compass: Stories for a life's journey.* New York: Simon & Schuster. Milgram, S. (1974). *Obedience to authority; An experimental view.* New York: HarperCollins. Posner, R.A. (2000). *An affair of state: The investigation, impeachment, and trial of President Clinton.* Cambridge, MA: Harvard University Press. Singer, P. (2004). *The president of good and evil: The ethics of George W. Bush.* New York: Dutton. Zimbardo, P.B. (1972). *The psychology of imprisonment: Privation, power and pathology.* Stanford, CA: Stanford University Press.

Robert W. Howard

Moral Conduct

Moral conduct may aptly be regarded as the ultimate expression of morality itself. Moral philosophers, psychologists, and educators alike typically agree that it is the manner in which a person lives one's life—or "conducts" oneself—in the context of social relations that distinguishes him or her as a moral person. In this respect, the quality of a person's moral conduct reflects the surest test of moral maturity, and it is the central goal of moral development and moral education.

Despite general consensus on its definitive status as a criterion of morality, moral conduct is a multifaceted concept that has been described from a variety of perspectives and categorized in many ways. Most broadly defined, it is often framed in terms of two well-established philosophical conceptions of morality. From the perspective of principles of "justice," it depicts qualities of interaction that emphasize respect for fairness and the rights of others (for example, treating people equally, keeping promises). Alternatively, when viewed from the perspective of "benevolence," it is directed toward the welfare and betterment of others (for example, being compassionate, helping a needy stranger).

Irrespective of these philosophical orientations, the literature on moral conduct also includes a spectrum of more specific categories of social interaction—ranging from "immoral" conduct, such as delinquency and aggression, at one extreme, to highly moral conduct, such as altruism and exemplary civic commitment at the other. Within this spectrum is an array of less extreme forms of behavior—including resistance to temptation, honesty, sexual promiscuity, political activism, social conformity, classroom behavior, illegal drug use, and more.

Not surprisingly, this diversity has raised questions concerning the legitimacy of some such categories as true representations of moral conduct. Accordingly, an additional and more significant layer of interpretation considers moral conduct from yet another perspective. Here, it is defined not on the basis of a specific classification (for example, honesty versus activism), but rather by the way it is carried out or "conducted" by a person. To some extent, such interpretations differ across varying psychological accounts of how morality develops (for example, social-learning versus cognitive-developmental theories).

Throughout the study of morality, the term "moral conduct" is often used synonymously with the terms "moral action" and "moral behavior." However, moral philosophers (for example, John Dewey, Alasdair MacIntyre) argue that there are meaningful conceptual differences between them. On their interpretation, moral behavior is most accurately defined as unmediated or unreflective "pieces of action," having little meaning in and of themselves, whereas moral action denotes behavior that is motivated by a person's deliberate intention and free will. Within the cognitive-developmental paradigm (for example, Jean Piaget, Lawrence Kohlberg), it is only when these criteria are met that a person's actions are deemed truly moral. In contrast, however, the term "moral conduct" means something still more than this. In its purest sense, it represents a sustained pattern of actions that emanates from a person's relatively stable disposition. Hence, it extends over time and across contexts, and is essentially embedded in one's personality. As such, it reflects the culmination and unity of a person's values, beliefs, and personal cares and commitments to conduct one's life in keeping with these internal standards. By this definition, the concept of moral conduct is closely aligned with that of "moral character," as elaborated by Dewey and some contemporary theorists.

Just as there are varying perspectives on the concept of moral conduct, so too have there been different approaches to the study of it. Most often, however, psychologists have adopted two diverse methodological approaches, both essentially observational and having relative strengths and weaknesses. The "quasi-experimental" approach examines moral conduct in a controlled "laboratory" environment, where participants are exposed to a specifically designed, simulated moral situation (e.g., a confederate in distress). Whereas these studies enjoy the advantages of scientific control, they are also necessarily restricted to isolated, contrived situations that are sometimes bland and artificial. In contrast, the "naturalistic" approach examines moral conduct in the context of naturally occurring activities, often observed over time and across situations. Here, conduct is defined as established traits or patterns of behavior, identified by classification, diagnostic systems, or public record (for example, delinquents, moral exemplars). Whereas this research may be more representative of real life, it is also more vulnerable to extraneous sources of variation and less reliable measurement techniques.

In sum, despite the status of moral conduct as a hallmark of moral maturity, it remains a somewhat elusive concept. It poses stiff challenges, but enduring rewards, for those who attempt to elucidate its meaning, study its development, and nurture it in our homes and schools.

Further Reading: Damon, W. (1988). *The moral child.* New York: Free Press. Dewey, J. (1908/ 1960). *Theory of the moral life.* New York: Holt, Rinehart and Winston. Eisenberg, N. (1992). *The caring child.* Cambridge, MA: Harvard University Press. Kohlberg, L. (1984). *The psychology of moral development.* San Francisco: Harper and Row.

Mary Louise Arnold

Moral Development

Moral development as a field of study examines processes of thoughts, issues, and considerations in the moral domain. Originally dominated by a structural, constructivist, cognitive Piagetian psychological model of increasing complexity of thought and operations about the sociomoral world and people's relationships with it, moral development is an interdisciplinary field that includes psychology, philosophy, sociology, political science, ethics, anthropology, and neuroscience. As such, moral development as a concept has grown to consider a multifaceted articulation of not only cognitive reasoning and justification but also intuition, emotion, social regulation and social interaction, and self-understanding. Each of these disciplines and facets contributes to a greater understanding of the transformations of understanding morality throughout the life span. These understandings include social-cognitive development of moral judgment about positive justice, self-development, self-understanding, perspective taking, interpersonal relationships, and faith.

Moral development from an individual standpoint is the change or transformation of thinking about moral issues, and is a function of maturation, social interaction, and interaction with the environment. This transformation includes increasing control of self and moral emotions, greater skills and variations in social interactions regarding moral issues and conventions, and changes in the structure and/or process of reasoning about and perspective of sociomoral issues involving the self and interpersonal and societal relationships.

The word "development" itself connotes improvement—individuals become better able to understand and construct meaning of the social and moral world by seeing more of the components that comprise what is moral from multiple perspectives (differentiation) and can interconnect those differentiated components into a coherent "sense" or system (integration) from which judgments can be made. This process has been described by Heinz Werner, Jean Piaget, and Lawrence Kohlberg, among others. The role of metacognitive reflection and coordination are important in that integration. Additionally, understandings of the social and moral world move from being externally derived to being internally constructed and understood from a personal interpretive standpoint. Meaning is constructed (not delivered from external authorities) and does not exist *a priori* within the mind. The individual is an active, rational interpreter of experience, and that experience includes the nonrational, intuitive, emotional, social, and cultural influences of oneself interacting with the environment. (See the entry on Cognitive Moral Development for a more detailed description of the development of making moral meaning.)

Conceptualizations of this process of development as a process of differentiation and integration and a movement toward increasing complexity accompany the theory of development as internalization. Internalization is described from a multitude of perspectives, including Piaget's reflexive and accommodative processes, nonrational compliance to external standards as with a behavioral perspective (e.g., B. F. Skinner), biologically based instinctual and/or affective emotion-based perspectives (e.g., Sigmund Freud, Jonathan Haidt, Nancy Eisenberg), and sociocultural appropriation (e.g., Lev Vygotsky, Barbara Rogoff). In addition, analytical domain theory (e.g., Elliot Turiel, Larry Nucci) and metacognitive reflection (e.g., David Moshman, Fritz Oser, Dawn Schrader) provide explanatory frameworks. Each of these perspectives, however, shares the common theme of a shift from an external or heteronomous way of understanding morality to an internal and autonomous regulation of thought and behavior. However, theorists offer differing explanations to account for the nature and type of moral development.

Moral development connotes directionality toward a goal or endpoint. This endpoint can be, for example, Kohlberg's principled moral judgment or postconventional level, which serves as the main argument for the concept of development, in contrast to simple change. However, a specific endpoint may not be required to count as development so long as the changes are progressive in some sense (Moshman, 2003). With change, no sense of "movement toward" something is required; for development, a valuation of the change as toward something "better" is implicated. Postmodern critiques would question what constitutes progress, though, since postmodern theorists claim assessments and judgments are always subjective and therefore no one approach is any better than another.

The question of universality across cultures (Shweder, 1990; Turiel & Wainryb, 2000) and gender (Gilligan, 1982; Walker, 2006) has likewise been debated as to how such factors affect the nature and trajectory of moral development. Voices from these perspectives claim that each culture or gender ought to be considered separately. Shweder states that moral development should be considered relative and particular to each culture; that morality can make sense only from each cultural point of view, thus invalidating a claim of universal moral development because of its Western, individualistic, androcentric bias.

Turiel and Wainryb present an alternative yet culturally sensitive viewpoint. Their analysis of moral development shifts away from looking at cultural patterning as a whole, to a focus on the diverse experiences people have while living in a culture that naturally consists of a variety of contexts within each culture. Their type of analysis explains moral development by examining the range of diversity within cultures, highlighting the ideas that participation and acceptance of norms and practices in culture plays as much a role in moral development as does the culture itself. They find that in both Western and non-Western cultures two age-related patterns develop: increased autonomy in adolescence and increased understanding of and concern for the social context. Turiel and Wainryb see autonomy and interdependence as interwoven rather than opposing moral developments. The implications for gender orientations that have characterized moral development for males and females as independent versus interdependent, respectively, are significant.

Walker's analyses on gender differences find that while there is little substantiation for Gilligan and colleagues' claims of gender differences in the trajectory of moral judgment development, dilemma effects exist. Thus, the type of dilemma considered may influence the reasons people give, causing researchers to categorize or evaluate moral reasoning and its development in a particular way. This supports the idea of consideration for context in the analysis of moral development, but the emphasis should be on the aspects of culture, its nature, one's participation in it, and the acceptance of norms, rather than on the culture or gender itself. Thus, future research on moral development lies in developing a more comprehensive perspective and explanation of the processes of development itself, and the full range of psychological and social processes that influence moral development.

Further Reading: Colby, A., & Kohlberg, L. (1987). *The measurement of moral judgment* (Vol. I). Cambridge: Cambridge University Press. Gilligan, C. (1982). *In a different voice: Psychological theory and women's development.* Cambridge, MA: Harvard University Press. Moshman, D. (2003). Developmental change in adulthood. In J. Demick & C. Andreoletti (Eds.), *Handbook of adult development* (pp. 43–61). New York: Kluwer Academic/Plenum Publishers. Piaget, J. (1932/1965). *The moral judgment of the child.* New York: Free Press. Shweder, R.A. (1990). Cultural psychology: What is it? In J.W. Stigler, R.A. Shweder, & G. Herdt (Eds.), *Cultural psychology: Essays on comparative human development* (pp. 27–66). New York: Cambridge University Press. Turiel, E., & Wainryb, C. (2000). Social life in cultures: Judgments, conflict, and subversion. *Child Development, 71,* 250–76. Wainryb, C. (2006). Moral development in culture: Diversity, tolerance, and justice. In M. Killen & J. Smetana (Eds.), *Handbook of moral development* (pp. 211–40). Mahwah, NJ: Lawrence Earlbaum Associates. Walker, L. (2006). Gender and morality. In M. Killen & J. Smetana (Eds.), *Handbook of moral development* (pp. 93–115). Mahwah, NJ: Lawrence Earlbaum Associates.

Dawn E. Schrader

Moral Discussion

As educators and psychologists became more and more interested in identifying the stages of moral reasoning according to Lawrence Kohlberg's theory of stages of moral reasoning development, they also became interested in how such reasoning developed. Moshe Blatt (see Blatt Effect) was a pioneer in using classroom discussions of moral dilemmas as an intervention to stimulate moral reasoning stage development. His work in the late 1960s and early 1970s helped spawn a large interest in utilizing teacher-led peer discussions of moral issues and problems in school (and other) settings.

The first wave of interest was largely in testing the effects of such implementation, and many studies were done showing that a series of such moral discussions could produce significant development of moral reasoning in students. In the early and mid 1970s, large scale studies were done in Boston and Pittsburgh by Ted Fenton, Kohlberg, and others. Interest was great and, as Jack Fraenkel claimed, many jumped on the "Kohlberg bandwagon."

This led to the second wave in the late 1970s and early 1980s, which produced workshops and guidebooks helping teachers learn the techniques of effective moral discussion facilitation. Samuel Gomberg (1980) and colleagues created a workbook and corresponding workshop. Arbuthnot and Faust (1981), Galbraith and Jones (1976), and others published "how to" books on leading moral discussions.

This in turn spawned a third wave that was more research-based. Numerous scholars turned their attention to understanding the causal processes that accounted for the effects of peer moral discussions on moral reasoning development. Led by the work of Marvin Berkowitz and John Gibbs on identifying developmentally stimulating forms of peer moral discussion (called "Transactive discussion"), researchers in the United States, Germany, and Switzerland primarily led this effort.

It has become clear that structured peer discussions of moral dilemmas stimulate moral reasoning development, especially for the lower stage students in the discussion and especially if the students engage in transactive discussion (really engage and analyze each other's arguments and reasoning). Researchers and practitioners have also been able to identify pedagogical strategies that seem to support the success of such discussions. Using moral dilemmas on which the group is split, directing discussants to try to reach consensus, focusing on reasoning, providing time for individual reflection, and so forth are effective strategies that teachers can employ.

The interest in moral dilemma discussions has diminished since its heyday in the 1970s and 1980s, in part because the focus on moral reasoning as an educational goal has lost ground to a broader emphasis on student character development and in part because Kohlberg and many of his followers were more interested in comprehensive school reform efforts (e.g., The Just Community) than the narrower focus on leading classroom discussions of moral dilemmas. In addition, numerous conceptual controversies arose. The best known is called the "Plus One Convention," which argued that a teacher needed to present moral arguments one stage above that of the student for the student to develop as a result of the moral discussion (see "Plus One Convention").

Nonetheless, Georg Lind at the University of Konstanz (Germany) has continued to study moral discussion and has generated a very helpful Web site and supporting materials for those interested in implementing this strategy (http://www.uni-konstanz.de/ag-moral/moral/dildisk.htm).

Further Reading: Arbuthnot, J., & Faust, D. (1981). *Teaching moral reasoning: Theory and practice.* San Francisco: Harper and Row. Berkowitz, M.W. (1985). The role of discussion in moral education. In M.W. Berkowitz & F. Oser (Eds.), *Moral education: Theory and application* (pp. 197–218). Hillsdale, NJ: L. Erlbaum. Galbraith, R.E., & Jones, T.M. (1976). *Moral reasoning: A teaching handbook for adapting Kohlberg in the classroom.* St. Paul, MN: Greenhaven.

Marvin W. Berkowitz

Moral Exemplars

Moral exemplars, also referred to as moral saints or moral paragons, can be conceptualized in two philosophical ways (Flanagan, 1991). First, a moral exemplar can be envisioned as a person who lives according to a unitary moral principle such as maximizing benefits and minimizing costs (i.e., utilitarianism). However, in such cases living life according to a single, unitary principle is neither desirable (see Wolf, 1982) nor psychologically realistic (see Flanagan, 1991): Who would and could live their daily lives according to a single principle?

Alternatively, a moral exemplar can be conceived of as a person who showcases a full complement of moral virtues such as trust, honesty, and integrity. Yet the problem with this approach is that it too seems psychologically unrealistic (Flanagan, 1991). For one, different moral virtues are often opposing: Leading a life of peace and solitude seems at odds with a life of conscientious activism. Moreover, a single person possessing all these ideal moral virtues seems impossible, and this leaves no allowances for flaws endemic in our nature (Flanagan, 1991). Therefore, looking to philosophers to help us define what a moral exemplar "ought to be" has met with minimal success.

While philosophers search for sound theories to help guide moral actions, moral psychologists have taken a different tack. For instance, Colby and Damon (1992) asked scholars in morality to generate features associated with moral exemplars. These scholars then used this list to nominate individuals. Their criteria included commitment to moral principles, behaving according to these principles, sacrificing self-interests, showing humility, and being inspirational. Similarly, Hart and Fegley (1995) had youth group and religious leaders and cultural psychologists generate their criteria in order to find caring exemplary ethnic youth. Their criteria list included community involvement, extraordinary family responsibilities, and volunteering. Thus, emerging from this research is the global impression that real-life moral exemplars are extraordinarily prosocially active in their family and/or community life, and possess specific characteristics such as being humble and selfless.

For the most part, the kinds of moral exemplars studied have been those people who perform "good deeds." For Colby and Damon, their adult moral exemplars were nominated largely due to their sustained involvement in issues around poverty, civil rights, health care, peace, and ethics. In studies by Matsuba and Walker (2004, 2005), their young adult moral exemplars showed extraordinary commitment to organizations such as Big Brothers Big Sisters. For Hart and Fegley (1995), their adolescent ethnic minority care exemplars were recognized for their contributions to a community gardening program and Special Olympics as examples. Beyond their prosocial work, however, is there more to know about the character of these moral exemplars?

Results from the above studies reveal additional information regarding the character of moral exemplars. For instance, Colby and Damon (1992) reported that their exemplars showed courage, certainty, positivity, and hopefulness in the face of challenging situations and personal sacrifices. Furthermore, in contrast to comparison individuals, moral exemplars were more agreeable (Matsuba & Walker, 2004), described themselves using more moral, caring personality traits, and emphasized more moral, caring goals (Hart & Fegley, 1995). Moreover, results reveal that moral exemplars' self-construction differs from comparison individuals. For instance, Hart and Fegley (1995) and Reimer and Wade-Stein (2004) showed that care exemplars' conception of their ideal self was more in-line with their actual self relative to comparison individuals. Matsuba and Walker (2005) found that moral exemplars uniquely constructed their life narratives: Relative to comparison individuals, moral exemplars reveal different life experiences such as witnessing the suffering of others in childhood and having experienced moments of empowerment. These kinds of life experiences seem to have shaped their life trajectory. Finally, Colby and Damon reveal that, over experiences, exemplars' moral commitments and personal goals became unified: Their actions defined who they were. Hence, their sense of moral duty no longer was in tension with their personal duty as often is portrayed in moral philosophy (e.g., Williams, 1981).

While psychological research continues to uncover the nature of a caring type of moral exemplar, many questions remain. Are there other ways to conceive of moral exemplars beyond the prosocial? (see Walker, 2002). Does culture matter? What are the costs of leading a morally exemplary life? These and other questions await answers.

Further Reading: Colby, A., & Damon, W. (1992). The development of extraordinary moral commitment. In M. Killen & D. Hart (Eds.), *Morality in everyday life: Developmental perspectives* (pp. 342–70). New York: Cambridge University Press. Hart, D., Yates, M., Fegley, S., & Wilson, G. (1995). Moral commitment among inner-city adolescents. In M. Killen & D. Hart (Eds.), *Morality in everyday life: Developmental perspectives* (pp. 371–407). New York: Cambridge University Press. Walker, L.J. (2002). Moral exemplarity. In W. Damon (Ed.), *Bringing in a new era in character education* (pp. 65–83). Stanford, CA: Hoover Institution Press.

References: Colby, A., & Damon, W. (1992). *Some do care: Contemporary lives of moral commitment.* New York: Free Press. Flanagan, O. (1991). *Varieties of moral personality: Ethics and psychological realism.* Cambridge, MA: Harvard University Press. Hart, D., & Fegley, S. (1995). Prosocial behavior and caring in adolescence: Relations to self-understanding and social judgment. *Child Development, 66,* 1346–1359. Matsuba, M.K., & Walker, L.J. (2004). Extraordinary moral commitment: Young adults involved in social organizations. *Journal of Personality, 72,* 413–36. Matsuba, M.K., & Walker, L.J. (2005). Young adult moral exemplars: The making of self through stories. *Journal of Research on Adolescence, 15,* 275–97. Reimer, K.S., & Wade-Stein, D. (2004). Moral identity in adolescence: Self and other in semantic space. *Identity, 4,* 229–49. Walker, L.J., & Pitts, R.C. (1998). Naturalistic conceptions of moral maturity. *Developmental Psychology, 34,* 403–19. Williams, B. (1981). *Moral luck: Philosophical papers, 1973–1980.* Cambridge, UK: Cambridge University Press. Wolf, S. (1982). Moral saints. *Journal of Philosophy, 79,* 419–39.

M. Kyle Matsuba

Moral Identity

For thousands of years, philosophers and theologians have been interested in the question of what motivates people to behave morally or to avoid behaving immorally—in other words, they have been interested in moral motivation. Over the past century, social scientists (e.g., psychologists) have taken up this question as well, and they have been forming and scientifically testing theories of moral functioning. Most of these theories, such as Lawrence Kohlberg's Cognitive Developmental Theory, propose that moral motivation stems from the understanding of moral principles. Essentially, when a person knows the moral thing to do in a given situation, he or she will be motivated to act consistently with that knowledge. Other theories suggest it is emotions that are primarily responsible for motivating moral action. In essence, feeling emotions such as guilt or empathy (often labeled "moral emotions") compels people to moral action. Finally, in recent years, some scholars have begun to argue that a person's identity may also play an important role in moral motivation. In fact, some even claim moral identity may be a stronger and more reliable source of moral motivation than moral understanding and moral emotion.

What Is Moral Identity?

People base their identities on various things such as values, goals, actions, and roles, which might be thought of as identity contents. So, a person has a moral identity to the extent that his or her identity is based on identity contents that might be considered moral. For example, someone for whom moral values (e.g., fairness, honesty, and kindness) are more central and important to his or her identity, in comparison to other values, might be said to have a moral identity. Similarly, an individual might be described as having a moral identity if moral roles (e.g., helping at a soup kitchen or donating blood) are central to his or her identity. It is doubtful that people either have or do not have a moral identity; rather, all people probably differ on a continuum regarding the extent to which their identity is morally based. Further, it is possible that the relevance of morality to one's identity fluctuates over time and across situations. Moral identity is a relatively new research area, so we still know little about what it entails and how it functions.

How Does Moral Identity Relate to Moral Action?

If moral identity is an important source of moral motivation, then it should be linked to moral action. Unfortunately, very few studies have examined links between moral identity and action; thus, we know little about how and to what extent moral identity compels moral action. Nevertheless, enough work has been done to suggest that moral identity may play an important role in morality. A few studies have involved examination of people identified as moral exemplars (that is, people who exhibit high levels of moral commitment), often in comparison to nonexemplars (that is, people who exhibit typical levels of moral commitment). These studies have all found that moral exemplars tend to define their identities and their personal goals and desires more in moral terms than nonexemplars. Other studies have assessed moral identity and moral action, and looked at links between the two directly. These studies have generally shown that individuals scoring higher on moral identity tend to exhibit or report higher levels of moral behavior than those scoring lower on moral identity. In short, there does seem to be a positive correlation between moral identity and moral action; but, the nature of this association has not yet been adequately elucidated. In other words, more work is needed to understand the causal nature of this relation (that is, does moral identity lead to moral action, does acting morally lead to moral identity, or is the association bidirectional?) and the mechanisms underlying it.

How Does Moral Identity Develop?

Little is known yet about how moral identity develops, although several theoretical models have been proposed. Primarily, it has been posited that identity and morality initially develop as two separate systems in childhood. Then, around adolescence the two developmental systems begin to converge in some individuals, such that their sense of morality becomes important to their sense of identity—which is moral identity. This fusion of morality and identity is enabled in adolescence because it is during this stage that the two systems both tend to become more ideological. In other words, people's sense of morality becomes based more on internal moral principles than on external things such as consequences of actions; similarly, identity becomes based more on internal belief systems than on external things such as physical characteristics or typical behaviors. Although studies have demonstrated these developmental changes in morality and identity, it is still unclear how the two merge to form a moral identity in some people.

What Factors Influence the Development of Moral Identity?

Several factors have been identified as influences on the development of moral identity, some individual and some contextual. At the individual level, things such as personality, cognitive development, attitudes and values, and broader self and identity development can impact moral identity development. For example, those more advanced in cognitive and identity development have greater capacities for moral identity development. Also, greater appreciation for moral values might facilitate their subsequent integration into identity. At the contextual level, one important factor is the person's social structure, including neighborhood, school, family, and institutions such as religious, youth, or community organizations. For example, a caring and supportive family environment can facilitate the development of morality and identity, as well as the integration of the two into moral identity. Additionally, involvement in religious and youth organizations can provide not only moral beliefs systems but also opportunities to act on those beliefs (e.g., through community involvement), which can aid their integration into identity.

How Can Moral Identity Development Be Facilitated?

If moral identity plays an important role in moral development and action, then present efforts for moral education and youth development may be aided by greater understanding of how to facilitate moral identity development. One of the most important ideas that has emerged thus far is that to form a moral identity youth not only must understand the objective importance of morality but also must gain a personal appreciation for morality and its relevance to them. This can be promoted by not only teaching moral principles but also providing opportunities to act on those principles. Such opportunities allow youth to gain a tangible appreciation for moral principles and see themselves as capable of and responsible for impacting others through moral action. A result of this process is that youth can then begin to integrate moral principles into their own identities, endowing them with greater motivation for subsequent moral action.

Further Reading: Colby, A., & Damon, W. (1992). *Some do care: Contemporary lives of moral commitment.* New York: The Free Press. Damon, W., & Gregory, A. (1997). The youth charter: Towards the formation of adolescent moral identity. *Journal of Moral Education, 26,* 117–30. Hardy, S.A., & Carlo, G. (2005). Identity as a source of moral motivation. *Human Development, 48,* 232–56. Lapsley, D.K., & Narvaez, D. (Eds.). (2004). *Moral development, self, and identity.* Mahwah, NJ: Lawrence Erlbaum Associates. Youniss, J., & Yates, M. (1997). *Community service and social responsibility in youth.* Chicago: The University of Chicago Press.

Sam A. Hardy

Moral Judgment

In contrast to the vernacular notion of "judgment," which connotes a verdict or conclusion, moral judgment includes social cognitive components that involve a complex constellation of reasons—regardless of whether the reasons themselves are not complex or philosophically elegant—about justice, rights, welfare, and rules in social interactions, as well as the reasoning processes involved in the contemplation of those reasons. Moral judgment, as a psychological construct, is the term used first by Jean Piaget and later by Lawrence Kohlberg, Elliot Turiel, and others in their investigations into the field of how people reason and make decisions about conflicts in the moral domain (see Cognitive Moral Development). These theorists pioneered the study of moral judgment in psychology, apart from, but grounded within, the sphere of philosophical inquiry.

Moral judgment in the psychological literature most often refers to Kohlberg's cognitive developmental definition of moral judgment. Kohlberg noted that, "it is only when social cognition is extended into prescriptive judgments as to what is right or good that we can identify a moral judgment" (Colby & Kohlberg, 1987, p. 10). Thus, prescriptivity, or the idea that there is an action that one "ought" to take in a certain situation, is the hallmark of moral judgments, and the prescriptivity arises from a moral principle, or a belief that one has about exactly what action one "ought" to take. Moral judgment, then, is the system of cognitive operations involved in reasoning about, understanding, and developing conclusions when thinking about dilemmas involving conflicts of ethics and morals. Moral judgment is a cognitive construct but is not without personal, emotional, and intuitive aspects (Nucci, 2004). Researchers have included the moral self, emotions such as guilt and empathy, and intuitions about moral principles without the underlying rational structure of them in their descriptions of moral judgment, especially when explaining the relationship between moral judgment and moral action.

A moral judgment can also refer to the unit of analysis within one's overall thinking about moral concerns, dilemmas, and issues. The ways that individuals reason about moral actions that should be taken in given situations, or make moral judgments, are seen to follow a developmental sequence, not unlike Piaget's theory of cognitive development. The sequence consists of three levels of perspective on social-moral convention: the preconventional, conventional, and postconventional levels; each comprising two stages (see Cognitive Moral Development). Moral judgment stages, according to Kohlberg, have four characteristics attributed to Piaget's requirements for stage structure. That is, each stage is qualitatively different from the other, the structures arise in an invariant sequence, and there is a coherent logic or thought organization of each stage so that it is a complete "structural whole" or system. Colby and Kohlberg (1987) articulate a comprehensive description and scoring manual for understanding individuals' moral judgment. As a methodological and analytic tool, Kohlberg's theory states that the study of moral judgment rests on three assumptions: (1) there is a phenomenological approach where individuals' judgments are seen in their own terms and from the individual's viewpoint, (2) moral judgments have a structure or underlying principles of thought patterns and are not solely content-based, and (3) moral judgments are constructed by individuals' active engagement with the world. The scoring manual operationalizes moral judgments as consisting of four components: issue, norm, element, and stage (Colby & Kohlberg, 1987). A moral judgment is an evaluation of the moral claims that are made in moral situations that include ideas of what action choice should be taken (issue), the moral reasons that justify why that action is the selected action choice (norm), moral and philosophical foundations that support the moral reasons that justify the action choice (elements), and the social perspective from which judgments are made (stage).

Third, moral judgment refers to the result of thinking about moral issues. When moral judgment refers to reasoning and understanding of thought processes and strategies of decision making regarding considerations of justice and fairness, it is considered cognitive moral judgment. However, a moral judgment refers to conclusions made or evaluation of behavior or norms in the moral domain, which is part of the larger social domain (Turiel, 1983). In this way, conclusions about social norms, dispositions, character, values, and the like are considered moral judgments in that they are judgments made in the moral domain but do not necessarily reflect structural cognitive components that follow along a cognitive moral developmental sequence such as outlined by Kohlberg. Although for researchers examining social conventions and morality a moral judgment is less specific, it is also a unit of analysis of moral considerations and conclusions. For many, including moral theorists and the general public, moral judgment connotes a valuation of the morality of a conclusion about something (reasons or reasoning processes or conclusions) in the moral domain. Or, moral judgment is also about valuing and caring in the moral domain such as Gilligan (1982) described and thus need not be cognitive-structural in a Piagetian or Kohlbergian sense but is still a result of thinking and reasoning. The field is currently moving toward a synthesis of the various perspectives of moral judgment to present a more comprehensive explanation of the concept.

Further Reading: Colby, A., & Kohlberg, L. (1987). *The measurement of moral judgment* (Vol. I). Cambridge: Cambridge University Press. Gilligan, C. (1982). *In a different voice: Psychological theory and women's development.* Cambridge, MA: Harvard University Press. Nucci, L. (2004). Reflections on the moral self construct. In D.K. Lapsley & D. Narvaez (Eds.), *Moral development, self, and identity* (pp. 111–32). Mahwah, NJ: Lawrence Erlbaum Associates. Piaget, J. (1965/1932). *The moral judgment of the child.* New York: Free Press. Turiel, E. (1983). *The development of social knowledge: Morality and convention.* Cambridge, UK: Cambridge University Press.

Dawn E. Schrader

Moral Judgment Interview

The moral judgment interview (MJI) is the instrument used to assess the stage of an individual's moral judgment. Lawrence Kohlberg originally designed the interview to explore how individuals make moral judgments. Analyzing the interview data that he collected from a cross-sectional sample of children and adolescents, he derived his first description of moral development for his 1958 doctoral dissertation. Later he administered the moral judgment interview to a longitudinal sample and further refined his descriptions of the moral stages.

The MJI follows the semiclinical model used by Jean Piaget to explore children's reasoning. The interview has a standardized format of dilemmas and questions that are presented to each participant. The interviewer asks participants "probe questions," which require them to elaborate upon or clarify their responses. The point of the clinical part of the interview is to understand how the participants arrive at their judgments; how do they see the values at stake in the dilemma, and what are the reasons that they use to justify their decisions? The greatest challenge for interviewers is to refrain from jumping to conclusions about what participants mean and to allow participants to express themselves as fully as possible in their own words. In a sense, the interview is like a conversation in which the interviewer is trying to ascertain as clearly as possible what the interviewee means.

Optimally MJIs are taped and transcribed for later coding. On occasion, experienced interviewers can write down the participants' responses verbatim. Sometimes, the interview is administered in writing but the quality of these interviews varies greatly. John Gibbs, a co-author of Kohlberg's standard moral judgment scoring manual, developed the Sociomoral Reflection Measure (SRM) for use as a written interview alternative to the MJI. The SRM does not use dilemmas but asks the participants to give reasons for upholding different moral values, such as obeying the law and keeping promises.

The MJI presents three moral dilemmas. Each moral dilemma presents a different moral problem involving several moral values. Currently the interview has three parallel forms (A, B, C). Form A is the most widely used and discussed version of the instrument. The interview begins with the well-known Heinz Dilemma in which a husband is forced to decide whether or not he should steal a drug to save his wife's life after having exhausted all other ways of obtaining the drug. The dilemma has no obvious right answer. Values can be evoked to support a decision to steal or not to steal the drug. For example, the values of respect for life, care, and a husband's duty support the decision to steal. On the other hand, the values of respect for property rights and the law support the decision not to steal. Dilemmas force hard choices and in doing so force participants to articulate how they understand the values at stake. Because there is no obvious "right answer" to the dilemmas, the respondents have to think carefully about their decisions and justify their positions. The dilemma format makes it difficult for participants to give merely what they consider to be the socially desirable "right answer." Removing the dilemma from participants' everyday experience (the protagonist's name, "Heinz," suggests that the dilemma is taking place in an unfamiliar location, life/death dilemmas are a rare occurrence, and the dilemma itself presents a hypothetical and not a real case) further encourages participants to think for themselves and to express what they believe is the right action (e.g., "Heinz should steal") in contrast to what they or others might do ["I (or Hienz) would let her die"].

The MJI is deliberately designed to assess moral reasoning competence, which is an individual's highest stage of moral judgment. Individuals may reason at lower stages in real life situations due to a variety of personality and contextual influences. Psychologists have debated, however, whether the MJI demands too much in asking individuals to articulate their justifications for their judgments. The reasoning elicited by the moral judgment interview may overemphasize moral reflection and fail to recognize tacit features of moral judgment. Instead of asking participants to answer open-ended questions, a production task, James Rest's Defining Issues Test (DIT) and Georg Lind's Moral Judgment Test (MJT) use a preference task, which asks participants to indicate their agreement with preselected moral positions.

Further Reading: Colby, A., Gibbs, J.C., Liberman, M., & Kohlberg, L. (1983). A longitudinal study of moral judgment. *Monographs of the Society for Research in Child Development, 48*(1–2), 1–124. Colby, A., & Kohlberg, L. (1987). *The measurement of moral judgment* (Vol. 1). New York: Cambridge University Press. Gibbs, J.C., Fuller, R.L., & Basinger, K.S. (1992). *Moral maturity: Measuring the development of sociomoral reflection.* Hillsdale, NJ: Lawrence Earlbaum Associates. Lind, G., Hartmann, H,A., & Wakenhut, R. (Eds.). (1985). *Moral development and the social environment.* Chicago: Precedent Publishing. Rest, J., Narvaez, D., Bibeau, M.J., & Thoma, S.J. (1999). *Post-conventional thinking: A Neo-Kohlbergian approach.* Maywah, NJ: Lawrence Earlbaum.

F. Clark Power

Moral Objectivism and Subjectivism

Moral objectivism and subjectivism are types of metaethical perspective, not themselves metaethical theories. Broadly speaking, the distinction concerns whether moral judgments are true or false, or whether the validity of moral standards such as rules and ideals depends on what people think. In analytic moral philosophy, these are called "moral cognitivism" and "noncognitivism," respectively.

Except in prototypical cases, these two types of perspective are not quite opposites. The dichotomy tends to require a kind of simplification that makes categorizing sophisticated perspectives difficult.

A paradigm case of subjectivism is emotivism. Emotivists hold that moral judgments express feelings or attitudes. The notion that your moral opinions are true for you and mine are true for me is interpreted by emotivists to mean that we approve of different things. A sentence like "She lied to you and that was wrong" may seem to report a fact about what she did, but actually it expresses the speaker's disapproval. There are simply no objective moral standards by reference to which there could be facts to state, any more than there are objective standards of beauty. Thus, the meaning of such statements is not their apparent content but rather their function. The function of moral judgments is to express feelings or attitudes.

A prototypical instance of objectivism is the view that there are moral absolutes. These moral standards, such as rules and ideals, are established and revealed by God and/or are discerned by reason. Whether anyone agrees or likes it is beside the point. Furthermore, the absolutes do not depend on context. Unprovoked violence against an innocent and vulnerable person is wrong, no matter what the circumstances. In clear cases at least, there is no room for interpretation or equivocation. Moral cognition may conform or not to these standards, but it does not affect them.

Another example of objectivism is realism. Realists hold that moral judgments have the same structure and truth conditions as observation statements. Moral judgments are propositions that report matters of fact in the world either accurately or inaccurately. If one speaker says, "She lied to you and that was wrong," and another says, "She lied to you and it was a permissible lie," then they cannot both be correct about the same event in the same respects, even if both are expressing their genuine feelings about what she did. Some forms of absolutism are compatible with realism, but the emphasis in absolutism is on absolute standards rather than on the existence of truth conditions for moral judgments.

A second type of moral subjectivism—or at least nonobjectivism—is prescriptivism. Prescriptivism like emotivism focuses on the meaning of moral language, but prescriptivists hold that moral judgments do not have a merely expressive function. Their function is to state prescriptions. Grammatically speaking, they have an imperative mood, such as "Do not lie," not a subjunctive mood, such as "Would that no one lied." Prescriptivists disagree with realists, holding that moral judgments do not have an indicative mood, such as "Her lie was wrong as a matter of fact." Descriptions may be true or false, but prescriptions cannot be. Since the function of moral language is to express prescriptions, moral judgments do not have truth conditions.

Two borderline cases may help illustrate the oversimplifying nature of the moral objectivism-subjectivism dichotomy: contractarianism and Aristotelianism.

According to contractarians, humans have a basic right to consent or not consent to any system of rules of conduct. No set of rules is binding that does not, or would not in the right conditions of rational discourse, gain consent. Moral standards, such as rules and ideals, and the judgments derived from them, are valid or invalid based on their having been accepted or their being acceptable, in the right conditions, to a reasonable person. Since consent is required, what people think is relevant. Since the reasonable person is a standard independent of any particular individual, however, there is some objective ground for moral judgments.

Aristotelians emphasize that what is right and good for humans depends on facts about the human species. Physical health is objectively preferable to infirmity or disease, all other things being equal. Thus, patterns of living that promote health are objectively better. Lying tends to erode trust, which is important for cooperation for common well-being, so lying is wrong, at least for the most part. The human good is determined by objective facts about the species and environment, and yet it is the human good that is central, which is at least partly a matter of human subjective experience.

Notice, finally, that any constructivist moral epistemology, any constructivist epistemology generally, is on these terms in a way both objectivist and subjectivist. A construction of reality, making the world intelligible, is always a human construction. On the other hand, some constructions are less adequate to reality than others, and the test is in organism-environment interactions, not in internal features of the constructions themselves.

Further Reading: Hare, R.M. (1952). *The language of morals.* Oxford: Clarendon. Sayre-McCord, G. (1988). *Essays on moral realism.* Ithaca, NY: Cornell University Press. Stevenson, C. (1944). *Ethics and language.* New Haven and London: Yale University Press.

Don Collins Reed

Moral Obligation

To have an obligation is to owe something, to be bound or in debt. So the question of moral obligation is, what are we morally bound to do and/or to refrain from doing?

For instance, Peter Singer (1972) has argued that we each have a moral obligation to contribute to famine and disease relief in developing countries, to the extent that we are able, without making a sacrifice of greater moral worth than the benefit done through our contribution. In a famous 1972 article, he compared our contributing from our comparative affluence to the act of saving a child from drowning in a nearby shallow pool, when doing so would soil our shoes and soak the bottom of our pants or skirt.

Two questions arise with this example. Are all moral obligations negative (not to do X), or are some positive (to do Y)? And are all moral obligations derived from an act of consent, or do some exist "by nature"?

No reasonable person would deny that one should refrain from unprovoked violence against a vulnerable, innocent person. But do I have a positive obligation as well? Am I obliged to intervene to prevent such harm from beginning or to stop it when it is occurring?

Some hold that there is an important distinction between duties and acts that go beyond one's duty, called "supererogatory." We might say that one who saved a drowning or starving child would be doing something praiseworthy but that no one has a moral obligation to do so, except perhaps the child's parent or someone else with whom the child is bound in a special relationship.

If, on the other hand, one had promised to provide such aid, or had voluntarily entered into an association or society one requirement of which was to provide such aid, then one has a moral obligation to help. Additionally, we might say that benefiting from such an association constitutes tacit acceptance of the obligations entailed by the relationship, even though no explicit commitment to those obligations has been made. Thomas Pogge (2002) has argued that affluent persons in developed countries benefit from global institutional structures that impede famine and disease prevention in developing countries and that on those grounds affluent persons have a moral obligation to make amends for the unjust consequences of the structures whose benefits they enjoy.

Moral obligations, then, may be negative only, or some may be positive. They may depend on explicit or tacit consent, a voluntary act taking on the obligation, but some may be "natural" rather than voluntary. Moral obligations may be distinct from praiseworthy acts that go beyond the call of duty. And they may include some "special obligations," which we have only to those with whom we are bound in special relationships, or such obligations may not be "moral" ones at all, but of some other type, since we might hold that all peculiarly moral obligations are universal and impartial.

We may also distinguish moral obligations from political and legal obligations. The laws of the state in which one lives, at least so long as these laws are duly enacted by a legislative authority that was duly constituted, impose legal obligations. According to some, political obligations are somewhat broader than legal obligations, including coming to the defense of one's state in the absence of a law requiring one to do so. Political and/or legal obligations are a subclass of special obligations, which extend to a state rather than to a family or other intimate association.

Finally, how one thinks about moral obligations, broadly speaking, depends on whether one believes that moral obligations bind independently of moral ideals or as the minimal conditions for possibly achieving moral ideals. Moral obligations bind independently only if there is some ground or warrant for them irrespective of one's goals and ideals. In liberal societies, where diverse peoples of different ethnicities live together, structuring their lives according to various worldviews and understandings of the human good, it has seemed imperative to suppose that there are universal moral rules that give rise to moral obligations that obtain whatever one's ethnicity. On morality we must all agree, it has been supposed, though on what makes life meaningful and worthwhile we may differ.

On the other hand, the failure of Kantians, utilitarians, contractarians, and other modern moral philosophers to agree, among themselves let alone with each other, is notorious. Aristotelians and other teleological ethicists understand moral obligations in relation to the minimal conditions for the possible achievement of the human good. Failing to fulfill moral obligations on this account is self-defeating. For some of these theorists, there is little importance in isolating a class of peculiarly "moral" obligations. The minimal conditions of achieving the human good are minimal "normally" and "for the most part" rather than absolutely, and so in that respect moral obligations are not clearly distinguishable from other obligations not usually considered moral, such as to maintain a healthy lifestyle and to develop one's talents.

Further Reading: Pogge, T. (2002). *World poverty and human rights: Cosmopolitan responsibilities and reforms.* Cambridge, England: Polity Press. Singer, P. (1972). Famine, affluence, and morality. *Philosophy and Public Affairs, 1*(1). Zimmerman, M. (1996). *The concept of moral obligation.* New York: Cambridge University Press.

Don Collins Reed

Moral Personality

In the most general sense, to speak of the moral personality is to refer to the organization of those psychological characteristics that affect a person's moral functioning (that is, his or her moral beliefs, emotions, and, particularly, moral action) and determine individual differences in this specific domain of human behavior. Though the concept of moral personality is as old as moral psychology, a more conscious and differentiated attention to it is relatively recent, a result of the theoretical vicissitudes in this area of psychology.

In a first phase, moral functioning was understood to be directly influenced by internalized moral demands, but it was taken for granted that moral demands were a part of the overall personality, operating in the context of, and in interaction with, the person's other psychological characteristics. This phase was theoretically dominated by the various psychoanalytic theories, on one side, and, on the other, by the different versions of behaviorism or learning theory. These two theoretical approaches are dramatically different in their conception of personality and yet look at morality in a rather similar way: objectively, as the set of conventional norms adopted in each society; psychologically, as the internalized reflection of such norms, subject to the need of internal and external adaptation. Most importantly, both theoretical approaches understood moral functioning in ways that make it unrecognizable from the perspective of people's common moral experience. The deterministic assumptions of both psychoanalytic and learning theories, and their skepticism about motives that, at least in part, would be independent of personal needs, excluded two essential criteria of morality, a genuine orientation to the moral good for its sake, and a certain capacity to choose and decide on moral grounds. In this first phase, then, the moral personality is personality with only a moral façade.

The cognitive revolution of the 1940s and 1950s and the increasingly dominant influence of cognitive-developmentalism corrected the previous distortions concerning the nature of morality and marked a second phase in the approach to the moral personality: Jean Piaget's emphasis on moral understanding, his work on egocentrism and on intentionality; Lawrence Kohlberg's insistence on moral reasoning and its logical organization; their—Piaget's and Kohlberg's—understanding of moral development as a result of the person's confrontation with the social and moral reality, provided a conception of moral functioning that is consonant with our everyday experience. In this conception, however, moral understanding became decontextualized from the person's overall psychological organization; moral cognitive structures were given complete, clearly unrealistic powers over moral functioning. Eventually the inadequacies of cognitive-developmentalism became obvious, especially when the theory was confronted with the complexities, detours, inconsistencies, and self-deceptions that people experience in their effort to live morally.

In the present third phase, efforts are being made to retain the essential truth of cognitive-developmentalism—that is, that genuine moral functioning must be based on some understanding of the nature of the moral good, informing moral intentions and actions—but to reintegrate moral understanding in the multilayered personality organization. These attempts, different as they are in their focus and questions, follow similar empirical and theoretical strategies. What needs to be understood and explained is the morally relevant action in all its variations, from the life inspired by moral concerns, to the immoral action performed in contradiction with one's understanding and values, to a life that is marked by open disregard of, and contempt for, morality and moral concerns.

The explanations for these differences, then, are constructed starting from the various personality variables, their developmental maturity and quality, their reciprocal interactions, and the quality of the overall personality organization. The questions that characterize the cognitive-developmental approach can still be pursued. However, from the perspective of the moral personality one can raise many other questions: for instance, concerning the independent role of moral motivation; the importance of moral motivation in relation to the person's other motives, their strength and organization; the influence of interpersonal attachments, and their supportive or obstructive role in moral functioning; the respective role of the person's responsibility system and control system; the importance of one's defensive and coping system, and so on.

Finally, it is important to realize that in approaching the moral personality in this way, one has to confront serious conceptual and theoretical difficulties, frequently a result of entrenched mental habits in psychology. In particular, a kind of paradox arises when moral functioning is seen in the context of personality, namely, the necessity to maintain the autonomy of morality, while at the same time recognizing its dependence on the organization of personality. Moral action ought to be autonomous in the sense that its cognitive validity and motivational force should not depend on its being an instrument to satisfy the person's various needs and desires. Functionally, however, morality must depend on other aspects of personality, which may, and frequently do, limit and even overwhelm moral demands. The situation is not that different from that of an office for scientific research, created to help governmental institutions in pursuing their goals according to reality conditions. Presumably the scientists are exclusively sensitive to the truth of their scientific information. And yet the executive agencies, more concerned with other goals, may want to ignore scientific information and may even pressure the scientists to suppress or alter their findings. The crucial difference in moral functioning is that, here, it is the same person who knows the validity of moral demands, is attracted by contradictory goals, and chooses to minimize, ignore, or distort moral understanding in order to pursue his or her individual self-interest.

Further Reading: Colby, A., & Damon, W. (1992). *Some do care. Contemporary lives of moral commitment.* New York: Free Press. Lapsley, D.K., & Narvaez, D. (Eds.). (2004). *Moral development, self, and identity.* Mahwah, NJ: Erlbaum. Lapsley, D.K., & Power, F.C. (Eds.). (2005). *Character psychology and character education.* Notre Dame, IN: University of Notre Dame Press.

Augusto Blasi

Moral Realism

In moral psychology, "moral realism" is a term that derives from Jean Piaget's (1932) research on moral development. It refers to young children's characteristic moral philosophy and, more specifically, to the developmentally typical way they comprehend moral rules. According to the moral-realist schema, moral rules are, first, heteronomous. That is to say, they are not susceptible to being sanctioned by the child him/herself but are viewed instead as being arbitrarily imposed by the external authority of parents and other adults. Heteronomy also implies that moral rules are good and command assent just in virtue of being authoritatively prescribed. Second, moral realism involves the belief in objective responsibility. Neither considerations of subjective intention nor considerations of circumstantial factors figure in young children's evaluations of moral responsibility. What counts is the degree to which the objective consequences of the violation of a moral rule deviate from what the rule commands. So, for instance, a child who steals a bun to give to a friend whose family has nothing to eat is no better or worse than a child who steals a ribbon because she thinks it would look nice on her dress. Similarly, a boy who breaks ten cups unintentionally is worse than the boy who purposely breaks only two cups. In other words, the moral realist tends to value the letter of the law (that is, the performance of the specific acts it commands or forbids) over the spirit of the law (that is, the specific human harms the law is intended to discourage, all things considered). Finally, moral realism is associated with what Piaget labeled immanent justice or the causal belief that retributive punishment unavoidably follows from the transgression of a moral rule. A cookie thief may get caught by an adult and punished or, if he does not, he might trip and hurt himself. He will not, however, get away with it. In this sense, the moral realist believes that moral rules are woven into nature's very fabric.

According to Piaget, the moral realism of children is partly a function of their general egocentric cognitive orientation. Cognitive and moral development are parallel processes insofar as both involve the emergence and growth of the ability to appreciate and coordinate various perspectives on a problem. It was thus highly significant for Piaget that common practices of moral socialization and the necessarily asymmetrical social relation between adults and children seem to support moral realism and, in so doing, to hinder rather than promote moral development. Heteronomy, most notably, is reinforced by adults' demand for unilateral respect: children are required to obey rules whose point they cannot possibly understand. Accordingly, they will tend to view punishments as arbitrary and expiatory even where efforts are made to connect punishment in a meaningful way to the nature of the transgression. Because mature conceptions of moral rules leave heteronomy behind, conditions that favor moral development are those where children are more or less free from adult influence. It is in the rough and tumble of peer interaction, not under the watchful eye of an adult authority, where children come to learn that moral rules are not arbitrary commands for obedience but more flexible social arrangements that serve pragmatic ends.

As it is employed in contemporary moral philosophy, "moral realism" has an altogether distinct signification. The ordinary language that people use to talk about morality is realist. People speak as if moral statements correspond to some real features of the world, features that exist independently of anyone's opinions or preferences. Just as the statement "The cat is on the mat" can be regarded as true only if the cat is, in fact, lying on the mat, a moral judgment such as "Alain is generous" is true only if it is the case that Alain actually is generous. Moral statements, like statements about the material world, report facts, and this suggests that there is some discernible truth about moral matters. Defending the possibility that moral judgments can be grounded in stable and objective truths rather than fleeting and subjective human reactions has always been a central concern of moral philosophy in the Western tradition.

The classical objection to moral realism starts from the observation that the human world is morally pluralistic: people's moral reactions, attitudes, and beliefs vary, and sometimes vary quite dramatically, from culture to culture and from individual to individual. From here it is often inferred that moral statements are true or false not in relation to objective standards but relative to either a set of cultural values (that is, social or cultural relativism) or one's personal beliefs and preferences (that is, individual relativism or subjectivism). Another possible response to moral pluralism is the claim that moral statements express subjective feelings, preferences, opinions, or prescriptions and only appear to report moral facts. This is the general tack of so-called "noncognitivist" theories of ethics such as expressivism, emotivism, projectivism, and prescriptivism. Against such claims, proponents of moral realism commonly point out that the mere fact that people disagree about moral matters does not in and of itself pose a problem for moral realism. Disagreement exists in all fields of human endeavor. Geophysicists disagree over the quantity of the world's remaining oil and gas reserves and historians disagree over the causes of the decline of the Roman Empire, but to conclude from this fact of disagreement that the answers to the geophysical and historical questions are relative to the personal beliefs and opinions of particular geophysicists or historians is obviously a false inference. Why should things be different in the moral arena? Presumably, this analogy would be convincing if, as is generally the case in geophysics and history, there were a tendency toward consensus when questions are subjected to close and protracted rational scrutiny. The onus falls on the moral realist to explain the striking failure of convergence in moral views on such vexed moral issues as capital punishment, abortion, and euthanasia even after protracted argument.

An important modern objection to moral realism acknowledges that moral statements at least purport to report facts but denies that anything exists in the world to which such moral claims might be found to correspond. "The cat is on the mat" makes reference to material objects describable in the language of science, but to what kind of object might the statement "Plagiarism is wrong" plausibly refer? As John Mackie (1977) argued, moral realism seems to entail the existence of "queer" entities or properties quite unrelated to everything else that is thought to exist. From this perspective, moral talk is just like talk about astrology, alien abductions, or where and when Harry Potter first met Ron Weasley: the facts to which it seems to refer are imaginary. Contemporary moral realists try to get around this problem by redefining moral facts as facts about what one would believe under conditions of ideal rationality—where one is fully and vividly aware of all relevant nonmoral facts and one's rational faculty is not impaired by such things as emotional disturbances, fatigue, compulsions, and the like. Such redefinitions, however, are prey to the objection that they are unsatisfactory as a justification of ordinary moral language because they are too far removed from what people seem to mean when they ordinarily talk about moral issues.

Further Reading: Mackie, J. (1977). *Ethics: Inventing right and wrong.* London: Penguin. Piaget, J. (1932). *The moral judgment of the child.* New York: Free Press. Sayre-McCord, G. (Ed.). (1988). *Essays on moral realism.* Ithaca, NY: Cornell University Press.

Bruce Maxwell

Moral Reasoning

Moral reasoning in its most general sense is a fundamental feature of moral functioning, and it has been the target of moral and character education efforts going as far back as Socrates. The importance given to moral reasoning varies according to the way in which morality itself is understood. If morality is simply the adherence to socially defined standards or intuitive or habituated responses, then moral reasoning has little relevance to the moral life. If, on the other hand, morality involves decision making, critical judgment, and justification, then moral reasoning is central to the moral life. The claim for the centrality of moral reasoning does not imply that some actions may be performed without forethought, that emotions and habits are not significant, or that social and cultural forces do not influence moral behavior. On the other hand, insofar as individuals strive to do what is right under conditions of uncertainty or disagreement, they not only think about what is right or wrong but also attempt to justify their conclusions in a reasonable way.

Because of the dominant influence of the cognitive developmental approach on moral psychology and education since the 1970s, moral reasoning has been a highly scrutinized and debated topic. Concerns have been raised that Lawrence Kohlberg's highly philosophical theory placed too much emphasis on the verbalizations of moral reasons. Individuals, especially children, may act on the basis of intentions that they cannot properly articulate. Although their functioning may be based in cognition, Kohlberg's account overlooks the tacit features of moral judgment. Kohlberg's theory, moreover, may distort the influence attributed to moral reasoning. However important moral reasoning may be, Rest (1986) illustrates that many noncognitive factors enter into the sequence of processes leading to moral action. On the other hand, he notes that cognition is present within all of the four components (sensitivity, judgment, commitment, and implementation). Rest makes clear that his model is a normative one: it describes how individuals should under normal circumstances act morally. He is aware, of course, that individuals can and often do fail to use their reasoning at any component of the process. Moral psychology wrestles with tension between idealized descriptions of how individuals should optimally function and actual descriptions of how they do function.

In his studies of the development of conceptions of distributive justice judgments, William Damon (1977) showed that even as toddlers children recognized the need to give reasons to justify their claims. While children at the earliest stage of development simply assert their claims on the basis of their desires (e.g., "I want the candy"), children at the following stage give some justification for the claim (e.g., "I should get the candy because I am the oldest"). Damon noted that at this stage, children typically give self-serving reasons, which they later understand are inadequate. At the later stage, they attempt to resolve disputed claims objectively by calling for strictly equal distribution and later for distribution based on merit and finally equity. Damon's research underscores the fundamental role of moral reasoning in moral functioning. Even very young children understand that the resolution of conflicting claims demands more than the assertion of their desires. At a very early age, they give justifications for their claims and soon find that self-serving justifications are unfair. Not surprisingly, Damon finds that children's performances do not always match their moral competencies. Children may maintain that it is fair to distribute goods impartially but, nevertheless, when given the opportunity may act in a self-serving way. Although moral reasoning influences how individuals believe they should act, moral reasoning only partly explains how individuals do, in fact, act.

In explaining the development of moral reasoning, Damon and other cognitive developmentalists, such as Jean Piaget and Lawrence Kohlberg, maintain that children advance by taking the perspective of others into account in order to reach a decision about what is fair. In this context, moral reasoning denotes a special kind of reasoning leading to justice. Kohlberg's stages of moral judgment describe the development of moral reasoning in this limited sense. Although Kohlberg, like Piaget, draws heavily on Immanuel Kant's moral philosophy for describing the features of moral reasoning, Kohlberg's stages include all considerations leading to prescriptive judgments of right and wrong.

Kohlberg, while acknowledging a wide diversity of reasoning in his stage descriptions (Kohlberg & Colby, 1987), also noted that reasons that appeared moral at one stage may be rejected as nonmoral at a higher stage. For example, the instrumental reasons often used to justify actions at stage 2 may be irrelevant or even immoral at stage 3 or higher. Kohlberg's hierarchical stage theory committed him to the controversial position that the higher stages were better stages of moral reasoning than the lower stages.

There are other ways in which reasoning is used in the moral life. In addition to deliberation about what should be done in a particular situation, reasoning may be used antecedently to determine whether a situation calls forth a moral response, whether one is responsible for taking action, and what would be the best way to execute the action. These kinds of reasoning used throughout this process may not all be moral in the strictest sense; for example, they may involve self-oriented considerations related to one's identity or pragmatic considerations about the most efficient way of carrying out a well-intentioned plan. Moral reasoning may also be used consequent to a moral action in self-evaluative judgments leading to shame, guilt, or self-approval.

Further Reading: Damon, W. (1977). *The social world of the child.* San Francisco: Jossey-Bass. Colby, A., Kohlberg, L., Speicher, B., Hewer, A., Gibbs, J., & Power, C. (1987). *The measurement of moral judgment, Vol. 1: Theoretical foundations and research validation.* New York: Cambridge University Press. Kohlberg, L. (1981). *Essays on moral development, Vol. I: The philosophy of moral development.* San Francisco: Harper and Row. Kohlberg, L. (1984). *Essays on moral development, Vol. II: The psychology of moral development.* San Francisco: Harper and Row. Piaget. J. (1965). *Moral judgment in the child.* New York: Free Press. Rest, J.R. (1986). *Morality development: Advances in research and theory.* New York: Praeger.

F. Clark Power

Mosher, Ralph L.

In his career, Ralph Mosher (1928–1998) was a leading figure in moral education, democratic schools, and counseling psychology. In moral education, Mosher was involved in curriculum development and in using the organization and governance of schools to promote human development. While he developed curricular materials—especially in counselor education—that promoted moral development, Mosher is best known for his research and influence on democratic schools, particularly with School Within a School and Brookline High School.

In democratic schools, Mosher emphasized the role of ethical issues in communities and the responsibility of schools to prepare students to develop as full and responsible democratic citizens with the requisite knowledge, skills, and dispositions. Mosher's theoretical approach was influenced by the work of John Dewey, especially the notion that learning democracy is akin to swimming in that both are best learned by doing, not on the sidelines (or shore) as observers.

Mosher was fond of quoting British historian, D. W. Brogan to make the point about democracy not being a spectator sport and that like the American Revolution teaching students to be democratic is never finished but is an ongoing process. Brogan describes totalitarianism as similar to the *Titanic,* majestic yet ill-fated. Mosher took the final sentence of the quote and made it the core of a title of one of his own publications, "Democracy is like a raft. It never sinks, but damn it, your feet are always in the water."

Mosher was not a theoretician alone; he was a regular attendee at democratic town meetings in democratic schools. Mosher, with a characteristic self-deprecating sense of humor, frequently referred to himself as a town meeting "groupie." Mosher's role was more accurately summarized as "guru." Mosher's involvement in democratic schools started at the School Within a School (SWS) program housed at Brookline (MA) High School. SWS is a school in which most governance decisions are made via direct, participatory democracy. All the members of the community meet and, with a one-person-one-vote system, debate and decide issues ranging from free speech, to group norms, to an admission process for incoming students.

Advocates of the three primary approaches to moral education—cognitive developmental, character, and caring—concur that a relationship exists between ethical issues and moral education. Within the field, differences exist about which is primary. Mosher emphasized democratic decision making as the primary focus of moral education rather than emphasizing moral dilemmas and related ethical issues (as was the case with many of the moral education curricula, programs, and initiatives of Lawrence Kohlberg). Mosher, recognizing that democracy includes both political and social democracy, and in the process of what Dewey called "conjoint living" ethical issues would inevitably arise and in this authentic context have added pedagogical force.

Mosher and Kohlberg also differed in the way they approached their roles as consultants to moral education programs. To what extent this was the result of personality and what extent pedagogy is an open question. In practice, Kohlberg was more active—serving as an advocate for justice. Mosher's contributions were subtler in public. Many of his contributions were provided before and after town meetings in structuring the issues, considering the democratic process, and afterward reflecting with the participants on the process and substance of the meeting. Following Dewey, Mosher saw today's end as a means to the next end-in-view.

When Brookline High School created a representative democratic model for governing the whole high school (town meeting members elected from the four houses in the high school plus SWS), Mosher was again both participant and researcher.

A Canadian born in Pittsburgh and raised in Nova Scotia, Mosher was educated at Acadia University earning both Bachelor's and Master's degrees. In Canada, Mosher was a high school guidance counselor and vice principal and served as an instructor at Nova Scotia Teachers College. He was at the Harvard Graduate School of Education from 1958 until 1972. During this time, Mosher was a member of the editorial board of the *Harvard Educational Review,* received a doctorate in education in 1964, and was invited to join the faculty. Mosher rose in rank to associate professor at the School of Education. In 1972, Mosher joined Boston University as professor of education where he chaired the department of counselor education/counseling psychology for several years and served as coordinator of programs in human development and education.

In his career, Mosher was responsible for 14 books as author and editor and was author of over 40 articles and chapters. In addition to publications, Mosher shared his research in professional conferences and consultation—formal and informal. A lifelong Canadian citizen (and having dual U.S.-Canadian citizenship until he turned 21), Mosher was a true believer in the principles undergirding the democratic experiment in the United States, which, arguably, started in 1776. Mosher's influence was international beyond North America. Many of Mosher's publications were translated into other languages. He participated in several international conferences, including two in Moscow in 1993 and 1994 where he and the organizers discussed the preparation of citizens in the post-Soviet Russia. Mosher was proud that his book *Preparing for Citizenship: Teaching Youth to Live Democratically*—co-authored with Robert A. Kenny Jr. and Andrew Garrod—was published in Russian during the same year it appeared in English.

Further Reading: Dewey, J. (1966). *Democracy and education.* New York: Free Press. (Original work published in 1916.) Mosher, R.L. (1981). A democratic high school: Damn it! Your feet are always in the water. In N. Sprinthall & R. Mosher (Eds.), *Value development as the aim of education.* Schenectady, NY: Character Education Press. Mosher, R.L. (1981). *How to teach your child right from wrong.* Minneapolis, MN: Winston Press. Mosher, R.L., Kenny, R.A., & Garrod, A.C. (1996). *Preparing for citizenship: Teaching youth to live democratically.* Westport, CT: Praeger Publishers. Mosher, R.L., Lickona, T., & Paradise, J. (1981). *Democracy with children.* Boston: Allyn and Bacon.

Robert W. Howard

Motivation

Motivation is the desire and the driving force that moves humans to strive for specific goals. The two types of motivation are intrinsic and extrinsic. Intrinsic is the motivation to engage in an activity for its own sake. The factors identified that support intrinsic motivation are competence, autonomy, and relatedness. Competence refers to feeling able to do certain tasks or attain specific goals. If the goals are personally valued, then there is a higher degree of intrinsic motivation. Autonomy is being able to perform a task or activity without help from others. Relatedness is feeling connected to one's social environment, oneself, and the world. The underlying motivation for relatedness is to avoid isolation.

Extrinsic motivation is the desire to engage in an activity as a means to an end. A common method of external motivation is using punishment and/or reward. Some might wonder, though, if extrinsic motivation precedes intrinsic motivation or vice versa. Students who study to receive an A grade instead of simply being interested in the material, for example, are thought to be extrinsically motivated. On the other hand, positive recognition by the teacher can begin to create and build the intrinsic motivation of the student. Extrinsic motivation in this sense taps the student's need for competence, autonomy, and relatedness.

Abraham Maslow's Hierarchy of Needs is considered to be one of the most influential theories of human motivation. His theory is framed in the classic pyramid design consisting of eight levels of human needs. The first four lower levels, what Maslow termed deficiency needs, are most fundamental to our existence. The first level of the pyramid represents the physiological needs of hunger, thirst, comforts, and so forth, that must be met before progressively higher order needs are sought. The second level is the need to be safe and secure without fear of danger. The third level of needs is love and belongingness. As social beings we strive to be accepted and affiliate with others. The fourth level is related to our esteem: the need to achieve our goals, to feel competent, and to be recognized for those accomplishments. The four higher level "growths" are the focus only when deficiency needs are met. The fifth level of the model and the first level of growth needs are cognitive related. The desire to know, explore, and understand are basic to growth needs. The sixth level refers to our need for symmetry and beauty in our world, commonly referred to as aesthetic needs. Self-actualization is the seventh level and is realizing and fulfilling one's potential. The final level and peak of the pyramid is self-transcendence that is to connect to something beyond the ego or to help others recognize their potential and find fulfillment. According to Maslow, wisdom is developed as a person becomes more self-actualized and self-transcendent. As a person's wisdom increases, the better prepared he/she is to handle different situations. Having wisdom is also considered a virtue and acts as a lens to view life and guide decision making. Additionally, demonstrating wisdom serves as a mentoring quality to others.

Other theorists have developed similar models suggesting human motivation based on specific and general needs. Ryan and Deci (2000) claim the fundamental needs to be autonomy, competence, and relatedness. Nohria, Lawrence, and Wilson (2001) state that humans have four basic needs: (1) to acquire objects and experiences; (2) to bond with others in long-term relationships of mutual care and commitment; (3) to learn and make sense of the world and of ourselves; and (4) to defend ourselves, our loved ones, beliefs, and resources from harm.

William James (1892/1962), one of the earliest theorists on motivation, identified three levels of human needs, material (physiological, safety), social (belongingness, esteem), and spiritual.

Although there are many theories on human motivation, a common theme among them is that persons need to belong to or to relate with others. Because we are social beings, this presents as a fundamental need to human existence and community building.

Further Reading: Deci, E., & Ryan, R. (1985). *Intrinsic motivation and self-determination in human behavior.* New York: Plenum. Maslow, A. (1943). A theory of human motivation. *Psychological Review, 50,* 370–96. Nohria, N., Lawrence, P., & Wilson, E.O. (2001). *Driven: How human nature shapes our choices.* San Francisco: Jossey-Bass. Ryan, R., & Deci, E. (2000). Self-determination theory and the facilitation of intrinsic motivation, social development, and well-being. *American Psychologist, 55*(1), 68–78.

Scott E. Hall

Multicultural Education

Multicultural education reflects a broad interest in helping all students succeed in school. But there are disparate views on what multicultural education should entail. Sleeter and Grant (2003) identify five basic approaches to multicultural education.

(1) *Adapt procedures to help the exceptional learn the traditional curriculum.* As the most conservative of the approaches to diversity, the primary value here is the traditions of the dominant culture. It considers the purpose of schooling to transmit the skills, discipline, and academics necessary to succeed in the mainstream culture. This approach pays attention to learning styles, uses curriculum that is sensitive to the student's background, and thereby provides motivation to the student; it accommodates to the skill level of the student, bridges the gap with second language families, avoids the boring and demeaning, makes connections with the child's home and community, and most especially focuses on building the cultural capital necessary for success in the macroculture. Culture is viewed as another individual difference. Even though this is the most conservative of approaches, it may be viewed as the moderate liberal approach. The rest of the approaches are further to the left.

(2) *Human relations: Foster respect for all people along with good feelings and skilled communication.* The primary value here is getting along with everyone. The purpose of schooling is to learn to get along with others and to nurture the uniqueness of each individual, to build nonjudgmental respect for self and others, no matter how different. Culture is viewed as another individual difference, like ability or personality, rather than the key feature of a person's life. The goals of this approach are to respect oneself and others, relate positively to other students, eliminate stereotypes that students often have of one another, improve self-concepts, especially in relation to individual or cultural differences, and promote positive intergroup communications. Schools often adopt curricula that reflect this approach.

(3) *Single group studies: Study one group in depth.* An anthropological approach, the primary value here is to learn respect for a particular culture other than the dominant one. This approach takes the perspective of the group that is studied, learns about their history and cultural contributions, and studies their current needs. There are a few schools that have adopted this approach, such as Afrocentric academies. Their goal is to provide a successful educational experience for African Americans who are the least successful group in public schools. These schools present an African-centered ideology, curriculum, and pedagogy. Single-group schools can offer an environment for these students to excel.

(4) *"Multicultural education" combines the first three and adds a focus on equal opportunity and cultural pluralism.* The primary value here is equal respect for all cultures. The goals of multicultural education are to promote an understanding and appreciation of America's cultural diversity; to promote alternative choices for people regardless of race, gender, disability, or social-class background; to help all children achieve academic success; to promote awareness of social issues involving unequal distribution of power or opportunity. The purpose of schooling is to make students aware of injustice so that they can do something about it.

(5) *"Multicultural education that is social reconstructionist" adds on to the previous four the development of political participatory skills.* The primary value here is changing society to be egalitarian. This approach focuses on modeling and celebrating diversity and equal opportunity, practicing democracy, analyzing students' own social inequalities, and encouraging social action. The purpose of schooling is to reform society toward justice.

Another theorist, Sonia Nieto, suggests that multicultural education is one of the basics important for all students, that it must be strongly antiracist, and that it must be infused throughout school practice as a continuous process and involve critical pedagogy. She goes a bit further in suggesting that her definition of multicultural education is the moral choice, that it is the only ethical option.

James Banks suggested a different framework for multicultural education. He lists the following as critical elements: (1) An equity pedagogy in which teachers adjust their teaching to facilitate the academic achievement of students from diverse groups; (2) Content integration concerns using examples and material from a variety of cultures in teaching; (3) Knowledge construction: teachers help students examine and determine how implicit cultural assumptions in a particular discipline influence the construction of knowledge in that discipline; (4) Prejudice reduction that focuses on the characteristics and modification of students' racial attitudes; (5) An empowering school culture in which all aspects of inequality are examined (e.g., grouping, labeling practices, achievement levels, participation in sports, interaction across group lines).

More recently the Multicultural Education Consensus Panel consisting of eight scholars in multicultural education (Banks et al., 2005) suggested 12 principles for making teaching culturally responsive. These include advice for teachers, students, schools, and their leaders.

In order to be effective multicultural educators, teachers must understand the complexities of ethnic groups within the United States and how race, ethnicity, language, and social class influence students. They must help students learn skills for getting along with others from different backgrounds. They should assess students with multiple and culturally sensitive methods. Students should learn about the values that all cultural groups share. They should understand that knowledge is socially constructed, as well as the effects that stereotyping has on relationships.

Schools should make sure that there are equitable opportunities and high standards for all students. Schools should provide activities outside of academics that foster positive intergroup relations. To improve social relations, schools can create groups around superordinate categories, such as a school chorus, that cut across ethnicity and other social categories. In fact, schools can intentionally structure interactions that reduce fear and anxiety. Moreover, schools should create caring communities that share decision making widely. All these activities should be supported by political and educational leaders who ensure equitable funding across schools.

The Multicultural Education Consensus Panel suggested that it is not enough to foster academic success in schools or minimal toleration of diversity. Instead, students need to learn to interact positively with diverse others, an essential characteristic of citizens in a flourishing democracy.

Further Reading: Banks, J.A., Cookson, P., Gay, G., Hawley, W., Irvine, J., Nieto, S., Schofield, J., & Stephan, W.G. (2005). Education and diversity (research and practice). *Social Education, 69*(1), 36–41. *Diversity within unity: Essential principles for teaching and learning in a multicultural society.* This source can be ordered from the Center for Multicultural Education, University of Washington. Sleeter, C.E., & Grant, C.A. (2003). *Making choices for multicultural education: Five approaches to race, class, and gender.* New York: John Wiley & Sons.

Darcia Narvaez

N

Narrative/Hermeneutic Approach

The narrative/hermeneutic approach to moral development and moral education has emerged over the past several decades in response to various critiques and criticisms of the cognitive-developmental paradigm (see Kohlberg, 1981, 1984). Among these critiques and criticisms, the most significant have come from those who have argued that the cognitive-developmental paradigm does not sufficiently acknowledge the multidimensional nature of the moral domain and disregards the profound ways in which contextual factors—including differences in gender, race, class, and culture—shape the meaning persons make of their lived moral experiences.

In response to many of these concerns, a new, interdisciplinary approach to the study of moral development and the practice of moral education has emerged (Day, 1991; Day & Tappan, 1996; Tappan, 1991; Tappan & Brown, 1989; Tappan & Packer, 1991). This approach focuses on the centrality of words, language, and forms of discourse—particularly narrative (storytelling)—in human life. It privileges language as fundamentally constitutive of meaning and assumes, therefore, that (moral) thoughts, feelings, and actions are semiotically mediated, and thus socioculturally situated. Moreover, it is because our thoughts, feelings, and actions are shaped by language that narrative—as a specific genre of discourse—is a primary scheme by which meaning is made. We are, by our very nature, "storytelling animals" (MacIntyre, 1981), and thus we understand our actions, and the actions of others, in and through narratives. Furthermore, because one of the functions of narrative in culture is to endow actions and events with moral meaning (White, 1981), this approach assumes that narrative provides a uniquely powerful vehicle for understanding human moral experience and moral functioning.

The narrative approach to moral development and moral education attends to lived moral experience as it occurs in the time, space, relational, and cultural contexts of everyday life—given that these are the primary dimensions of narrative. It appreciates the multifaceted character of the moral domain, reflecting an awareness that there are many different stories that can be, and are, told about the moral lives of human beings. And it focuses methodological attention on the "hermeneutic problem" (or the "problem of interpretation")—that is, on the ways in which researchers interpret and understand the meaning of others' moral experiences, calling, in so doing, for researchers to acknowledge how their own prejudices, assumptions, and moral commitments influence and affect their understanding of others' moral stories (see Tappan, 1990).

The narrative/hermeneutic approach also focuses attention on a particular conception of the moral self (Day & Tappan, 1996). This is the dialogical self, in contrast to the cognitive-developmental view of self as an epistemic subject (Kohlberg, 1984). From a narrative perspective self is thus understood not as a "prelinguistic given" that merely employs language as a tool to express internally constituted meanings, but rather as a product of language from the start—arising out of semiotic, discursive, and communicative practices (Kerby, 1991).

Several implications for empirical research in moral development and moral education follow directly from these theoretical turns. First, instead of seeking to assess a unitary "deep structure" that is assumed to underlie an individual's moral reasoning in response to hypothetical dilemmas at any given point in the life cycle (see Kohlberg, 1984), researchers from the narrative perspective are interested in identifying the multiplicity of voices that constitute the moral dialogues that mediate and shape persons' lived moral experience (see Day, 1991; Tappan, 1991). Once dialogue, rather than monologue, becomes the focus of empirical attention, a whole host of interesting developmental questions come to the fore, including: At what age are such dialogues first evident? What are the vicissitudes of such dialogues as they unfold over the course of the life cycle? What is the relationship between a person's dialogue(s) with others and his dialogue(s) with himself? What are the effects of gender, class, and cultural differences on persons' moral dialogues?

Second, such a focus on dialogue necessarily moves the researcher away from charting individual developmental trajectories, toward identifying what might be called "shared" or "distributed" developmental trajectories. Development, from a narrative/dialogical perspective, does not go on within persons so much as it goes on between persons, in the relationship and conversation that they share. This suggests that researchers should explore the dynamics of moral action that emerges from discourse and dialogue between persons engaged in genuine and mutual interchange, thereby extending Vygotsky's (1978) concern with how, in the "zone of proximal development," the more competent can assist the less competent to advance to a higher developmental level (see also Tappan, 1998).

Finally, these research questions call for a method for interpreting narratives and dialogues that does not ask "coders" to match key words, phrases, or target sentences to a predetermined set of categories (see Colby & Kohlberg, 1987). Rather, research from a narrative perspective requires a method that is sensitive to the fundamentally polyphonic nature of discourse (Bakhtin, 1981), a method that thus captures, fully, the personal, relational, and cultural dimensions of psychic life (see, for example, Brown, Debold, Tappan, & Gilligan, 1991; Brown & Gilligan, 1991, 1992; Brown, Tappan, Gilligan, Miller, & Argyris, 1989). Only by using such a method can the complexity of persons' narratives of lived moral experience be fully honored and appreciated.

Further Reading: Bakhtin, M. (1981). In M. Holquist (Ed.), *The dialogic imagination* (C. Emerson & M. Holquist, Trans.). Austin: University of Texas Press. Brown, L., Debold, E., Tappan, M., & Gilligan, C. (1991). Reading narratives of conflict and choice for self and moral voice: A relational method. In W. Kurtines & J. Gewirtz (Eds.), *Handbook of moral behavior and development: Theory, research, and application.* Hillsdale NJ: Lawrence Erlbaum. Brown, L., & Gilligan, C. (1991). Listening for voice in narratives of relationship. In M. Tappan & M. Packer

(Eds.), *Narrative and storytelling: Implications for understanding moral development* (New directions for child development, No. 54). San Francisco: Jossey-Bass. Brown, L., & Gilligan, C. (1992). *Meeting at the crossroads: Women's psychology and girls' development.* Cambridge, MA: Harvard University Press. Brown, L., Tappan, M., Gilligan, C., Miller, B., & Argyris, D. (1989). Reading for self and moral voice: A method for interpreting narratives of real-life moral conflict and choice. In M. Packer & R. Addison (Eds.), *Entering the circle: Hermeneutic investigation in psychology.* Albany: State University of New York Press. Colby, A., & Kohlberg, L. (1987). *The measurement of moral judgment* (Vols. 1 & 2). New York: Cambridge University Press. Day, J. (1991). The moral audience: On the narrative mediation of moral "judgment" and moral "action." In M. Tappan & M. Packer (Eds.), *Narrative and storytelling: Implications for understanding moral development* (New directions for child development, No. 54). San Francisco: Jossey-Bass. Day, J., & Tappan, M. (1996). The narrative approach to moral development: From the epistemic subject to dialogical selves. *Human Development, 32,* 67–82. Kerby, A. (1991). *Narrative and the self.* Bloomington, IN: Indiana University Press. Kohlberg, L. (1981). *Essays on moral development, Vol. I: The philosophy of moral development.* San Francisco: Harper & Row. Kohlberg, L. (1984). *Essays on moral development, Vol. II: The psychology of moral development.* San Francisco: Harper & Row. MacIntyre, A. (1981). *After virtue: A study in moral theory.* Notre Dame: University of Notre Dame Press. Tappan, M. (1990). Hermeneutics and moral development: Interpreting narrative representations of moral experience. *Developmental Review, 10,* 239–65. Tappan, M. (1991). Narrative, language, and moral experience. *Journal of Moral Education, 20,* 243–56. Tappan, M. (1998). Moral education in the zone of proximal development. *Journal of Moral Education, 27,* 125–45. Tappan, M., & Brown, L. (1989). Stories told and lessons learned: Toward a narrative approach to moral development and moral education. *Harvard Educational Review, 59,* 182–205. Tappan, M., & Packer, M. (Eds.). (1991). *Narrative and storytelling: Implications for understanding moral development* (New directions for child development, No. 54). San Francisco: Jossey-Bass. Vygotsky, L. (1978). In M. Cole, V. John-Steiner, S. Scribner, & E. Souberman (Eds.), *Mind in society: The development of higher psychological processes.* Cambridge, MA: Harvard University Press. White, H. (1981). The value of narrativity in the representation of reality. In W. Mitchell (Ed.), *On narrative.* Chicago: University of Chicago Press.

Mark B. Tappan

Naturalistic Fallacy

You cannot deduce a "should" from an "is," a prescription from a description. To do so commits the naturalistic fallacy. But we do it all the time, fallaciously. We hold that because some people are capable of helping others in need, they have a responsibility to do so. Because people are talented, they should develop and use their talents—because they have potential they should realize it. Of special ethical importance, some hold that because people greatly and enduringly disagree on what is morally right or wrong, that there is no "fact of the matter," or that we should not prescribe a particular moral code as if it were true or valid. Put more fittingly for this fallacy—the fact of disagreement of divergence (descriptive relativity) does not imply the validity of disagreement or relativism.

Like many distinctly philosophical ideas now prominent in moral psychology and education, this fallacy was imported by Lawrence Kohlberg primarily, and the Piagetian school of cognitive development. Kohlberg entitled a classic 1974 article, "From Is To Ought: How to Commit the Naturalistic Fallacy in the Study of Moral Socialization and Get Away With It." Kohlberg argued that his empirical observation of moral stage development in the moral reasoning of children also showed how children should develop morally—also how they should be taught ethics. A temporally later stage of moral development, in fact, is a better or more morally competent stage of reasoning. Therefore, it is desirable for, even incumbent on, teachers to speed this natural course of development in the classroom without altering it. Indeed, because this natural or spontaneous course of development is self-created or cognitively constructed by children as they resolve everyday moral problems, the only ethical approach to morally educating them is to stimulate this development. Any other approach imposes an outside view of morality on them indoctrinatively. It thereby violates the ethical principles (of freedom) it hopes to teach.

Kohlberg argues against moral relativism in this same article. This is the view that ethics is neither true nor false, valid nor invalid. It is simply a matter of cultural convention, personal taste or preference, or group interest. He cites the naturalistic fallacy as the basis for a common cross-cultural rationale used to support relativism. This is the view that because people within any society have different ethical views than any other society, there is no generally valid ethical viewpoint. By contrast, Kohlberg argues that the factual diversity of ethical beliefs—even among individuals within the same society—simply does not speak to the validity of a general or universal principle. This principle might be currently posed or as yet uncovered. Neither would the factual observation of there being a principle we all held in common, either within a society or cross-culturally. Again, this is because normative validity (what we really should do) is not determined by factual observations (what we believe or do not believe about shoulds or oughts, duties and obligations, right and wrong). We can, in fact, all happen to adopt the same principle for accidental "reasons," or for practical, not moral, reasons. The fact that we all hold it does not show that we should, that it is valid. Apparently the widespread or universal belief once was that "natural" tragedies like floods or tsunamis were moral condemnations from God.

Our diversity of beliefs can show that some of us are correct and others incorrect about ethics. But it may also be that none of us are correct. If we share certain basic values or principles, we can still all be incorrect. This is the case even in so-called factual belief and science. It was commonly believed that the world was flat—everybody knew that and considered it obvious. Scientific revelation at that time believed as gospel that the sun revolved around the earth. It was once believed that our personality was a function of four humors in the body—like phelgm and bile.

We have risen above these false beliefs, along with the false beliefs that competed with them. But even now we are finding that despite all we know about the physical matter in the universe, perhaps three-quarters of it is actually made of something else, something unseen and unknown—dark matter. In our meticulously detailed studies of matter—not just molecules, atoms, and electrons, but subparticles in their nucleus and the strange forces that bind them—in tracing the big bang down to a microsecond, then tracing its course of spreading stuff and its congealed particulates—we just did not happen to notice most of reality at all. None of the hotly contested rival theories of these many centuries noticed it either.

These are powerful conceptual insights into relativism, physical and moral. But like the naturalistic fallacy itself, the points involved may be wildly overstated. It is certainly not irrelevant to ethical validity that almost no one believes certain things, or almost everyone does, or that there is wide disagreement on an ethical value. The most plausible explanation of widespread agreement normally is that it captures the truth. That is how reliable observation is measured in part—what it is based on—and why it is used in science after all. If a wide variety of standard, neutral, or diverse (randomly selected) observers all see the same thing—if measuring machines do too—then the best explanation is that there is something there. It is likely that something is there—and something somewhat like what is seen to be there. Otherwise, what would account for this amazing coincidence of observation?

Of course, there are other explanations—the relevant observers could all be limited in the same way, their observational powers similarly skewed. They could all be using common internal expectation to project features of observation on the objects being observed. Even in assuming that there is a distinction between observer and objects, they may be doing so—with objects really "out there" in a separate world, which we observe "in here," in our minds. Ultimately, this may not be the case. But we often can research and analyze these alternative explanations further, trying to see which can be verified better, and decide that one is more likely.

In ethics people often share opinions because they are socialized (brainwashed) to do so. They believe it because it is conventional to do so. They have never thought it out, never thought critically or skeptically about it. They act on it similarly because this is "what is done" or "how it is done." They may never have thought to act unconventionally. Or they may hold a value in common because it addresses a common need or fear, not because it is really valuable in itself. This would also explain why certain conventional values arise and are sustained over time.

Conversely, when people have diverse and conflicting ethical beliefs, we have reason to wonder if there is any "fact" of the matter—or valid value in this area. If there were one, we should expect people to see it, to agree on it, especially after long thinking, research, and discussion of the matter. Again, alternative explanations are possible and have been found correct in the past. People deceive themselves on matters of value and principle, refusing to see the truth even when it is right before them. People "imagine things," holding a range of flowery ideals that are unreachable or ironically mean spirited. Whisk these away and few alternatives remain.

Some people were right about slavery—it is wrong—while most others were morally incorrect in their views. The same is true about sexism and racism, which were once not only approved of, but held up as required ethical practice. (Sexism still is held up now in certain religious traditions especially.)

As commonly conceived and used, the naturalistic fallacy goes too far. For the most part this is because it really applies only to logical deduction, a very narrow and strict form of inference. One cannot deduce an "ought" statement from an "is" statement. But in ethics, like science, we rarely come across a strict deduction—even within technical moral philosophic writings. Instead, in every other form of inference or reasoning, principles similar to those above on plausibility, weight of evidence, probability calculation, and the like apply. Facts and observations simply do make certain ethical views, values, or principles more plausible, or less. If it is true, as psychological egoism holds, that humans are hardwired to be predominantly self-interested, then altruism-tending ethical principles are implausible. These ethics simply put too much burden on us to be moral, making morality our harsh taskmaster, not also our chosen tool. These ethics are not fit to us, well-designed for beings like us, but for masochists, self-flagellators who enjoy feeling guilty, or hopeless dreamers.

There was a time in moral philosophy when the naturalistic fallacy dominated discussion. It does not do so anymore. But that obsession with metaethics is no more. And one reason is that many ways were found to blur the distinction between fact and value and to infer norms from facts in the looser ways we actually reason. The great ethical traditions are founded on doing so. Aristotle's view of human nature does in treating adaptability as a fact—indeed, functional explanation in the life sciences generally does, as a matter of routine.

Kohlberg's blurring of the fact or value on this point has much still to bring social science and education. Without making questionably positivistic assumptions about facts, it is difficult to avoid empirical observations of values and norms. These are many of the "facts" gathered by social science. If any sort of physical, psychological, or socioeconomic development occurs, then empirical science must chart the fact that such change is *progressive*. It goes from worse to better, less able or competent to more. It does not simply change. In the moral sphere, development and education go not only from less psychologically adequate in one's thinking about morality but also in the adequacy of one's moral judgment and reasoning themselves. This is what the data and the facts show when one looks at learning without value-neutral blinders on. At least this is an empirical and scientific plausibility.

Further Reading: Searle, J.R. (1964). How to derive "ought" from "is." *The Philosophical Review, 73*(1), 43–58. Wilson, D.S., Dietrich, E., & Clark, A.B. (2003). On the inappropriate use of the naturalistic fallacy in evolutionary psychology. *Biology and Philosophy, 18,* 669–681.

Bill Puka

Neural Basis of Moral Cognition

Like all other cognitive abilities, the ability of humans to make complex moral judgments is brain based. Every time teachers lead a moral dilemma discussion, neural connections in the brains of their students are literally changed. Similarly, there are maturational changes in the brain that are assumed to subserve the increases in moral reasoning ability that occur during childhood and adolescence. When the change is sufficient, be it gradual or sudden, we call it a new moral stage. Understanding how morality is neurally mediated is fundamental to moral psychology and moral education.

Case studies of persons with brain injuries have shown that some brain areas are more involved than others with moral cognition. Persons with damage to the prefrontal cortex, in particular, frequently have problems in moral judgment and behavior and are described as having "acquired sociopathy." The first such case, published in 1868, is that of railroad worker Phineas Gage, who survived the passing of an iron rod through his skull, which resulted in extensive damage to the prefrontal cortex. After this injury, the once courteous and diligent man exhibited a marked deterioration in his social-moral judgment and character, although other cognitive abilities were preserved.

Lesion studies have provided evidence that the prefrontal cortex is vital for moral reasoning, and also for moral development. Compared to patients who acquired frontal lobe lesions during adulthood, persons with early childhood lesions have even more flagrant deficits in moral behavior later in life. Nevertheless, to date, no case has been described in which a lesion resulted in the selective impairment of the ability to make moral decisions.

Brain imaging studies, made possible by technological advances, have revolutionized neuroscience research. Noninvasive functional magnetic resonance imaging (fMRI) scanners make it possible to obtain images of the soft-tissue neural structures of any person's brain and to establish correlations between behavior (e.g., skilled movement) and neural functioning (e.g., activation of motor cortex) within specific brain structures. The majority of fMRI experiments are based on a subtractive method. For instance, one could compare the brain activity when a person is thinking about a statement with moral content to brain activity when the person is thinking about a statement without moral content, such as, "The elderly are useless" as opposed to "The elderly are 20 percent of the population." By subtracting the latter from the former, one can determine the activation that is unique to the moral task.

The first fMRI study of morality appeared in 2001 and, to date, a dozen such studies have been published. In addition to confirming the importance of the prefrontal cortex, the collected studies have identified moral activations in at least nine brain areas and, of these, three areas have shown significant activations across a clear majority of the studies. These "moral brain" areas are described as follows.

1. Medial frontal gyrus. Two studies by Jorge Moll and colleagues showed that this gyrus (ridge) on the frontal cortex was associated with greater activation for moral content (relative to nonmoral content, unpleasant conditions, or faces). Tom Farrow and colleagues documented greater activation for forgiveness moral judgments (relative to social reasoning judgments and empathic judgments). Joshua D. Greene and colleagues also demonstrated greater activation in the medial frontal gyrus for personal-moral dilemma tasks, relative to impersonal or nonmoral dilemmas. Carla L. Harenski and Stephan Hamann used photos of moral and nonmoral situations; when the research participants viewed the moral stimuli, they showed relatively greater activation in the medial frontal gyrus. Hauke R. Heekeren and colleagues replicated these findings by demonstrating greater activation for moral judgments than semantic judgments. Diana Robertson and colleagues used contextually standardized, real life moral (care/justice) dilemmas to study moral sensitivity, which is the ability to recognize a moral dilemma. They found that moral (care/justice) issues prompted greater activations in the medial frontal gyrus (relative to neutral issues and strategic/tactical issues). When care and justice were compared directly, no significant differences were found in terms of their activation of the medial frontal cortex.

More generally, prior research has shown that the medial prefrontal cortex has been significantly associated with diverse brain functions, especially cognition (attention, error detection, evaluative judgments, explicit memory, working memory, social cognition, temporal sequencing of behavior, thinking about and access to knowledge about the self, processing rewarded behavioral outcomes). The medial prefrontal cortex has also been associated with action (imagination, inhibition, imitation) and emotion (emotional response monitoring, pain perception).

Most of the general functions of the medial frontal cortex are relevant to the field of the psychology of morality, including the development of both justice and care judgments, because both orientations include theories about the moral self and social role taking, and both require an ability to imagine or predict another's perspective, intentions, or actions.

2. Posterior cingulate cortex and retrosplenial area. Research by Greene and colleagues found that activation of the dorsal and ventral posterior cingulate cortex was specifically associated with evaluating the appropriateness of solutions to personal moral dilemmas compared to impersonal and nonmoral dilemmas. Farrow and colleagues found that forgivability judgments induced stronger activations in the posterior cingulate cortex than did social or empathic judgments, and Harenski and Hamann found the same activation pattern for the task of watching moral emotional pictures as for watching nonmoral emotional pictures. Robertson and colleagues replicated these results and also found that implicit recognition or sensitivity to justice moral dilemmas alone and to care moral dilemmas alone each significantly activated the posterior cingulate cortex, compared to neutral issues. Recognition of care moral dilemmas also showed greater activation than recognition of justice moral dilemmas in the retrosplenial cortex.

The posterior cingulate cortex has been associated especially with cognition (explicit memory, including the successful recall of emotional memories, episodic memories, autobiographical memories, self-reference, language recall, semantic categorization, and metaphors), but also with emotion (anger, happiness, rest) and perception (olfaction, visual motion). More generally, the posterior cingulate cortex functions as an interface between emotion and cognition.

From the perspective of moral psychology, the observed activation of the posterior cingulate cortex may reflect the dependence of moral sensitivity on access to one's cognitive, emotional, and somatic experiences related to previous moral conflicts. The posterior cingulate cortex may mediate the process by which the memory of past moral dilemmas and decisions is used to guide an interpretive awareness of moral situations. Furthermore, the posterior cingulate cortex may contribute to moral evaluations made by taking a first-person perspective and predicting one's own responses, emotional or otherwise, to a specific moral action.

3. Posterior superior temporal sulcus. This sulcus (groove) on the surface of the temporal lobe has shown significant activation by personal moral dilemmas (relative to impersonal and nonmoral dilemmas), moral claims (relative to nonmoral neutral and unpleasant claims), and moral pictures (relative to unpleasant pictures and nonmoral emotional pictures).

Heekeren and colleagues partially replicated the above findings by demonstrating greater activation in the left posterior superior temporal sulcus for moral decisions than for semantic decisions. Robertson and colleagues also found that implicit recognition of moral dilemmas, relative to neutral events or nonmoral dilemmas, showed greater activation in the posterior superior temporal sulcus. Recognition of care dilemmas alone and of justice dilemmas alone both replicated this finding. Finally, when justice and care dilemma recognition were directly compared, there was a preferential activation for justice issues in the left superior temporal sulcus. Qian Luo and colleagues investigated the neural basis of implicit moral attitude by comparing visually depicted legal and illegal behaviors. Performance on illegal relative to legal trials showed significantly greater activity in the superior temporal gyrus, but not in the adjacent superior temporal sulcus.

The posterior superior temporal sulcus has been implicated in social cognition (activated during effort related to assessing the intentions of other individuals, violating expectations, or representing a historical figure's mental states), emotion (viewing happy, sad, and disgusting films; viewing emotional film versus recalling film), and perception (cortex within and adjacent to the superior temporal sulcus is activated by social signals involving expressive "biological motions" of the face, hands, mouth, and eyes).

Posterior superior temporal sulcus activations are consistent across tasks that require cognitive, emotional, and perceptual perspective taking. The role of the posterior superior temporal sulcus in multimodal sensory integration suggests that it also may function to integrate perspectives taken from these different vantage points. From a moral psychology perspective, the posterior superior temporal sulcus has a clear role in social perspective taking in the service of moral sensitivity. This interpretation is consistent with Lawrence Kohlberg's theory of moral judgment in which he considered the ability to perceive the perspectives of others essential to moral development.

Despite a wide variety of moral stimuli and tasks between studies, the cumulative research findings have been remarkably consistent. Moral reasoning activates different brain areas than reasoning without a moral component does, and those variations in moral tasks correlate with corresponding variations in neural activity. What is emerging is an understanding of a distributed neural network of brain areas that compose the moral mind. To bridge the gap between moral biology and moral education, however, future fMRI research should address the comparative effectiveness of different approaches to moral education by collecting, for instance, pre- and postintervention neuroimaging data.

Further Reading: Greene, J., & Haidt, J. (2002). How (and where) does moral judgment work? *TRENDS in Cognitive Science, 6*(12), 517–23. Mobbs, D., Lau, H., Jones, O., & Frith, C. (2007). Law, responsibility, and the brain. *PLoS Biology, 5*(4), 693–700. Robertson, D., Snarey, J., Ousley, O., Harenski, K., Bowman, D., Gilkey, R., & Kilts, C. (2007). The neural basis of moral sensitivity to issues of justice and care. *Neuropsychologia, 44*(4), 755–66.

John Snarey

The Nicomachean Ethics

The Nicomachean Ethics is the best known of Aristotle's (384–322 B.C.E.) writings on moral philosophy, the other two being the *Eudemian Ethics* and the *Magna Moralia.* Its title reflects the general belief that it was edited by Aristotle's son Nicomachus. Although this belief is not firmly established, there is no doubt that the *Nicomachean Ethics* is the most complete and structurally solid of the three works, as well as the one that has had the greatest impact on contemporary theorizing about ethics and personality development.

Contents

The Nicomachean Ethics comprises ten books, each of which contains several chapters. Book I lays out Aristotle's general views regarding the human *telos* (goal orientation) and the accompanying concept of *eudaimonia* (human flourishing). Books II–IV discuss the moral virtues, first in general terms and then by analyzing specific personal virtues such as courage and temperance. The remaining six chapters discuss what might be called the social dimension of ethics, which includes justice (Book V), prudence (Book VI), evil (Book VII), friendship (Books VIII–IX), and politics (Book X).

The Human Function and the Concept of Flourishing (Eudaimonia)

To identify the goal of human life, Aristotle asked what are the specifically human capacities or functions; that is, what it is that only humans can do. His answer was quite simple: only humans are able to reason, and so the human function is "activity of the soul in conformity with reason" (Bekker, 1098a7). (Note: All modern editions or translations of Aristotle intended for scholarly readers use Bekker numbers, in addition to or instead of page numbers, so that citations can be checked without having to use the same edition or translation that the author used.) This is not to say, as Plato did, that the human function is to reason and only to reason, since life consists in many kinds of activity, including "animal activities" such as eating and drinking. But it is to say that in their properly human exercise these various activities are directed by reason and as a consequence are, in fact, considerably more than brutish animal behavior. For instance, human meals are typically social events, in which people share stories, celebrate successes, commemorate anniversaries, and so on.

Closely allied to the concept of a thing's function is the concept of its good, which in Aristotle's teleological theory is defined as "what everything seeks" (1094a1). Since the activities of human life are multiple and diverse, each activity carries with it its own end and hence has its own good. For example, the end goal of medicine is health, that of strategy is victory, that of economics is wealth, and so on. Although there is a plurality of goods, they are all relative in the sense of being a stepping-stone to other goods. However, there must also be a final or highest end, one that is desired for itself. This would be not just one more good, but rather a "sovereign good," to which all other goods are subordinate. Aristotle calls this highest end or sovereign good *eudaimonia,* a Greek word variously translated as "flourishing," "living well," or simply (and somewhat misleadingly) "happiness."

The Virtues

Since human reason is exercised only in the practice of virtue (*arête*), the "human good proves to be activity of the soul in accord with virtue" (1098a16). Following his division of the soul into Will and Reason, Aristotle distinguishes two classes of virtues, moral and intellectual. The moral virtues are the result of custom and constitute a settled disposition or habit that Aristotle describes somewhat paradoxically as "a second nature." A virtuous act is one that maintains the "golden mean," which is the midpoint between excess and deficiency in human actions or passions. Three of the most important moral virtues described at length in the *Nicomachean Ethics* are courage, temperance, and justice, of which friendship is an important special case. (Aristotle also discusses other virtues such as generosity, magnificence, magnanimity, and, somewhat more briefly, veracity, ingenuity, amiability, and humility.) A fourth virtue, prudence (*phronesis*), is both moral and intellectual, since it provides the rational dimension of any virtue. It is practical knowledge about how the principle of the golden mean applies to particular, concrete cases, and so stands in contrast to the other major intellectual virtue, wisdom (*sophia*), which is the theoretical and contemplative knowledge that Aristotle considered the capstone of human flourishing, that is, *eudaimonia.* But since prudence is a necessary condition for moral virtue and virtue is a constitutive condition of *eudaimonia,* it follows that one can be prudent without being wise, but it is not possible to be wise without being prudent.

Friendship

Aristotle's discussion of friendship is relatively self-contained and has been the subject of many scholarly treatises as well as popular works on love. He distinguishes three kinds of friendship, the paradigm case of benevolence and the two derivative cases of friendship based on utility and friendship based on pleasure. Like the other moral virtues, friendship in the first sense is a settled disposition or habit, in this case the disposition to will the good of another for his or her own sake. But unlike the other virtues, it is also a condition that makes being good possible, in that friends cultivate each other's virtue, although if a friend's character changes for the worse and cannot be saved, then virtue requires that one leave the friend (1165b12–31). Also—and again unlike the other virtues, which bring pleasure simply because we enjoy any activity that we do well—the company of friends is pleasurable for other reasons as well, and its exercise makes life enjoyable. These are only some of the reasons that Aristotle offers in support of his claim that the good person cannot hope for *eudaimonia* without friendship. Among the reasons not discussed here is one that is particularly apt in our own time: given the fact that human beings are inherently political, it is better, he argues, to live with friends than with strangers whose character is unknown.

Further Reading: Aristotle. (1999). *Nicomachean Ethics* (T. Irwin, Trans.). Indianapolis: Hackett Publishing. Broadie, S. (1995). *Ethics with Aristotle.* Oxford: Oxford University Press. Cooper, J. (1977). Friendship and the good in Aristotle. *Philosophical Review, 86,* 290–315. Hardie, W. F. R. (1980). *Aristotle's ethical theory* (2nd ed.). Oxford: Oxford University Press. Sherman, N. (1989). *The fabric of character: Aristotle's theory of virtue.* Oxford: Oxford University Press. Urmson, J. O. (1988). *Aristotle's ethics.* Oxford: Blackwell.

Ana Laura Santamaría and Thomas Wren

Noddings, Nel

Nel Noddings is among the leading contemporary figures in the fields of educational and moral philosophy. She received her Ph.D. from Stanford in 1975, after spending the first part of her career as an elementary and high school mathematics teacher and school administrator. Noddings taught at Pennsylvania State University and the University of Chicago (where she directed the University's Laboratory School), before returning to Stanford in 1977. At Stanford she received the Award for Teaching Excellence three times, and she served as Associate Dean and as Acting Dean of the School of Education for four years. In 1992 Noddings was named the Lee L. Jacks Professor of Child Education—a chair she occupied until she retired in 1998. Since her retirement from Stanford, Nodding has held positions at Teachers College, Columbia University (as Professor of Philosophy and Education); at Colgate University (as the A. Lindsay O'Connor Professor of American Institutions); and at Eastern Michigan University (as the John W. Porter Distinguished Chair in Urban Education). She is also a past president of the Philosophy of Education Society, the John Dewey Society, and the National Academy of Education.

Over the course of her long and productive career Noddings focused her primary attention on the significance of caring and the caring relationship both as an educational goal and as a fundamental aspect of the teaching-learning process. For Noddings, to care and to be cared for are fundamental human needs: we need to care for others in order to live a full and fulfilling life, and we need care from others in order to survive. Not only has Noddings provided an extensive philosophical analysis of the roots of the care perspective, she has also considered the implications of this perspective for the practice of moral education, focusing on four central components of a caring pedagogy: modeling, dialogue, practice, and confirmation.

As a result, Noddings's work has become a primary source of insight and inspiration for those interested in the ethical and moral dimensions of teaching, schooling, and education broadly conceived. Her books include an attempt to articulate an "ethic of care" and to explore its implications for ethics and moral education (*Caring: A Feminine*

Approach to Ethics and Moral Education [1984]—her most important and well-known book); an attempt to explore evil from the perspective of women (*Women and Evil* [1989]); and a series of books that seek to expand and extend her work on care, focusing on the educational implications of the "ethic of care" across a variety of educational levels, contexts, and issues (*The Challenge to Care in Schools* [1992]; *Educating Moral People* [2002]; *Starting at Home: Caring and Social Policy* [2002]; *Happiness and Education* [2003]; and *Critical Lessons: What our Schools Should Teach* [2006]).

Further Reading: Noddings, N. (1984). *Caring: A feminine approach to ethics and moral education.* Berkeley: University of California Press. Noddings, N. (1989). *Women and evil.* Berkeley: University of California Press. Noddings, N. (1992). *The challenge to care in schools: An alternative approach to education.* New York: Teachers College Press. Noddings, N. (2002). *Educating moral people.* New York: Teachers College Press. Noddings, N. (2002). *Starting at home: Caring and social policy.* Berkeley: University of California Press. Noddings, N. (2003). *Happiness and education.* New York: Cambridge University Press. Noddings, N. (2006). *Critical lessons: What our schools should teach.* New York: Cambridge University Press.

Mark B. Tappan

O

Obedience

Obedience is, and has always been, deeply embedded in schooling. Emile Durkheim, the influential moral education theorist (1858–1917), believed that to obey rules, no matter how petty, was the hallmark of a virtuous child. However, he claimed as well that a teacher's expressed authority is merely derivative, for it emanates from a higher power. Teachers are more agents than authors of the schools' standards (1961); like the children, they too are obliged to obey the transcendent social norms. Durkheim's religious overtones are made explicit in the writings of leading nineteenth-century American educators. William T. Harris, a prominent leader and U.S. Commissioner of Education, for example, maintained that the school, though independent of formal religion, is founded on divine principles. Because schools are subservient to, and instruments of, the divine will, absolute obedience to educational authorities is required of all students unconditionally (1888). This expectation of total obedience survived the decline of public schools' overt religiosity and prevails today in many Student Conduct Codes. It is thus not uncommon to see language in contemporary codes holding students responsible for obeying every instruction that may be given by any school employee—including teacher, substitute teacher, student teacher, teacher assistant—in any classroom, hallway, bathroom, auditorium, school grounds, or school transportation.

Intrinsic to obedience is the suspension of judgment and the relinquishment of will. Though initially submission may be an act of individual choice, it is inconsistent with vigilant appraisal and independent judgment. According to Simone Weil (1909–1943), the spiritual French writer, obedience presupposes a general prior consent, not a considered review of every order issued by an authority. Fealty to the authority of person or institution is such that once given the consent becomes permanent. For Weil, and many others, submission is an expression of faith and love (not fear of punishment or promise of reward). As such, it feeds the soul and is a condition of the fulfilled life. To obey God, teachers, parents, laws, and rules means to accept another's judgment even though it may not fit one's own. True, it requires placing the will of another before one's own, but no one assumes dictatorial power for everyone, those in charge as well as those charged, is committed to a hierarchy of submission, to obeying the demands of a more ultimate power. This requirement that yokes obedience and submission nullifies the because-I-say-so rationale sometimes resorted to by teachers. It protects children against arbitrary or willful actions of school personnel.

Yet, even given this protection, we cannot so easily dispense with reason, judgment, personal agency, and responsibility. Heedless deference to authority results in obvious evil whether it be Rudolph Eichmann sending millions of Jews to death camps on the orders of his superior (Arendt, 1963), submission to orders of wrongdoing from a professional (Milgram, 1974), or simply doing what the boss says without applying a moral filter. While God may be all good, the same cannot be said of ordinary authorities. Rules must sometimes be resisted. The solution, said Martin Luther King Jr., is to obey rightful authority and to obey unless a command is contrary to conscience. As he wrote in *Letter from Birmingham Jail* (1963), one can divide laws into those that are just and unjust. Any law that humiliates and degrades the human person is unjust. As one has an absolute moral responsibility to obey just laws, one has the same responsibility to disobey unjust laws. How does this bifurcation fit educational settings?

Schools are strongly hierarchical institutions with continual obedience demanded of children and teachers. Obedience is an instrumental requirement for effective functioning and, often, is considered an independent virtue. Submission, with its close connection to love and trust, is thought to be a desired mental habitus for learning. But blind obedience, the total suspension of judgment, results in the loss of those qualities—agency and autonomy—that schools want to encourage. Obedience, then, is not a virtue *per se*. As the philosopher Bernard Williams (1985) observed, it is an executive virtue. Executive virtues—courage and self-discipline are others—do not have intrinsic objectives or worth but take on worthiness through the objectives they assist in realizing. Obedience can enable goodness or evil; it can be character building or character defeating.

Many school rules are matters of convenience—requirements of attendance and dress; conduct in hallways, outdoor spaces, and classrooms. Submission to them, although sometimes perceived by students as assaults on individuality, does not degrade human personality. Other rules, however, are matters of morality—prohibitions on speech, controls on relationships, and conditions of discipline—that may seriously impinge on human personality. Children (depending on age) and teachers deserve some outlet for questioning, disputing, and participating in rule development, even, under particular circumstances, resisting that which affronts conscience. To construct school policies that serve justice as well as obedience is one of educators' continuing challenges.

Further Reading: Arendt, H. (1963). *Eichmann in Jerusalem: A report on the banality of evil.* New York: Viking Press. Durkheim, E. (1961). *Moral education.* Glencoe, IL: The Free Press of Glencoe. Harris, W.T. (1888). Moral education in the common schools. United State Bureau of Education, Circular of Information, No. 4, pp. 81–91. Reproduced in C.H. Gross and C.C. Chandler (Eds.), (1964), *The history of American education through readings* (pp. 249–58). Boston: D.C. Heath. King, M.L., Jr. (1963). Letter from Birmingham Jail. In M.L. King, Jr. (Ed.), *Why we can't wait* (pp. 77–100). New York: Harper and Row. Milgram, S. (1974). *Obedience to authority, an experimental view.* New York: Harper and Row. Weil, S. (1978). *The need for roots: Prelude to a declaration of duties towards mankind.* New York: Routledge and Kegan Paul. Williams, B. (1985). *Ethics and the limits of philosophy.* Cambridge, MA: Harvard University Press.

Joan F. Goodman

Obligations for Character Education

Character education is not a new idea in American schools or through history. From the time of Plato, societies have realized that moral education was an important goal in preparing future citizens who might strive to make the world a better place. Both Aristotle and Plato discussed the need to educate emotional responses that would lead to a virtuous character (Homiak, 2003). Early education in America was infused with moral education. Moral lessons were found in all types of textbooks, not just readers (McClelland, 1992).

As public schools became the preferred educational institutions, moral education was forced to compete with a diverse curriculum meant to prepare citizens for an industrial and scientific age. In the 1960s and 1970s, the focus became rights more than responsibility, and freedom more than commitment (Lickona, 1991). At this time, schools began to practice "values clarification," an approach that teachers used to help students learn how to understand (clarify) their own values rather than be taught lessons about what was right and what was wrong. Kohlberg's cognitive-developmental approach was similar in that it focused on Socratic peer discussion of value dilemmas (Noel, 1997). With the lack of focus on moral and character education in schools, however, along with the changing patterns of American family life, came a significant increase in juvenile crime, drug use, and generally antisocial behavior in young people. Thus, with the 1980s came a renewed interest in character education, and in 2001, President Bush endorsed character education within the No Child Left Behind Act and through the establishment of a federal grant program offering millions of dollars for schools wishing to educate for character.

With the renewed societal interest in character education came an interest at the state legislative level for creating new character education laws or revisiting and reviving older laws that had a connection to moral or civic education (Glanzer & Milson, 2006). Between the years of 1993 and 2004, 23 states passed character education laws. Unfortunately, there is little consistency between states as to what constitutes character education and how to provide it effectively. Some states mandate that character education happen, specifying particular virtues or traits that should be taught. Other states suggest that schools approach character education by addressing school climate, working systemically, and incorporating certain social and emotional learning skills. In general, character education has not been integrated at the legislative level into other education legislation (Glanzer & Milson, 2006). Almost no states have provided funding for their character education requirements.

Teachers are generally not receiving professional instruction for moral or character education at the preservice level in their teacher education programs. In a survey done with 600 deans of education in 1999, over 90 percent of them responded that they supported the need for character education in K–12 schools, but only 13 percent were satisfied with their institution's efforts to integrate character education within their teacher education programs (Bohlin, Dougherty, & Farmer, 2003).

Further Reading: Bohlin, K., Dougherty, S., & Farmer, D. (2003). *Practices of teacher educators committed to character.* Washington, D.C.: Character Education Partnership and the Center for the Advancement of Ethics and Character. Glanzer, P.L., & Milson, A.J. (2006). Legislating the good: A survey and evaluation of character education laws in the United States. *Educational Policy, 20*(3), 525–50. Homiak, M. (2003, Spring). Moral character. *The Stanford Encyclopedia of Philosophy.* Retrieved May 2, 2004, from http://plato.stanford.edu/archives/spr2003/entries/moral-character/ Lickona, T. (1991). *Educating for character.* New York: Bantam Books. McClelland, B.E. (1992). *Schools and the shaping of character: Moral education in America, 1607–present.*

Washington, D.C.: Office of Educational Research and Improvement. Noel, M. (1997). *Morality in Education* (Historical Materials No. SO 029 489): EDRS.

Merle J. Schwartz

Original Position

The term "original position" refers to a particular doctrine in the general and classic theory of justice presented by John Rawls. But this position itself is a reinterpretation of an ethical view postulated by Immanuel Kant that combines his "veil of ignorance" and "kingdom of ends." It also represents the so-called state of nature conceptions crucial to various social contract theories for legitimating government structures.

Kant's "veil of ignorance" is a conceptual device that aims to reduce the tendency to favor our own personal interests when making moral judgments. The reasoning of the moral agent when under the veil of ignorance is uncontaminated by bias. Rawls's original position upgrades this aspect of the device by identifying self-interest, envy, and even risk-taking as tendencies especially dangerous to equality and fairness. One is enjoined to reason about moral issues blind to one's own self-interest.

Kant's "kingdom of ends" represents the overall moral community—all beings capable of moral understanding and choice. When we decide how to act, we realize that we should consider everyone involved and whether they would agree to the way we are treating them. It is only fair that everyone's perspective be considered, that everyone have a say, at least ideally or in principle. For Kant (and Rawls), this perspective views people as ends in themselves, or beings with their own ends or goals that they are capable of determining for themselves. They are not just tools for us to use as means to our ends. To say that we are free is to say that we are all kings or rulers of our own domain, or should be seen and treated that way.

Rawls's Original Position refines the personal qualities of free beings situated in a negotiation that can express their self-determination in mutual respect for self-determination. Kantians like Rawls imagine how it would be possible to develop ethical and political ground rules we could all voluntarily agree on. Moral agents, assuming the original position prior to society, deliberate on the justice of social arrangements, but shielded from the bias of their own self-interest by the veil of ignorance.

They recognize that such deliberation might ideally involve our agreeing on the shared purposes ethical and governmental institutions must serve. To get agreement, we must drastically reduce the dizzying array of differences and conflicts we show in our ethical opinions and political standards. But several giant steps can make the path much shorter, putting an end in sight. The first is to limit our decision-making process, requiring it to be rational logically and reasonable motivationally. Centuries of analysis has provided shared ground rules on such matters among theorists that are largely reflected in our social norms and expectations. The veil of ignorance can be used to rule out the use of information that allows us to rationalize nonrational or irrational notions as well as partisan interests.

Obviously any standards we could agree on unanimously in the original position would be extremely minimal. Such standards would grant latitude for personalized value systems. It would allow individuals and social groups their own stylized ethics "on the side," elaborating shared ground rules, certainly, but also adding all manner of content and flourish, tailored to the exigencies of their particular contexts. We see this latitude in the freest of societies but also in the most authoritarian and traditional ones as well. We typically accept similar ground rules for different reasons, from different perspectives. We compromise on ground rules that we would never choose for ourselves ideally, but find acceptable for common purposes where we do not expect to make all the rules. We recognize that we can often diverge without conflicting. And we can deal with likely conflicts among different ethical systems by remaining independent of each other, working only in tandem, not interactive cooperation.

Rawls's original position is an attempt to specify and make plausible Kantian ethical agreement behind a veil of ignorance, by the universe of moral agents, with the end of formulating common ground rules for interaction.

Further Reading: Johnston, J.S. (2005). Rawls's Kantian educational theory. *Educational Theory, 55,* 1–25. Korsgaard, C. (1996). *Creating the kingdom of ends.* Princeton, NJ: Princeton University Press. Rawls, J. (1999). *A theory of justice.* Cambridge, MA: Harvard University Press. Regan, T.J. (1996). Animating Rawls's original position. *Teaching Philosophy, 19,* 357–70.

Bill Puka

Oser, Fritz

Fritz Oser is Professor of Education and Educational Psychology at the School of Education in Friborg University, Switzerland, and has been a leading international scholar in moral and religious psychology and education since the 1980s. A cognitive developmental theorist, Oser was deeply influenced by his compatriot, the renowned Swiss psychologist, Jean Piaget. Oser's research studies are as wide-ranging as they are groundbreaking. He has made outstanding contributions to the fields of religious development and education, moral development and education, teacher education, and civic education. The University of Mainz, Germany, conferred upon him an honorary doctorate in 1987; and in 2003, the Association for Moral Education gave him the Kuhmerker Award for excellence in and service to the field of moral education.

Oser received his Ph.D. from the University of Zurich in 1975. He did postdoctoral research in moral development at Harvard University with Lawrence Kohlberg and in teacher education at the University of California at Los Angeles with Richard Shavelson in the late 1970s. Both Kohlberg and Shavelson had a profound and enduring influence on Oser's own scholarship.

In the 1970s, when cognitive developmental research into social interaction and morality was flourishing and James Fowler was beginning to elaborate his theory of faith development, Oser began a highly original research program to study the development of what he called religious judgment. Presenting participants with religious dilemmas in an interview similar to the one Kohlberg designed, Oser described an age-related sequence of stages of religious thinking. On the basis of cross-sectional and longitudinal studies, Oser claimed that these stages are "mother-structures," not reducible to stages of social perspective taking or moral development.

Although deeply influenced by Christian theology, Oser studied religious development in a wide variety of religious traditions and also explored the psychology of atheism. In keeping with the cognitive developmental tradition, he argued that, although the content of religious judgment may vary from religion to religion, religious stages are universal. Oser's focus on how individuals integrate explicitly religious concepts with moral judgment complements Fowler's focus on faith as implicit in an individual's self-understanding and worldview. Taken together, Oser and Fowler's theories have changed the landscape of religious psychology and have called attention to the positive role that religious faith can play throughout the life span. Oser's theory with its attention to religious concepts has had a particularly strong influence on the practice of religious education, particularly in Europe.

While he was developing his theory of religious judgment, Oser undertook a series of research projects that enriched and, in certain respects, transformed the cognitive developmental approach to education. A sympathetic critic of aspects of Kohlberg's theory, Oser found the early work on moral education to be overly dominated by a concern for stage change with little exploration of other variables related to moral discourse, such as tolerance or ethical sensitivity. Oser also argued that Kohlberg's theory gave insufficient attention to the role of emotions in moral interactions.

Integrating the cognitive developmental theory within a broader framework of educational psychology, Oser was one of the first to explore the professional role of the teacher as moral educator. Early research on moral discussions focused exclusively on procedures and methods without attending to what the teacher contributed to the process. Oser linked specific moral education techniques within an encompassing framework of competent teaching in which teachers integrated theoretical knowledge and practical know-how in all of their interactions with students. He maintained that teachers have a moral responsibility not only to foster their students' moral development but also to teach their students as well as possible. This means that teachers need to determine what practices will work best with which students. It also means that teachers need to undertake their specifically moral role more reflectively and with a commitment to moral dialogue. In his studies of teachers and teacher education, Oser demonstrated that many teachers were simply unprepared for the ethical demands of the teaching profession. He devised teacher education curricula that sensitized teachers to the moral demands of their role and gave them tools for leading discussions. Finally, Oser proposed a bold new approach to teacher training that broke through the theory-practice divide to inform teachers as they are engaged in the actual practice of teaching.

In the latter part of his career, Oser turned to the study of students' political development and how schools can promote civic knowledge and engagement in democratic societies. He stressed the importance of discussing political issues in an open and critical way and of fostering a sense of responsible citizenship oriented to justice and social care.

Further Reading: Oser, F.K., Dick, A., & Patry, J.-L. (Eds.). (1992). *Effective and responsible teaching: The new synthesis.* San Francisco: Jossey-Bass. Oser, F.K., & Gmünder, P. (1991). *Religious judgment: A developmental approach.* Birmingham, AL: Religious Education Press. Oser, F.K., Achtenhagen, F., & Renold, U. (Eds.). (2006). *Competence oriented teacher training: Old research demands and new pathways.* Rotterdam: Sense Publishers. Veugelers, W., & Oser, F.K. (Eds.). (2003). *Teaching in moral and democratic education.* New York: Peter Lang.

F. Clark Power

P

Parent Education

The very notion of parent education or, more commonly, education for parenthood is a creation in and of late industrial polities. For previous generations the thought of formalizing the preparation of adults for their role as parents was largely inconceivable since the art and techniques of parenting were deemed to be capacities that emerged out of the lived experiences in vertical communities. Of course, different kinds of communities had very different views as to what might entail learning how to be a parent. For those whose lives were marked by hard labor and material insufficiency, parenting probably consisted of managing to raise one's children to a stage where they could go out to work. For others, at the far end of the continuum the task was frequently delegated to wet nurses, nannies, governesses, and private education. Of course, there is a somewhat romanticized view that in aboriginal societies the whole community raised a child; children were not, in that sense, exclusively the offspring of their parents (see, for example, Booth & Crouter, 2001) but were members of the tribe. No doubt there is something to be said for such an analysis, but it suffers the perpetual danger of being exaggerated. In any event, to be a parent was to occupy a position rather than, as tends to be the case in contemporary liberal democratic polities, have assigned to one particular practicalities, responsibilities, and capacities.

Prior to the nineteenth century children were deemed to inhabit the largely private domain of the family, and childhood was for some, such as Rousseau, an idyll that should be as free as possible from the interference of adults. But the advent of industrialization alongside two changes in social and political life brought about increased state interest in children and consequently in parenting. Emerging awareness that children were being exploited and abused in factories, mills, and agriculture coupled with the perceived growing economic need to create a literate and numerate workforce meant that the state began to see parenting in a more active light. Parents started to become publicly responsible for their children's welfare and education. Indeed, in many countries the last decades of the nineteenth century saw children removed from their parents to be educated in state-sponsored and state-financed environments. Further shifts took place in the post–Second

World War period in liberal democratic polities wherein the urbanization that began with the late-eighteenth-century industrial revolution gathered pace and vast sprawling cities and their suburbs evolved. With these changes came increased movement of people with a consequent dislocation and severed ties with traditional vertical communities, which we might suppose offered (if only in a culturally imagined way) the "village based" community upbringing so ingrained in the modern social imaginary.

The loss of such a world (probably partly imagined and partly actual) where parents, grandparents, neighbors, extended family, and community were active participants in the upbringing of children has led to a sense of social emergency in late industrial liberal democratic polities. Adolescents are often cast as unruly and in need of firm upbringing; many parents are deemed dysfunctional, and increasingly the state demands that parents do certain kinds of things to secure the welfare of and an education for their children. Indeed, a substantial number of liberal democratic polities have experienced an acute sense of social emergency around the perceived ill behavior of young people and a sense that parents have themselves lost the capacity for parenting. Consequently there is a growing sense that parenting itself needs to be taught as it can no longer be acquired as a natural outcrop of living in an intergenerational community.

In discussions surrounding the need for and shape of education for parenthood, the state tends to see itself not only as the guarantor of last resort with respect to any individual child but also the court of first instance. Some would argue that these historical and cultural developments have led to a diminution of parental capacity. Moreover, it may be argued that the state has arrogated to itself too much control over the education of children and is in danger of expanding its grip far beyond the confines of school. Parents deemed incapable of exercising appropriate educational and social control over their children may have their children removed. Indeed, in 2007 a British court initially ruled that a child who was deemed excessively obese should be removed from his parents and placed in protective custody since the parents were failing to discharge their duty of care. This, and a host of other cases where parents are deemed incapable and/or inadequate, has led to widespread calls for formal and formalized programs in parental education focused on child rearing and, perhaps more poignantly, on developing the capacity to assume responsibility for the children they bring into the world.

So loud had the chorus for parental education become in the first decade of the twenty-first century that the former British prime minister, Tony Blair, instituted a series of enforceable measures requiring parents to undertake certain kinds of activities to control and take responsibility for their children. More recently this has evolved into suggestions that parents of children seen to be vulnerable or at risk of antisocial or criminal behavior should have to undertake preventative programs that are intended to teach them appropriate skills in social and moral upbringing. Of course, such calls are not unproblematic since there are many parents who require no such program, a lot of them likely to see the move toward this as unnecessary meddling by government in the private affairs of the household. And, of course, if the sense of a social emergency reflects some deep cultural shifts in behavior, then governments themselves may not be immune from criticism since a raft of legislation and deregulation around the evolution of free markets would appear to have nurtured a rather more selfish and self-indulgent society than that of the immediate postwar period where austerity and self-control represented important social and personal forces constraining the behaviors of parents and their offspring. Moreover, in most industrially developed countries, and as a consequence of deregulation, family lifestyle, including such basics as housing, appear to require dual incomes. This in turn means that in many instances family units are rather more fragmented than heretofore. Infants are placed in nurseries from their earliest months. This move also means that it is increasingly difficult for parents to function as educators of first resort. Yet there is substantial evidence to suggest that both educational and sociomoral functioning is critically dependent upon thoughtful parenting.

The challenge amid all this ambiguity is to know what parent education might entail. We know that parental characteristics, discursive practices, and engagements have a profound effect on how children eventually come to assume responsibility in and for the world. Since such matters offer children certain kinds of feedback it might be useful to have some grasp of what parents need to know. While it is not easy to classify and delimit the kinds of things entailed in education for parenthood, nevertheless we can make some pertinent observations. A useful starting point might be Maslow's hierarchy of needs, which requires that more basic physiological and security needs are met before nurturing and facilitating the development of social, ego, and self-actualization needs. Such a schema offers something like a map of what might be required in and of parent education. Moreover, arguably being a prudentially and ethically good parent is not the expression of a set of demarcated skills but is rather the manifest expression of a set of dispositions toward one's child and, in its turn, the world. We also know from modern neurophysiology that the relationship between lower and higher functions is complex. For this reason such a hierarchy of needs, which is not naïvely determinist, is to be preferred to some of the more populist behaviorist approaches to such matters.

Parents need to understand how to nurture their children physiologically and nutritionally as some of the higher order engagements are significantly dependent upon more basic nurture. This might appear rather obvious, but much research suggests that many modern socioindividual ailments such as attention deficit disorder are linked to nutritional deficiencies. This would suggest that the collapse of traditional communities of memory around food and eating has implications beyond the child and the immediate family. Consequently, parents need some introduction into food and nutrition. Similarly, children who are not equipped to enter meaningfully into social life are unlikely to become self-actualizing. Parents then need to know how to cultivate a set of social manners that help children to understand the need for the negotiation of desires and the accommodation of the other in one's own plans. Of course, there is much detail that needs to be put on such claims, but it is clear that parent education is becoming increasingly necessary in late industrial societies.

Further Reading: Booth, A., & Crouter, A. (2001). *Does it take a village? Community effects on children, adolescents and families.* New Jersey: Lawrence Erlbaum.

James C. Conroy

Parental Rights

Parental rights generally refer to the wide range of claims parents may have with respect to their relationship with not only their own children but also the state where this entails consideration of children's well-being. There are, for example, the rights of parents to maternity/paternity leave, the rights of noncustodial parents to access, the rights of parents to bring children up in a particular faith/ideological tradition, and the rights of parents to determine educational provision for their children. It is not always self-evident where each of these rights claim is best located. Are they inalienable rights of the parent or state endowments, or indeed the right of the child? Talk of rights is not always or inevitably straightforward.

There has been much dispute over parental rights, and disagreement has tended to center on the extent to which children themselves possess certain rights to self-determination that supersede parental rights. As with many debates and issues in moral education and moral development, the argument can become polarized along politico-ideological lines. Although never universally the case, those on the political Right tend to regard parental rights as superordinate. Parents, they argue, have the responsibility and duty, and in consequence, thereof, the right to nurture their children as flourishing human beings and good citizens.

Those on the political Left generally wish to place quite robust limitations on parental rights, suggesting that children have significant rights independent of their parents. Such rights they argue must be determined and upheld irrespective of certain kinds of parental wishes and desires. While such wishes and desires may be important for parents in so far as they reflect their ethical and cultural affiliations, this, they argue, does not imply that children must necessarily be subjected to these. In late industrial polities the emphasis on autonomy as a liberal Right appears to have subordinated historically more robust accounts of parental rights where children were deemed to be inheritors of particular traditions and where expectations of intergenerational continuity were high.

Following from this, we may see the battle lines between Left and Right thicken around issues of schooling (McLaughlin, 1984), religion, and sexual ethics where increasingly liberals on the Left argue that parents have minimal rights with regard to the religious upbringing of children on the grounds that beliefs about such matters are contingent and accidental features of an individual's being and consequently should not be seen as ineluctably attached to the equally contingent beliefs of another. Moreover, and even more politically charged is the claim that the state itself embodies and has certain superordinate responsibilities that should, when appropriate, eclipse parental rights. However, some might argue that only when parents manifestly fail to discharge their obligations may they be held accountable by the state, which may then intervene to secure and protect the position and rights of the child. Of course, the very possibility of such state intervention itself implies that parental rights are provisional and conditional rather than absolute and unequivocal.

While those on the Left might desire a state of affairs where children's rights are entirely independent of parents' rights it is not entirely clear how this would work. For example, is the claim that a parent has a right to maternity/paternity leave a claim that the child has a right to parental presence during the first months of life or is it a claim that the parent can levy a right that the state/employer must support the parent in his/her desire to spend time with the children? Much talk of rights with regard to parents is apt to be confused if we are not clear about the grounds on which these are to be claimed or indeed which and whose right is being exercised. Sometimes certain kinds of perceived social or cultural goods are confused with rights. While it may be of benefit to a child (and indeed society) that his/her parent get maternity/paternity leave, it is not entirely clear that this is a right in the strong sense. It may, of course, be a delegated right in the sense that the state obliges employers to make available such leave and gives employees the right to request such leave. However, delegation by the state rests on the belief that the state itself holds such power as a matter of right: a view that is not shared by many who would prefer to follow Paine's (1876) view that parents have had their rights displaced by the state's assumed rights, which are actually no more than the arrogation of power. In an echo of Rousseau's (1997) "Social Contract" the "will of the people" is deemed to be more important than that of the individual or any group of subordinate individuals, and the "will of the people" is embodied in the state.

Of course, there is an argument that parental rights may not be reduced to the capacities of one person to have responsibility over another (less powerful) but on a sense of attachment. The discussion so far concerning parental rights hinges on a mixture of social goods and individual protections but this may not be the whole story. Parents may be attached to their children through bonds of love and affection that transcend the claims of Rousseauian justice. Hence, in a liberal democratic polity there might be a claim that all children should be treated the same and consequently be sent to the same school. This seems to accord with the principles of justice and equity. However, I might wish to send my child to a different (say private or religiously denominated) school because I have an instinct that it will better suit his/her capacities and temperament. I have intimate knowledge about my child's capacities, abilities, and dispositions, and so this privileged access enables me to make a judgment in the context of the particular, whereas the state can only do so with respect to the general. Thus, we see that there is no clear account to be had of parental rights. The appropriate mixture is a subtle blend of children's rights to certain freedoms, the parents' rights to discharge their responsibilities of care, and the state's obligation to protect the weak.

Further Reading: McLaughlin T.H. (1984). Parental rights and the religious upbringing of children. *Journal of Philosophy of Education, 18*(1), 75–83. Paine, T. (1976). *Common sense.* Harmondsworth, England: Penguin. Rousseau, J.J. (1997). *The social contract and other later political writings* (V. Gourevitch, Ed.). Cambridge, England: Cambridge University Press.

James C. Conroy

Peace Education

Peace education is based on an inquiry into the principles of nonviolence, human rights, and social, economic, and political theories of justice that inform normative critiques of international security policies. The pedagogy of peace education is primarily directed toward developing student capacities for critical thinking and reflection upon various global issues perceived as obstacles to peace. Peace educators seek to facilitate the development of alternative strategies to achieve international peace accords and avoidance of all forms of direct and indirect violence (Burns, 1996).

Peace education pedagogy supports teaching and learning methods that stress student participation and respect for differences. Curriculum developed for peace education should seek to enable children to put peacemaking into practice by learning to resolve conflicts in the classroom, schools, and in the local community. Curriculum planning should also include opportunities for professional development and continuous learning for all staff and teachers involved with peace education programs. There are several organizations (both American and international) that are committed to the promotion of peace education and professional development for peace educators and curriculum designers. For example, in the early 1980s, Educators for Social Responsibility (ESR) initiated violence prevention programs for use in American secondary schools. The ESR network supports high school reforms with the purpose to create safe and respectful learning environments. Through their school redesign training program called Partners for Learning, they provide technical support and training for secondary teachers, staff, and administrators to help implement positive changes for a respectful learning environment. Creating positive learning cultures that promote peace requires a commitment to reduce intolerance, harassment, and other aggressive student behaviors. The Educators for Social Responsibility organization helps students to develop more effective interpersonal social skills, self-discipline, and emotional competence by fostering safe and welcoming learning environments.

Since its establishment in 1945, the United Nations (UN) has been an organization that is also instrumental in the promotion of peace education, especially in the areas of study related to global governance and the emergence of global civil society. Creating a culture of peace requires the intentional commitment of progressive educators who can teach the values, standards, and principles articulated in fundamental UN documents such as the Universal Declaration of Human Rights, the World Declaration on the Education for All, and the Convention on the Rights of the Child, to name but a few.

These documents collectively describe peace education as educational initiatives that (1) develop and support "zones of peace" where children are safe from violent conflict, (2) uphold children's basic rights as outlined in the Convention on the Rights of the Child, (3) create an environment where peaceful and respectful behavior is modeled by all members of the learning community, (4) demonstrate the principles of equality and nondiscrimination in administrative policies and practices, (5) build upon the knowledge bank in peace research that articulates best practices in conflict resolution rooted in local cultures, (6) resolve conflicts in ways that respect the rights and dignity of everyone involved, (7) integrate the topics of peace, human rights, social justice, and global issues throughout the curriculum, and (8) create opportunities to encourage explicit dialogue about the values of peace and social justice (Levine, 2000).

Acting in partnership with the United Nations and its Nongovernmental Organizations, the efforts of committed educators, researchers, and citizen organizations have advanced education for peace by linking ideals with extensive research (Levine, 2000). The Hague Agenda for Peace and Justice for the 21st Century is a significant example of efforts to develop peace and human rights education programs for all institutions, including law schools and medical schools internationally. The International Peace Research Association, founded with support from UNESCO, has a Peace Education Commission that serves as a network helping educators from around the world work together to promote a culture of peace. The Peace Education Network, based in London, also works closely with the UN to develop and support peace education programs.

These and various other organizations point to the fact that the participation of all global citizens and nationalities is essential in order to develop a global culture of peace in which all citizens live by international standards of human rights, dignity, and respect for each other. Organizations committed to promoting global peace understand that the content knowledge and pedagogy of peace education should strive to counteract the dehumanizing effects of global poverty, prejudice, discrimination, rape, violence, and war, and to promote dialogue that reaffirms the dignity and worth of all persons and strengthens tolerance and friendship among all nations.

Further Reading: Burns, R.J. (1996). *Three decades of peace education around the world: An anthology.* New York: Garland. Fry-Miller, K., & Myers-Walls, J. (1988). *Young peacemakers project* *book.* Elgin, IL: Brethren Press. Guinan, K. (1994). *Celebrating peace: Young peacemakers club.* Independence, MO: Herald Publishing House. Levine, D.A. (2000). *Teaching empathy.* Ontario, Canada: Blue Heron Press. Reagan, T., Harris, I.M., & Morrison, M.L. (2002). *Peace education.* Jefferson, NC: McFarland & Company.

Monalisa M. Mullins

Peer Influence

Peers are individuals of similar age, status, or maturity level. Peer relationships emerge in childhood and continue throughout the developmental life span as an integral part of one's social experiences. Peer relationships are a pervasive social force in a developing child's life—spending time with peers on the phone, playing team sports, attending school activities, or just hanging out. Williams and Stith (1980) outlined five functions of childhood peer relationships: (a) provide companionship; (b) create a context for testing new behaviors; (c) serve as a source of social knowledge; (d) teach logical consequences and rules of acceptable social conduct; and (e) reinforce gender-role behaviors. Within peer relationships, children learn communication skills and how to resolve conflicts, and begin to appreciate the value of assuming the perspective of another. Successful (i.e., close, stable, satisfying) childhood and adolescent peer relationships have been linked to social adjustment and positive mental health. Poor peer relationships, in contrast, are associated with school dropout, delinquency, and depression. For example, Bagwell and colleagues (1998) found that children reporting a stable best friend in fifth grade had greater self-worth as adults (as assessed 12 years later) than their fifth grade counterparts who did not report a stable peer relationship.

As children transition from childhood to adolescence, more and more time is spent with peers. Families do exert an influence on the peer development, however (Frabutt, 2001). Parents sometimes provide direct coaching for children's peer behavior, offering advice and supervising and commenting on peer play. Families also provide the context for peer development by arranging social contacts and opportunities with other peer play partners. Parents indirectly influence peer relations through their own parenting practices and parent-child interaction style. Both the social content and affective tone of the parent-child bond create a template that children use as a model for their own personal relationships with peers.

Much inquiry has been directed at understanding peer status, how children are perceived within the broader social network by their peers. The field of sociometry quantifies the differences in social status among peer groups by asking children to name their peers who are liked most and liked least. Four peer statuses have been identified (Wentzel & Asher, 1995). Popular children are named by many others in the peer group as a friend and are well liked by others. Compared to unpopular children, popular children are more physically attractive, friendlier, and more outgoing. Neglected children do not receive many nominations and are not positively or negatively chosen. Neglected children tend to be socially isolated within the peer social network. Rejected children are actively disliked by others and receive very few nominations as someone's best friend. Rejected children are more likely than popular children to exhibit aggressive behavior, engage in antagonistic behavior, or act impulsively and in a disruptive manner. Notably, rejected status consistently predicts academic failure and school dropout. Controversial children are highly disliked by some of their peers and are highly liked by some of their peers. These children have some prosocial skills but do not exhibit them effectively in all contexts.

Peer relationship problems are caused by several possible factors. One is poor social cognition among children and adolescents—in appropriate thinking about social interactions. For example, when presented with an ambiguous peer interaction (e.g., a peer knocks a ball out of your hand), children with social skills deficits may immediately assume hostile intent when, in fact, the contact was accidental. Children with social information processing deficits do not assess the social context effectively, do not generate and assess different social reactions, and may act impulsively, often with aggression or hostility. They may not have good emotional regulation and thus fail to limit their level of emotion expressiveness in certain social situations. Approaching and entering an already started social interaction is a particular challenge, as these children rely on ineffective strategies (e.g., negative self-presentation) to enter the group.

Because the developmental impacts of poor peer relations are so great, program developers have created several possible interventions for children with social skills deficits. These programs essentially provide social coaching to improve social skills. Through discussions, role plays, and encouraged reasoning about appropriate and inappropriate modes of expression, children can increase their self-control, group awareness, and social problem-solving ability.

Further Reading: Bagwell, C.L., Newcomb, A.F., & Bukowski, W.M. (1998). Preadolescent friendship and peer rejection as predictors of adult adjustment. *Child Development, 69,* 140–53. Frabutt, J.M. (2001). Parenting in contemporary society: Exploring the links with children's social, moral, and cognitive competence. In T.C. Hunt, E.A. Joseph, & R.J. Nuzzi (Eds.), *Handbook of research on Catholic education. The Greenwood educators' reference collection* (pp. 181–204). Westport, CT: Greenwood Press. Wentzel, K.R., & Asher, S.R. (1995). The academic lives of the neglected, rejected, popular, and controversial children. *Child Development, 66,* 754–63. Williams, J., & Stith, M. (1980). *Middle childhood behavior and development* (2nd ed.). New York: MacMillan.

James M. Frabutt

Peters, Richard S.

The English philosopher Richard Stanley Peters played a leading role in establishing the analytic approach to the philosophy of education, a highly influential style of inquiry into conceptual problems in education in Britain and the United States in the second half of the twentieth century.

Born in 1919, Peters was educated at Clifton College, Oxford. He served during the Second World War in an ambulance unit and after the war worked as a schoolteacher at Sidcot School, an historic private school founded by Quakers. During this time, he continued to study philosophy at Birbeck College, London, where he was eventually appointed as lecturer in philosophy. In 1962 Peters was selected as the inaugural Chair of Philosophy of Education at the University of London's Institute of Education. In this position he worked tirelessly to demonstrate the importance of conceptual clarity in teaching, teacher education, and education policy and to establish the philosophy of education as an autonomous subdiscipline of applied philosophy. Declining health forced him into an early retirement in 1983.

When Peters came of age academically, the central preoccupation of educational philosophy in Britain and the United States was the history of educational ideas. Research and teaching consisted primarily in studying great thinkers in the Western philosophical canon and considering the meaning of their work for education. Emboldened by the way that linguistic analysis, at that time already a staple of mainstream philosophy, had shed new light on old philosophical problems, Peters sought to introduce the method into the philosophy of education.

Analytic philosophy's fundamental idea is simple: ill-defined problems yield erroneous solutions. Early analytic philosophers such as G. E. Moore, Bertrand Russell, and Ludwig Wittgenstein believed that many of the problems that had for centuries beleaguered philosophers were the result of language used poorly and that such problems would not as much be solved as dissolved—shown to be pseudo-problems—by being correctly formulated in plain language. Moore, for instance, famously dismissed Descartes's classical problem of solipsism (the postulate that no good reason can be found to believe that anything other than oneself and one's inner experiences exist) by simply presenting his hand for inspection. "Here is a hand" is a common sense proposition with an ordinary meaning. A hand is an external object that by definition does not exist in one's mind. Thus, in conceding that Moore is, in fact, showing his hand, one is at the same time logically committed to the belief that at least one external object exists, namely Moore's hand.

At the Institute of Education, Peters built up a department staffed by faculty members who were trained both as teachers and as analytic philosophers. They believed that the clarification of key concepts in education—teaching, learning, skill, achievement, aims, indoctrination, and the like—could contribute significantly to the improvement of educational practice and policy. Peters took a special interest in analyzing the concept of education itself. He saw the increasing tendency for education to become specialized, vocational, and geared to the economy militates against a clear-sighted conception of the very meaning of "education." According to his analysis, in ordinary language "education" implies the intentional transmission by ethical means of knowledge that is valuable to those who become acquainted with it. Its value derives from being conducive to a general "understanding of the world and one's place in it" (Peters, 1966). Under critical pressure, Peters and like-minded philosophers of education came to concede that conceptual analysis in education does more than simply clarify conceptual schemes. Analytic philosopher's so-called "linguistic arguments" can also provide tacit support for the controversial normative assumptions about the nature of persons, language, knowledge, society, and moral values that are embedded within those schemes. Nowhere is this point more clearly perceptible, perhaps, than in Peters' own rather traditionalist conclusion that the educated person is a knowledge generalist initiated into various aspects of high culture.

Peters's most important contribution to moral education is his treatment of what he called "the paradox of moral education" (1981). Most people agree that the *non plus ultra* goal of moral education should be moral autonomy: the rational, free, and intelligent adherence to a moral code. However, moral education so construed faces at least two strategic difficulties. First, very young children are impervious to moral reasoning. That is, they are not yet cognitively able to grasp a moral rule's rationale and must therefore be made to conform to rules they cannot understand. Second, and as Aristotle pointed out long ago, if people are not trained from an early age to imitate the affective and behavioral responses typical of a person of good moral character, they are unlikely to develop them as spontaneous responses in adult life. This is the paradox: the use of constraint and habituation seems inevitable in moral education, but their use would also seem to create conditions that are detrimental to the emergence of moral autonomy down the road. Peters proposed to resolve it by attending to the distinction between learning "to act in *accordance with* a rule" and "learning to act *on* a rule" (Peters, 1981). Whereas acting in accordance with a rule means merely to behave blindly as the rule prescribes, acting on a rule means to adopt it as an intelligent guide to one's behavior, or flexibly, intentionally, and with an understanding of its point. Echoing both Jean Piaget and John Dewey's work on the moral development of the child, Peters advanced that children learn to understand moral rules and to apply them intelligently by trying to use them in actual social contexts. From this perspective, being forced or drilled to act in accordance with a moral rule, far from being antithetical to moral autonomy, is developmentally necessary to its achievement. "Young children," Peters (1981) said memorably, "can and must enter the palace of Reason through the courtyard of Habit."

Further Reading: Hirst, P.H., & White, P. (1998). The analytic tradition and philosophy of education: An historical perspective. In *Philosophy of education: Major themes in the analytic tradition* (Vol. 1, pp. 1–12). London: Routledge. Peters, R.S. (1966). *Ethics and education.* London: George Allen & Unwin. Peters, R.S. (1981). *Moral development and moral education.* London: George Allen & Unwin. White, J. (2001). R.S. Peters. In R.A. Palmer (Ed.), *Fifty modern thinkers on education* (pp. 118–22). London: Routledge.

Bruce Maxwell

Piaget, Jean

Jean Piaget was born in Neuchâtel, Switzerland, on August 9, 1896. His work on children's moral development was part of a seven-decade career of research and writing that resulted in the publication of more than 60 books and several hundred articles. Piaget's interest in science began in childhood. With the support of one of his uncles he began to study the local wildlife near his home, and he published his first article at age ten on the sighting of an albino sparrow. During adolescence he studied the adaptations of mollusks to life in the fresh water lakes of the Alps. This led to a part-time job with the director of Neuchâtel's Museum of Natural History, where he published a series of scientific papers earning him a reputation among European scientists who assumed he was an adult. He received his doctorate in science from the University of Neuchâtel at the age of 22.

Piaget's early interest in biological sciences was counterbalanced by his parents' focus upon religion and philosophy. For the young Piaget, philosophy proved to be unsatisfactory as he weighed the arguments presented by proponents of empiricist and rationalist accounts of epistemology (the study of knowledge) with their emphases on experience on the one hand and presumed innate structures of logic on the other. Piaget turned to his fascination with biological adaptation as a way to resolve these competing explanations of how knowledge develops in individuals.

Piaget proposed that children's thinking undergoes a sequence of transformations, or developmental stages, that constitute increasingly adaptive structures of logic and understanding. Piaget's study of children's morality, published in 1932, predated his work on children's logical structures, but contained some of his basic insights into the nature of cognitive development. It was Piaget's basic contention that, although children acquire information from the outside environment, their understandings or interpretations of things are the result of the child's own efforts to explain or make sense of the world.

Piaget devised a series of studies designed to get at their understandings of moral rules, moral intensions, distributive justice, and responses to wrongdoing. What Piaget concluded was that children's moral thinking may be characterized in terms of two moralities. According to Piaget, young children begin in a "heteronomous" stage of moral reasoning, characterized by a strict adherence to rules and duties, and obedience to authority. This heteronomous morality gives way in later childhood to an autonomous morality based on mutual respect and reciprocity.

The heteronomy Piaget observed in young children was thought to stem from two factors. The first factor is the young child's cognitive structure. According to Piaget, the thinking of young children is characterized by egocentrism. That is to say that young children are unable to simultaneously take into account their own view of things with the perspective of someone else. This egocentrism leads children to project their own thoughts and wishes onto others. It is also associated with the unidirectional view of rules and power associated with heteronomous moral thought, and various forms of "moral realism." Moral realism is associated with "objective responsibility," which is valuing the letter of the law above the purpose of the law. This is why, according to Piaget, young children are more concerned about the outcomes of actions rather than the intentions of the person doing the act.

The second major contributor to heteronomous moral thinking in young children is their relative social relationship with adults. In the natural authority relationship between adults and children, power is handed down from above. The relative powerlessness of young children, coupled with childhood egocentrism feeds into a heteronomous moral orientation.

The shift to autonomous morality involves changes in the child's cognitive structure, along with shifts in his/her social relations through interactions with peers. Peer interactions reduce the power differential experienced in adult-child exchanges, and foster mutual give-and-take as children attempt to resolve their interpersonal disputes. Engagement with other children results in situations in which there needs to be common ground for solutions that all parties will accept. In this search for fair resolution, children find strict heteronomous adherence to rules sometimes problematic. As children consider these situations, they develop toward an "autonomous" stage of moral reasoning, characterized by the ability to consider rules critically, and selectively apply these rules based on a goal of mutual respect and cooperation.

The ability to act from a sense of reciprocity and mutual respect is associated with a shift in the child's cognitive structure from egocentrism to perspective taking. Perspective taking allows the child to differentiate his or her own needs and point of view from those of others. This new cognitive ability permits the child to coordinate perspectives and to arrive at solutions to interpersonal disputes based on reciprocity. The relative equality in power relations among peers, and this emergent cognitive ability to engage in reciprocity results in a morality based on mutual respect and fairness rather than adherence to external authority and social convention.

Piaget engaged in his research on moral development partly as a response to a book on moral education published by the eminent sociologist Emile Durkheim (1925). Durkheim proposed that moral development was the result of socialization processes that built from children's natural tendencies toward attachment to groups, an attachment that manifests itself in a respect for the symbols, rules, and authority of the group. Schooling allows for children to participate in a broader group context that more closely resembles the broader society than the interactions that take place in the family. Attachment to group life within the school context, according to Durkheim, promotes the child's attachment to society and respect for its rules, norms, and authority. Through moral education, children were also said by Durkheim to develop a spirit of discipline needed to control behavior and conform to society's norms. Durkheim's position on moral education is consistent with some traditional approaches to character education.

In contrast with Durkheim, and in line with the findings from his developmental research, Piaget argued that moral education should foster the child's moral autonomy. At young ages in particular, schools and teachers need to minimize their power relative to children, and foster the peer interactions and interpersonal problem solving necessary to stimulate the development of autonomous morality. The role of the teacher in a Piagetian classroom is to engage children in actively arriving at fair resolutions to interpersonal disputes rather than imposing adult solutions. Students in Piagetian classrooms are also to be involved in actively evaluating and altering classroom rules and norms from a position of reciprocity and mutual respect, rather than top-down compliance with teacher authority. Since moral development also involves shifts in social cognition, uses of the curriculum would serve to raise issues for moral discussion and debate rather than solely as sources of information about existing social norms and standards. An excellent contemporary adaptation of Piaget's theory for moral development of young children may be found in DeVries and Zan (1994).

Further Reading: DeVries, R., & Zan, B. (1994). *Moral classrooms, moral children: Creating a constructivist atmosphere for early education.* New York: Teachers College Press. Durkheim, E. (1961). *Moral education.* Glencoe, IL: The Free Press. (Original work published 1925.) Piaget, J. (1932). *The moral judgment of the child.* New York: Free Press.

Larry Nucci

Plagiarism

Plagiarism is the act of using and passing off as one's own the words or ideas of another without properly acknowledging the original author or source. Common forms of plagiarism include (1) failing to cite, or improperly citing, a quotation, paraphrase, summary, data, idea, or any other piece of information that is not one's own or is only partially so; (2) using parts of texts or an entire paper procured through the Web or a term paper service; and (3) allowing or employing a third party to do some or all of the research and writing required of an assignment. Third parties include friends, fellow students and acquaintances, businesses, and parents. Plagiarism is a form of academic dishonesty. To avoid plagiarism, students must pay scrupulous attention to citation rules when using printed material as well as orally presented information, for example, material in books, journals, graphs, tables, visual art, music, audio lectures, lecture notes, lab notes, personal conversations and correspondence (including emails), on-line chats and bulletin boards, the Web, CD-ROMs, and other telecommunication sources. In plagiarizing, a person misrepresents one's knowledge and can be found guilty of academic dishonesty or academic fraud.

Plagiarism occurs at all levels of education, but extant research mainly focuses on the problem at the high school and undergraduate levels. Plagiarism in education is a problem for many reasons. One, in the exchange of knowledge, the academic integrity of all parties involved (scholars, researchers, faculty, students, and parents) is essential. Two, students are supposed to grow intellectually and accumulate a body of knowledge that is truly their own, and faculty are asked to evaluate their growth. If students are not honest about what they know, then the accuracy and validity of the evaluation process is undermined, and the degrees awarded by educational institutions become suspect. By properly citing sources of information in their academic work, students document that work and enable their teachers to validate their interpretations of that work. Moreover, by providing accurate citations, students contribute to the transfer of knowledge.

There are many underlying causes of plagiarism besides a willful intention to deceive or a desire to edge out the competition, as the research of McCabe (2005), Breen and Maassen (2005), and Ercegovac and Richardson (2004) illustrates. Students may be unaware of how or when to use citations, they may genuinely misunderstand what constitutes plagiarism, or they may lack confidence in themselves in the art of academic writing. Other causes include carelessness, poor time management, stress over grades, laziness, immaturity, and faulty moral reasoning. Students in educational institutions that do not have an honor code are more likely to plagiarize; and students in majors such as business, science, and technology are more likely to plagiarize. If students perceive the faculty as not attending to academic integrity or if the same assignments are given in a course, semester after semester, the students are more likely to use others' work. In addition, students inexperienced with standard English writing and citation conventions, especially students from abroad, are more likely to plagiarize than other students.

Responses to plagiarism vary among students, faculty, and institutions (McCabe, 2005; Ercegovac & Richardson, 2004). Students may be surprised that they plagiarized, or they may underestimate the seriousness of the problem. Faculty, already feeling overburdened with teaching and research, often prefer not to get involved, especially if it entails holding discussions in ethics and instructing students in writing technique. Faculty also may not want to pursue alleged instances of plagiarism because the process is too long and complicated; or faculty may try to handle it themselves, without due process. Faculty may also not perceive the administration as supportive or consistent in prosecuting cases. Responses at the school level will vary depending on whether there is an honor code policy to which everyone actively adheres and whether there are fair procedures in place for handling the problem.

To avoid problems, schools and individual faculty may increase surveillance of students and threaten strong sanctions. They may also employ Web-based detection services to determine the authenticity of students' papers. However, such measures do not help students to avoid inadvertent acts of plagiarism nor do they encourage students' ethical development. McCabe (2004, 2005) recommends that schools that have an honor code policy and where faculty and students openly value and maintain academic integrity are the most likely to keep plagiarism cases to a minimum. Breen and Maassen (2005) find that special tutorials to teach students to identify obvious and subtle forms of plagiarism and develop better research and writing skills also decrease the likelihood of the offense. These authors as well as model programs on academic integrity, such as Princeton University's, provide excellent guidelines and information for students, faculty, and schools.

Research in moral development in general suggests that in order to help students develop their thinking about ethical issues, time must be taken to grapple with the issues involved. To accomplish this, students need faculty who see themselves as significant guides in their students' ethical development. Besides responding to incidents when they arise, faculty can forestall the problem by instructing students properly and by making clear their expectations at the start of each semester. Though the principle of subsidiarity is advisable, attention should be paid to formal due process so that all parties involved feel heard, the offense is documented, and the offender is instructed and/or admonished. Consequences should be determined on the basis of important information, such as the severity of the act and whether the student has a record of past offenses. Whether a school is proactive or reactive in handling plagiarism, for students to develop ethically, the emphasis must be on educating students and not merely punishing them.

Further Reading: Breen, L., & Maassen, M. (2005). Reducing the incidence of plagiarism in an undergraduate course: The role of education. *Issues in Educational Research, 15*(1), 1–16. Ercegovac, Z., & Richardson, J.V. (2004). Academic dishonesty, plagiarism included, in the digital age: A literature review. *College & Research Libraries, 65*(4), 301–18. McCabe, D. (2005). It takes a village: Academic dishonesty and educational opportunity. *Liberal Education, 91*(3), 26–31. McCabe, D.L., & Pavela, G. (2004). Ten (updated) principles of academic integrity: How faculty can foster student honesty. *Change, 36*(3), 10–15.

Ann Marie R. Power

Plato

Plato (ca. 428–347 B.C.E.) was the first author in the West to write about a wide range of philosophical questions—ethical, political, aesthetic, metaphysical, and epistemological—relating considerations on one type of question to those on another. His writings exhibit not only philosophical insight but also narrative artistry and an appreciation for the relationship between personal character and philosophical conviction.

With rare exceptions, Plato wrote dramatic works called "dialogues" rather than treatises in a monologue style. The central character in most of these conversations is Socrates, an Athenian who fascinated Plato as a youth but who was executed legally by the city when Plato was in his mid- to late-twenties. One of Plato's students, Aristotle, never met Socrates. He arrived in Athens as a teenager from the court of King Philip of Macedon to study in Plato's Academy. He studied Plato's dialogues and heard many stories about the enigmatic Socrates.

Plato stands between Socrates and Aristotle. Socrates wrote nothing and famously claimed to know nothing. He nonetheless dazzled those who listened to his philosophical conversations with leading persons in fifth century Athens. Aristotle, on the other hand, wrote volumes of lectures and lecture notes. Some collections of these set the basic structure of knowledge in scientific, ethical-political, and aesthetic fields for centuries.

Plato was not as open-ended in his inquiries as Socrates, seeming at some points in his writings to develop a set of doctrines into a coherent perspective on reality, knowledge, and the good. But he was more open-ended than Aristotle, writing dialogues that without exception require the reader to take the reflections further than the dialogues took them. Plato was intentionally less didactic than Aristotle but also cautiously, deliberately more systematic than Socrates.

Plato's dialogues are traditionally grouped into three time periods: early, middle, and late. A fourth period is inserted by some between the first and second: transitional dialogues that diverge from the early dialogues in content and style but that appear less seasoned than the middle dialogues. The middle dialogues are taken to give full expression to Plato's genius and to present what has long been called "Platonism."

The order within the four groups is a matter of dispute, and there is some disagreement about whether particular dialogues belong in one group or the other. As arranged by

C.D.C. Reeve (2006), the early dialogues are *Alcibiades, Apology, Charmides, Crito, Euthyphro, Hippias Major, Hippias Minor, Ion, Laches, Lysis, Menexenus,* and *Theages.* The transitional dialogues are *Euthydemus, Gorgias, Meno,* and *Protagoras.* The middle dialogues are *Cratylus, Phaedo, Symposium, Republic, Phaedrus, Parmenides,* and *Theaetetus.* And the late dialogues are *Timaeus, Critias, Sophist, Statesman, Philebus,* and *Laws.*

This arrangement makes central the development of Platonism. The early dialogues were "Socratic" in the sense that in most of them the character Socrates employs a method of refutation of the theses presented by his interlocutors without defending views of his own. The discussion typically ends without resolving the dispute that is its focus, usually involving the attempt to define some concept such as beauty, courage, or holiness.

In the middle dialogues, however, most commentators find Platonism, consisting of three main metaphysical and epistemological theses: (1) the soul is imprisoned in a body but is itself immortal and passes from life to life in new incarnations; (2) knowledge acquired in previous lives is retained unconsciously as the soul begins a new incarnation, and learning consists of recollecting ideas from previous lives, not of getting something new into the head; and (3) the real objects of our knowledge are abstract ideas or "forms." These objects are intelligible or thinkable but not visible, the way the equilateral triangle and H_2O are thinkable, in the abstract, but in matter are only instanced. When one knows anything, one has the "form" as one's idea, and so one's intellect participates in the form immaterially the way a physical object of its type participates in the form materially. When, for instance, one knows water, one has "what it is to be" water, H_2O, as one's thought—though, of course, one does not thereby have water on the brain.

Few of the middle dialogues mention more than one of these three theses, let alone explain all three, but taken as a set the middle dialogues return to these theses often enough that commentators have typically supposed Plato was in this period of his writing developing his own philosophy. A common though questionable inference is that Plato was in these dialogues using Socrates merely as his mouthpiece. A closer reading suggests to some that, even in these dialogues, Plato wants his readers to question some of Socrates's assertions.

In three of the six late dialogues, Socrates is not a main speaker. The late dialogues are viewed by some as more tedious and less focused on the development of a philosophical perspective. Others find Plato moving further away from Platonism.

Plato traced his ancestry on his mother's side back two centuries to Solon, the author of Athens' constitution, and on his father's side back five or six centuries to an early king of Athens. His stepfather was a friend of the influential statesman, Pericles, some 20 years Plato's senior. He seems to have intended originally to enter political life himself but to have been dissuaded from this by the events of and following the Peloponnesian War, including Socrates' execution. Plato devoted himself instead to writing a new genre of philosophy and founded the Academy in about 388 B.C.E. Nonetheless, the next year he visited the court of Dionysius I, tyrant of Syracuse, and made two later trips to Sicily in apparent efforts to influence political events for the better.

For his efforts he was held in prison more than once but escaped the fate of his mentor, Socrates. As other-worldly as Platonism may seem, Plato himself seems not to have had his head entirely in the clouds.

Nonetheless, according to the standard account, Plato and Aristotle were diametrically opposed. For instance, in Platonism, the forms exist separately, accessible only by thought, and horses, for instance, are mere imitations of what it is really to be a horse. In

Aristotelianism, on the other hand, the forms exist in the physical things themselves, as constituent features of things. What it is to be a horse exists as the "formal cause" or defining structure of each horse, with a particular body being the "material cause" of each horse. In Platonism, if horses became extinct, what it is to be a horse would be entirely unaffected. In Aristotelianism, what it is to be a horse would continue to exist only in a secondary sense, as a notion humans have.

Aristotle criticized the separateness and other aspects of the forms as well, but his account of the role of contemplation in the best human life has seemed to some Platonic. He would have studied the early to middle dialogues as a student in the Academy, and he was engaged in discussion and disagreement with Plato as Plato wrote the late dialogues. Aristotle sided with Plato rather than his pupil Alexander the Great on the civic locus of the best life.

Plato's dialogues presented incomplete inquiries. Aristotle went one direction. Plato would call each of us, perhaps in cooperation, to work out our own—and in that he was ever a true Socratic.

Further Reading: Cooper, J.M. (Ed.). (1997). *Plato: Complete works.* Indianapolis, IN: Hackett Publishing. Gadamer, H. (1980). *Dialogue and dialectic.* New Haven, CT: Yale University Press. Nails, D. (2002). *The people of Plato.* Indianapolis, IN: Hackett Publishing. Pickstock, C. (2007). *A short guide to Plato.* New York: Oxford University Press. Plato. (2004). *Republic* (C.D.C. Reeve, Trans.). Indianapolis, IN: Hackett Publishing.

Don Collins Reed

Pluralism

Pluralism is used in many different contexts to refer to deep-seated multiplicity. Pluralism is the opposite of monism, which regards multiplicity as mere appearance and all reality as one. Most contemporary discussions of pluralism focus on its social reality and moral and political significance. We take cultural diversity for granted in thinking about our nation and our world. Yet we have very different views about how deep cultural differences run and the possibilities for achieving a mutual understanding and respect. Cultural differences include not only language and customs but also deeply held metaphysical, moral, and religious beliefs. The social sciences, particularly anthropology, have taught us to understand and tolerate cultural diversity. The dominant view among the social sciences is that values are relative to each culture, and no culture should be considered superior to another. Some object to this relativism on the grounds that in insisting upon tolerance, it falls prey to the absolutism that it decries.

In philosophy, there are different ways to approach the moral pluralism. Monists debate whether values or goods are ultimately one, as Plato maintained, or whether there are radically different values or goods, as Aristotle argued. More frequently philosophers accept moral pluralism as a social fact and examine its moral implications. Are culturally and religiously based moral systems, principles, and values irreducible and incommensurate? Are they ultimately irreconcilable, or can one be a moral pluralist and find agreement on fundamental principles? Many philosophers argue that moral pluralism need not necessarily imply moral relativism insofar as different moral systems, principles, and values may be based on a common universal moral core (Walzer, 1996). In other words, acknowledging the reality of moral diversity does not commit one to regard all moral values as equal worth or to accept a cultural practice as moral simply because it is a cultural norm. The recognition of pluralism need not imply relativism. For example, some African societies require that young girls approaching puberty have a clitorectomy, a form of female circumcision, which is often done within a ritual of initiation into womanhood. A moral pluralist, while recognizing that this practice has moral value within certain cultures, may, nevertheless, find the practice morally objectionable.

Pluralism raises particularly vexing challenges in the political sphere. *E Pluribus Unum* is a motto of the United States and appears on its currency. The phrase comes from the Latin meaning "out of many, one." All societies must achieve a unity among their diverse cultural groups or face dissolution. Yet how is this unity to be achieved? Should society act as a "melting pot" in which distinct cultures gradually surrender their identity? Is the analogy of a melting pot a euphemism for describing assimilation into the dominant culture? Should society allow cultural groups to maintain their distinctiveness by encouraging separatism, and how much separatism can a society allow?

Pluralism is used to describe what is and to prescribe what should be. Regarded as a fact, pluralism means nothing more than the existence of diverse groups with different cultural identities. Regarded as an ideal, pluralism is a way of respecting and "engaging" diversity (Eck, 2006). In response to W. E. B. DuBois's agonized questions: "What after all am I? Am I an American or am I a Negro? Can I be both? Or is it my duty to cease to be a Negro as soon as possible and be an American?" (p. 11), the ideal of pluralism affirms that one can be a citizen without having to renounce one's racial or ethnic identity. Moreover, the ideal pluralism maintains that civil society is enriched by diversity in dialogue because it is only through dialogue that respect and trust can emerge.

Moral education can help young people to live in a pluralistic society by identifying ways in which they can participate fully within their own cultural and religious groups while still taking responsibility for contributing to the ideal of pluralism in the wider society. In order to live in peace and justice, religious and cultural groups must look within their own traditions to find the resources that can support and even nourish multicultural understanding and communication.

Further Reading: DuBois, W. E. B. (1989). *The souls of Black folk.* New York: Penguin. (Original work published 1903.) Eck, D. L. (2006). *On common ground: World religions in America.* New York: Columbia University Press. Leicester, M., Modgil, C., & Modgil, S. (2000). *Moral education and pluralism: Education, culture and values.* New York: Flamer Press. Power, F. C., & Lapsley, D. K. (1992). *The challenge of pluralism: Education, politics, and values.* Notre Dame, IN: University of Notre Dame Press. Walzer, M. (1996). *Thick and thin: Moral argument at home and abroad.* Notre Dame, IN: University of Notre Dame Press.

F. Clark Power and Nicholas J. Houpt

Plus One Convention

With the large interest in the psychological study of the development of moral reasoning in children and adolescents during the 1960s, 1970s, and 1980s came a similar interest in educational applications of Lawrence Kohlberg's theory of stages of moral reasoning development. There were two related forms of application of Kohlberg's psychological theory to educational practice (comprehensive school reform in the form of Just Community Schools and classroom discussions of moral problems). The latter (see Moral

Discussions and Blatt Effect) produced many implementation studies and educational curricula and supports, as well as research.

Based in large part on the pioneering basic research of Elliot Turiel and James Rest in the early and mid 1960s, it was assumed that part of the mechanism of stimulating moral reasoning development through peer discussions of moral problems (moral dilemmas) was the exposure of the individual child to moral arguments one developmental stage higher than his/her own level of moral reasoning. This was called the "Plus One" strategy. Beginning in the mid 1960s and continuing undaunted through the 1970s and into the early 1980s, the Plus One Convention went largely unchallenged, with one exception. The only real challenge was the argument that it was impractical or even impossible for most teachers to generate Plus One moral arguments for their students.

In the early 1980s, Berkowitz published a set of papers revisiting the Turiel and Rest research, as well as the seminal classroom intervention research (see Blatt Effect) and concluded that the Plus One Convention was largely a myth. Not only was it impractical for teachers to do what some (e.g., Arbuthnot & Faust, 1981) were prescribing, namely spontaneously generating and inserting Plus One arguments into classroom discussions of moral dilemmas, but the research that had been invoked to justify the soundness of this technique in fact did not actually support arguments for the technique. In other words, teachers could not reasonably be expected to implement the Plus One Convention, and they did not need to anyhow as it was not really supported by research.

The general acceptance of the Plus One Convention did not die easily as it was quite widely and unreflectively held. However, with the relative decline in interest in the pedagogical strategy of moral discussions in classrooms and the recognition that Plus One was both impractical and unsupported, it has largely died out both in the literature and in the classroom.

Further Reading: Arbuthnot, J., & Faust, D. (1981). *Teaching moral reasoning: Theory and practice.* San Francisco: Harper and Row. Berkowitz, M.W. (1981). A critical appraisal of the educational and psychological perspectives on moral discussion. *The Journal of Educational Thought, 15,* 20–33. Beyer, B.K. (1978). Conducting moral discussions in the classroom. In P. Scharf (Ed.), *Readings in moral education* (pp. 62–75). Minneapolis, MN: Winston.

Marvin W. Berkowitz

Political Development

Aristotle's writing about *polis*—or the city-state—led to the English word political. In current parlance, to label something political or someone a politician is as often as not meant in a pejorative manner. In his *Politics,* Aristotle philosophized about the nature of a governed city-state and speculated about which form of governing would be most likely to achieve the desired end (*telos*): a society in which citizens are virtuous and lead satisfying lives. The role of politicians was to create a constitution that provides the infrastructure for society: providing laws, institutions, and, most importantly, education generally and moral education particularly.

Aristotle described three different options for the constitution of societies: (a) rule by one person, (b) rule by a small number of rulers, and (c) rule by many persons. Aristotle recognized that the number of rulers was just one dimension and whether the society was positive or negative would be a separate question. Accordingly, he described rule by one as either (a1) a kingship or (a2) a tyranny; rule by a few as (b1) aristocracy based on merit as the positive and (b2) oligarchy the negative. The positive outcome of rule by many would be (c1) polity with (c2) democracy as the negative. Of the six, as one might infer from the names, aristocracy was the type of constitution that Aristotle would consider preferable in the best of all possible worlds; however—given human fallibility—polity was in Aristotle's conclusion the best practical option. Polity is a word that is relatively rare in current usage. That democracy would be a corrupt version of rule by the many would likely be viewed as suspect by the average person on the streets of the United States. The difference between polity and democracy would be determined by whether the citizens made decisions and acted for the common good (polity) or whether self-interest motivated decisions.

Any comprehensive political philosophy must also deal with the challenge to sustain the constitution over time. For Aristotle the solution included: (a) enforcing laws both big and small, (b) not allowing office holders to profit from public service, (c) including the members of marginalized classes/groups in the government as minor office holders. However, the most important solution is (d) providing education. Aristotle believed that education must be universal for citizens and not left to families, and he argued that education should shape each citizen and cause him/her to act for the common good. Aristotelian educational prescriptions included physical education and favored practical knowledge over the theoretical. Aristotle did not include all inhabitants of the city-state as citizens (excluding women, slaves, and the young). Citizens, in Aristotle's view, had a positive obligation to serve the duties as a citizen—that is, citizenship is as much a verb as a noun.

The issues raised by Aristotle are generic and remain current in United States history and remain open questions today. In 1835, Alexis de Tocqueville, a French Aristocrat, visited the United States and wrote at great length of what he observed and concluded. Relevant here are the observations de Tocqueville made about the disposition of U.S. citizens to place their own individual interests in a context of what was in the interest of the community as a whole. What he called the "habits of the heart" are the tendency that—in Aristotelian terms—created more of a polity than corrupt democracy (again to use Aristotle's definition).

How society is organized, who benefits, and how resources are distributed are fundamentally ethical questions and, in both analyzing current events and examining history, provide opportunity for moral reflection and education. For example, the U.S democracy and society places great value on freedom (including the pursuit of happiness through free choice) and equality. Whether that equality should be equality of opportunity (in which merit is rewarded) or equality of outcome (leading to a system of equity) is frequently controversial. Social policies that include equity-based affirmative action programs are a current example. To read a major newspaper on any given day will generate a list of controversial ethical issues that raise questions about how best to organize society in terms of the constitutional infrastructure, laws, and social policy including: Which groups of society should be taxed and at what rates? What people should be able to get married? What structures of government should be created (and by whom) in nations where regimes have been changed by acts of war? Will foreign and military policies be established to promote democracy in other nations or to protect a source and low price for fossil fuels for the United States? What portion of governmental coffers should support education and the least-advantaged members of a society and what should be used for other purposes and to benefit other citizens (and corporations)?

Turning to development and how it applies to politics, two types can be considered: the development of society and the development of individuals. While the generic issues raised in Aristotle's *Politics* remain current, progressive political development is evident in that many societies (including the United States) no longer exclude women from citizenship nor sustain a system of slavery. In terms of individual development, moral educators should prepare students to recognize, discuss, deliberate, and act (individually and in groups) on moral issues; in Aristotelian terms, this is to be virtuous and to prepare themselves and others in the community to live satisfying lives.

Further Reading: Aristotle. (1996). *The politics and the constitution of Athens* (S. Everson, Ed.). Cambridge, England: Cambridge University Press. Noddings, N. (2004). *Starting at home: Caring and social policy.* Berkeley: University of California Press. Nozick, R. (1974). *Anarchy, state, and utopia.* New York: Basic Books. Nussbaum, M.C. (2004). *Hiding from humanity: Disgust, shame, and the law.* Princeton, NJ: Princeton University Press. Rawls, J. (2001). *Justice as fairness: A restatement* (E. Kelly, Ed.). Cambridge, MA: Belknap Press.

Robert W. Howard

Positive/Distributive Justice (Stages of)

Positive justice is a domain of study within moral development that focuses on how children think about and resolve conflicts that arise in prosocial interactions. A special case of positive justice concerns fair sharing or "distributive justice." Although children are enjoined by parents to share their belongings, for example, it is not always clear on what basis one should share, especially when there are many claimants who want to be treated fairly. Distributive justice, then, is the problem of how to distribute property, goods, and favors in a way that is fair when there are conflicting and competing claims.

Jean Piaget did the first studies of distributive justice in young children, although his studies focused more on what children considered to be the fair distribution of punishment rather than the fair sharing of goods and favors. In his view distributive justice is a matter of equal treatment. But young children do not insist on equal treatment but rather confuse fairness with adult authority. For a young child what the adult commands is judged fair even if adult judgments are arbitrary, unequal, and harsh. Piaget thought this was because young children have unilateral respect for adults that encourages their cognitive egocentrism. It is not until children have greater experience with equality in peer interactions that their notion of justice changes to favor equal treatment. Later still, in early adolescence, the principle of equal treatment gives way to a greater appreciation of equitable treatment. Here it is understood that treating everyone the same is not always fair given extenuating circumstances so that the application of strictly equal justice must be corrected with considerations of equity.

Damon (1977) identified a stage sequence of distributive justice reasoning about fair sharing that parallels Piaget's sequence. At stage 0-A, the sharing criteria is self-interest ("I should get more because that's what I want"). At stage 0-B, self-interest is defended on external, physical, or observable grounds ("All us boys should get more"). At 1-A, the notion of strict equality is endorsed—everybody must get the same. At 1-B, this concern for strict equality is modified in the direction of merit or desert—those who worked harder deserve more; those who were lazy deserve less. What about competing claims to merit? At 2-A, there are attempts to work out an equitable compromise, which is then perfected at stage 2-B where one takes into consideration the larger goals and purposes of the group. So the sequence moves from egocentrism and physical notions of fairness (Level 0) to strict equality (Level 1) and then to equity (Level 2). Typically the summit of distributive justice reasoning is within reach of children by age 8 to 10. This is worth saying because children are credited with more sophisticated understanding of fairness in the distributive justice domain than by Lawrence Kohlberg's famous theory of moral development. By middle childhood, children can think about fair sharing in ways that are sensitive to issues of equality and equity. In contrast, Kohlberg's theory groups children of this age into preconventional stages, perhaps because the moral dilemmas of concern to Kohlberg are more substantial and require greater ability to articulate sophisticated moral justifications.

Research on distributive justice reasoning has relied on two methods: a clinical oral interview method pioneered by Piaget; and also an objective, standardized instrument called the Distributive Justice Scale (Enright, Franklin, & Manheim, 1980). The sequential properties of the distributive justice stage sequence have been attested by longitudinal research. Children who show change over time tend to move to the next highest stage. Distributive justice reasoning is also associated with cognitive development, particularly with logical reciprocity and the ability to take the perspectives of others. For this reason children at higher distributive justice stages also appear to be more socially competent. However, growth in distributive justice reasoning over time does not seem to be merely the result of growing verbal ability. Growth in distributive justice reasoning might be more rapid at younger ages than older ages and is sensitive to contextual effects. For example, research shows that lower class children may lag behind their middle class peers. That said, the distributive justice sequence has been observed in both Sweden and Zaire, which supports claims regarding the universality of social cognitive developmental stage sequences.

The distributive justice stage sequence does not have exacting assumptions about stage development, unlike Kohlberg's moral developmental stage theory. The distributive justice stages are a taxonomy of various sharing criteria that seem absent a notion of hierarchical integration, or a notion of why one stage must give way to the next, or why reasoning at one level is preferred or better than the reasoning of a lower stage—and in what sense "lower"? Clearly the complexity of justice reasoning and its development requires stage theories of different kinds.

Further Reading: Damon, W. (1977). *The social world of the child.* San Francisco: Jossey-Bass. Damon, W. (1988). *The moral child: Nurturing children's natural moral growth.* New York: Free Press. Enright, R.D., Franklin, C.C., & Manheim, L.A. (1980). Children's distributive justice reasoning: A standardized and objective scale. *Developmental Psychology, 17,* 555–63. Lapsley, D. (1996). *Moral psychology.* Boulder, CO: Westview Press. Piaget, J. (1932). *The moral judgment of the child.* New York: Norton.

Daniel K. Lapsley

Positive Psychology

For much of the twentieth century, psychology focused on what was wrong with people, on fixing disorder and disease. The positive psychology movement, initiated by Martin Seligman when he was the president of the American Psychological Association in 1998, is about rebalancing the field of psychology to focus on strength and virtue, and making people's lives better with positive prevention and increased well-being.

Positive psychology claims that there are buffers against psychopathology, traits that individuals can develop to foster resiliency. One of Seligman's areas of study is learned optimism. He shows that people can learn to be optimists, thereby preventing depression and anxiety. There has been great growth in educating children for resiliency, including online sources for self-help.

Much of positive psychology focuses on the individual (like psychology in general)— how do I flourish and feel great? These address such notions as "flow," well-being, self-esteem and coping, creativity, self-efficacy, authenticity, and toughness. But there are some branches of positive psychology that focus on more morally relevant constructs, such as moral emotions like gratitude, forgiveness, compassion, empathy, and positive emotions such as joy, interest, hope, contentment, and humor. Positive affect generally is related to prosocial behavior (Isen, 2002).

Positive psychology's relevance to moral education is easy to see in Peterson and Seligman's compendium of character strengths and virtues in which, using stringent criteria, they identified 24 virtues or strengths of character. The criteria for including a virtue in the list were that it contribute to fulfillments that comprise a good life, it is valued for its own sake, its display in one person does not diminish others, it is manifest in a range of behavior, and it is distinctive from other virtues. Peterson and Seligman discuss how it is important to identify and strengthen the virtues a person has.

The strengths are grouped into six categories. The first category is called wisdom and knowledge, which includes the cognitive strengths associated with acquiring and using knowledge. The strengths included here are creativity, which has to do with imagining novel and productive ways to conceptualize and do things; curiosity, which means being interested in ongoing experience for its own sake; open-mindedness, which includes examining things from multiple perspectives and making judgments based on a careful weighing of evidence; love of learning, which involves the tendency to systematically refine what one knows; and perspective or wisdom, which is used to counsel others or interpret the world.

The second category of strengths are unified under the title of courage, emotional strengths that help one accomplish goals. These include bravery, acting on convictions and not avoiding threat and difficulty; persistence, which involves taking pleasure in and completing goals; integrity, which concerns being genuine and taking responsibility for one's actions; and vitality, responding to life wholeheartedly.

The third category of strengths is called humanity and involves caring for others. The strengths here include love, which involves being close to people; kindness, doing things for others; and social intelligence, knowing how to get along well with others.

The fourth category of strengths is called justice, which entails civic strengths important for a healthy community life. These strengths include citizenship, bearing one's share of upholding community welfare; fairness, giving others a fair chance and not playing favorites; and leadership, organizing groups to get along and accomplish goals.

The fifth category of strengths is called temperance, protective strengths against excesses. These strengths include forgiveness and mercy, not seeking revenge but giving others a second chance; humility/modesty, not regarding oneself above others; prudence, having to do with not taking undue risks; and self-regulation, being disciplined.

The sixth category is called transcendence. Its strengths include appreciation of beauty and excellence, perceiving and appreciating beauty and outstanding performance; gratitude, taking time to express thanks; hope, expecting good outcomes; humor, liking to laugh and bringing it about in others; and spirituality, having a sense of purpose.

Ultimately positive psychology is about optimal human functioning. There were "three pillars" of positive psychology initially proposed by Seligman and Csikszentmihalyi: positive subjective experience, strengths and virtues, and positive institutions and communities. The focus thus far has been on the first two. However, the latter focus, on communities and institutions, has been addressed by the Search Institute and asset building within communities.

Along with other researchers into prevention science, the Search Institute focuses on fostering human strengths in order to cultivate resiliency in stressed or at-risk youth. Forty assets have been identified, 20 external and 20 internal. The 20 external fall into four categories: support (e.g., family, neighborhood), constructive use of time (e.g., youth program), boundaries and expectations (e.g., adult role models), and empowerment (e.g., service to others). The 20 internal assets include commitment to learning, positive values, social competencies, and positive identity. Students with more assets achieve better grades and procure better life outcomes. Communities all over the world adopt an asset-building approach to youth development.

Further Reading: Benson, P.L., Galbraith, J., & Espeland, P. (1994). *What kids need to succeed: Proven, practical ways to raise good kids.* Minneapolis, MN: Free Spirit Publishing. Isen, A.M. (2002). A role for neuropsychology in understanding the facilitating influence of positive affect on social behavior and cognitive processes. In C.R. Snyder & S.J. Lopez (Eds.), *Handbook of positive psychology* (pp. 528–40). Oxford, England, and New York: Oxford University Press. Peterson, C., & Seligman, M. (2004). *Character strengths and virtues: Handbook and classification.* Washington, D.C.: American Psychological Association and Oxford University Press. Seligman, M.P., & Csikszentmihalyi, M. (2000). Positive psychology: An introduction. *American Psychologist, 55,* 5–14. Snyder, C.R., & Lopez, S.J. (2002). *Handbook of positive psychology.* New York: Oxford University Press.

Darcia Narvaez

Postmodern Ethics

Postmodern ethics is a post–World War II way of thinking about morality and ethical decision making. It is a direct outgrowth of the fact that Western societies today tend to be secular rather than theocratic, and pluralistic rather than monistic in their religious, philosophical, and political worldviews. Because there is no metaethical narrative that will be able to secure the universal approval of every individual and group in these postmodern times, and because all the old metaphysical and moral certainties have been largely questioned, debunked, and banished forever, according to such thinkers as Derrida (1976), Lyotard (1984), Nash (2002), and Rorty (1979), then ethics becomes mainly a consensual, culturally constructed, pragmatic activity.

What constitutes an acceptable framework of moral rules, principles, and theories is a project to be worked out among diverse individuals and groups, who, on matters of morality, ethics, politics, and religion remain "strangers" to one another. The key for postmodern ethicists is to reach an unforced agreement in the ethical arena on what might work, in what specific situations, and under what circumstances—rather than attempting to universalize, make absolute, and, then, impose and enforce, a uniform set of moral rules and principles on everyone.

It is not uncommon for postmodern ethicists to use such terms as "language games," "narratives," "myths," and "functional fictions" in describing ethical and moral paradigms. What all of these terms share in common is the underlying assumption that morality and ethics can never be separated from their context-specific languages, unique historical conditions, socialization habits and practices, and local political, religious, culture, class, race, and gender interests. Hence, postmodern criteria for the use of such hot-button moral terms as "right" and "wrong," "good" and "bad," "defensible" and "nondefensible," "moral" and "immoral," "unethical" and "ethical," tend to be both contextual and pluralistic.

In spite of many technically subtle, philosophical differences, most postmodern ethicists tend to identify as nonessentialists and antifoundationalists. They do this particularly when one ruling group or another is prone to make a definitive religious claim in order to ground their putative ethical and moral truths in some kind of once-and-for-all, supernatural revelation or authoritative magisterial teaching. For postmodern ethicists, there is no essential, unchanging human nature located somewhere above or beyond the contingencies of particular times and places. Neither are there essential supernatural truths that must be accepted unconditionally by believers and nonbelievers everywhere.

There is no supra-objective, metaphysical reality that is situated beyond the ebb and flow of constantly changing human discourse and moral preference. There is no unimpeachable, absolutely certain, divine foundation for ethical decision making. Everything is up for grabs—everywhere and always. All ethical decisions are subject to continual critique and reconstruction, depending on additional knowledge, more effective argumentation, and greater functional utility. When all is said and done, morality is nothing more than a particular construction made by particular people living in particular communities at particular times in order to solve problems and guide ethical decision making. No core of moral or ethical values is ever irrefutable or immutable. There is no final word, and no conversation-stopping bottom line, when it comes to moral and ethical discourse. There is always something more that can, and will, be said.

Postmodern ethicists often rely on the assertion—"It all depends. . ."—when pushed to legitimate a code of moral beliefs or to validate a particular ethical decision, judgment, or action for everyone, everywhere. Ethical decision making is relativistic for postmodern ethicists, particularly when some pontifical authority claims to be in the exclusive possession of "Moral Truth" or "Right Ethical Discernment." What makes these absolutistic claims anathema to postmodern ethicists is their conviction that it is impossible for any authority to step outside of personal histories, cultural contexts, and bounded interpretive frameworks when thinking about, and doing, ethics. There is just no "God's-eye" view of the perfect way to settle moral disputes or to solve ethical dilemmas. The best that people can do is to work together to reach some kind of functional moral consensus on how they ought best to treat one another.

Postmodern ethicists are not always relativistic, however, because, in the twenty-first century, people must be able to arrive at some type of consensually agreed upon, and universally supported, sets of ethics and norms. They will need to work hard to achieve this consensus because, without a set of guiding moral ideals that people can support, and live by, everywhere, regardless of their differences, then they will continue to inflict terrible pain and humiliation on one another. Thus, the most useful postmodern ethic is the one that respects moral pluralism but one that is, also, capable of arriving at defensible ethical positions with the moral suasion to hold all people accountable for treating one another with respect and compassion.

Further Reading: Derrida, J. (1976). *Of grammatology.* Baltimore, MD: Johns Hopkins University Press. Lyotard, J. (1984). *The postmodern condition: A report on knowledge.* Minneapolis, MN:

University of Minnesota Press. Nash, R.J. (2002). *"Real world" ethics: Frameworks for educators and human service professionals.* New York: Teachers College Press. Rorty, R. (1979). *Philosophy and the mirror of nature.* Princeton, NJ: Princeton University Press.

Robert J. Nash

Postmodern Virtues

Postmodernism as an approach to moral education, ethics, and the formation of character can be summed up in Jean Francois Lyotard's famous phrase "incredulity toward meta-narratives." Unpacked, this phrase suggests the following: (1) There is no longer an all-encompassing explanation for what ought to be the good, the true, and the beautiful that will hold for everyone in all times and places—especially so in the world of the twenty-first century with its cacophony of pluralistic philosophies, moralities, religions, and politics; (2) People do not discover or receive moral truth and meaning, as they did when metamoral narratives of various types carried the day; now, they create and construct morality. Objectivism (the truth is out there to be found) is out; constructivism (the truth is in here to be created) is in.

Moreover, (3) What is left for us in a postmodern world, amidst the ruins of the older, unquestioned, traditional moral truths, is to work together to create some useful narratives that feature overlapping values, ideals, and virtues that people might be able to agree on in order to avoid doing violence to one another because of their religious, political, or philosophical differences. (4) In order to keep this collective morality-construction project from becoming merely one more "grand moral vision," superimposed on everyone by fiat and threat, people will need to learn how to converse with one another across their differences, regarding their common convictions about how to live together in some kind of solidarity and mutual benefit.

Finally, (5) There are a number of postmodern virtues that all of us, especially educators, parents, and human service leaders, can help one another to cultivate in order to create a moral social disposition that cherishes such virtues as pluralism, flexibility, compassion, personal responsibility, sensitivity to difference, and respect for multiple versions of truth, justice, and love. These are the virtues that grow out of a moral uncertainty, and they reflect a willingess to experiment with alternative perspectives and practices.

Many postmodern philosophers and moral educators, despite their differing perspectives on how best to form the moral virtues, do agree with Aristotle that a virtue is a habit, disposition, quality, or skill that needs to be practiced before it can become an integral component of moral character. Practice makes perfect in the Aristotelian sense. Good human beings are good because they do the good, often and over a lifetime, and not merely because they know the good and can defend it intellectually.

Also, most postmodernists, who are interested in this topic of moral formation in the young (and in all others as well), would agree that fostering the democratic dispositions are a good place to begin. Why the democratic virtues? Because, according to these postmodernists, if nobody has an indisputable corner on truth, then it will only be through the art of moral conversation and gentle persuasion that people will be able to come to some type of unforced agreement on the moral norms that will direct their lives. This, after all, is the rationale for democracy.

In order to engage successfully in this type of democratic conversation, however, we will need to develop, and practice, certain virtues. These include such moral qualities as hope and confidence, friendship and trust, humility and caution, honesty and integrity, a sense of social justice and equity, civility, a respect for difference of opinion and individual autonomy, goodwill and generosity, and, above all, a spirited yet open sense of inquiry. These are what some postmodernists call the postmodern virtues.

What does a good postmodern conversation look like vis-à-vis the democratic virtues necessary to achieve it?

- We show respect for others by working hard to understand them on their terms as well as on our terms.
- We acknowledge openly that we do not possess any unimpeachable version of The Truth. At most we can only express our preferred truth and hope to be understood.
- We maintain a stance of open-mindedness at all times regarding the possibility of learning something new about ourselves and others in the conversation.
- We make a conscious effort to refrain from imposing our conception of morality on anyone else, simply because it may not fit.
- We make a heroic effort to listen intently in order to grasp the narrative meaning of other people's moral visions. In other words: Why does the speaker believe with such conviction and passion that this particular moral language is preferable to any other one?
- We realize that clarifying, questioning, challenging, exemplifying, and applying moral ideals and visions are activities always to be done in a self- and other-respecting manner.
- We occasionally allow our democratic conversations to get off course because a spirit of charity, intellectual curiosity, and, at times, playfulness will characterize moral conversation.
- We understand that it will always take time to get to know one another before we can actually engage in the type of democratic conversation that is robust, candid, and challenging, without any of us being seen, and dismissed, as offensive, hostile, or arrogant.

Further Reading: Grenz, S.J. (1996). *A primer on postmodernism.* Grand Rapids, MI: Eerdmans. Nash, R.J. (1997). *Answering the virtuecrats: A moral conversation on character education.* New York: Teachers College Press. Natoli, J. (1997). *A primer to postmodernity.* New York: Blackwell Publishers, Inc. White, P. (1996). *Civic virtues and public schooling: Educating citizens for a democratic society.* New York: Teachers College Press.

Robert J. Nash

Power, F. Clark

F. Clark Power is one of the central figures in the field of moral education. Currently he serves as Professor of Liberal Studies, Concurrent Professor of Psychology, and Faculty Fellow in the Institute for Educational Initiatives at the University of Notre Dame. He also serves as Co-Director of the Center for Ethical Education, which he co-founded. A native Philadelphian, Power studied philosophy and theology earning his B.A. from Villanova University (1970) and his M.A. in theology from the Washington Theological Union (1974).

Power came to the study of moral development and education through religion and philosophy. While teaching middle school students in a Catholic school, he realized that they did not understand matters of right and wrong in the same way he did. So he went to Harvard University to study moral development at Kohlberg's Center for Moral Development and Education at the Harvard University Graduate School of Education, where he ultimately earned his doctorate in education (1979). Power quickly became a key player in Kohlberg's team during the height of the Center's influence, the middle to late 1970s. Power's dissertation was at the heart of Kohlberg's most important educational project, the Just Community School. Power brilliantly conceptualized and assessed the development of collectivity and community in these experiments in high-school-based democracy. His analysis of the psychology and sociology of shared moral norms and understanding remain the most intelligent and complex work on this topic nearly 30 years later, and are clearly presented in his book (with Kohlberg and Ann Higgins) *Lawrence Kohlberg's Approach to Moral Education* (1989). The Just Community School remains one of the most ambitious, theoretically grounded, research-supported, and daring experiments in education. Furthermore, the theoretical underpinnings of the Just Community model (including Jean Piaget, Emile Durkheim, John Dewey, and others) continue to influence progressive thinking in school reform today.

Power has also significantly influenced the field of moral education through his various roles with the Association for Moral Education, an organization founded by the Kohlberg group while Power was Kohlberg's doctoral student (1976). Power therefore was at the heart of the AME from its inception. As President of the Association for Moral Education in the late 1980s, he organized the first fully international AME conference, taking the organization to a new level of international collaboration and influence. This ultimately led to its remaining an extremely international organization, which now meets triennially outside of North America.

Since arriving at the University of Notre Dame in 1982, Power found in the Program in Liberal Studies a vehicle for the integration of his social justice orientation and his diverse scholarly interests in philosophy, theology, psychology, and education. While teaching classical texts to Notre Dame students, he also founded the World Masterpieces Seminar at South Bend Center for the Homeless, where he has co-taught classics to homeless adults since the late 1990s. Power has continued his work in school democracy and moral development in many diverse but interconnected ways. Power has repeatedly expanded moral development theory and moral education into novel but related areas. His early work with Kohlberg, Fritz Oser, and James Fowler on the interface of religion and moral reasoning, especially his work with Kohlberg on the place of religious concepts in Kohlberg's model of moral reasoning development, helped legitimize an integration of theology and the cognitive-developmental theory of moral reasoning. His lifelong passion for sports (as an athlete and as a fan) helped kindle his interest in the role of sport in moral development. Consequently he co-founded the Mendelson Center for Sports, Culture and Character at the University of Notre Dame, bringing distinguished colleagues (Brenda Bredemeier, Matthew Davidson, David Shields) from around the United States to Notre Dame to staff the Center.

Power has also done substantial scholarship in studying the moral self (he was co-editor with Daniel Lapsley of *Self, Ego and Identity: Integrative Approaches,* 1988), including the relation of self-esteem to moral development. And, of course, he has continued working on school democracy, including Just Community Schools. Through all this he has remained a leading voice in the fields of moral development and moral education, as witnessed by his receipt of the prestigious Kuhmerker Award for lifetime achievement from the Association for Moral Education (1997).

Power's scholarship is impressive both in its depth and quantity, and reflects his unique blend of intelligence, interdisciplinary orientation, ethical commitment to improving the world, and sincere devotion to the scholarly pursuit of knowledge, all of which are echoes of his mentor, Kohlberg. In this sense, he may be one of Kohlberg's greatest living legacies, carrying on the brilliant, innovative, justice-driven, scholarship and application that was at the heart of Kohlberg's Center for Moral Development and Education. A prolific scholar, Power is the co-author of two books and co-editor of four more. He has published over 60 journal articles and book chapters, some of which have been translated into diverse languages (e.g., German, Spanish, French, Japanese, and Hungarian).

Power remains the leading thinker on democratic school reform. Power's unique blend of philosophy, theology, psychology, sociology and education positions him as one of the most intelligent, innovative, and thoughtful scholars grappling with core issues in how children and adolescents develop a moral sense and how schools can responsibly and effectively support such development.

Further Reading: Power, F.C., Higgins, A., & Kohlberg, L. (1989). *Lawrence Kohlberg's approach to moral education.* New York: Columbia University Press. Power, F.C., & Khmelkov, V.T. (1997). The development of the moral self: Implications for moral education. *International Journal of Educational Psychology, 27,* 539–51. Power, F.C., & Fallon, S.M. (In press). Teaching and transformation: Liberal arts and the homeless. In G. Guttierez & D. Groody (Eds.), *The preferential option for the poor and the university.*

Marvin W. Berkowitz

Practical Wisdom (*Phronesis*)

In the *Nicomachean Ethics,* Aristotle identifies *phronesis* as the fundamental moral mode of practical knowledge and understanding. Indeed, in some opposition to what he takes to be a Platonic account of moral reflection focused more upon theoretical definition of the good, Aristotle insists that phronesis has the primarily practical purpose of assisting us to become good. This immediately gives phronesis or practical wisdom a primary role in the development of those character traits presupposed to the acquisition of Aristotelian moral virtue. Indeed, although practical wisdom is distinguished as an intellectual disposition from the other three main "moral" virtues of temperance, courage, and justice, Aristotle nevertheless regards it as one of the four key or "cardinal" virtues.

Moreover, although the virtue of practical wisdom is of a somewhat different logical order from the moral virtues, Aristotle holds that it cannot develop in the absence of the basic training required for the acquisition of moral virtues: apart from the framework of right values and commitments that such training provides, the practical reason of phronesis would be more or less indistinguishable from the more narrow prudential calculation that Aristotle refers to as "cleverness." No less significantly, there can be no "complete" acquisition of the moral values of temperance, courage, and justice without moral wisdom, since such wisdom is also presupposed to genuine knowledge of how to act temperately, courageously, or justly. Practical wisdom is at least partly designed to help us know what to do—not least in the face of moral uncertainty—and for Aristotle a key respect in which a practical moral "syllogism" differs from a theoretical argument is that its conclusion is an "action" not merely a decision or other "judgment."

That said, phronesis should not be regarded as concerned only with establishing what to do, and it is important to see how Aristotle's notion of phronesis differs from many later concepts of practical moral reason. For example, on Kant's later view of moral reason, practical deliberation is exclusively concerned with deciding what should be done to fulfill a moral duty grounded in rationally disinterested and dispassionate reflection. Moreover, even on the rival ethical perspective of modern utilitarians, which shares some common naturalistic and teleological features with virtue ethics, and which is significantly inspired by ideals of universal benevolence, the actual process of moral deliberation is largely a matter of the exercise of calculative reason in the interests of securing right or beneficial consequences.

To see how Aristotle's phronesis differs from such modern rationalistic accounts of reason, however, one must appreciate: first, the relationship of practical wisdom to the moral virtues of courage, temperance, justice, and so on; second, the place of affect—desire or emotion—in moral virtue. Basically, for Aristotle, the moral virtues are regarded as particular orderings of human appetite, sentiment, and sensibility. According to Aristotle's celebrated doctrine of the mean, a virtue is a state of character lying in a mean between deficiencies or excesses of emotion or feeling, and the role of phronesis or practical wisdom is precisely to determine the right course between such extremes. Thus, the courageous agent feels neither too much fear nor too little; the temperate person indulges the appetites neither too much nor too little; the generous are neither too profligate nor too stingy; and so on. But one consequence of this role of phronesis in the cultivation of virtue is therefore that it is no less character forming than action guiding. In short, Aristotelian practical wisdom is tied to an essentially aretaic ethics of good character, more than a Kantian or utilitarian deontic ethics of right action.

All the same, phronesis is nevertheless a form of knowledge or reason, and almost everything remains to be said about the rational basis of practical wisdom, deliberation, and judgment. In fact, latter day virtue ethicists are mostly divided over the nature and source of the principles upon which phronesis draws for correct moral deliberation and judgment—if not, indeed, over whether it is appropriate to talk of phronesis as drawing on principles at all. For some contemporary followers of Aristotle, phronesis employs principles grounded in considerations regarding the "natural" basis of human flourishing. For others, who hold that human nature is a social construction, there can be no such "natural" conception of human flourishing. On this view, virtuous principles are apt to be seen as resting on socially conditioned—and perhaps widely divergent—cultural perspectives and traditions. However, for yet others—also claiming Aristotelian ancestry— it is a mistake to regard virtuous knowledge as a matter of appreciating rules or principles at all: on the contrary, the wisdom of phronesis is better understood as capacity for more contextualized "particular" judgment that by its very nature resists codification in terms of any and all rules or principles.

Further Reading: Dunne, J. (1993). *Back to the rough ground: "Phronesis" and "techne" in modern philosophy and in Aristotle.* Notre Dame, IN: University of Notre Dame Press.

David Carr

Pragmatism

Taken within the American context, pragmatism can be understood as a philosophy shaped by the work of its three founding geniuses: Charles Sanders Peirce, William James, and John Dewey. As we shall see, both James and Dewey made explicit contributions to areas related to educational theory and practice. Yet both readily acknowledged that these contributions find their ground in Peirce's work in abstract areas of philosophy such as logic, semiotics, metaphysics, and the philosophy of science.

According to his good friend James, Peirce first founded pragmatism as a theory of meaning. That is, pragmatism was to be understood as a means by which philosophers and other theorists could separate sense from non-sense within theory and related practice. Moreover, meaning was to be understood in terms of consequences. If a term's presence makes no difference in the way we go about evaluating the truth of claims about what the term refers to, it is meaningless. On the surface this may look like the famous "verification principal" of the twentieth-century logical positivists, but placed within Peirce's overall stress on evolutionary processes, the place of mind in the word of nature and fallibility rather than certainty, the result is much different.

In a useful summary of pragmatism as a philosophy of education, Jim Garrison (in Garrison & Neiman, 2005) points out the extent to which Pierce's pragmatism marks a radical departure from traditional Western philosophy. For example, the tradition, following Plato, had typically understood philosophy, including philosophical ethics as the theoretical uncovering of "pre-existing" entities or essences, such as "God, Being or the Good." Pragmatism would focus instead on action rather than contemplation. Second, traditional philosophy had tended to understand "belief" in terms of the assent of a purely nonbodily soul to this or that belief (e.g., "I believe that it is raining, or that pleasure is the good"). However, Peirce takes belief to be better understood as embodied habits of action that inherently involve emotion, habits involving the whole person in community. For Peirce, truth points to a future ideal, the coming together of beliefs within the evolving and intelligent scientific community, rather than correspondence to some nonhuman reality.

Thus pragmatism is prone, in ethics, to reject views of the good as fixed for all time in some supernatural or natural essence or command. Ethics must relate to the human person, whatever else he or she might be, as a part of a nature to which Darwin must be given his due. In his *Talks to Teachers on Psychology* (1983), William James developed these notions in terms of a "first principle of learning": useful habituation of belief, the fruitful relationship of the nervous system toward the useful, true, and good. However, given James's own sophisticated understanding of Darwinism in his great *Principles of Psychology* (1981), such habituation could work only if the teacher understood the human person and human mind as something more than the mechanical, passive stimulus response machine imagined by modern behaviorism. There is all the difference in the world between mechanical and intelligent adaptation.

Pragmatism as a philosophy of education culminates in the work of John Dewey, especially his *Democracy of Education* (1966). In his philosophy of education, Dewey expands upon James's idea of intelligence and Peirce's idea of community to ground his ideas in that of democracy. Democracy, for Dewey, cannot be understood simply as a procedure or set of procedures meant to procure representation in policy making. Instead, Dewey's idea is that true democracy is a way of life, of living in community. This idea is the key for grasping Dewey's still underutilized notion of creating good citizens.

Democracy, for Dewey, is best understood in terms of social practices that allow for the full and free expression and participation of all citizens in self and community life and rule. Here Dewey comes close to echoing Peirce's definition of "reality" and "truth" in terms of what will be agreed upon in the future by the ideal scientific community, as well as an Aristotelian concept of the virtues. However, neither James nor Dewey could accept a view that made the scientific way of knowing so dominant.

Contemporary pragmatists have often focused on forms of oppression, be it of women, people of color, the poor, and so forth, which limit the free and open dialogue required for full expression of the virtues in the democratic classroom (Martin, 1994).

Further Reading: Dewey, J. (1966). *Democracy of education.* New York: Free Press. Garrison, J., & Neiman, A. (2005). Pragmatism and education. In N. Blake et al. (Eds.), *The Blackwell guide to the philosophy of education.* Malden, MA: Blackwell Publishing Company. James, W. (1981). *The principles of psychology.* Cambridge, MA: Harvard University Press. James, W. (1903). *Talks to teachers on psychology.* Cambridge, MA: Harvard University Press. Martin, J.R. (1994). *Changing the educational landscape.* New York: Routledge.

Alven Neiman

Prejudice

Prejudice is most widely thought of as a negative feeling or belief held by an individual that is associated with that individual's categorization of a member of another social group. This definition is based in large part on Gordon Allport's classic (1954) definition that viewed prejudice as antipathy toward an individual based on erroneous and rigid overgeneralization. More neutral definitions de-valence the term, pointing to the bases of the English word from Latin and its component parts—a prejudgment, or a judgment based on one's preconceptions. Most psychological and educational scholarship, however, concerns itself with the social problems associated with prejudgment of an individual based on ascribed group membership and thus adhere more closely to the purposefully valenced definition offered by Allport.

Prejudice has been distinguished from the highly related concepts of stereotypes and discrimination. Stereotypes are an attributed set of characteristics to members of a group that one may or may not also endorse, whereas prejudices are seen as personally held beliefs, that is, a fact or set of facts that one endorses. In other words, these concepts are distinct in that one can be aware of the existence of a stereotype and not evidence the prejudice associated with it (Devine, 1989). Definitions of discrimination tend to emphasize unequal or biased treatment of an individual based on her or his attributed group membership. That is, discrimination usually is defined as a behavioral display of unequal treatment, whereas prejudice is viewed as an internally held attitude. One may hold prejudicial attitudes and beliefs and not act on them, and one may engage in differential or discriminatory treatment of individuals and not hold corresponding prejudicial views.

Scientists' understanding of the nature of prejudice continues to develop alongside evolving sociocultural norms regarding the expression of prejudice as well as technological advances in psychological measurement. In the mid-1900s, burgeoning interest in prejudice, spurred in large part by blatant and hostile expressions of prejudice such as the Holocaust and American civil rights unrest, focused on the development and testing of theories regarding the notion of a psychoanalytically motivated prejudiced personality type (Adorno, Frenkel-Brunswik, Levinson, & Sanford, 1950). The "prejudiced personality" was seen as the culmination of a convergence of a number of traits such as conformance, intolerance for ambiguity, and conventionalism, and viewed as entailing a safe projection of one's unconscious rage onto those perceived as socially beneath oneself because of an inability to express that rage at its causal source, such as a parental or other dominant figure. The original work, though criticized on methodological and political grounds, spurred numerous lines of fruitful research. Growing attention in the latter portion of the century to the cognitive aspects of prejudice, such as low tolerance for ambiguity and the need for cognitive closure, expanded earlier thinking. Emerging theories of group behavior such as "Social Identity Theory" stated that people tend to see themselves and others in terms of "us versus them" group memberships (see Tajfel & Turner, 1979). This provided a firm foundation for today's conceptualizations of prejudice. Over time, too, overt expressions of prejudice in American society have begun to give way to more covert expressions, characterized by subtlety, ambiguity, and prefacing disclaimers. Such "modern prejudice" is much more difficult to discern and, thus, to measure. This modern expression of prejudice appears to be characterized by a clash between people's desire to release the tension associated with negative group-based views of others, such as prejudiced thoughts, and a desire to maintain and convey positive personal principles about the self (Crandall & Eshleman, 2003). Measures of explicit prejudice commonly employed in earlier research (e.g., traditional self-report measures) are beginning to be coupled with and, in some cases, replaced by measures of "implicit" prejudice (e.g., the Implicit Association Test; Banaji & Hardin, 1996), tests that are purported to reveal the hidden, private, unmoderated, and, even, unconscious prejudices that most, if not all, humans are believed to harbor.

Further Reading: Adorno, T.W., Frenkel-Brunswik, E., Levinson, D.J., & Sanford, R.N. (1950). *The authoritarian personality.* New York: Harper and Row. Allport, G. (1954). *The nature of prejudice.* Reading, MA: Addison-Wesley. Banaji, M.R., & Hardin, C.D. (1996). Automatic stereotyping. *Psychological Science, 7*(3), 136–41. Crandall, C.S., & Eshleman, A. (2003). A justification-suppression model of the expression and experience of prejudice. *Psychological Bulletin, 129*(3), 414–46. Devine, P.G. (1989). Stereotypes and prejudice: Their automatic and controlled components. *Journal of Personality and Social Psychology, 56*(1), 5–18. Tajfel, H., & Turner, J.C. (1979). An integrative theory of intergroup conflict. In W.G. Austin & S. Worchel (Eds.), *The social psychology of intergroup relations.* Monterey, CA: Brooks/Cole.

Alexandra F. Corning

Principles of Effective Prevention

While there exist many definitions and models, from a public health perspective prevention is usually divided into three types: (1) primary prevention, which focuses on intervening with a broad, universal population to keep something from happening in the first place; (2) secondary or selected prevention that intervenes with individuals already exhibiting risk related to the outcome in question; or (3) tertiary or targeted preventive interventions, which provide services (i.e., treatment) to individuals already engaged in the identified problem behavior. This entry will focus specifically on the first two approaches of prevention related to moral reasoning and development.

If the goal of prevention is to keep something from becoming a problem in the first place, then it makes sense to try to reach as many individuals as possible as opposed to selecting persons for special treatment. Universal prevention programs can be public health campaigns to improve health (e.g., smoking is bad for you) or reduce injury (wear your seat belts). Universal prevention programs can also focus on improving or increasing the social, emotional, and behavioral competencies that promote prosocial, moral reasoning and development. Fortunately, there exists an increasing emphasis on these programs, most of them based in schools, and many show promising evidence of effectiveness.

The role of universal preventive efforts in improving moral reasoning and development is more indirect than direct, as most young elementary school age children are not yet developmentally able to reason at a high moral level given limited social cognitive and information processing skills. What young children are capable of, however, is to behave in a socially competent, respectful, and efficacious manner. As adults (parents, teachers, mentors) we have a responsibility to socialize our children to become competent and productive adolescents and adults, and we can begin via early identification and prevention to enhance child social and emotional development. We can also seek to foster those skills, values, attitudes, and environmental supports that protect against high-risk behaviors and prevent problems that reduce the likelihood a child will act in a prosocial, moral way toward others (Benson et al., 1999). The development of social-emotional competencies is critical to laying a protective foundation that can foster positive youth development (Catalano, Berglund, Ryan, Lonczak, & Hawkins, 1998; Weissberg, Kumpfer, & Seligman, 2003).

Most primary, universal prevention programs operate in schools, because this is one setting highly conducive to reaching a large number of youth with appropriate organizational and adult supports (Flannery et al., 2003). Attachment to school is also one of the most important protective factors for positive developmental outcomes for youth (Blum, McNeely, & Rinehart 2002; Resnick et al., 1997). Of course, this does not mean that prevention occurs only in one setting. In fact, the most effective prevention programs operate at more than one level (individual, family, neighborhood), in more than one setting (school, home, community), and focus on more than one positive behavior outcome or risk reduction strategy.

Effective prevention programs also focus on strengthening social, emotional, and/or behavioral competencies, seek to improve self-efficacy (vs. self-esteem, for example), advocate for the development of prosocial norms for appropriate behavior, provide opportunities for healthy prosocial involvement by others (e.g., teachers, parents), and provide immediate recognition and reinforcement for positive behavior.

An important context for effective prevention is to consider the specific approach used to enhance competency. The two most commonly utilized approaches in schools are those that focus on environmental or organizational change strategies (e.g., improving school climate or culture or classroom strategies to alter peer norms and perceptions) and those that focus primarily on skill-focused interventions such as decision-making skills, self-regulation (impulse control), coping, and refusal-resistance skills.

Clearly, the themes from prevention research show that positive social and emotional youth development is a multifaceted endeavor that can have many outcomes essential to positive moral development and reasoning (Cicchetti et al., 2000; Durlak & Wells, 1997; Elias et al., 1997). Some general characteristics of effective prevention efforts (Benson et al., 1999; Collaborative for Academic, Social, and Emotional Learning, 2003; Flannery, 2006; Flannery & Huff, 1999; Flay, 2002; Greenberg et al., 2003; Kumpfer & Alvarado, 2003; Nation et al., 2003; Pittman et al., 2001) include:

1. Programs that focus on enhancing protective factors and social competencies as well as on risk reduction.
2. Programs that are based on scientific evidence (research-based) and are implemented with high quality and fidelity.
3. Programs that target multiple outcomes at multiple levels (e.g., combine school and family/community efforts).

4. Programs that are culturally sensitive and developmentally (age) appropriate.
5. Programs or services that help youth learn how to apply social-emotional skills and ethical values in daily life.
6. Activities that encourage responsibility, connection to prosocial peers, attachment to institutions (schools, churches), and relationships with prosocial adult mentors, all of which can decrease the likelihood of risky behavior.

Young people will perform better academically and function more effectively on a day to day basis if they learn to recognize and manage their emotions, establish positive goals, make good decisions, and handle interpersonal situations and conflicts, all related to positive moral reasoning and development.

Examples of effective school-based prevention programs to improve social-emotional competencies, problem-solving skills, and prosocial behavior related to later moral reasoning and development include: Peacebuilders (Embry et al., 1996; Flannery et al., 2003), the Linking of Interests of Families and Teachers (LIFT) program (Reid, Eddy, Fetrow, & Stoolmiller, 1999; Stoolmiller, Eddy, & Reid, 2000), many elements of the Fast Track prevention trial (Conduct Problems Prevention Research Group, 1999), the social-emotional learning movement (CASEL, 2003; Weissberg & Greenberg, 1998), which includes programs like Promoting Alternative Thinking Strategies (PATHS; Greenberg, Kusche, & Mihalic, 1998) and efforts that have been broadly characterized as Character Education, although the effects of these programs is just recently being investigated in more rigorous efficacy trials.

Further Reading: Flannery, D.J. (2006). *Violence and mental health in everyday life: Prevention and intervention strategies for children and adolescents.* Walnut Creek, CA: Altamira Press. Nation, M., Crusto, C., Wandersman, A., Kumpfer, K.L., Seybolt, D., Morrissey-Kane, E., et al. (2003). What works in prevention: Principles of effective prevention programs. *American Psychologist, 58,* 449–56. Pittman, K.J., Irby, M., & Ferber, T. (2001). Unfinished business: Further reflections on a decade of promoting youth development. In P.L. Benson & K.J. Pittmann (Eds.), *Trends in youth development.* Norwell: Kluwer. Wandersman, A., Morrissey, E., Davino, K., Seybolt, D., Crusto, C., Nation, M., et al. (1998). Comprehensive quality programming and accountability: Eight essential strategies for implementing successful prevention programs. *Journal of Primary Prevention, 19,* 3–30.

Bibliography: Benson, P.L., Scales, P.C., Leffet, N., & Roehlkepartain, E.G. (1999). *A fragile foundation: The state of developmental assets among American youth.* Minneapolis, MN: Search Institute. Blum, R.W., McNeely, C.A., & Rinehart, P.M. (2002). *Improving the odds: The untapped power of schools to improve the health of teens.* Minneapolis, MN: Center for Adolescent Health and Development, University of Minnesota. Catalano, R.F., Berglund, L.M., Ryan, J.A., Lonczak, H.S., & Hawkins, D.J. (1998). *Positive youth development in the United States: Research findings on evaluations of positive youth development programs.* Report to the U.S. Department of Health and Human Services, Office of the Assistant Secretary for Planning and Evaluation and National Institute for Child Health and Human Development. Cicchetti, D., Rappaport, J., Sandler, I.N., & Weissberg, R.P. (Eds.). (2000). *The promotion of wellness in children and adolescents.* Washington, D.C.: Child Welfare League of America Press. Collaborative for Academic, Social, and Emotional Learning. (2003). *Safe and sound: An educational leader's guide to evidence-based social and emotional learning programs.* Chicago: Mid-Atlantic Regional Education Laboratory, The Laboratory for Student Success. Conduct Problems Prevention Research Group. (1999). Initial impact of the fast track prevention trial for conduct problems: I. The high-risk sample. *Journal of Consulting and Clinical Psychology, 67,* 631–47. Durlak, J.A., & Wells, A.M. (1997). Primary prevention mental health programs for children and adolescents: A meta-analytic review. *American Journal of Community Psychology, 25,* 115–52. Elias, M.J., Zins, J.E., Weissberg, K.S., Greenberg, M.T., Haynes,

N.M., Kessler, R., et al. (1997). *Promoting social and emotional learning: Guidelines for educators.* Alexandria, VA: Association for Supervision and Curriculum Development. Embry, D., Flannery, D.J., Vazsonyi, A.T., Powell, K., & Atha, H. (1996). Peacebuilders: A theoretically driven, school-based model for early violence prevention. *American Journal of Preventive Medicine, 12*(5), 91–100. Flannery, D.J. (2006). *Violence and mental health in everyday life: Prevention and intervention strategies for children and adolescents.* Walnut Creek, CA: Altamira Press. Flannery, D.J., & Huff, C.R. (Eds.). (1999). *Youth violence: Prevention, intervention and social policy.* Washington, D.C.: American Psychiatric Press. Flannery, D.J., Vazsonyi, A., Liau, A., Guo, S., Powell, K., Atha, H., et al. (2003). Initial behavior outcomes for the peacebuilders universal school-based violence prevention program. *Developmental Psychology, 39,* 292–308. Flay, B.R. (2002). Positive youth development requires comprehensive health promotion programs. *American Journal of Health Behavior, 26,* 407–24. Greenberg, M.T., Kusche, C., & Mihalic, S. (1998). *Blueprints for violence prevention, Book ten: Promoting alternative thinking strategies (PATHS).* Boulder, CO: Center for the Study and Prevention of Violence. Greenberg, M.T., Weissberg, R., O'Brien, U., Zins, J., Fredericks, L., Resnik, H., et al. (2003). Enhancing school-based prevention and youth development through coordinated social, emotional, and academic learning. *American Psychologist, 58,* 466–74. Kumpfer, K.L., & Alvarado, R. (2003). Family-strengthening approaches for the prevention of youth problem behaviors. *American Psychologist, 58,* 457–65. Nation, M., Crusto, C., Wandersman, A., Kumpfer, K.L., Seybolt, D., Morrissey-Kane, E., et al. (2003). What works in prevention: Principles of effective prevention programs. *American Psychologist, 58,* 449–56. Reid, J., Eddy, J.M., Fetrow, R., & Stoolmiller, M. (1999). Description and immediate impacts of a preventive intervention for conduct problems. *American Journal of Community Psychology, 27,* 483–517. Resnick, M.D., Bearman, P.S., Blum, R.W., Bauman, K.E., Harris, K.M., Jones, J., et al. (1997). Protecting adolescents from harm—Findings from the national longitudinal study on adolescent health. *Journal of the American Medical Association (JAMA), 278,* 823–32. Stoolmiller, M., Eddy, J.M., & Reid, J. (2000). Detecting and describing preventive intervention effects in a universal school-based randomized trial targeting delinquent and violent behavior. *Journal of Consulting and Clinical Psychology, 68,* 296–306. Wandersman, A., & Florin, P. (2003). Community interventions and effective prevention. *American Psychologist, 58,* 441–48. Wandersman, A., Morrissey, E., Davino, K., Seybolt, D., Crusto, C., Nation, M., et al. (1998). Comprehensive quality programming and accountability: Eight essential strategies for implementing successful prevention programs. *Journal of Primary Prevention, 19,* 3–30. Weissberg, R.P., & Greenberg, M.T. (1998). School and community competence-enhancement and prevention programs. In E. Siegel & K.A. Renninger (Eds.), *Handbook of child psychology* (Vol. 4, pp. 877–954). New York: Wiley. Weissberg, R.P., Kumpfer, K., & Seligman, M. (2003). Prevention that works for children and youth: An introduction. *American Psychologist, 58,* 425–32.

Daniel J. Flannery

Prosocial Reasoning

Psychology has a rich history of attempting to understand the cognitive, or thinking, side of prosocial behaviors (acts that benefit another person). Much of the research on moral cognitions has focused on people's responses to dilemmas developed by Lawrence Kohlberg. Kohlberg theorized that moral reasoning progressed through a series of stages, and that once a person attained the next stage, reasoning from the prior stage is left behind. However, critics of Kohlberg's theory have noted that, among other problems, the dilemmas used to assess moral reasoning levels are focused on issues of justice and laws. These are not the type of moral dilemmas that the majority of people confront in their daily interactions with others. Rather, people are more frequently confronted with situations in which they can choose either a prosocial act or a self-serving act. While such choices are difficult for people, they do not involve breaking laws or other such extreme circumstances. Scholars have noted that understanding how people reason about dilemmas involving prosocial acts can tell us about how people make moral decisions in their everyday lives.

Nancy Eisenberg has been the primary theoretical force behind understanding prosocial moral reasoning (Eisenberg, 1992). Eisenberg proposed that prosocial moral reasoning gradually progresses from lower to higher levels of maturity. That is, there is a developmental progression both in terms of when particular types of reasons first begin to be used, as well as in the relative frequency with which a person uses reasons from each level. For example, while adults may tend to rely on more advanced levels, they may also make use of the lower levels. However, it would be unusual to see a child using reasons from the higher levels. Moreover, people use different levels of prosocial reasoning across the life span.

There are five levels of prosocial reasoning. The lowest level, hedonistic, is focused on the consequences of the action to the self. Level Two, needs-oriented, involves taking into account the needs of others. However, this is done in a relatively simplistic way. Reasoning at the third level, approval and interpersonal, focuses on issues of approval from others. Stereotypical reasoning, also at the third level, is exemplified by stereotypical conceptions of how "good" people and "bad" people behave. Level Four A is a self-reflective empathic orientation and is characterized by a consideration of other's needs and emotions. Level Four B is a transitional orientation where people are beginning to show a tendency to reason based on internalized values or concern for the broader society. In Level Five, the strongly internalized orientation, there is a clearer idea about maintaining the broader social contract and living up to one's own beliefs and values.

Eisenberg's original research on prosocial reasoning used interview responses to verbal dilemmas. Her interview measure can be used with children as young as four to five years of age. Carlo, Eisenberg, and Knight (1992) later developed a paper-and-pencil measure of prosocial moral reasoning (PROM) that can be used with older children and with adults. The PROM assesses people's preferences for moral reasons at each level, rather than spontaneously generated reasons. There is evidence that the PROM is reliable and valid to use. Individual's responses to either assessment technique are categorized according to the level of prosocial reasoning exhibited. It is then possible to determine which level of prosocial reasoning is predominant across contexts.

One of the primary reasons for seeking to understand prosocial reasoning is to gain insight into decision making about moral actions. Although there are many influences on moral behaviors, prosocial reasoning has been shown to be one predictor, especially when the behavior requires cognitive effort. The research on prosocial reasoning shows that there are individual and group differences (including gender and cultural differences) in its use and that there are personal (e.g., empathy) and environmental (e.g., family and peers) variables associated with such differences. Prosocial reasoning also relates more strongly to prosocial action for older adolescents and adults than for younger children (Eisenberg, Guthrie, Cumberland, Murphy, Shepard, Zhou, & Carlo, 2002).

Further Reading: Carlo, G. (2006). Care-based and altruistically based morality. In M. Killen & J. Smetana (Eds.), *Handbook of moral development.* (pp. 551–580). Mahwah, NJ: Lawrence Erlbaum Associates. Carlo, G., Eisenberg, N., & Knight, G. P. (1992). An objective measure of adolescents' prosocial moral reasoning. *Journal of Research on Adolescence, 2,* 331–349. Eisenberg, N. (1992). *The caring child.* Cambridge, MA: Harvard University Press. Eisenberg, N., Guthrie, I.

K., Cumberland, A., Murphy, B.C., Shepard, S.A., Zhou, Q., & Carlo, G. (2002). Prosocial development in early adulthood: A longitudinal study. *Journal of Personality and Social Psychology, 82,* 993–1006.

Brandy A. Randall and Gustavo Carlo

Prudence

Prudence is the quality of behaving thoughtfully and exercising good judgment. In the philosophical tradition as influenced by Aristotle and Thomas Aquinas, prudence not only is one of the four cardinal (meaning a hinge or pivot) virtues but is, in the words of Aquinas, the "mother" of all the virtues. Within this tradition, prudence is the virtue of practical wisdom. We may think of it as the virtue of the decision-making component of virtue. The Thomistic scholar Pieper (1966) argues that our common understanding of prudence gets in the way of our appreciation of its full philosophical and even theological significance in an earlier tradition. In order to appreciate what prudence means as a cardinal virtue, we must first understand what we mean by the term and its moral significance in contemporary moral philosophy as it has been influenced by Immanuel Kant.

In ordinary usage, prudence is an admirable trait, but one we would hardly associate with moral heroism. The prudent person thinks before acting, looks beyond immediate gratification, and evaluates the consequences of possible actions. The prudent person is cautious and careful, acts with restraint, and shuns extravagance. Pieper (1966) notes that not only do we tend to confuse prudence with temperance but that we can even think of prudence as restraining certain kinds of virtuous acts if they demand too great a personal sacrifice.

We generally think of prudence today as a virtue of enlightened self-interest. Prudence leads us to decide what is good for us in particular circumstances. It is generally prudent to treat others well because they will reciprocate in some way. The prudent merchant will find that "honesty is the best policy" because honesty attracts customers. What motivates the exercise of prudence is not moral duty or a concern for others but what is good for oneself. The great enlightenment philosopher Immanuel Kant believed that in order to think clearly about moral matters a sharp division had to be made between the right and the good. Decisions about what is right had to do with one's moral duty, which was dictated by the categorical imperative. Kant believed that decisions about the good were based in self-interests that varied according to different individuals and circumstances. Moreover, decisions about the good do not seem to bind in the same way or with the same force with those of morality. For example, physicians today recommend getting 30 minutes of exercise a day for good health. Would it be wrong to exercise only twice a week or for only 15 minutes a day? Would this be the moral equivalent of hurting another person, even in a slight way by, for example, hurting another's feelings?

Kant certainly believed that we should all practice the virtue of prudence in attempting to pursue our own happiness, but he did not think of prudence as a moral virtue because he believed that self-interest and not duty ultimately motivates prudence. Although Kant's conception of happiness may have been dominated by what philosophers call hedonism or the pursuit of pleasure, Kant's basic distinction between moral duty and personal happiness (however understood) still holds. I must treat others honestly not because having an honest reputation will help my business but because I have a moral duty to be honest even if that would not be to my advantage. Kant recognized that we may well find happiness in treating others with respect and kindness. He insisted, however, that we not confuse the motive of self-interest with the motive of duty.

This notion of prudence as the virtue of rational self-interest is very different from Aristotle and Aquinas's view of prudence as practical wisdom or rational decision making. Aristotle and Aquinas did not reserve prudence for the pursuit of self-interest. Prudence was also essential for choosing what is just in a particular circumstance. Prudence is thus an executive virtue. It interacts and directs the other virtues. We often think of the virtues in isolation from each other. Thus, for example, we might think of soldiers as brave even if they are fighting in an unjust war. Aristotle and Aquinas, however, held that the virtues, especially the cardinal virtues, work in harmony. Within this framework, one could not maintain, as Kant did, a divergence between the right and the good. A decision could not be prudent if it were not just.

Ironically, character educators, who rightfully evoke Aristotle's emphasis on the role of habit in virtue, sometimes neglect Aristotle's emphasis on the role of reason, and specifically the intellectual virtue of *phronesis,* which is often translated as prudence. Aristotle recognized that the practice of the virtues required the disposition to make sound decisions in particular circumstances. Prudence is thus nothing other than the well-formed conscience and the cultivation of deliberation is essential for character education.

Further Reading: Aristotle. (1999). *Nicomachean ethics* (T. Irwin, Trans.). Indianapolis, IN: Hackett. Den Uyl, D.J. (1991). *The virtue of prudence.* New York: Peter Lang. Nelson, D.M. (1992). *The priority of prudence: Virtue and natural law in Thomas Aquinas and the implications for modern ethics.* College Station, PA: The Pennsylvania State University. Pieper, J. (1966). *The four cardinal virtues.* Notre Dame, IN: University of Notre Dame Press.

F. Clark Power

R

Raths, Louis E.

Louis E. Raths (1900–1978) was born in Dunkirk, New York. Because of the necessity of earning money to support his mother and younger brothers and sisters, he was unable to attend college until the age of 24. He received his B.A. degree in 1927 from Antioch College in Yellow Springs, Ohio, his M.A. in 1930 from the University of Chicago where he worked in the University's Laboratory School, and his Ph.D. in 1933 from The Ohio State University under the tutelage of Ralph Tyler. Upon completion of his studies in 1933, he remained at Ohio State until 1947 as an assistant professor, eventually becoming a full professor. During his time in Ohio, beyond normal teaching responsibilities, he led the reconstruction of the Ohio Soldiers and Sailors Orphans Home in Xenia, Ohio (1933–1934) as the principal and Director of Academic Education as well as holding a position as a Research Assistant in the Bureau of Educational Research. In 1935, Ralph Tyler asked him to join the evaluation team as Associate Director, Evaluation Staff of the Eight Year Study under the auspices of the Progressive Education Association. While having the title of Associate Director, in actuality Raths became the active director. He served in this capacity until 1938. In 1947, Raths moved to New York University as professor and Director of Research where he remained until his official retirement in 1962. During his tenure at NYU, he taught one night a week in the Master of Arts Teaching program at Yale University. In the fall of 1962 he took a position as Distinguished Professor of Education at Newark State College (now Kean University, Union, New Jersey) where he remained until 1966 when he retired once again. He returned to his hometown of Dunkirk in 1966 and, until his death in 1978, continued to work with graduate students in his capacity as Adjunct Professor of Education and Consultant to the Faculty at Fredonia State University.

Throughout his career Raths had teaching and administrative experience in elementary, junior, and senior high schools. In addition, he provided consultant services to churches, numerous colleges, universities, school districts, as well as to state, federal, and nongovernmental agencies. He was the recipient of numerous awards including Great Teacher Award, New York University, 1962; Honorary Doctor of Humane Letters, Upsala

College, Orange, New Jersey; Honorary Doctor of Letters, Kean State University, 1976; Distinguished Graduate, Antioch College, 1976; Honorary Life Member, Phi Delta Kappa, Fredonia State University, 1976; and Hall of Fame, College of Education, The Ohio State University, 1989.

Raths authored or co-authored eight books, 10 articles or chapters in edited books, and some 70 individual articles. Additionally, he developed four tests (The Scale of Beliefs, The Ohio State Social Acceptance Test, The Wishing Well, and The VANPIT Thinking Test) and in conjunction with others developed media and curriculum materials.

While teaching at Ohio State, Raths's colleagues included his Ph.D. advisor Ralph Tyler and fellow faculty member Carl Rogers. Through them, he was exposed to Rogers's client-centered therapy and Tyler's rationale for evaluation and curriculum development. He also came to know of the work of the Superintendent of the Winnetka Schools Carleton Washburne and his Winnetka Plan for progressive educational practice. When these notions were coupled with an understanding of Sigmund Freud's conceptualization of deprivation and emotional security and John Dewey's ideas on thinking and values, Raths crystallized three interrelated educational theories of emotional needs, thinking, and valuing as related to behavior all in the service of human empowerment.

In the Needs Theory the meeting of affective needs of children is critical for successful learning to occur. The deprivation of emotional security may lead to student behavior characterized on the one hand by aggression, if not violence, and on the other hand by submissive obedience, alienating withdrawal, and/or physical sickness. Regardless of the direction, when these conditions occur, both children and learning suffer. Their struggle to overcome the emotional barriers blocks attention paid to educational endeavors and reduces any sense of personal efficacy, which results in disempowerment. Thus, it is mandatory for teachers to pay as close attention to the emotional as well as the academic needs of the student.

Related to the Needs Theory, Raths developed a Thinking Theory. Just as in the Needs Theory, he attributed the lack of effective student thinking to student frustration and emotional deprivation. His interest was in exploring why some students, when presented with a problem, are able to grasp implications, question assumptions, and generate various hypothetical solutions to the problem. Other students, however, seem frozen in response. These behaviors signify a lack of cognitive power characterized by an inability to "make purposeful choices, to connect means with ends, to identify similarities and differences in seemingly analogous situations, to suspend judgment in the presence of contradictory data, to design and carry out plans for projects or investigations" (Wassermann, 1987, p. 461). For the classroom teacher, Raths identified behavior markers of thinking deficits. These include impulsivity, overdependence, inability to connect ends with means, narrow comprehension, dogmatism and closed-minded belief systems, rigidity, inflexibility, and fear of being wrong.

In Values Theory, Raths was concerned for the means by which individuals are truly free to reflect upon and come to clarity about choices related to their life experiences. The operational word here is "free." Rather than accept imposed values, individuals should be able to make value meanings unencumbered by external influences. To accomplish this goal, Raths offered a sevenfold process of value clarity or, as it became known, Values Clarification (VC). A true value was chosen from alternatives; considered with the consequences of the alternatives; chosen freely; prized and cherished; publicly affirmed; acted on repeatedly; and acted on with consistency. Of the three theories, VC became the most criticized, not for its theoretical basis as conceptualized by Raths but rather for what it seemed to become as seen by its critics (see Values Clarification).

Embedded in all of Raths's work is a fundamental respect for individual capacity and ever-developing autonomy free of manipulation, imposition, and external control. The glue that binds Raths's three theories together is a concept of empowerment by which one empowers the self rather than is empowered by someone else. It is in this sense that Raths can be considered as a moral educator.

Further Reading: Raths, L. (1969). *Teaching for learning.* Columbus, OH: Charles Merrill. Raths, L., Harmin, M., & Simon, S. (1969). *Values and teaching.* Columbus, OH: Charles Merrill. Raths, L., Wassermann, S., Jones, A., & Rothstein, A. (1967). *Teaching for thinking: Theory and application.* Columbus, OH: Charles Merrill. Wassermann, S. (1987, February). Teaching for thinking: Louis E. Raths revisited. *Phi Delta Kappan, 68,* 460–66. Wassermann, S. (1991). Louis E. Raths: Theories of empowerment. *Childhood Education, 67*(4), 235–39.

Tom Wilson

Rawls, John

Imagine that you and others in your community are called upon to create a government from scratch. In the history of many countries, this actually happened. A political revolution took place after which a new type of government—often a democracy—had to be designed and instituted. It occurred during the American and French Revolutions, and in many revolutions (violent or velvet) in South American, African, and eastern European countries, extending to the old Soviet Union. The process was going on in Iraq and Iran in 2006, though less from an internal revolution than an outside military incursion.

Further, imagine that to create a legitimate government you had to negotiate a shared ethic, a basis for legitimacy in the process and the result, assuring a just government. You had to create an agreed upon ethic of justice that was not only new but very faithful to our actually held ethical beliefs and traditions—and ethically legitimate in itself.

Think about what this project would mean for issues like conventional or common-sense morality and the widespread centuries-old debate over moral relativism. The project would declare first that, though we share certain basic moral values and principles as a society, due to socialization, and these are a great help in devising a more broadly shared ethic on purpose, we are now going to transform what came to us by social tradition and socialization. We are going to reshape our social ethos into an ethic we can consciously agree on. And we are going to base that agreement on those shared reasons and purposes that will come to light in focused social discussion. In a way, this is turning social ethics into something like a social constitution. This constitution can then be used as a justice groundwork for a just political constitution, itself the groundwork for just laws.

Whether there is no fact of the matter about valid or shared ethics—whether we differ greatly in our ethical beliefs due to differences in personal upbringing, ethnic affiliation, gender, enculturation, personal experience, and reflection—we are going to make a fact of the matter of ethics. This is our project. We are going to stipulate, based on whatever shared purposes and rationales for having ethics we can find that ethic X will be our standard for moral intercourse. Why? Because we need it to be—we need some common ethical way to resolve conflicts and communicate mutual expectations for trusting cooperation. And because our attempt to create such standards comes to this, ethics X, ethics X is valid as such. No doubt, one of the best ways to achieve such agreement is to provide a lot of leeway or personal freedom, for each individual to hold his/her own personal value code, and pursue it nonharmfully. This is the importance of rights.

The "social contract" project outlined above is the focus of John Rawls's classic tome, *A Theory of Justice*. Rawls's theory brought together a host of crucial ideas from ethics and political theory that were never gathered together in such a way before. It afforded audiences of many sorts a new perspective on how ethics and politics hang together, especially given the many conflicting theories in both fields. Rawls's views are referred to constantly in several main branches of moral education and psychology, not to mention philosophy, law, and public policy. His notion of "justice as fairness" is a central pillar on which stands Lawrence Kohlberg's "Just Community" approach to moral education, and Kohlberg's depiction of ultimately adequate moral reasoning. Indeed, Rawls's theory was well-known, and its lore widely circulated a decade before it was published. It took Rawls 20 years to write and get right. And it integrated the critical reactions and suggestions of many colleagues worldwide by the time it finally came out. Several other books followed, focused more on details of political theory.

There are hosts of particular insights in Rawls's volume, suggestive for moral education. In fact, a whole section of the book is devoted to moral development and education. But it is derived from the prescientific views of Jean-Jacques Rousseau especially, like the Kantian perspective on which it so relies. Many in psychology and education have therefore ignored this section, trying to derive more state-of-the-art implications from Rawlsian principles. Here are the main Rawlsian ideas of more general import and influence.

First, the principle of "mutual respect," derived by Immanuel Kant from "the golden rule" is argued as the foremost basis for (Western) justice, rights, and democracy. Only this principle provides a solid, inherent basis for going right when we try to build a social ethic together. Only this basis allows us to build our shared ethic ethically—with mutual self-determination. All other leading ethics imply objectionable forms of mutual threat, coercion, authoritarianism, or oppression on the way to ethical ends. Rawls's book is often used as the standard reference for comparing the leading rival theories in ethics—utilitarianism, Kantian contract theory, intuitionist virtue theory, moral perfectionism, and libertarian rights—gauging their comparative adequacy and inadequacy. Rawls rates each tradition on a single set of adequacy criteria, derived both from philosophy's "metaethical" research, but from unshakable core assumptions or "considered judgments" about how morality functions. These are determined, in turn, by the way our most unchangeable or implastic needs—psychologically and socially—reflect in the core purposes that any ethic must serve. As noted, chief among these purposes are (a) resolving conflicts of interest, and of different personal value systems themselves, and (b) providing a firm and public ground of mutual trust for building social cooperation. If we used any other ethical viewpoint but respect for persons, Rawls argues, we would have to deceive each other, to threaten or coerce some, to acquiesce to others, in achieving "accord." And he demonstrates how and why this happens in a simulated social negotiation—the Original Position (OP).

To understand every aspect of the OP, we must recall that, like Kant and Rousseau, Rawls not only pictures democracy as a kind of implicit social contract. Rather he builds the contract back into ethics itself—at least that part of ethics needed for building a legitimate political system. He takes us step by step through this long preconstitutional convention, specifying exactly how the "founding fathers (and mothers)" should reason, what knowledge they should have, what their legitimate motivations should be, what information should be excluded because it would bias negotiation, and so forth. And he makes the process as hard as he can for himself, requiring fully unanimous agreement for conventioneers or negotiators (OP parties) under conditions of great uncertainty, and the stipulation that their decision is a one-time test that must stand for all time.

Anyone considering the prospect of such a negotiation seriously would be understandably defeatist. But instead of focusing on agreement per se, Rawls focused on the main obstacles to agreement, the main sources of disagreement, and addressed them one by one. The nonmoral and irrational "temptations" that would cause some of us to seek power advantages over others were his favored targets. Rawls simply rules out some of the most blatant sources of bias—physical threat and coercion, vengeful or envious thinking, and irrational risk taking in negotiations. But like Kant, he draws down the "veil of ignorance" to do most of the work, which means eliminating the information we would need to rig the negotiation or contract in our favor. If you cannot be sure which interests or goals any particular contractors favor during negotiations, then you cannot single them out for special treatment. And rules imagine an "original (contracting) position" in which the contracting parties do not even know whom they are or what they want. All they know is that they need an ethic that will perform certain functions anyone needs to make social life livable and even mutually beneficial. (Even thieves need protections against thievery in society to protect the goods stolen.)

A legal trial procedure in many ways serves as a model for Rawls's approach. Rules of evidence keep clearly biasing information from jurors, even when it is relevant information. The judge further allows or restricts information as litigators present rival legal theories (and support for them), trying to win the jury's accord. (Rawls continually presents the utilitarian case against his own Kantian case at each juncture in theory building.) The OP parties are sequestered, the way juries often are, so that outsiders who might bribe, threaten, or misinform them are kept at bay. And jurors are given directions by the judge for how to reason fairly in a way germane to the purpose of their deliberations—determining guilt or innocence beyond reasonable doubt. With all these safeguards and protections in place, to ensure due process, but very few (if strict) directives on how to proceed, the jury is set free to reason or deliberate as it will, presuming a wide range of opinions and perspectives. In some cases it must reach a unanimous decision to return a verdict. Focusing on procedure in this way is what Rawls's express notion of "justice as fairness" comes to.

While this "social contract negotiation" is consciously designed to be hypothetical, and intellectually idealized, one could imagine adapting it to the classroom. This is especially true for later stages in the "four-stage sequence" of negotiation specified by Rawls. While working with Lawrence Kohlberg, Al Erdynast engaged research subjects in a version of this contracting situation. This simulated gaming showed the capacity of people (with similar and high competence in moral perspective taking) to reach surprising consensus. Erdynast, like many, has become a lifelong student of Rawls's writings.

Rawls concludes that two main ethical guidelines or general principles would come out of the original position under a veil of ignorance. The primary one would ensure strict equality in shares of liberty, including both positive and negative rights of various scopes. (These are rights to needed resources and rights against certain violations, respectively.) The second would be a strict equality in welfare distributions or share (one's piece of the economic pie). This equality is defined chiefly in terms of opportunity, but also actual goods (income and wealth). "Primary goods" compose most of these shares, such as decent living conditions, income needed to fulfill basic needs, resources prerequisite to retaining a sense of self-esteem and belonging, worth and meaning in one's life. Justice, unlike utility, is not an ethic that promotes maximum social welfare or happiness, but assures the freedom to pursue such goals in whatever way one chooses. It ensures that we are not interfered with in that pursuit, nor allowed to languish helplessly without at least minimal wherewithal to engage in the pursuit.

Rawls provides a "difference principle," posed as a rider on the second principle, for making exceptions to equal shares. It allows the distribution of greater material incentives to the most productive or likely to produce insofar as this measure will generate more overall wealth for all in society—but especially for the least advantaged. This is seen as Rawls's biggest theoretical innovation though it was tacked on rather late in his theory's development, and apparently suggested by a colleague. The idea can also be found in such mundane historical locations as President Andrew Jackson's inaugural address.

Perhaps a more innovative contribution is Rawls's discussion of "natural talents" and "unearned social advantages." By tracing the degree to which our earning and accomplishments are greatly influenced by others—by our biological and social inheritance—Rawls hoped to overcome our powerful belief that we should get what we deserve through our individual work-effort and earning. Rawls makes excellent notice of the fact that what counts as a valuable product, valuable work effort that went into it, or the talent that allowed that effort to bear desired fruit depends largely on consumer whims. It is not found in the qualities of the productive. In one society, spending one's life trying to stuff a round object into a hoop hung above one's head would be considered a wasted, perhaps deranged way of life. In other societies, it is the basis for being a rich celebrity—a professional basketball star. By enlarging the hoop, and speaking of hula dancing, one can also make a quick fortune—for little apparent reason.

The main substantive criticisms of Rawls's view are (a) that it allows too much economic inequality to be just; (b) that it is basically an apology for liberalism and the social contract position, starting with assumptions and ground rules that ensure this conclusion; (c) that his view is not sufficiently respectful of individual rights, especially property rights, allowing the scope of individual liberty to be adjusted as suits social welfare; (d) on the other hand, that justice as fairness is too individualistic, violating communitarian and socialist sensibilities that recognize the primarily sociocentric notion of social ethics; and (e) despite contrasting itself with utilitarianism, it is in many ways a covert and indirect version of that defamed view.

On the methodological side, Rawls's use of the veil of ignorance is said to render the whole view too abstract and vague, therefore practically useless. It is a moral "View from Nowhere" as some critics put it (Nagel, 1986). It provides us insufficient information, and therefore insufficient justification for taking anything that happens in the negotiation as relevant to our actual ethical choices. So many shortfalls and inconsistencies have been alleged of this yet magnificent general theory that some believe it shows the futility of pursuing general ethical theories. Some have suggested that we instead consider different principles for different spheres of justice—governmental, workplace, family, community—which present different sorts of ethical demands (Walzer).

Further Reading: Nagel, T. (1986). *The view from nowhere.* New York: Oxford University Press.

Bill Puka

RCCP (Conflict Resolution)

The Resolving Conflict Creatively Program (RCCP) is a comprehensive, school violence prevention program that emphasizes conflict resolution and intercultural understanding. Its primary goal is to help young people reduce violence and prejudice and form caring relationships by teaching and modeling appropriate social and emotional skills. The program began in 1985 as a collaboration between the New York City Board of Education and Educators for Social Responsibility's New York chapter. In 1993, a national center for RCCP was established to create and maintain multiyear partnerships with school districts across the country, including New York, Louisiana, Alaska, Georgia, and California.

RCCP uses a whole-school approach, meaning that its focus is on changing the total school environment to create a community of peace and nonviolence. The program demands a long-term commitment, requires support at the highest levels within the school system before implementation, and asks that the school district make RCCP part of its vision for school change. Its comprehensive approach includes five components:

(1) Professional training and ongoing support for teachers. RCCP provides teachers with 24 hours of introductory training in conflict resolution theory and skills, intercultural understanding, emotional and social literacy, and infusion strategies for integrating these skills into the regular academic curriculum (e.g., social studies, language arts). Each teacher is also provided with a staff developer, who visits the school several times each year to assist with preparation, observe classes, and discuss concerns.

(2) A classroom curriculum. Themes throughout the curriculum are peace and conflict, communication, fostering cooperation, working with feelings, negotiation and mediation, appreciating diversity, bias awareness, and countering bias. Examples of specific skills within these themes include active listening, perspective taking, empathy, assertiveness, negotiation, cooperation, and bias-countering skills. Lessons for teaching these skills involve role-playing, interviewing, group discussion, brainstorming, capitalizing on "teachable moments," and other experiential learning methods.

(3) A student-led mediation program. A group of students is selected by classmates and teachers to be peer mediators. Their role is to be an objective third-party that assists the individuals in conflict to resolve their differences constructively using negotiation. This component provides a peer model for constructive conflict resolution and reinforces students' skills in working out problems on their own.

(4) Administrators' training. Workshops are provided to administrators to introduce the concepts of conflict resolution and intercultural understanding and show how their leadership can encourage the school community to embrace and model peace and nonviolence.

(5) Parent training. Workshops for parents involve training in the skills and concepts of conflict resolution and intergroup relations so they can make their homes peaceful and reinforce what their children are learning at school about nonviolence. Examples of skills taught in parent workshops include active listening, using "I-messages" to communicate what they want and need, and win-win negotiation techniques.

Many of the sites (e.g., school districts in New York City, Anchorage, and Atlanta) have conducted evaluations of program effectiveness. Evaluation findings vary somewhat from site to site (e.g., student and teacher attendance improving in RCCP schools in Atlanta, reading scores positively related to level of RCCP implementation in Anchorage). A common finding across all sites was children and teachers feeling safer and more appreciative of one another.

At the New York site, a recent rigorous, independent evaluation of RCCP was conducted. The study included over 11,000 students in the first through sixth grades and 300 teachers in 15 elementary schools, which had varying levels of implementation, from none at all to integration of all program components. Data were collected over a two-year period, assessing children's academic achievement (specifically math test scores) as well as their social and emotional learning via child- and teacher-report assessment. Three distinct profiles of exposure to RCCP emerged from the data: (1) high lessons, in which children received greater than the average number of RCCP lessons but their teachers received only average amounts of RCCP training, (2) low lessons, in which children received only a few RCCP lessons but their teacher received greater than the average amount of RCCP training, and (3) no RCCP intervention. Of the three groups, the high lessons group had the greatest increases in math test scores. In addition, the high lessons group had the most positive changes in children's social and emotional developmental trajectories. Thus, children receiving higher levels of RCCP lessons from their teachers had the most positive outcomes that reduced the risk of future school failure and aggressive behavior. However, it should be noted that, because of the study's quasi-experimental design, the outcomes may be due to unobserved characteristics of the high lesson teachers rather than to the RCCP lessons per se. Nonetheless, RCCP shows promise as an effective program to teach students positive, nonviolent social skills.

Further Reading: Brown, J.L., Roderick, T., Lantieri, L., & Aber, J.L. (2004). The resolving conflict creatively program: A school-based social and emotional learning program. In J.E. Zins, R.P. Weissberg, M.C. Wang, & H.J. Walberg (Eds.), *Building academic success on social and emotional learning: What does the research say?* (pp. 151–69). New York: Teachers College Press. Lantierni, L., & Patti, J. (1996). *Waging peace in our schools.* Boston: Beacon Press. Selfridge, J. (2004). The resolving conflict creatively program: How we know it works. *Theory into Practice, 43,* 59–67.

Tonia Bock

Reciprocal Justice

The word reciprocal comes from the Latin *reciprocus,* which literally means to go backwards and forwards. The association of reciprocity with justice goes back to the *lex talonis,* "an eye for an eye and a tooth for a tooth," a principle that limited the scope of revenge. Later religious and cultural codes from around the world defined reciprocal justice as the golden rule, "do unto others as you would have them do unto you." The golden rule does not prescribe a tit-for-tat concrete equality in exchanges but an ideal mutuality. Applying the golden rule obliges us to treat others as we desire them to treat us or, to quote another verse from the Bible, to "Love your neighbor as yourself." Even if we have received ill treatment in the past, we are not to repay them in kind but to treat them, as we would want them to treat us.

In the *Nicomachean Ethics,* Aristotle discusses the relationship of reciprocal justice in economic exchanges. He resolves the problem of commercial transactions involving different kinds of goods by showing how the value of the goods themselves depends on the value they have to the parties in the exchange. For example, suppose a farmer wants to buy some goblets from the local potter. The buyer and the seller determine a just exchange by reaching an agreement on how much wheat a goblet is worth.

Reciprocal justice is not only a key economic principle; it plays a fundamental role in societal functioning. In a classic article in sociology, Alan Gouldner (1960) proposed that society depends upon a norm of reciprocity. If someone does you a kindness, you will feel that you should return the favor in the future. Those who take advantage of the kindness of others by not reciprocating are regarded as deviant. The norm of reciprocity thus acts as an informal mechanism for maintaining social stability.

How the norm of reciprocity gets established and is sustained has been the topic of considerable attention in the social sciences. How can we explain the felt obligation to reciprocate? Sociobiologists claim evidence for a norm of reciprocity in various nonhuman species. Citing examples from birds and fish as well humans, Robert Trivers (1971) argued from a Darwinian perspective that reciprocal altruism brings with it an evolutionary advantage. Reciprocity increases survival value as long as there is a way of monitoring those who return favors and those who do not.

Cognitive developmentalists, such as Jean Piaget and Lawrence Kohlberg, regarded reciprocity as a principle of rationality and not simply as an inherited instinct. In their view, reciprocity is an essential feature of morality; and it is also key to their explanation of how morality develops. According to Piaget (1932), morality develops from nonreciprocity to reciprocity, from unilateral respect to mutual cooperation. Piaget believed reciprocity develops as children interact and are challenged to take others' perspectives and to coordinate them with their own. Lawrence Kohlberg similarly maintained that perspective taking or role taking is at the cognitive core of the stages of moral development. For example, at stage 1, children take only their own perspective into account. At stage 2, they consider the perspective of others and recognize that others may not want what they want. This leads children to an instrumental and concrete sense of reciprocity, "I'll scratch your back, if you scratch mine." At stage 3, children not only recognize that others have perspectives different from their own but also recognize that perspective taking can be mutual. This mutuality leads to golden rule reciprocity.

In articulating his notion of justice as reciprocity, Kohlberg drew heavily on the philosopher John Rawls's *Theory of Justice*. Rawls (1999) argued that principles of justice should be determined impartially "under a veil of ignorance" in which parties to the social contract do not know the characteristics of those whom they represent. In a just society, moreover, individuals must view each other not only as free and equal but as willing to enter into and to abide by cooperative arrangements that they agree are fair. Reciprocity, Rawls contends, is a criterion of moral reasonableness that demands that individuals abide by such arrangements even when it may be in their self-interest to violate them.

Further Reading: Gouldner, A.W. (1960). The norm of reciprocity: A preliminary statement. *American Sociological Review, 25,* 161–68. Kohlberg, L. (1981). Justice as reversibility: The claim to moral adequacy of a highest stage of moral judgment. In *Essays on moral development: Vol. I. The philosophy of moral development* (pp. 190–226). New York: Harper and Row. Piaget, J. (1932). *The moral judgment of the child.* New York: Free Press. Rawls, J. (1999). *A theory of justice* (Rev. ed.). Cambridge, MA: Harvard University Press. Trivers, R.L. (1971). The evolution of reciprocal altruism. *Quarterly Review of Biology, 46,* 35–57.

F. Clark Power

Relativism

Moral relativism refers to the position that there is no objective or universal moral truth. This position should be distinguished from moral pluralism, which admits to multiplicity of moral viewpoints without denying the possibility of objectivity or universality. Moral relativists claim that there are fundamental and irreconcilable disagreements about right and wrong. The source of the disagreement is not in the facts, which may be shared by both parties, but in the ethical standards themselves. For example, two persons may agree in all respects about the facts of eating meat (e.g., the pain inflicted on animals, the extent of world hunger, nutritional alternatives) but disagree about whether eating meat is morally right. In discussing their positions, they may put forth very different opinions about the value of animal life and their responsibilities to alleviate world hunger. Can any common moral standard be established? Are there overarching principles or values that would allow them to agree on whether they should or should not eat meat? Moral relativism maintains that there is no privileged standpoint from which we can ultimately make moral judgments.

Some may adopt moral relativism because they believe that respect for others means that we must tolerate value differences. How people dress, wear their hair, and spend their free time is a matter of personal choice. Although we may not like or be comfortable with others' choices, we should not criticize them because they do not agree with us. Relativism in this sense is a way of honoring individual freedom and practicing tolerance of others. This kind of values relativism can lead to problems, however, if we do not distinguish among different kinds of values. Individuals are free to express themselves in many different ways and to pursue many different kids of activities. Are they free, however, to cheat on a test, to bully another person, or to take a person's property? We experience some values as duties. While we may have a certain amount of freedom over our lives, we do not have complete freedom over the lives of others. What sense are we to make of our experiences of moral duty? They appear to be very different from preferences. Are they the products of reason or intuition or some combination of both? To what extent if any do they reflect an objective moral order or reality?

Even if there are moral rules that do not reduce to value preferences, do such moral rules bind in all circumstances? Some moral rules and values would appear to conflict with others. Suppose, for example, that during the Second World War, members of the Gestapo went door to door looking for Jews. Would it be wrong to tell a lie to protect human lives? There are, in fact, many instances in which moral rules that normally apply might have to be broken to serve a higher good. This seems to indicate that there are no moral absolutes, or does it? Although moral rules may not hold absolutely, there may be more abstract, higher order moral principles that do hold in some absolute or objective sense. One may reject the absolutism of moral rules without rejecting all standards of right and wrong. On the other hand, one may argue that moral principles are themselves imbedded in culture-bound theories or particular philosophical systems (e.g., McIntyre, 1989; Rorty, 1989). Jurgen Habermas (1984) has proposed that moral agreement can, nevertheless, be reached through principled communication.

Cultural relativists reject moral objectivism not because particular rules do not apply absolutely but because societies have such very different rules. Cultural relativists locate the source of moral duties and moral authority in the society or culture in which we live. Anthropologists have discovered that different societies have widely divergent moral codes. Social scientists generally take the view that standards of right and wrong originate within society. Individuals acquire their moral and nonmoral values through processes of socialization in which social norms, beliefs, and values are internalized. On the other hand, social scientists have also produced evidence for cultural uniformity, such as the prevalence of the golden rule. Many social scientists adopt relativism as a method, which allows them to be open and nonjudgmental in exploring differences. Yet should a stance that is useful for gathering information lead to the conclusion that cultural values are beyond a critical moral appraisal?

If moral standards are simply relative to one's culture, what does this mean for the way we think about the Nazi's campaign of genocide or of racist laws in the United States? How is it possible to criticize laws that emanate from society, if society is the source of morality? In his renowned *Letter from a Birmingham Jail,* Martin Luther King Jr. argued that the racist laws of the South violated a natural law binding on all. He went so far as to claim that a law in violation of the natural law is not a law at all. Moral heroism, such as Martin Luther King's, seems to come from a belief that justice is not the arbitrary belief of an impassioned reformer, of a social movement, or of a particular philosophical stance.

Moral relativism can play an important role in how we think about moral education. In the 1970s, the values clarification approach provided exercises for students to explore their own value choices and to respect the choices of others. Moral educators from a variety of perspectives criticized this approach as relativistic for failing to distinguish between moral and nonmoral values. Values clarification endorsed tolerance as an absolute value without providing a way in which students might consider the grounds on which tolerance itself could be justified. Moreover, values clarification also had no way of teaching students to approach moral values critically. Respecting individuals does not mean that we must respect their choices, especially if their choices are harmful to themselves or others. Accepting values as they are confirms the status quo. Character education approaches that mandate teaching the consensual values of society may be vulnerable to many of the same criticism levels as values clarification. Teaching that one must conform to values of one's society without attending to whether or not the values of one's society are themselves moral is to teach cultural relativism.

If moral education is to address moral relativism, it must engage moral differences through a respectful and critical dialogue, which presupposes that, in spite of our differences, we may be able to reach agreement on basic principles guaranteeing human rights and dignity.

Further Reading: Bernstein, R.J. (1985). *Beyond objectivism and relativism.* Philadelphia: University of Pennsylvania Press. Habermas, J. (1984). *The theory of communicative action: Vol. 1. Reason and the rationalization of society* (T. McCarthy, Trans.). Boston: Beacon Press. McIntyre, A.C. (1989). *Whose justice? Which rationality?* Notre Dame, IN: University of Notre Dame Press. Rorty, R. (1989). *Contingency, irony, and solidarity.* Cambridge, England: Cambridge University Press. Wong, D.B. (1986). *Moral relativity.* Berkeley, CA: University of California Press.

F. Clark Power and Nicholas J. Houpt

Religion

Religion is a set of beliefs, encompassing convictions about the existence of a supernatural being or beings, a moral code of conduct held to be in congruence with the will of the deity, and a prescribed order for worship or prayer in order to communicate with the supernatural. These beliefs in a god or gods, a moral order, and a way of worship give rise to a general world view or philosophy for living that help to explain one's place in the universe. Religion can serve as an organizational principle for society, create a unifying theme for various social efforts, and help support believers in the struggles, problems, and challenges they encounter in daily living. The shared beliefs, values, and practices of a particular religion can create a strong social grouping that serves to strengthen the bonds of community within the group and marshal appropriate resources as needed for the group's advancement and care.

A basic organizing principle for most religions is the existence of god, defined as a supernatural being. Some religions are polytheistic, claiming the existence of many gods, each with their own respective spheres of influence. Monotheistic religions believe in a single and omnipotent deity. Religions tend to locate and explain the presence and action of the deity in different ways. Theologians refer to three major groups of religions, distinguished by their perspective on the divine presence: sacramental, prophetic, and mystical.

Sacramental religions tend to look toward signs in concrete, physical objects that are said to somehow communicate the divine presence or put believers in touch with the deity. Statues, crucifixes, cows, water, bread, wine, and totems are examples of objects thought to manifest the divine presence in a way that is tangible and helpful for believers. The Hebrews of the Old Testament revered a decorative box known as the Ark of the Covenant as the dwelling place of their god among them. Hindus believe that the god Shiva resides in a special way in the Ganges River, prompting believers to bathe in the river to access the god's healing powers. Catholics believe that bread and wine become the body and blood of Jesus during their ritual prayers commonly known as the Mass. The material, sacramental object is routinely understood as a symbol of the divine and often as its direct embodiment.

Prophetic religions rely on the conduct of human society and the unfolding of human history as a source for divine revelation and intervention. Prophetic religions look to the major events in history and especially to the inspired words and teachings of great leaders to uncover the divine power and presence in the world. Prophets, thought to be messengers sent from god, help believers to discern and interpret the ongoing revelation of god through history.

Mystical religions, in contrast to the concrete and historical nature of sacramental and prophetic religions, depend on the personal and private religious experience of believers. Mystics are individuals to whom god is said to speak privately and spiritually, revealing what is essential and true. Mystical experiences by definition go beyond words and public religious rituals. Mystics are believed to have privileged access to the divine and are pervaded and transformed by the intimate, personal knowledge of and contact with the deity.

The moral code of religions is manifested in creeds, or statements of doctrine that delineate the beliefs of the group. While the origin of doctrine differs across religions, doctrine is essential for establishing the general parameters of religious practice and the content of the moral code. The support of the moral code and its efficacy is directly related to the ability to connect the moral norms expected with doctrine and the deity.

Worship activities are common across religions and vary according to the focus and needs of the group. Sacramental religions typically have elaborate, prescribed ceremonies, often thought necessary for contact with the divine. Prophetic traditions rely heavily on the spoken word, often preached in the form of a well-articulated homily or sermon. Mystical religions look more to the personal spirituality and earnestness of the mystic themselves as a way to ensure meaningful communication with the divine.

Religion remains a complex and often contentious topic in public discourse. Because of constitutional protections in democracies such as the United States, public or federal support for any particular religion is prohibited. Since many citizens, however, are religious people and members of particular religions, conflicts often arise about the place of religion in civic life. Issues related to religious practices in such venues as public schools, civic gatherings, graduations, military service, and courthouse squares are frequently litigated.

Further Reading: Edwards, P. (Ed.). (1967). *The encyclopedia of philosophy.* New York: Macmillan. James, W. (1902). *The varieties of religious experience.* New York: Modern Library. Kant, I. (1934). *Religion within the limits of reason alone* (T. Greene & H. Hudson, Trans.). Chicago: Open Court. Schleiermacher, F. (1958). *On religion: Speeches to its cultured despisers* (J. Oman, Trans.). New York: Harper.

Ronald J. Nuzzi

Religious Education

Religious education refers to the systematic presentation of the tenets of a particular faith via an organized curriculum and educational process. Religious education can be classroom-based as in the case of private, sectarian schools, or it can be field- and experiential-based, involving faith-based, liturgical rituals, worship of deities, and social gatherings of a community of believers.

Because constitutional protections prohibit the federal government of the United States from advancing any particular religious tradition, religious education is most often found in church-affiliated schools, social service agencies, and community action networks. The largest system of private schooling in the United States, and particularly the largest sector of the private school market—Catholic schools—historically have their origin in the widespread dissatisfaction with religious education in public schools. Catholic leaders and educators found early American schools highly influenced by Protestant theology and, absent the political influence to change public schooling, opted instead for the establishment of their own schools. In 2006–2007, nearly 2.5 million students attended Catholic schools at the K–12 level.

Private schools, especially those founded by religious groups, and Catholic schools include the teaching of religion as a regular, often daily, academic subject along with other required classes. Nationwide, a large, highly competitive network of textbook publishers exists, producing the curriculum materials needed for religious education at every level. In Christian traditions, typical curricular components include: the Bible; the life of major biblical characters and the narratives surrounding them; the life of Jesus and the apostles; morality and ethical norms; and particular teachings regarding current issues of the day such as social justice, war and peace, sexual ethics, medical ethics, and environmental ethics. Service programs are also a common part of religious education. Students learn the tenets of the faith and then, infused with that knowledge, go out into the community to provide some service or social good work, usually directed to the benefit of others, at no charge. Examples of such service includes visiting the homebound, sick, or institutionalized, hand making gifts for the needy, delivering goods such as food or clothes to the poor, writing letters of advocacy on behalf of a worthy cause, or cleaning a public park or street. Larger group efforts at providing service include major undertakings such as rehabilitating a house or entire neighborhood, or even traveling abroad to work with the poor on special projects to help address their needs.

Religious education includes instruction in the beliefs, traditions, and values of a particular faith, but it is not limited to that. In addition to religiously inspired service for others, religious education often includes explicit religious practice, or worship, whereby believers gather together to perform a ritual that has common meaning, reinforces the faith of the community, and helps advance the bonds between members of the faith. This religious practice animates the Sunday worship practice among Christians, the Sabbath observance among Jews, and the Friday prayers of Islam. Such public worship practices serve to instill a comfortable manner of practicing one's faith, bolster the religious identity of practitioners, and create a shared sensed of mission among believers. Public worship is also an effective way to demonstrate the power of shared religious convictions and to reaffirm the importance of holding fast to particular teachings. Ritualized public worship regularly includes recitations from the sacred texts of the community as well as some explanation of the sacred texts and discussion of its implications by the religious leadership.

Religious education has been identified as an academic discipline in some research (Schweitzer, 2006), though this claim is highly criticized by others. Historical research is the most common scholarly work supporting religious education as a discipline, although increasingly empirical studies have been undertaken to assess the impact of religious affiliation on a broad range of social behaviors. Such studies are important in that they can help religious and civic leaders understand if there are certain religious traditions that tend to produce similar public behaviors among their believers. It is common practice to study religious affiliation and strength of affiliation, for example, in examining voter patterns, charitable giving tendencies, and support or opposition to social issues (Campbell, 2006).

Education in faith has evolved from focusing exclusively on learning doctrine, prayers, and rituals of a particular faith to highlighting a comprehensive framework of meaning and values that is able to guide the believer in everyday life, to provide an anchor of meaning in a pluralistic society. Churches and private religious educators are aware of the need for high quality religious education programming in schools, and are heavily invested in the preparation and formation of adult leaders to teach these classes and direct such programs. Understood as a process of lifelong formation, religious education is relevant to children and adults alike, though school- and church-based programs often focus on the young. Religious education for adults is a growing field, receiving more attention across various faith traditions.

Further Reading: Berryman, J. (1991). *Godly play: A way of religious education.* San Francisco: Harper. Brelsford, T. (2004). Editorial. *Religious Education, 99*(1), 1–3. Campbell, D. (2006). *Why we vote: How schools and communities shape our civic life.* Princeton, NJ: Princeton University Press. Horell, H. (2004). Fostering hope: Christian religious education in a post-modern age. *Religious Education, 99*(1), 5–22. O'Murchu, D. (1997). *Reclaiming spirituality: A new spiritual framework for today's world.* Dublin: Gill and Macmillan. Schweitzer, F. (2006). Research in religious education: Perspectives for the future. *Religious Education, 101*(2), 166–69.

Ronald J. Nuzzi

Reparation

Reparative justice is concerned with the problem of giving meaning to punishment via reciprocity or equity. Reparation means the opportunity for restitution to the victims and the community. In the *Moral Judgment of the Child,* Piaget (1932/1977) observed that reparation is part of retributive justice thinking, particularly concerned with "putting things right." Considering that the bond of solidarity is broken when a person transgresses moral norms, punishment is justified as a responsibility to others and the collective (see Retributive Justice). Reparation relates punishment to the idea of restoration via equality for compensation or restitution, or equity after harm, which creates a developmental pattern of values—from equality to equity. Values development is related to heteronomy and autonomy, moral orientations, and the concepts of distribution and retribution.

In the domain of retribution, the morality of heteronomy submits the child to adults' authority. Heteronomy intrinsically connects reparation with expiatory punishment. Adult constraint influences a child to believe that rules are legitimate and sacred. Thus, violation of the rules justifies punishment by strict equality (eye-for-an-eye justice) or expurgating wrong by suffering. Punishment by strict equality makes reparation after compensation (to give something of equal value) or restitution (bringing back what was taken away). Consequently, relationships are restored as a reward. This shows that young children do not differentiate punishment from vengeance, nor is the notion of moral values different from the value of material goods. During childhood, a genuine belief that violations to adults' rules justify expiatory punishment by reciprocity makes children accept suffering as moral and obligatory because that is the only way a person can repair wrongdoing.

Moral heteronomy is superseded by the morality of autonomy, in which individual conscience is the real source of justice reasoning. Autonomy brings to young adolescents the idea of equality by reciprocity and equity. Adolescents understand that rules are intrinsically connected to affective ties in interpersonal relationships and collective obligations. Mutual respect, cooperation, trust, and reciprocity are values in the morality of solidarity. For example, young adolescents understand that lies are a breach of trust. Considering that the collective has a moral responsibility to the person, lying should not be accepted by the group for the sake of solidarity. Thus, violations to the norms are perceived as a breach to the bonds of solidarity toward the collective. Nevertheless, socialization agents (family, schools, etc.) and the community have the moral obligation to provide viable possibilities to reparation when moral transgression occurs. Autonomy of thinking gives the person the ability to take societal perspective, which gives meaning to values. Transgressions should follow with punishment and responsibility. For the sake of conscience in the person, punishment should fit the crime. A person should also have access to reparation that can be offered through different means. For example, accepting responsibility, apologizing, and showing repentance and remorse are means to psychological and moral reparation.

However, psychology has investigated justice reasoning and the role of reparation to the self and in interpersonal reconciliation between victims and offenders. Now, what should be the role of reparation leading a person on the way to return to society after transgression?

The idea is that society should adopt equity, which is justice with mercy, as a form of societal justice. Equality by reciprocity no longer attends the demands of justice that to be fair needs equity (Piaget, 1932/1977). Since antiquity Greek and Roman philosophers and rulers (Seneca, Marcus Aurelius) have advocated a view of justice via equity, which includes reparation. Historical documents such as the Babylonian code of Hammurabi (1700 B.C.); the Sumerian Code of UrNammu (2060 B.C.); the Roman Law of the Twelve Tables (449 B.C.); the Law of Ethelbert (A.D. 600); and the Hebrew concept of Shalom (Van Ness et al., 1997) include societal reparation.

What equity does is take personal circumstances into account to make equality effective and to provide meaning to punishment. Therefore, equity is justice thinking that brings relativity to equality (Colby & Kohlberg, 1987). Equity gives a morally autonomous person the feeling that punishment should be relative to the crime. This kind of justice is also known as restorative justice.

Restorative justice is the new paradigm of reparation. Reparation in restorative justice connects punishment with redemption and forgiveness. As we said in the beginning, reparation means the opportunity for restitution to the victims and the community. In restorative justice, reparation elevates the role of the offenders by giving them a chance for redemption and forgiveness. Reparation also elevates the role of victims by involving them in the process. Reparation does not pose the rights of victims against the rights of offenders but instead addresses the principle that the collective should function by bonds of solidarity. In summary, psychology has dedicated attention to the role of reparation in justice reasoning and individual development. To our knowledge there is no research in psychology, law or education dedicated to investigating the role of societal reparation for when a person takes responsibility for transgressions and wants to return to society after punishment.

Further Reading: Colby, A., & Kohlberg, L. (1987). *The measurement of moral judgment: Vol. 1. Theoretical foundations and research validation.* New York: Cambridge University Press. Piaget, J. (1977). *The moral judgment of the child.* New York: Free Press. (Original work published 1932.) Van Ness, D., & Heetderks-Strong, K. (1997). *Restoring justice.* Cincinnati, OH: Anderson Publishing.

Júlio Rique and Julian Bruno Gonçalves Santos

Republic

The title of this dialogue by Plato (ca. 428–347 B.C.E.) is the word in ancient Greek for the city. The dialogue is ostensibly about justice, since in the first of ten books or chapters, the discussion focuses on arriving at a satisfactory definition of justice and an answer to the question whether a life of justice or injustice is more profitable. But to answer this question and to provide a definition, the character Socrates begins an account of the ideal or best city that frames most of the rest of the dialogue.

Plato wrote the *Republic* in about 380 B.C.E. when he was in his late 40s. The problem to which the dialogue is meant to provide an answer is a set of related concepts of justice and of the best human life that are as prevalent today as they were when Plato wrote. Those concepts are articulated by the character Thrasymachus in Book One and refined and sharpened in Book Two by characters representing Plato's older brothers, Glaucon and Adeimantus, as follows: "justice" is defined by the people in power who control "the justice system," the legislative and judicial processes that supposedly seek true justice but actually serve the interests of the powerful; furthermore, no one, powerful or not, desires genuinely to be just but only to have the advantages of a reputation for justice while securing also the advantages of a life of unfettered injustice.

In response to this popular opinion, the Socrates of the *Republic* presents the following theses: Humans naturally depend on each other, since none of us is self-sufficient either at birth or in adulthood. The best life for humans is a life lived in a good community, contributing to the shared good of the whole as one is best able. Educators must discern the natural talents of each child and nurture those specific talents so that each is enabled to be their best and to make their best contribution to the network of interdependence for the common good. And though education should foster specific skills relating to each person's natural talents, the general aim of education is the cultivation of human virtue, producing both psychic and civic harmony. Thus, a conception of justice that makes self-gratification the highest priority is fundamentally wrongheaded.

The *Republic* is not, however, a lecture merely rearranged into dialogue form. Plato lays several traps for uncritical readers, and it is likely that the text was written in part at least to provide intellectual challenges to his students in the Academy—including Aristotle beginning in his late teens.

It is important in this connection to notice that in Book One a useful and still accepted definition of justice is considered and rejected. The character Polemarchus attributes to the poet Simonides the claim that justice is to give to each what is owed. Prompted by Socrates, he clarifies that he thinks we owe benefit to friends and harm to enemies, but when Socrates convinces him that it is unjust to harm even our enemies, they do not return to the poet's definition. Thrasymachus interrupts, and the discussion comes to focus instead on Thrasymachus's anticonventional definition and Socrates's attempt to refute it.

The best known theses in the *Republic* are not about education or even justice and the best city but are about knowledge and reality. Socrates offers the famous myth of the cave and the diagram of the line as part of an attempt to persuade Glaucon and Adeimantus that true knowledge moves beyond illustrations or examples of any kind, to the realities themselves.

Books Five through Seven where the so-called "theory of the forms" is presented are formally a digression from the main argument—prefaced by Socrates's nervous warnings that on these matters he is most insecure. Late in Book Five, Socrates observes that the best city cannot be realized unless rulers become philosophers and philosophers become rulers. To explain this absurd statement, he has to explain why genuine knowledge of the good and other abstract realities is required for good ruling.

The "forms" are abstract rather than concrete entities. For instance, the equilateral right triangle is thinkable but not perceivable. You can try to draw one, but it will only be an approximation. Today we might say that H_2O is "what it is to be" water, the form of water. Extending Socrates's account to our molecular concept of water, a sample of water is merely the reflection in the perceivable realm of "the what it is to be" water, H_2O, in the intelligible realm. When we have scientific knowledge about water, H_2O is what we know, not any particular sample, which we can only perceive, because H_2O is universal and changeless and thus a proper object of knowledge.

The supreme form is the form of the good. If the best city is to survive, its rulers must be able to appreciate the good itself, in virtue of which all good things are good. Having the forms as one's thoughts, and appreciating the form of the good, requires many years of mathematical and philosophical training—hence rulers must be philosophers.

However, early in Book Ten (*Republic* 597b–d) Socrates states, in an almost offhanded way, the grounds for a critique of the theory of forms later stated in Plato's *Parmenides* and made famous by Aristotle as the Third Man Argument. The *Republic* ends with a finger-wagging tale about the afterlife and how the unjust get what they deserve in the end.

Plato leaves the conversation unfinished, intentionally incomplete. He was even here a true Socratic. We must think for ourselves about what should be saved from Socrates's theses in the *Republic*. We cannot simply treat the dialogue as a lecture.

Further Reading: Annas, J. (1981). *An introduction to Plato's Republic.* New York: Oxford University Press. Ferrari, G.R.F. (Ed.). (2007). *The Cambridge companion to a Plato's Republic.* New

York: Cambridge University Press. Pickstock, C. (2007). *A short guide to Plato.* New York: Oxford University Press.

Don Collins Reed

Resilience

Resilience is defined as adaptive functioning despite adversity and is evidenced by competence in certain domains, such as effective management of psychological processes or behavioral self-regulation (Masten, 2001; Masten, Best, & Garmezy, 1990). Consistent with a developmental psychopathology framework, Egeland, Carlson, and Sroufe (1993) described resilience as resulting from a developmental process involving a complex set of transactions between the individual and the environment, conceptualizing resilience as a process, as opposed to a characteristic residing within the individual. Thus, resilience may be viewed as the individual's use of available resources to facilitate positive developmental outcomes, which may enhance the individual's functioning and increase resources for successful adaptation to the next developmental stage.

Further defining resilience, resilience phenomena include good outcomes in high-risk children, sustained competence in children under stress, and recovery from traumatic experiences. In order for development to be considered resilient, both (a) significant risk must have been present at some point in the developmental process and (b) current functioning must be competent. In terms of age and gender differences, adversity during later childhood or adolescence is linked with worse outcomes than in earlier childhood, and boys' responses to stress tend to be more external (e.g., disruptive and aggressive behavior), whereas girls' responses tend to be more internal (e.g., anxiety and depression). Moreover, it appears that girls are more resilient than boys in childhood, but more vulnerable in adolescence.

Two constructs that are closely related to resilience are risk factors and protective factors. Risk factors are those that are statistically linked with negative outcomes (e.g., poverty, low birth weight). Not surprisingly, the presence of multiple risk factors appears to be linked with poorer outcomes than the presence of only one risk factor. In contrast, protective factors are those that alter the effects of risks, such that development is more positive than it would otherwise be. One protective factor that is critically important to children's resilience is quality of caregiving, which facilitates the development of self-esteem, social skills, a sense of trust in others, and engagement with the environment. Other important protective factors include intelligence and problem-solving skills, competence, and likability. In terms of the broader context of development, schools, neighborhoods, and churches can also serve as protective agents.

Overall, the empirical literature suggests that, in the absence of permanent damage or extremely harsh early experiences, humans are highly resilient in the face of adversity. Nevertheless, little competence has been observed in children exposed to severe risk, with protective factors in this context serving primarily to diminish negative outcomes, rather than contributing to resilience. In any case, the goodness-of-fit between the developing individual and the environment (e.g., the fit between child emotional development and caregiving strategies) is particularly important in determining resilience. That is, there is no single route to resilience, but rather it is the interaction among multiple factors that, in concert with one another, produce development.

Research suggests that such psychosocial factors as caregiver quality, intellectual functioning, and self-concept are critically important in protecting children from the effects of adversity. In a longitudinal study of competence, Masten, Hubbard, Gest, Tellegen, Garmezy, and Ramirez (1999) found that resilient children were distinguishable from maladaptive children by their high levels of psychosocial resources, which were comparable to those of competent, low-adversity children. Moreover, the levels of competence in resilient children vary across domains, such that resilient children may show substantial difficulties in some areas while concurrently showing high levels of functioning in other areas (Luthar, Doernberger, & Zigler, 1993). Furthermore, although resilient children show competence at some developmental points, their competence varies over time (e.g., increasing emotional distress over time), highlighting the need to view resilience as a multidimensional construct.

Therefore, in terms of intervention, some at-risk children who are functioning well may have hidden needs in some domains, which should be targeted by intervention programs. Three approaches to fostering resilience include: (a) adding more assets or resources; (b) strengthening existing assets and/or weakening the existing risk factors; and (c) preventing adverse circumstances from occurring. Moreover, the most comprehensive intervention programs stem from viewing development as a system, and consequently target multiple aspects of the individual's environment. Relatedly, the empirical literature suggests that designing intervention efforts for specific circumstances increases their effectiveness. To advance the field by building on current knowledge of how and why resilience develops, delineating the factors, processes, and pathways to resilience is an important direction for future work, toward the goal of developing effective interventions to foster the development of resilience.

Further Reading: Egeland, B., Carlson, E., & Sroufe, L.A. (1993). Resilience as process. *Development and Psychopathology, 5,* 517–28. Luthar, S.S., Doernberger, C.H., & Zigler, E. (1993). Resilience is not a unidimensional construct: Insights from a prospective study of inner-city adolescents. *Development and Psychopathology, 5,* 703–17. Masten, A.S. (2001). Ordinary magic: Resilience processes in development. *American Psychologist, 56,* 227–38. Masten, A.S., Best, K.M., & Garmezy, N. (1990). Resilience and development: Contributions from the study of children who overcome adversity. *Development and Psychopathology, 2,* 425–44. Masten, A.S., Hubbard, J.J., Gest, S.D., Tellegen, A., Garmezy, N., & Ramirez, M. (1999). Competence in the context of adversity: Pathways to resilience and maladaptation from childhood to late adolescence. *Development and Psychopathology, 11,* 143–69.

Alice C. Schermerhorn

Respect

Simply defined, respect is showing regard for the intrinsic value of someone or something, including respect for persons, for animals, for property, for the environment, as well as respect for oneself. Self-respect is the form of respect that prevents persons from allowing themselves to be treated in a way that demeans, denigrates, or insults. Theoretical and practical applications of respect represent a primary interest of moral and political philosophers, as well as theologians. Respect is also a civic virtue with imminently practical implications for human communities.

In a human sense exhortations for respect can be viewed as pleas for justice (i.e., giving a person his/her due). Calls for respect are frequently articulated by those who feel disrespected (i.e., not valued) based on their gender, age, sexual orientation, or economic status. In a 2002 Public Agenda poll on the state of respect in the United States, nearly 8 in 10 adults (79 percent) agreed that "the lack of respect and courtesy is a serious problem in our society." Seventy-four percent said that Americans used to treat each other with more respect in the past. Whether levels of respect have actually declined, what seems clear is that the norm of respect remains important.

On the one hand, the virtue of respect might rightly be considered universal (we will that all people show respect) and reversible (we would wish to be treated with respect). As such, respect represents the heart of the golden rule ("do unto others as you would have them do unto you"). On the other hand, conceptions of what deserves respect and how those displays of respect should be made manifest are very much a local construction. Within any particular culture norms and rituals of respect vary dramatically. Whether to take off ones shoes or hat or leave them on, whether to make eye contact or not, when to stand or sit, to hug, kiss, shake hands, or wave—these and countless other applications are social constructions of respect that are painstakingly conceived, conveyed, and enforced.

These local applications of respect are often referred to as "common courtesy," "civility," or "good manners" (or "rudeness" if omitted or misapplied). In a moral sense these applications are not universal, and yet within a particular culture they are considered essential for peaceful coexistence. Social and emotional skills are the operational skills, or building blocks of respect. We must learn and master the skills of respect, including how to interrupt, how to apologize, how to disagree, for example.

Even in "antisocial" cultures such as gangs, norms of respect and disrespect are significant for establishing and maintaining cultures. Actions or attitudes that appear to disrespect, or "dis," are commonly understood and strictly enforced by community members. In this way we see respect as the cornerstone of culture—both those that would be considered prosocial and those that would be considered antisocial.

British educator David Isaacs (2001) argues that there are three essential applications of respect: (1) a general respect we owe to every human without exception, (2) respect for persons based on the role they occupy, and (3) respect as an inner attitude. Individuals do not need to "earn" respect in the way that admiration or esteem is earned; we deserve such respect simply by virtue of being human. In the face of commonly held moral maxims such as "You've got to give respect to get it" and "respect is earned not given," philosophers such as Immanuel Kant argue for the centrality of respect due persons (including oneself) simply because of the inherent value of every individual equally, as an end in itself, not as a means.

Parents, teachers, and public officials, for example, deserve this respect because of the special authority and responsibility they have for the welfare of others. Parents, teachers, public officials, and religious leaders are given respect because of the particular authority represented by their office. Even if we disagree with the particular person, we nonetheless demonstrate respect for the office or position.

We are not being truly respectful toward other persons if we are inwardly contemptuous of them, even if we do not show that attitude by our actions. However, respect includes the right of conscience to disagree respectfully with others' beliefs or behaviors. Respect for someone's human rights and dignity does not require us to accept or approve that person's behavioral choices.

Further Reading: Isaacs, D. (2001). *Character building: A guide for parents and teachers.* Portland, OR: Four Courts Press. Lickona, T. (1991). *Educating for character: How our schools can teach respect and responsibility.* New York: Bantam. Lickona, T., & Davidson, M. (2005). *Smart & good high schools: Integrating excellence and ethics for success in school, work, and beyond.* Cortland, NY: Center for the 4th and 5th Rs (Respect & Responsibility)/Washington, DC: Character Education Partnership.

Matthew L. Davidson

Responsibility

Responsibility literally means the "ability to respond." Responsibility defines our duty or positive obligations. It calls us to fulfill our commitments, to intervene when necessary to stand up for what is right, and to correct what is wrong—even when helping carries a cost. Responsibility describes our dependability or trustworthiness, our ability to carry out our duties and fulfill our obligations—at home, in the workplace, in our communities. Practically speaking, a person is judged responsible if he/she can be counted on to do his/her part for a group; however, it is this same simple concept that a person is judged to be responsible on larger issues. Can individuals be trusted to do their part for the human community and for the environment that sustains them? If so, they are considered responsible; if not, they are considered irresponsible.

A sense of responsibility inspires ethical intervention. It is at the core of moral courage. It can be helpful to examine the virtue of responsibility by investigating instances where individuals chose not to respond in upholding their obligations to prosocial norms. For example, the Third Reich of Nazi Germany systematically murdered 11 million human beings, including 6 million Jews. Although the vast majority of people did nothing to help those who were being persecuted by the Nazis, others chose to respond. Why? An examination of their motives helps us to better understand the nature of responsibility.

Samuel and Pearl Oliner (1988) investigated 406 rescuers who had helped to save Jews in Nazi-occupied Europe, comparing these individuals with 126 nonrescuers. The Oliners found three kinds of "moral catalysts," sometimes operating in combination, that moved people to respond: norm-centered responsibility (acting in accord with the values of a particular group), empathic responsibility (moved by another's distress), and principled responsibility (commitment to a universal ethic).

"Collective responsibility" is a term for defining a norm-centered motive based on an allegiance to the shared code of a particular group. For example, members of a particular church, team, or organization may be motivated to act according to a particular code or set of shared norms and a strong sense of attachment to others. These norms demand the individuals weigh their personal interests with the interests of the group, a notion that is often used in reference to the ideals of teamwork or citizenship. This can be true of groups with both prosocial and antisocial purposes (e.g., members of a team versus members of a gang or cult).

Unlike those motivated to respond by a sense of collective responsibility, for others personal empathy provides the motivation to respond for others. Personal empathy includes the ability to feel or relate to different people and groups and their experience, especially to internalize their suffering and to feel called to respond. For this type of individual simply knowing that others are suffering or in need provides the motivation required for action. This empathy can be indirect (simply learning of a need may lead to response), or direct (an experiential encounter may motivate response).

Motivation to respond may also be based on a belief in a universal ethic or principles like justice or peace. For example, social responsibility is based on orientation to help others even when there is nothing to be gained personally; further, it tends to involve the commitment of personal resources and the incurrence of personal risk. All of which suggests a deeper motivational principle or ethic, qualitatively different from personal responsibility (for example, for one's own children) or collective responsibility (for example, to one's religious or ethnic group).

Thus, one may be said to have a responsibility to oneself, as well as a responsibility to others. We have a responsibility to act in a way that attends to our personal needs; so too responsibility requires the ability to respond for the welfare of others, including those outside one's immediate family and community circle. Ultimately, responsibility is not simply a matter of balancing different kinds of responsibilities—personal, collective, social, and so forth—since these different types often exist in tension with one another, so much as it is possessing some capacity for each type of responsibility.

Further Reading: Colby, A., & Damon, W. (1992). *Some do care: Contemporary lives of moral commitment.* New York: Free Press. Lapsley, D.K. (1996). *Moral psychology.* Boulder, CO: Westview Press. Lickona, T. (1991). *Educating for character: How our schools can teach respect and responsibility.* New York: Bantam. Lickona, T., & Davidson, M. (2005). *Smart & good high schools: Integrating excellence and ethics for success in school, work, and beyond.* Cortland, NY: Center for the 4th and 5th Rs (Respect & Responsibility)/Washington, DC: Character Education Partnership. Oliner, S.P., & Oliner, P.M. (1988). *The altruistic personality: Rescuers of Jews in Nazi Europe.* New York: Free Press.

Matthew L. Davidson

Rest, James R.

A moral psychologist who developed the Defining Issues Test (DIT) of moral judgment development and created the "Minnesota approach" to the study of moral development, James R. Rest was born in 1941 and grew up in New Orleans. He studied history and philosophy at Tulane University and after a brief flirtation with seminary entered the clinical psychology program at the University of Chicago. At Chicago, Rest met and began working with Lawrence Kohlberg whom he followed to Harvard University for postdoctoral studies. In 1970 he was recruited to the University of Minnesota and the Department of Educational Psychology where he quickly rose to full professor in 1977.

Rest's early work was in the Kohlberg tradition, and he was intimately involved with the Harvard group's interview-based scoring procedures for moral stage. At the same time, Rest's moral comprehension studies led him to believe that there were other methods for assessing moral judgment development. At Minnesota, his first order of business was to explore these various measurement options. Rest's motivation to create an alternative measure of moral thinking in the Kohlberg tradition was twofold. First, during the late 1960s when Rest was finishing his dissertation work, the Kohlberg group had come to the conclusion that measurement issues had to be addressed prior to any further focus on theoretical considerations. Rest agreed but was concerned about the adequacy of the then current interview scoring process and the direction Kohlberg and his colleagues were taking to shore it up. Particularly troublesome to Rest was his perception that the Kohlberg group uncritically viewed spontaneous production as the most theoretically consistent means to define and score moral stages. Further, Rest questioned the Kohlberg group's strong views on the importance of distinguishing between the content of a moral dilemma and organizing structure in the scoring process. Second, Rest was concerned that the field needed a more accessible measure in order to stimulate research in moral judgment development. The result of this work became the DIT.

At first, the DIT was viewed by those in the field as simply a "quick and dirty" method for measuring Kohlberg's stages. However, this assumption overlooked some significant differences in the theoretical underpinnings of the Kohlberg and Rest approaches as Rest made clear in his 1979 book describing the first phase of work on the DIT. Chief among these differences was the developmental model assumed by each group. Kohlberg argued for a step-by-step invariant stage sequence, while Rest favored a continuous model where different organizations of thinking shift from immature to more complex forms. Over time, the differences between Rest and Kohlberg grew wider.

During the 1980s Rest increasingly became convinced that a singular focus on moral judgment development was insufficient to explain moral functioning. He developed this view in a major review of the moral domain for Carmichael's *Handbook of Child Psychology* in which he identified four component processes that were central to the production of moral behavior. These components are moral sensitivity, moral judgment, moral motivation, and moral character. Known as Rest's Four Component Model, this work stimulated a wave of new measurements designed to assess the different components and new approaches to moral education. Much of the work leading up to and stimulated by Rest's model was published in his 1986 book and 1994 edited volume. As a result of these shifts in theoretical focus, the field recognized Rest's work as a distinct branch of moral psychology, and it became common to see references to the "Minnesota approach."

The 1990s saw further elaboration of the four moral components and additional attention to theory. This focus led to a 1999 book in which Rest and his colleagues looked back over the Kohlberg and Minnesota traditions and with attention to current advances in cognitive sciences developed a neo-Kohlbergian theory of moral thinking. This view continues to influence research and educational practice. Rest died in 1999, having suffered from a degenerative neurological disorder.

Further Reading: Rest, J. (1979). *Development in judging moral issues.* Minneapolis, MN: University of Minnesota Press. Rest, J. (1983). *Morality.* In P.H. Mussen (Series Ed.) & J. Flavell & E. Markman (Vol. Ed.), *Handbook of child psychology: Vol. 3. Cognitive development* (4th ed., pp. 556–629). New York: Wiley. Rest, J.R. (1986). *Moral development: Advances in research and theory.* New York: Praeger. Rest, J. & Narvaez, D. (1994). *Moral development in the professions.* Hillsdale, NJ: Lawrence Erlbaum Associates. Rest, J., Narvaez, D., Bebeau, M., & Thoma, S. (1999). *Postconventional moral thinking: A neo-Kohlbergian approach.* Mahwah, NJ: Lawrence Erlbaum Associates. Thoma, S.J. (2002). An overview of the Minnesota approach in moral development. *Journal of Moral Education, 31,* 225–246.

Stephen J. Thoma

Restorative Justice

Restorative justice is an alternative paradigm of justice and programs of community responses to crimes. In the restorative paradigm, a crime is defined as a broken tie between a person and his or her community. Thus, to be fair, justice should have the responsibility of repairing and restoring the bonds between offenders and their communities by creating opportunities for dialogues between victims and offenders, as well as having equity and mercy as the guiding principles for punishment. The operative principles of restorative justice programs are based on cooperation (between victims, offenders, and community leaders), redemption (of offenders), and reintegration (of offenders into the community and of reconciliation with victims) in association with punishment.

In restorative justice, community cooperation is expected to occur via restorative circle meetings involving victims, offenders, lawyers, and community leaders. The community takes responsibility for the process by creating new relationships and capacitating offenders with new skills and competencies. For offenders, this is a way to earn redemption. Redemption should occur when one takes responsibility for his or her actions and accepts punishment with meaning, which is obtained via dialogues and justifications for punishment given during restorative circle meetings. Punishment in restorative justice can take many different forms: incarceration according to the law, community service, compensation, reparation, or restitution. Reintegration is both the community's responsibility, by having social programs helping offenders back to society after one pays its duty to justice, and the offenders' responsibility, by demonstrating redemption and new competencies. Reconciliation, though desirable, might occur between victims and offenders but is not a necessary condition for offenders' reintegration.

Restorative justice stands in opposition to retributive justice. Punishment in retribution is expiatory. Punishment in restorative justice is equitable, a way to earn redemption, reintegration, and reconciliation. Societies believe that retribution will deter one from committing crimes by fear of punishment. However, society also lives with the fear of crimes, as retributive justice only takes the perspective of offenders. Retributive justice systems bear no responsibility to victims, who are left on their own, or to the community, for retribution is not responsible for prevention or rehabilitation. Communities are left under the care of a justice philosophy that has no mercy. Restorative justice takes a multidimensional and communitarian perspective by involving the community, victims, and offenders in restorative circles. Thus, it is a collaborative system of repairing damaged relationships via justice.

Restorative justice stems from ancient practices. Premodern societies functioned under two principles of justice: vengeance and reparation. Reparation is the ancient form of restorative paradigms. Reparation means the opportunity for restitution to the victims and the community. Reparation is found in many historical documents (Van Ness et al., 1997): the Babylonian code of Hammurabi (1700 B.C.); the Sumerian Code of UrNammu (2060 B.C.); the Roman Law of the Twelve Tables (449 B.C.); the Law of Ethelbert (A.D. 600); and the Hebrew concept of Shalom, which means an ideal state in which a community should function and live.

Restorative justice came back internationally during the 1990s, as a "new" movement for alternatives in justice systems. Across nations, restorative justice has received different labels (community justice, alternative justice, etc.) and has reached different levels of influence. For example, in the United States, it is common to find small courts of restorative justice functioning at the community level under the supervision of state attorneys. Usually, in America, the community and the justice system decide which cases are allowed to be part of restorative programs. In New Zealand, Canada, Australia, and also some states in the United States, restorative justice has reached a high institutional level, playing an influential role in criminal justice law and social policies. The movement has reached South America with programs being implemented in several states in Brazil.

Values and social movements are usually at the root of social changes. Values are motivational forces that give rise to social movements. Restorative justice has a new set of values that aims to shift the justice paradigm and create a new system. Defenders of restorative justice believe that without a change of values, structural reforms of current systems are meaningless with respect to elevating society to a new level of human capacity. The Human Rights movement presently has been a strong voice of resistance against expiatory punishment and has supported restorative justice. Restorative justice programs are effectively showing lower recidivism rates for adolescents. Domestic violence can also be reduced with counseling for victims and offenders within the community. It is the outcome of those programs associated with social movements that are influencing changes in the system and educating society toward embodying new values. Historically, punishments, rights, mercy, reparation, forgiveness, and equity have been concepts debated in every nation's justice system. Bits and pieces of those concepts are found universally but are used scarcely because they have not become popular for conflict resolution yet.

Further Reading: Braithwaite, J. (1989). *Crime, shame, and reintegration.* New York: Cambridge University Press. Bazemore, G., & Schiff, M. (1996). Community justice/restorative justice: Prospects for a new social ecology for community corrections. *International Journal of Comparative and Applied Criminal Justice, 20*(1), 311–35. Van Ness, D., & Heetderks-Strong, K. (1997). *Restoring justice.* Cincinnati, OH: Anderson Publishing. Zehr, H. (1990). *Changing lenses. A new focus for crime and justice.* Scottsdale, PA: Herald Press.

Júlio Rique

Retributive Justice

A theory of punishment addresses three ethical problems: (1) distinguishing between punishments and other types of sanctions (e.g., penalty or revenge); (2) specifying good or moral punishments; and (3) justifying punishment. Retributive justice is concerned with the third problem of justifying punishment. Historically two conflicting theories have attempted to justify punishment: the retributive theory and utilitarian theory.

The retributive theory holds that the only defensible justification of a punishment is the culpability of the person to be punished. The theory further stipulates that the severity of the punishment should be proportional to the severity of the act punished. Hence every retributive consideration is contained in the character of the offense itself, with no other consideration to be admitted. For this reason the retributive theory has been called "backward looking" since one is entitled to punish an offender in light of (looking back over) the facts of the case. The retributivist approach to punishment typically requires a punishment to involve a deprivation of a good, such as liberty or property. It must be for violation of legally established rules and not for moral culpability; that is, punishment should be for an offense involving an offender and not for "sins" or of "sinners." Finally, punishment must be distinguished from direct action of an aggrieved person, which is considered revenge and not punishment.

There are several variations of retributive theory. One is called "repayment theory." Repayment theory reflects the standard usage of retribution. Punishment is inflicted, on the repayment view, in order to make the offender pay for the offense. A second variation is "desert theory." Punishment is inflicted because it is deserved. According to this view the core meaning of retributivism involves the notion of just deserts. To give as a justification for punishment that it is deserved by offenders is retributivism. A third usage is called "penalty theory." Here punishment is viewed as an automatic penalty, the justification of which is guaranteed simply by knowing that the offense was committed. A fourth variation is "annulment theory." This position holds that punishment must annul a crime and restore the right by making restitution.

It is clear that a unidimensional theory of retribution does not exist. In general, however, retributivism involves paying for a crime. It involves a retrospective association of a punishment with its offense. The punishment must be for legal (but sometimes moral) culpability, which is then administered through the offices of an authority—though in some cases punishment may be for violation of orders or for evident violations in the absence of explicit prohibition. Finally, punishment must set the wrong to right, give comfort to the victim, and be proportional to the original offense. Only when some or all of these criteria are satisfied can a given punishment be morally justified.

In contrast to the retributivist position, the utilitarian view can be stated simply. Punishment is justified entirely by its consequences. A punishment is just if it serves to reduce the incidence of lawbreaking. There is no thought of bringing suffering to bear on guilty miscreants as a justification for punishment, but only a concern for the deleterious effect on future criminal activity. Thus, where retributivists are "backward-looking," utilitarians are "teleological"; that is, they have the future "end goal" (the *telos*) in mind, which is a reduction of offending. They are concerned only with deterrence.

The utilitarian view leads to some interesting complications. For example, if it is the desirable consequences of punishment that justify it, and not the fact that anyone has committed an offense, then what prevents us from punishing anyone at all, even the innocent, if to do so favors deterrence? And would not utilitarian theory also justify severe and ghastly punishment, for the same reason? One could evade this criticism by insisting on the moral or legal guilt of the victim, but then we are surrendering to a retributive principle and not a utilitarian one.

Of course, utilitarians could reply that arbitrary or severe punishment is not acceptable on the good utilitarian grounds that all unnecessary suffering is undesirable, say, because it undermines respect for the law. Utilitarians also argue that retributivists cannot logically match the severity of punishment to the magnitude of an offense, and that they have not advanced an ethical argument at all but only a logical one. In other words, the meaning of "punishment" logically entails reference to past guilt. Logically one can punish only the guilty, but this need not imply that we ought to punish them. For this we need to appeal reasons of utility and deterrence.

Some attempts at compromise have been undertaken. One prominent view suggests that utilitarian theories can be invoked to justify the institution of punishment, but that the retributive theory is required to justify the distribution of punishment in particular cases (Hart, 1968).

Further Reading: Cottingham, J. (1979). Varieties of retribution. *Philosophical Quarterly, 29,* 238–46. Day, J.P. (1978). Retributive punishment. *Mind, 87,* 498–516. Hart, H.L.A. (1968). *Punishment and responsibility.* New York: Oxford University Press. Marshall, J. (1984). Punishment and moral education. *Journal of Moral Education, 13,* 79–85. Oldenquist, A. (1988). An explanation of retribution. *Journal of Philosophy, 85,* 464–79.

Daniel K. Lapsley

Reverence

Reverence is a form of respect and honor, felt and often exhibited as a way of expressing a deeply held conviction of awe or veneration. Reverence includes the inner disposition or feeling of respect for another as well as the outward manifestation of that respect in the form of deferential behaviors. Reverence can be directed toward other persons because of their roles, status, or history, and to God or to other deities as a form of worship and obedience.

Reverence is an ancient virtue, present in the political, civic, and religious ceremonies of humanity for thousands of years. It serves a useful purpose in the organization of society and its institutions, is helpful in the designation of various roles within that order, and serves to motivate all members of a social group to undertake responsibilities that will preserve the good of the social order. Reverence is one way in which social stratification is accomplished and reinforced. Leaders are due reverence, and followers revere their leaders. While the presence of excessive reverence for leaders has been problematic in some cultures, a necessary degree of reverence has historically helped cultures to function more efficiently. Once leaders lose or forfeit such respect, and followers no longer revere their leaders, chaos often follows.

Reverence also describes the relationship within various religions of individual believers toward God or other deities. Institutionalized religious practices are frequently public rituals of reverence, organized public displays of respect and honor for God. Similar to reverence in the social and political order, public acts of reverence for God tend to strengthen the bonds of community among believers and reinforce their commonly held convictions about God. Such reverential acts often result in increased respect not only for members of the religion, but also for the respect accorded the group by the wider society. Reverence occupies an important place in religious traditions as a way of understanding the human relationship to God. It prescribes certain immanence in God, an otherness, to which the proper and most appropriate response is respect. Ritualized acts of reverence —songs, dancing, lighting a candle or a fire, drumming, or keeping a watchful silence— can provide an experience of transcendence, helping believers to achieve insight into their lives in respect to the gods they worship.

Reverence can also refer to the honor and respect afforded to certain individuals with whom we have special, personal relationships. It is a common norm across cultures to show reverence for one's ancestors. This norm would include respect, honor, and deference to one's parents, grandparents, and extended family as well as to earlier and long-deceased ancestors. Reverence requires a certain level of compassion and understanding be afforded to one's ancestors, their values, and their traditions. This often includes the preservation of specific physical artifacts or land, the telling of ritualized anecdotes and their important lessons, and the maintenance and decoration of grave sites.

Recent scholarship has described reverence as the ability to understand and act upon the inner conviction that there is something larger than a human being, and therefore something larger than oneself, in any given interaction. Such a posture allows us to attempt to balance our own personal desires and ambitions with the conviction that we are in a context that is larger than simply ourselves (Goodenough & Woodruff, 2001).

Some scholars have argued that one of the purposes of education is education for reverence, that is, learning who and what it is that deserves our reverence and respect and, conversely, that which should inspire our contempt. Educating for reverence includes the development of character and a set of shared values that serve as the source for generating reverence. Reverence so understood involves a well-developed moral character and an active engagement with the community where life is shared. Because such reverence is understood to animate every human interaction, and because all person's are due respect for their unique personhood and participation in the human family, reverence can be seen as operational in every human relationship.

Further Reading: Goodenough, U., & Woodruff, P. (2001). Mindful virtue, mindful reverence. *Zygon, 36*(4), 585–95. Gross, V. (1989). *Educating for reverence: The legacy of Abraham Joshua Heschel.* Bristol, IN: Wyndham Hall. Hauerwas, S. (1981). *A community of character: Toward a constructive christian social ethic.* Notre Dame, IN: University of Notre Dame Press. Ostwald, M. (1962). *Aristotle: Nicomachean ethics, translated with introduction and notes.* Indianapolis, IN: Bobbs-Merrill. Woodruff, P. (2002). *Reverence: Renewing a forgotten virtue.* London: Oxford University Press.

Ronald J. Nuzzi

Role Taking

Role taking or perspective taking means considering the viewpoints of other persons and is at the core of cognitive developmental theories of social and moral development. Role taking is also a key process for social and moral education. As James Mark Baldwin and George Herbert Mead noted in their seminal theories, to take the role of another is the first step in developing an understanding of oneself. It is also the first step in developing an understanding of the other as a subject similar to the self. Coordinating the perspectives of self and others makes possible morality as well as enduring interpersonal and societal relationships.

We can appreciate the importance of role taking for social and moral development by observing how children play a "hide-and-go-seek" game with an adult. When it is their turn to hide, very young children will often go behind a chair or a table where they remain partially in view. For toddlers, hiding means to find a place where the adult seeker is out of view. They assume that if they cannot see the adult, the adult cannot seem them. Their assumption that the other's perspective is the same as their own is evidence of what Jean Piaget calls egocentrism, an inability to differentiate the self's perspective from that of the other. Piaget identified egocentrism in children's speech (failing to take into account the needs of the listener when telling a story) as well as in their play. Piaget went so far as to claim that young children's conversations are actually "collective monologues" in which the children make sense to themselves but not to each other.

Among adults, we also speak of egocentrism as a failure to consider the interests or concerns of the other. For example, consider the young man who makes a reservation to take his date to a seafood restaurant because he likes fish. She may have an allergy to fish or may not like fish. We would say that he should have consulted with her ahead of time about her food preferences. Was he being selfish? Egocentrism and selfishness may be related insofar as both put the self before the other. Selfishness, however, is generally the more pejorative act because selfishness involves an unwarranted pursuit of self-interest. In the case of choosing the restaurant, the young man may well have wanted to please his date, and he may have been disposed to put her interests above his. His egocentrism was due to his blindness to her perspective rather than to his conscious choice. Egocentrism is thus a kind of ignorance, which may or may not be blameworthy. The success of relationships depends upon taking the perspective of the other into account. In adult relationships, we assume that each party has at least the capacity for role taking. The young man is aware that others' needs and preferences may be different from his own. He is also aware that caring for another means attending to his/her needs and preferences. His egocentrism is, therefore, due, to a failure to apply his role-taking ability to this particular situation. In the case of children, however, role-taking ability is a basic competence, which is developed in stages through years of social interaction. Egocentric children simply cannot take the role of the other, which at times may confound unsuspecting adults. Evidence of childhood egocentrism may be found on the soccer fields of children under the age of seven who "swarm" to the ball in spite of their coaches' instructions to stay in position. Young children do not have the role-taking competence to understand the advantages of spreading out to receive a pass or to defend against a child who may break free of the swarm with the ball. In fact, young children do not understand competition either because in a game competition is a form of cooperation, an additional concept not yet understood. To compete, one has to take the role of the other in order to understand the other's intentions and strategies. Psychologists have found games to be a window into children's role-taking abilities.

In seeking to understand children's role-taking abilities, we should take care to understand the relationship between role taking and the related notion of empathy. Children manifest signs of empathy at very young ages. For example, consider how Don (age two) responded to his one-and-half-year-old sister, Karen, who was crying in pain from a stomachache. Don became distressed when he saw her, toddled over to her crib, and gave her his blanket. Although this is an example of empathy, what does it tell us about Don's ability to take Karen's role? The fact that Don brings Karen his blanket and not hers tells us a great deal about his level of role taking. Don assumes that Karen wants what he wants when he is in pain and brings Karen his blanket, even though he knows that she has her own blanket. Later in his development, Don will be able to distinguish the two perspectives, and his empathy will lead him to more adequate response.

Jean Piaget, John Flavell, Robert Selman, Lawrence Kohlberg, Michael Chandler, Monica Keller, and many other cognitive developmental psychologists have helped to chart the developmental trajectory of role taking from infancy into adulthood. The development of role taking proceeds from an initial stage of egocentrism in which no distinction is made between the point of view of the subject and that of the other. Subjects may be aware that others have a point of view, but they simply identify it with their own. At the next stage, subjects are aware that others have a different point of view, but do not take that consideration into account. For example, a young soccer player may acknowledge that his/her opponent wants to win too but does not alter his/her play. At the following stage, subjects take into account that others have different perspectives. In a soccer game, a player may notice that his/her opponent fakes one way and goes in the opposite direction. He/she will then begin to anticipate what the opponent is about to do. Finally, subjects develop to a stage of mutuality in which they become aware that the other is also engaged in role taking. The soccer player who successfully anticipated his/her opponent fake now comes to the realization that his/her opponent is able to anticipate his/her reactions. Now, instead of faking one way and going the opposite, he/she may not fake at all. But then again, he/she may fake if he/she is aware that his/her opponent is also aware that he/she may be trying to outwit him/her by not making a fake at all. Mutual role taking leads to an impasse in competitive games. In sociomoral development, mutual role taking leads to the golden rule, which underlies a commitment to such interpersonal values as trust and care and to such societal values as respect for the rule of law. Mutual role taking is also at the heart of Lawrence Kohlberg's postconventional stages of morality, which require taking a prior-to society perspective.

Encouraging children to take the role of others through role play and discussions of literature, historical issues, and moral dilemmas is at the heart of many programs fostering children's social and moral development. It has also proven to be an effective way of helping children who are struggling with interpersonal problems and poor social skills.

Further Reading: Flavell, J.H. (2004). Theory-of-mind development: Retrospect and prospect. *Merrill-Palmer Quarterly, 50*(3), 274–90. Kohlberg, L. (1984). *Essays in moral development, Volume 2: The psychology of moral development.* New York: Harper and Row. Mead, G.H. (1934). *Mind, self, and society.* Chicago: University of Chicago. Selman. R.L. (1980). *The growth of interpersonal understanding: Developmental and clinical analyses.* New York: Academic Press.

Brooke Crawford and F. Clark Power

Ryan, Kevin

Kevin Ryan was born on October 7, 1932, in Mt. Vernon, New York. Recipient of the Boston University Scholar-Teacher Award in 1989, the 1990 Association of Teacher Educators citation as one of America's Outstanding Educators, the 1998 National Award of Distinction by the University of Pennsylvania Graduate School of Education, the 1998 Award for Educational Excellence by the Paideia Society, and the 2000 Sanford N. McDonnell Lifetime Achievement Award in character education, Ryan has written and edited 20 books, written over 100 articles and developed several sets of instructional materials. Ryan has taught on the faculty of the University of Chicago, The Ohio State University (where he also served as the School of Education's Associate Dean), and Boston University.

He has served as a consultant to the United States Department of Education and the state departments of education of New York, Massachusetts, California, Georgia, South Carolina, New Hampshire, Maryland, Alabama, and Virginia. Ryan has worked overseas with educators in Portugal, Germany, Egypt, Finland, Australia, Japan, Korea, Taiwan, and Spain.

Ryan completed his Bachelor of Arts degree in English and Psychology in 1955 at St. Michael's College of the University of Toronto. Upon graduation he enlisted in the U.S. Navy and became a naval officer. Ryan earned his Master's in Teaching from Columbia Teachers College and taught high school English in Suffern, New York, for four years.

In 1963, Ryan received a Ford Foundation Fellowship to pursue doctoral work at Stanford University, and in 1966, he was offered the directorship of the University of Chicago's Master of Arts in Teaching Program. Ryan's initial research and writing at Stanford and the University of Chicago focused on the education of teachers.

In 1970 he was granted an Alfred North Whitehead Fellowship at Harvard University. A landmark moment in his professional life, he redirected his scholarly work toward moral education and came to know Lawrence Kohlberg, B.F. Skinner, Jerome Bruner, Lawrence Tribe, and others. He completed *Those Who Can Teach* with James Cooper (now in its eleventh edition, this book remains one of the leading texts in teacher education) and became interested in how a person develops moral self-regulation. When he returned to the University of Chicago, he started his first graduate seminar on theories of moral education and launched a new academic trajectory.

Ryan regards *Character Development in Schools and Beyond* (edited with George McLean and its second edition edited with Thomas Lickona) his single most important publication. He explains,

> While the volume never made much of an impact on the educational community, it did a great deal for the people involved. Among the group were Tom Lickona, Ed Wynne, William Kirk Kilpatrick, Clark Power and six or seven others. We met yearly in Washington during the early and mid-1980s and learned a great deal from one another. We also forged some deep friendships. A major intellectual outcome was to broaden our understanding of moral and character education. It helped many of us break out of the intellectual straightjacket of psychology (Values Clarification and Kohlberg's stages of moral development, both of which I found inadequate and not particularly useful in schools) and to appreciate that philosophy, theology and literature have much to offer both the study of human character and the moral life. (K. Ryan, personal correspondence, April 9, 2007)

In 1989 Ryan founded the Center for the Advancement of Ethics and Character at Boston University, the first academic center in the country to focus on the preparation of teachers as moral educators. The Center's primary mission is to support elementary and secondary school teachers in their fundamental work: helping children acquire sound moral judgment and the enduring habits of good character.

In 1993 he wrote *Reclaiming Our Schools: A Handbook for Teaching Character, Academics and Discipline* with Edward Wynne, offering educators and school leaders a clear mandate to reclaim the moral purposes of education. The title of one of his most frequently delivered talks captures this well, "Character Education: The School's Latest Fad or Oldest Mission?" In his 1996 "Character Education Manifesto" he writes,

> Character education is about developing virtues—good habits and dispositions that lead students to responsible and mature adulthood....Character education is not about acquiring the right views—currently accepted attitudes about ecology, prayer in school, gender, school uniforms, politics, or ideologically charged issues.

Ryan's publications continue to draw the distinctions among virtues, values, and views into sharp relief. His 1999 *Education Week* article with Karen Bohlin, "Virtues, Values or Views," argues that teaching virtues, such as diligence, responsibility, kindness, and honesty, provides a more reliable framework for character education in public schools than promoting subjective values or political viewpoints. In his 1999 book, *Building Character in Schools: Practical Ways to Bring Moral Instruction to Life,* Ryan and co-author, Karen Bohlin, provide school leaders and teachers with a blueprint for teaching virtue.

In August 1999, Ryan became an emeritus professor and the emeritus director of the Center for the Advancement of Ethics and Character. In December 2000, the Trustees of Boston University established the Kevin Ryan Library for Ethics and Education. From 1998 to 2000 Ryan served as President of the Character Education Partnership. Ryan remains a leader in character education and, as underscored in a recent interview, charges the next generation of academics and educators interested in developing the terrain of moral education with the following:

1. Read the Ancients and great literature for an understanding of human character and the moral life.

2. Come to understand and acknowledge the immense limitations of trying to help a young person acquire a strong character and a moral compass without engaging the deepest meaning structure of their lives (i.e., his or her religious beliefs or sense of "who am I?). Realize, too, that in trying to influence a person's character one is, indeed, treading on sacred space.
3. Respond to the fact that our character consists largely of our habits and consider approaching character education from the perspective of helping children acquire the skills of habit formation.

Being selected a member of the Pontifical Academy for the Social Sciences by Pope John Paul II in 2003 is the professional appointment about which Ryan says he is most proud. Here he enjoys collaborating with a group of international scholars to study and address world problems.

Ryan currently lives in Chestnut Hill, Massachusetts, and writes a regular column on education and family for the *Pilot* with his wife Marilyn. The greatest joy of his life, Ryan says, is his family—his wife, two married daughters, his son, and his grandchildren. "Just being in their presence, hearing them talk and laugh and get on so well with one another is the most satisfying part of my life" (K. Ryan, personal correspondence, April 9, 2007).

Further Reading: Bohlin, K., Farmer, D., & Ryan, K. (2003). *Building character in schools resource guide.* San Francisco: Jossey-Bass. The Center for the Advancement of Ethics and Character at Boston University, http://www.bu.edu/education/caec. Ryan, K., & Wynne, E. (1997). *Reclaiming our schools: A handbook for teaching character, academics and discipline* (2nd ed.). Columbus, OH: Prentice Hall/Merrill.

References: Ryan, K., Bohlin, K., & Thayer, J.O. (1996, February). *Character education manifesto.* Retrieved from The Center for the Advancement of Ethics and Character at Boston University Web site, http://www.bu.edu/sed/caec/files/manifesto.htm. Ryan, K., & Bohlin, K. (1999, March 3). Virtues, values or views? *Education Week, 18*(25), 49, 72. Ryan, K., & Bohlin, K. (1999). *Building character in schools: Practical ways to bring moral instruction to life.* San Francisco: Jossey-Bass. Ryan, K., & Cooper, J. (2007). *Those who can, teach* (11th ed.). Boston: Houghton-Mifflin. Ryan, K., Lickona, T., & McLeon, G. (Eds.). (1988). *Character development in schools and beyond* (2nd ed.). New York: Praeger.

Karen E. Bohlin

S

Schemas

The notion of schemas is one that has driven research in cognitive psychology for decades since Frederic Bartlett (1932). Jean Piaget described schemas as cognitive structures that organize an individual's operational activities. Classic schema theorists like David Rummelhart describe schemas as general knowledge structures residing in long-term memory. Schemas are sets of expectations, hypotheses, and concepts that are formed as the individual notices similarities and recurrences in experience. A schema consists of a representation of some prior stimulus phenomenon that organizes or guides the application of prior knowledge to new information (sometimes referred to as "top-down" or expectation-driven processing). Activated automatically without awareness, schemas operate constantly in the mind, being evoked by current stimulus configurations that resemble the stimuli that created the schema in the first place. Schemas decrease the amount of processing needed for encountered stimuli and are considered to be part of every encounter with the environment.

Schemas are essential to human understanding because they serve so many functions. Schemas likely operate in important ways during moral behavior, by interrelating different stimuli, filling in missing information, guiding attention and directing problem solving. Moral schemas can be described as general knowledge structures used in social information processing and cooperative behavior. Moral schemas are built from experience in social interaction. They are constructed automatically from the brain's noticing the elements in the socially relevant environment that co-vary and the cause-consequence chains that obtain from particular actions.

Piaget described intelligence as adaptation, which involves the operations of schemas in two co-occurring ways, assimilation and accommodation. Assimilation is a process of maintaining existing schemas and adapting environmental input to them. Accommodation involves modifying existing schemas in light of new information from the environment. Only a more or less stable equilibrium between them constitutes a complete act of intelligence. When assimilation outweighs accommodation, then thought evolves in an egocentric direction. When accommodation outweighs assimilation, thought evolves in the direction of imitation.

Modern schema theorists have provided more concrete descriptions of schemas. Derry's (1996) Cognitive Schema Theory outlines a hierarchy of schemas: (a) memory objects (specific small units of related characteristics), (b) cognitive fields (an activated set of memory objects), and (c) mental models (an overall meaning structure of a particular situation or experience). According to Cognitive Schema Theory, we might say that those with more complex moral judgment have a larger and better organized set of memory objects that can be activated within multiple cognitive fields and form part of complex mental models. An expert has more complex and elaborate mental models that can be activated in any number of ways because the architecture is so rich and interrelated. Those with lower levels of moral judgments have a more limited set of possible activations (fewer memory objects, cognitive fields, and mental models).

Schema structures that parse incoming sensory data are themselves unconscious and are activated automatically when their patterns match the pattern of incoming data (bottom-up activations; Marcel, 1983). The perceived regularities may or may not activate linguistic centers and, as a result, may or may not be accessible for verbal description (McCloskey & Kohl, 1983; diSessa, 1982). As Keil and Wilson (2000) point out, individuals are often able to understand something without being able to explain it to others. Keil and Wilson distinguish between two types of schema knowledge: a basic explanatory set of schemas, present even in infants, and more advanced explanatory schemas that include statements of principles and are evident through verbal performance.

Keil and Wilson's theory can help explain the disparity in findings between two measures of moral judgment development: Kohlberg's Moral Judgment Interview (MJI) and Rest's Defining Issues Test (DIT). The MJI presents moral dilemmas and requires respondents to articulate reasons for moral decisions. The MJI is scored according to Kohlberg's stage theory. The DIT is a recognition test that provides options from which respondents select. It is scored according to neo-Kohlbergian theory; items reflect three schemas: Personal Interest, Maintaining Norms, and Postconventional (formerly categorized as Kohlberg stages 2 and 3, stage 4, and stages 5 and 6, respectively). Whereas it is difficult to find anyone scoring at stage 5 on the MJI, Postconventional thinking is found to be more widespread using the DIT, especially in measuring changes based on higher education. Individuals who display Postconventional thinking on the DIT but not on the MJI may not have put their understanding into words. The DIT taps into tacit understanding, schemas that are not necessarily available in words (Narvaez & Bock, 2002).

In moral education, the development of schemas occurs on multiple levels. Students develop schemas for moral sensitivity, judgment, motivation, and action. For example, as students develop moral sensitivity from positive interaction with others who are different, they move beyond stereotyped response (assimilation: strong and narrow schema activation) to notice when someone else is in need (accommodation).

Further Reading: Derry, S.J. (1996). Cognitive schema theory in the constructivist debate. *Educational Psychologist, 31,* 163–74. diSessa, A. (1982). Unlearning Aristotelian physics: A study of knowledge-base learning. *Cognitive Science, 6,* 37–75. Keil, F.C., & Wilson, R.A. (2000). *Explanation and cognition.* Cambridge, MA: MIT Press. Marcel, A.J. (1983). Conscious and unconscious perception: Experiments on visual masking and word recognition. *Cognitive Psychology, 15,* 197–237. McCloskey, M., & Kohl, D. (1983). Naive physics: The curvilinear impetus principle and its role in interactions with moving objects. *Journal of Experimental Psychology: Learning, Memory, & Cognition, 9,* 146–56. Narvaez, D., & Bock, T.S. (2002). Moral schemas and tacit judgement or how the defining issues test is supported by cognitive science. *Journal of Moral Education, 31*(3), 297–314.

Darcia Narvaez

Secular Humanism

Secular humanism is an approach to life that exalts the power of reasoning and science with specific exclusion of any reference to a transcendent deity. It focuses on the actualization of the full personhood of individuals through the use of their natural and earthly abilities without appeal to any god or divine authority for human behavior.

Secular humanism can be understood as an evolving philosophy with many and varied manifestations. For the early part of America history, a religiously Protestant cultural hegemony was an important part of daily American life (Toumey, 1993). Other religious groups such as Catholics, Mormons, and Jews existed in highly developed subcultures, having withdrawn from the mainstream Protestant culture. This was the case in the United States through the 1950s.

In the late 1950s and early 1960s, cultural mores began to shift. The sexual revolution, including the advent of widely available birth control, the influence of mass media, rock music, and increased drug use all contributed to an enormous cultural shift. Political upheavals resulting from war protests and ongoing dissatisfaction with government added to the questioning of previously unchallenged beliefs.

Legal events in this period also contributed to the development of secular humanism. Several freedom-of-religion cases in the U.S. Supreme Court served to precipitate a reconsideration of the place of religion in American public life. *Engel v. Vitale* in 1962 (370 US 421) and *Abington v. Schempp* in 1963 (374 US 203) concluded that public schools must not force either group prayer or Bible devotions on their students.

A third U.S. Supreme Court case is the origin of the term "secular humanism," at least as it appears in scholarly literature. In *Torcaso v. Watkins* (367 US 495) in 1961, Judge Hugo Black used the term alongside Buddhism, Taoism, and Ethical Culture as examples of religions in the United States that do not teach what would generally be considered a belief in the existence of God. Although the court's decision did not define secular humanism, its comparison of secular humanism to Buddhism and Taoism suggested that it was marginal to American culture.

In the *United States v. Seeger* (380 US 163) decision of 1965, the Supreme Court ruled that a strongly held, sincere personal belief in a Supreme Being constituted a sufficient and compelling reason for conscientious objector status for draftees. An atheist could not be granted such status based on *Seeger.* Whether or not the legal precedents provided by these Supreme Court decisions helped or hindered religion's cause is a subject of ongoing debate in scholarly circles. Nonetheless, the decisions did appear to expand the validity and appeal of theistic religions vis-à-vis nontheistic ones by giving a special, government-sanctioned status to those who profess a personal belief in God.

Today, secular humanism is a popular way to describe a way of thinking and living that aims to bring out the best in people so that everyone can enjoy a high degree of happiness, success, and fulfillment. Secular humanists reject the claims of most theistic religions, especially supernatural and authoritarian beliefs. They affirm that self-responsibility is paramount and that all persons must take responsibility for their own lives, needs, and problems. Secular humanism emphasizes reason and scientific inquiry, individual freedom and responsibility, human values and compassion, and the need for tolerance and cooperation.

Religious persons are critical of secular humanism because of the exclusion of any belief in God as well as any way of relating to the transcendent. Moreover, the reliance on self-determination and self-actualization when taken to extremes can harm community and social life. In some sense, religionists argue, the denial of the existence of God is in itself a religion, with characteristics, logical consequences, and behavioral mandates that suggest an organized religious faith. Moreover, theologians counter that the theism versus atheism debate is not defined totally by disagreement about the existence of a Supreme Being. Rather, theism includes this belief plus convictions about the orderly nature of the universe, the meaning of life, the value of suffering, and the unfolding of God's will in the ordinary events of life as well as the major movements of history. Conversely, atheism involves more than just the denial of the existence of God. It includes presumptions about the nature of the universe, the narrowly described meaning of life as limited to what is seen, the avoidance and disvaluing of suffering, and the solely scientific explanation of human history.

Secular humanism understood as nonreligious is a part of modern society and contemporary cultural mores. Secular humanism experienced as antireligious continues to be a source of political and religious contention and will likely remain so as theistic believers try to support and implement educational programs and public policies that are at odds with secular humanism.

Further Reading: McGraw, O. (1976). *Secular humanism and the schools: The issue whose time has come.* Washington, D.C.: The Heritage Foundation. Roszak, T. (1972). *Where the wasteland ends: Politics and transcendence in post-industrial society.* Garden City, NY: Doubleday. Toumey, C. (1993). Evolution and secular humanism. *Journal of the American Academy of Religion, 61*(2), 275–301.

Ronald J. Nuzzi

Self-Awareness

Self-awareness refers to the mental representation of the self, the substance and content of self-understanding. For example, a 10-year-old boy understands that he is a student, a soccer player, a family member, and an iPod lover. A 14-year-old girl understands that she is a daughter, in the midst of puberty, a basketball player, and a music lover. Self-awareness is based, in part, on the various roles and membership categories that define who we are (Silvia & O'Brien, 2004). There are three facets of self-awareness: (1) personal memories, which consist of individual's autobiographical episodes that are important in thoughts about self, (2) representations of the self, which include the generalized conceptions individuals make about their selves, and (3) theories of the self, which enable an individual to identify which characteristics of the self are relevant, organize these characteristics in hierarchical order, and make claims about how these characteristics are related to each other (Fletcher & Baldry, 2000).

Self-awareness is mainly constructed by oneself and is influenced by developmental changes. Infants are not able to describe with language their experiences of themselves. Therefore, researchers use infants' visual self-recognition to assess their self-understanding. Infants are presented with images of themselves in mirrors, pictures, and other visual media. Infants who have a sense of self recognize their own images in the mirror and coordinate the images they see with the actions of touching their own bodies. Infants, therefore, initially develop a sense of rudimentary self-awareness called self-recognition at approximately 18 months of age (Duval & Silvia, 2002).

As they get older, children's self-awareness shifts from mainly self-recognition to include physical actions, body image, and material passions. For example, a 4-year-old child would describe himself as "a boy, strong, with brown eyes, swimmer, and has a hamster." Self-evaluations in early childhood tend to be unrealistically positive and represent an overestimation of personal attributes. But in middle and late childhood, self-evaluations become more realistic, partly because of increased social comparison and perspective taking. Children also begin to distinguish between their real and ideal selves. They begin to define themselves in terms of internal characteristics; for example, a 10-year-old girl might say, "I am smart, friendly, and popular" (Nezlek, 2002).

Self-awareness becomes more integrated in adolescence. Because of their advanced cognitive ability, adolescents begin to use abstract and idealistic labels in self-description. Adolescents become more self-conscious about and preoccupied with their self-understanding (Silvia & O'Brien, 2004). Their self-understanding fluctuates across situations and across time; for example, they can be cheerful one moment and moody the next. They start to construct ideal selves in addition to actual ones (Nezlek, 2002). As individuals move into adulthood, they begin to engage in self-reflection, and self-awareness is now focused more on psychological makeup. Adults are more likely to accept both their positive and their negative characteristics, and they also examine their possible selves—what they might become, what they would like to become, and what they are afraid of becoming (Fletcher & Baldry, 2000). Self-awareness in adulthood also includes life review, which involves looking back on one's life experiences, evaluating them, interpreting them, and in some cases reinterpreting them (Duval & Silvia, 2002).

Beside developmental changes, self-awareness is influenced by the sociocultural contexts. As individuals grow and construct multiple selves, self-awareness can vary across relationships and social roles (Nezlek, 2002). Fletcher and Baldry (2000) argue that selves emerge as individuals adapt to their cultural environments and are culture specific. Different cultures emphasize different values. Whatever the context, an accurate self-awareness is strongly correlated with psychological well-being. To possess an accurate self-awareness is to possess the ability to recognize and acknowledge one's strengths as well as one's areas of challenge. It is accepting one's current reality, as well as striving toward one's future potential. Individuals who possess an accurate self-awareness will embrace their strengths and will see them as tools to help themselves and to help others. Furthermore, those individuals will not be filled with false pride, but rather will be filled with the conviction that they have value and worth in society. As a result, these individuals will not display false modesty or self-devaluation that rob them of their strengths and crushes their hopes (Duval & Silvia, 2002).

Further Reading: Duval, T.S., & Silvia, P.J. (2002). Self-awareness, probability of improvement, and the self-serving bias. *Journal of Personality and Social Psychology, 82*(1), 49–61. Fletcher, C., & Baldry, C. (2000). A study of individual differences and self-awareness in the context of multi-source feedback. *Journal of Occupational and Organizational Psychology, 73,* 303–19. Nezlek, J.B. (2002, April). Day-to-day relationships between self-awareness, daily events, and anxiety. *Journal of Personality, 70*(2), 249–75. Silvia, P.J., & O'Brien, M.E. (2004). Self-awareness and constructive functioning: Revisiting "the human dilemma." *Journal of Social and Clinical Psychology, 23*(4), 475–89.

Winnie Mucherah

Self-Esteem

Self-esteem refers to a person's evaluation of self, also called self-worth or self-image. Self-evaluation is based on many domains of one's life: academic competence, athletic competence, physical appearance, social competence, close friendships, romantic appeal, and job competence (Harter, 1999). Individuals have both a general level of self-esteem and varying levels of self-conceptions in particular domains in their lives. However, self-esteem appears to have an especially strong association with self-perception in the domain of physical appearance. For example, Harter (1999) found that among adolescents, overall self-esteem is correlated more strongly with perceived physical appearance than with academic competence, social competence, behavioral conduct, or athletic competence. Self-esteem may vary with age; it appears to be high in childhood, then it declines in adolescence and increases in adulthood until late adulthood, when it declines again. Although self-esteem may decrease in adolescence, the drop is very slight (Baldwin & Sinclair, 1996).

Self-esteem is profoundly affected by feedback from significant others and peers. Parental warmth, approval, and appropriate expectations predict high self-esteem in childhood and adolescence. Encouragement from teachers is also linked to a favorable self-image. However, when support from significant others or peers is conditional (withheld unless the individual meets very high standards), individuals oftentimes engage in behaviors they consider "false"—not representative of their true self. Individuals who frequently display false-self behavior because others devalue their true self suffer from low self-esteem, depression, and pessimism about the future. Feelings of self-esteem proceed from a sense of acceptance by others (Michie, Glachan, & Bray, 2001). Successes and failures, therefore, bolster or undermine feelings of self-esteem precisely because they affect one's expectations of being accepted or rejected by others. The specific content of these contingencies may vary, depending on one's culture and upbringing, but most people would have no difficulty identifying socially desirable traits and behaviors (e.g., success, competence, physical attractiveness, and social skills) that generally lead a person to be accepted and included by others.

Individuals differ in the degree to which they anticipate that interpersonal acceptance is conditional versus unconditional. The sense that one's social world is characterized by highly conditional acceptance contributes to self-esteem problems, depression, and anxiety (Harter, 1999). This type of expectation can make an individual overly concerned and perfectionistic about their performance outcomes, highly vigilant for interpersonal feedback, and prone to instability in self-esteem and related affects (Moneta, Schneider, & Csikszentmihalyi, 2001). Ultimately, repeated experiences of conditional acceptance can produce chronically low self-esteem, as the individual learns that he or she is less worthy as a person if failing or not performing the behaviors desired by others (Harter, 1999).

The larger social environment also influences one's sense of self-worth. Caucasian American adolescents' self-esteem, for example, is less positive compared to that of African Americans, who benefit from warm, extended families and a strong sense of ethnic pride (Moneta, Schneider, & Csikszentmihalyi, 2001). Overall, adolescent girls' self-esteem is lower than that of boys. This may be due to the fact that teenage girls worry more about their physical appearance and feel more insecure about their abilities. White girls are far more likely to show declines in early adolescence than are Black girls, who are more satisfied with their physical appearance and peer relations (Moneta, Schneider, & Csikszentmihalyi, 2001). Moreover, adolescents who attend schools or live in neighborhoods where their socioeconomic status or ethnic group is well represented have fewer self-esteem problems because they have more opportunities for friendship, social support, and a sense of belonging (Baldwin & Sinclair, 1996). Therefore, it appears that schools and communities that accept the teenager's cultural heritage support a positive sense of self-worth.

Self-esteem is linked to individual's psychological well-being. High self-esteem is associated with self-confidence, an optimistic outlook on life, and a belief in the ability to cope with life's problems. And low self-esteem is linked to anxiety, depression, and increasing antisocial behavior over time (Baldwin & Sinclair, 1996). Self-esteem can be enhanced through (1) identification of the causes of self-esteem and the areas of competence significant to the individual, (2) provision of emotional support and social approval—individuals with low self-esteem come from conflicted environments in which emotional support is unavailable, (3) achievement through direct instruction, and (4) coping skills (Harter, 1999).

Further Reading: Baldwin, M.W., & Sinclair, L. (1996). Self-esteem and "if...then" contingencies of interpersonal acceptance. *Journal of Personality and Social Psychology, 71*(6), 1130–1141. Harter, S. (1999). *The construction of self: A developmental perspective.* New York: Guilford. Michie, F., Glachan, M., & Bray, D. (2001). An evaluation of factors influencing the academic self-concept, self-esteem and academic stress for direct and re-entry students in higher education. *Educational Psychology, 21*(4), 455–72. Moneta, G.B., Schneider, B., & Csikszentmihalyi, M. (2001). A longitudinal study of the self-concept and experiential components of self-worth and affect across adolescence. *Applied Developmental Science, 5*(3), 125–42.

Winnie Mucherah

Self-Understanding (Stages of)

The notion of self-understanding encompasses all that an individual can articulate about his or her self. Our self-definitions tell us who we are, as well as how to think and act—it provides the teleological values that inform goal-directed behavior and the deontological guidelines that regulate interpersonal relationships. It is in this way that self-understanding enters the moral domain.

James's (1890) classic taxonomy of the self is the point of departure for many contemporary theories of self-understanding, particularly the distinction between the self-as-knower (or "I-Self") and self-as-known (or "Me-Self"). The I-Self includes notions (or "schemes") of agency, distinctiveness, continuity, and reflection. The Me-Self is the self-concept that includes recognition of one's material characteristics, preferred activities and capabilities, along with social characteristics and relationships and spiritual or psychological traits. Thus, the content of self-understanding is operationalized as the eight different schemes.

Meanwhile, the structure of self-understanding is operationalized as stages of sociocognitive complexity with which an individual reasons about his or her self. Damon and Hart (1988) proposed a developmental model that charts progressive understanding of I-Self and Me-Self from early childhood to early adulthood. Similarly, Selman (1980) describes a sequence of self-understanding as one of four domains of interpersonal understanding. Both developmental models assume that self-understanding is highly organized as structures of social cognition, and that these structures undergo modification that can be characterized in terms of a stage. The notion of stages assumes that development proceeds discontinuously, where a transition to the next higher stage is followed by a period of consolidation at the new stage.

For Damon and Hart's model, the four levels (referred to as "self-theory") represent a sequence of progressively more sophisticated justifications for one's self-statements. At Level 1 categorical identifications have no further meaning than the label itself. A Level 2 (first present at age 9) response entails defining oneself in comparison or competition with other traits, people, or norms. In Level 3 (age 11), the self is understood in terms of interpersonal implications where the emphasis shifts to belonging. And in Level 4 (age 13), the adolescent uses systematic beliefs and life plans to justify his or her self-statements. Here, the self is understood relative to personal or moral evaluations.

Development through these four levels occurs for each content scheme. For example, self-understanding within the physical scheme develops from a simple identification of one's possessions or body (Level 1), to physical attributes that influence one's capabilities (Level 2), to explaining the significance of one's possessions in terms of social appeal (Level 3), and to finally seeing the significance of physical attributes in terms of a personal ideology or moral standard (Level 4; "I feel proud that I live in the United States... because we're free here."; Damon, Hart, Pakula, & Shupin, 1988, p. 17). Of primary importance here is that advancement in level—regardless of the scheme—is associated with moral functioning (Hart & Fegley, 1995).

Selman's developmental model of self-awareness is couched within his broader theory of interpersonal understanding. The theory describes the growth of a single sociocognitive construct through five stages and is applied simultaneously across four domains: individual (self-awareness), friendship, peer group, and parent-child (the former of which is most relevant to self-understanding). For the domain of self-awareness, children at Stage 0 see inner psychological and outer physical experiences as inextricably fused, such that emotions or thoughts are expressed physically ("My mouth told my arm [what to do]"; Selman, 1980, p. 95). In progressing through the stages, children come to see their inner experience as independent from the outer world such that lying becomes possible (Stage 1, ages 5 to 9). A Stage 2 child (ages 7 to 12) is able to see his or her Me-Self by stepping mentally into the I-Self, such that one's inner state is seen as being diverse and multiply motivated (e.g., excited but scared). Able to now see both the Me-Self as well as the I-Self, the Stage 3 (ages 10 to 15) child is aware of a volitional agency that directs his or her own behavior. And finally, an individual in Stage 4 (age 12 to adult) recognizes an unknowable aspect of his or her inner functioning beyond the I- and Me-Selves (i.e., the unconscious).

Empirical work has supported two important findings relevant to moral psychology and moral education. First, the stages/levels are developmental, that is, related to age and stage-like. And second, both content (scheme) and structure (level) are related to moral functioning such as caring action (Hart & Fegley, 1995), honesty (Derryberry & Thoma, 2005), and peer relations (Selman, 1980). With the realization that rationality does not capture all that there is to know about moral functioning, Blasi (1993) has posited that identity mediates the sometimes disjunction between what we judge to be right and how we actually behave. The stage models of self-understanding give life to Blasi's notion and, in doing so, make a significant contribution to the fields of moral education and to developmental psychology in general.

Further Reading: Blasi, A. (1993). The development of identity: Some implications for moral functioning. In G.G. Noam & T.E. Wren (Eds.), *The moral self* (pp. 99–122). Cambridge, MA: MIT Press. Damon, W., & Hart, D. (1988). *Self-understanding in childhood and adolescence.*

New York: Cambridge University Press. Damon, W., Hart, D., Pakula, K., & Shupin, J. (1988). *Scoring manual for self-understanding.* Unpublished manuscript, Clark University, Worcester, MA. Derryberry, W. P., & Thoma, S. J. (2005). Moral judgment, self-understanding, and moral actions: The role of multiple constructs. *Merrill-Palmer Quarterly, 51,* 67–92. Hart, D., & Fegley, S. (1995). Prosocial behavior and caring in adolescence: Relations to self-understanding and social judgment. *Child Development, 66,* 1346–1359. James, W. (1890). *The principles of psychology.* New York: Holt. Selman, R. L. (1980). *Growth of interpersonal understanding: Developmental and clinical analysis.* New York: Academic.

Jeremy A. Frimer

Selman, Robert L.

Robert Selman's richly textured theory based on the development of the individual's capacity to coordinate social perspectives has provided the field of developmental psychology with a powerful way to understand the development of moral character, as manifest in respectful and mature interpersonal relationships. Selman's seminal contributions have linked theory, research, and practice to suggest how children growing up can more adequately come to understand, manage, and make personal meaning of the interpersonal and moral dilemmas they face.

Selman, a professor of psychology and education at Harvard University, was born in 1942 in New York City, majored in psychology at Cornell University, and received his Ph.D. in clinical psychology at Boston University. In early clinical placements, he was struck by the inability of sociopathic prison inmates and "troubled" children to consider the point of view of other people. Selman began his research career in 1969 as a postdoctoral fellow with Lawrence Kohlberg, who became his mentor, longtime friend, and colleague. Interested in the developmental stage approach of Jean Piaget and Kohlberg, and also influenced theoretically by George Herbert Mead and Harry Stack Sullivan, Selman worked on two assumptions: that the essence of morally and socially advanced reasoning is composed of the capacity to more adequately coordinate and balance the social perspectives of all persons involved, and that peer relationships are a particularly critical arena in which normal and abnormal social capacities develop.

At the heart of Selman's theory of interpersonal development is the core perspective coordination operation—the developing ability to differentiate and coordinate the points of view of self and others through an understanding of the thoughts, feelings, and wishes of each person. Preschool children cannot clearly differentiate social perspectives psychologically, but older children learn to first differentiate one perspective (that of self or other), then to coordinate perspectives. Adolescents become able to take a "third-person" or mutual perspective on relationships, then develop interdependent perspective coordination, in which an individual's perspective is understood in the context of multiple points of view at an in-depth, societal, "generalized other" level.

Selman's research has been based in the Human Development and Psychology area (of which he was Chair from 2000 to 2004) at the Harvard Graduate School of Education and the Judge Baker Children's Center at Harvard Medical School (where he directed the Manville School for children with severe social and emotional problems from 1975 to 1990). Working in these therapeutic and academic contexts, Selman and his collaborators in the Group for the Study of Interpersonal Development moved through three phases in a practice-based research program that constructed a complex yet elegant theoretical model. Each of the three phases investigated a theoretical construct that emerged from research embedded in clinical/educational practice, which both informed and was enriched by the theory.

Using Kohlberg's interview methodology, Selman first investigated the growth of inter-personal understanding by assessing children's and adolescents' knowledge of social rela-tions through their reasoning about hypothetical social-moral dilemmas. Reasoning about friendship, for example, evolves from egocentric and one-way to more reciprocal and mutual conceptions. Ratings and observations of the children's social interactions revealed that high level interpersonal understanding does not guarantee good peer rela-tionships (known as the "gap" between thought and action), but that those with low level understanding invariably have difficulties getting along with their peers.

In a second research phase, the social perspective coordination levels were used to inves-tigate the relationship between interpersonal understanding and social action. This work constructed an analysis of levels of interpersonal negotiation strategies, in which conflict in relationships is resolved at developmental levels (impulsive, unilateral, reciprocal, col-laborative) that parallel those of interpersonal understanding. A major impetus and source of data for this phase of theoretical work was the development of pair therapy, a therapeu-tic treatment in which pairs of children who have difficulties in their peer relationships meet with an adult therapist trained to help them learn how to have fun and resolve con-flicts together. This author was an active partner in the research and theorizing done in this phase.

The third component of the theoretical model, personal meaning, is the intensity and quality of emotional investment an individual is able to make in a specific relationship. Developmental levels of personal meaning awareness were constructed in studies of ado-lescents' risk-taking behavior in the context of their relationships. Maturity—or lack thereof—of personal meaning awareness explains gaps between social thought and action, and plays an essential role in how persons manage risk.

Extending his efforts to link theory and practice, Selman recognized the implications of the "Risk and Relationship" framework for prevention and founded (and directed in the 1990s) the Risk and Prevention program at Harvard. This one-year master's degree pro-gram trains graduate students to promote the development and integration of academic and social competence in children and adolescents in a three-way partnership of university academic study, mental health agency supervision, and urban public school service. One prevention service directly influenced by the theoretical model is a literacy and ethics cur-riculum that uses high quality children's literature depicting compelling social issues to help children develop an "ethic of social relationship" and put into action their evolving awareness of respectful ways to get along with other people.

Selman's most recent work, with colleagues and students, focuses on research that inte-grates contextual and developmental influences on the social choices youth make, for in-stance, in intergroup or peer relationships, and the justifications they give for their actions. Selman's body of work is innovative in the recognition that the social-cognitive capacity of social perspective coordination is foundational for both social and moral development. His developmental theory of social awareness and the clinical/educational practices based on it hold unlimited potential to help students of moral development understand and promote sociomoral development.

Further Reading: Selman, R.L. (1980). *The growth of interpersonal understanding: Developmen-tal and clinical analyses.* New York: Academic Press. Selman, R.L., & Hickey Schultz, L. (1990). *Making a friend in youth: Developmental theory and pair therapy.* Chicago: University of Chicago

Press. Selman, R.L., Watts, C.L., & Hickey Schultz, L. (Eds.). (1997). *Fostering friendship: Pair therapy for treatment and prevention.* New York: Aldine de Gruyter. Selman, R.L. (2003). *The promotion of social awareness: Powerful lessons from the partnership of developmental theory and classroom practice.* New York: Russell Sage.

Lynn Hickey Schultz

Service Learning

Service learning is a pedagogy that engages students in forms of service to enhance their understanding of academic issues and social realities. Distinct from volunteerism, service learning is a more formally structured practice that integrates reflection and analyses of the issues students and community members encounter in addressing a public or human need. Service learning is credit-bearing (usually course-based) and built on collaboration with local agencies and human service providers. Academic credit is offered not for the experience per se, but for the learning fostered, so that assessment is a key component. While not a new concept, service learning initiatives have expanded rapidly in both secondary schools and colleges since the 1990s.

Service learning may be understood as a subset of both experiential learning (see the work of David Kolb) and community-based learning. Service learning methods are consistent with and supported by developmental theory (see Brandenberger, 1998). Jean Piaget described intelligence as an activity, emphasizing that human knowledge is developed through interaction. Human beings act on their environment to build personal understanding of reality in a process known as constructivism. Similarly, Erik Erikson described the role of agency in relation to social contexts as fundamental to personality and identity development in youth. Further, John Dewey's emphasis on the role of experience in education and the social purposes of education provide important grounding for service learning.

Advocates of service learning emphasize its reciprocal nature: when student development goals and positive community outcomes are integrated, learning is optimal. Either implicitly or explicitly, service learning is consistently framed as a means to foster citizenship or social change. And since students are placed in relational contexts, service learning has implications for moral education. Service learning offers opportunities to enhance: (1) moral sensitivity through exposure to community issues and ethical challenges; (2) moral judgment through ongoing encounters with multiple alternative perspectives; (3) moral motivation and focus through connections with people and issues that take on personal meaning; and (4) moral behavior and expertise through practice in complex contexts. Research by Boss (1994) suggests that service learning presents opportunities for both cognitive and social challenge—and related support—in a manner that prompts significant moral development.

As service learning has grown in recent decades, so has related disciplinary research examining potential outcomes (see Eyler and Giles, 1999). Best practices have been identified (see Howard, 1993), yet challenges remain. Various initiatives are labeled service learning without theoretical grounding or consistent implementation, with a subsequent impact on student outcomes (and research clarity). Some suggest that service learning may lead to an individualistic focus, circumventing attention to the role played by social structures and political forces—though many advocates use service learning to explicitly draw attention to such factors. Another challenge is to consistently attend to the community perspectives raised within the many partnerships necessary for service learning, and define reciprocal institutional roles (see Bringle, Games, & Malloy, 1999).

In sum, service learning is a creative pedagogy with implications for moral education and, more broadly, institutional ways of knowing. As an alternative to traditional expertise models and classroom practices, service learning emphasizes that context matters, that social problems have complex etiologies, and that enhanced solutions come from dialogue and cooperation.

Further Reading: Boss, J. (1994). The effect of community service work on the moral development of college ethics students. *Journal of Moral Education, 23*(2), 183–98. Brandenberger, J. W. (1998). Developmental psychology and service-learning: A theoretical framework. In R. G. Bringle & D. K. Duffy (Eds.), *With service in mind: Concepts and models for service-learning* (pp. 68–84). Washington, D.C.: American Association for Higher Education. Bringle, R. G., Games, R., & Malloy, E. A. (1999). *Universities and colleges as citizens.* Boston: Allyn & Bacon. Eyler, J., & Giles, D. E. (1999). *Where's the learning in service-learning?* San Francisco: Jossey-Bass. Howard, J. (Ed.). (1993). *Praxis I: A faculty casebook on community service learning.* Ann Arbor: Office of Community Service Learning Press, University of Michigan.

Jay W. Brandenberger

Sex Education

Sex education programs are often designed to reduce unwanted sexual activity, unintended pregnancy, the incidence of sexually transmitted diseases (STD), and the risk of HIV infection and AIDS. Some are also designed to improve relationships among young people.

Many research studies have demonstrated that sex education programs have become increasingly effective at meeting those goals. Nearly two-thirds of evaluated programs successfully reduce sexual risk taking by delaying sex, reducing the frequency of sex (including the return to abstinence), reducing the number of sexual partners, or increasing either condom or other contraceptive use. A few programs even have significant positive effects on more than one of these behaviors. Research studies also demonstrate that sex education programs, including those that focus more on use of condoms or other forms of contraception, do not increase sexual behavior.

In addition, studies demonstrated that at least some programs positively influenced factors demonstrated to affect adolescent sexual behavior or the quality of that behavior. For example, nearly all programs increased knowledge about various sexual topics and many clarified or improved values and attitudes about sexual behavior and contraceptive use, perceptions of peer norms about sexual behavior, self-efficacy to refuse unwanted sex, self-efficacy to use condoms or contraception, and motivation or intention to abstain from sex or use protection against pregnancy and STD. Some also increased communication with parents or other adults about sexual topics.

Sex education programs are quite robust. Some had positive behavioral effects that lasted for two or three years or more. Some were effective with both low- and middle-income youth, in both rural and urban areas, with girls and boys, with different age groups, with sexually experienced and inexperienced youth, and in school, clinic, and community settings. When programs found to be effective in one state were subsequently implemented in other states, they were also found to be effective there, provided they were implemented as designed.

Programs that are effective typically share common characteristics. For example, they focus on avoiding unintended pregnancy or STD, give a clear message about behaviors that either encourage or prevent these health outcomes, focus on more than just knowledge (e.g., perceived risk, values, norms, attitudes, and skills) and use interactive instructional methods that involve youth and help them personalize information.

Support for sex education and STD/HIV education in the schools is strong. A nationwide survey conducted in 2004 revealed that 93 percent of parents of junior high school students and 91 percent of parents of high school students believed it is very or somewhat important to have sexuality education as part of the school curriculum. Thus, the controversies surrounding sexuality and HIV education programs do not focus on whether these programs should be offered in school, but rather on what topics should be taught and emphasized. Despite the controversies widely emphasized in the media, 95 percent of parents of junior high school students and 93 percent of parents of high school students believed that birth control and other methods of preventing pregnancy are appropriate topics for sexuality education programs in schools.

Given the need for effective educational programs, schools have responded. Surveys show that most schools offer sexuality or HIV education. According to a 1999 nationwide study, of those schools teaching any topics in sexuality education, between 85 and 100 percent included instruction on consequences of teenage parenthood, STD, HIV/AIDS, abstinence, and ways to resist peer pressure to have sex. Between 75 and 85 percent of the schools provided instruction about puberty, dating, sexual abuse, and birth control methods. Teachers reported that the most important messages they wanted to convey were about abstinence and responsibility.

Despite the fact that most adolescents receive at least a minimum amount of sexuality or HIV education, it is widely believed by professionals in the field that most programs are short, are not comprehensive, fail to cover some important topics, and are less effective than they could be. For example, only half to two-thirds of the teachers covered how to use condoms or how to get and use other methods of contraception.

In sum, sex and STD/HIV education programs have been demonstrated to be successful at increasing knowledge, improving other factors that reduce sexual risk taking, and thereby actually reducing sexual risk-taking behavior. Contrary to the fears of some people, programs that emphasize abstinence as the safest and best approach for young people, but also encourage the use of condoms and other forms of contraception for sexually active youth, do not increase sexual behavior. Given widespread support for comprehensive sex and STD/HIV education in schools, these programs should be implemented more broadly in schools. In particular, either schools and communities should implement programs that have already been demonstrated to be effective with populations similar to their own or they should implement programs that incorporate the common characteristics of effective programs.

Douglas Kirby

Sexual Orientation

Sexual orientation is an enduring erotic, romantic, sexual, or affectionate attraction toward members of the same sex, the opposite sex, both sexes, or neither sex. It may be grouped under the larger umbrella term "sexuality," but it differs from other components of sexuality including but not limited to gender identity, which is one's psychological awareness of being male, female, some combination of both, or neither gender, and gender role, which is behavior typically associated by society as masculine or feminine. In research, the most common method to assess sexual orientation is to ask individuals how they self-identify (that is, gay, lesbian, bisexual, homosexual, heterosexual) or with whom they engage in sexual relations (behavior). These and other indirect methods of assessment falsely suggest synonymy with sexual orientation.

Sexual identity is any socially recognized label that organizationally names sexual feelings, attractions, and behaviors. The initialism LGBTQQ encompasses many of the current socially recognized sexual identities including lesbian, gay, bisexual, transgender, queer, or questioning. Initial research on sexual identity described a categorical distinction between proportions of heterosexual and homosexual sexualities, and regarded homosexuality and heterosexuality as opposites on the same continuum. However, Alfred Kinsey found that aspects of sexual orientation are neither proportional to nor necessarily consistent with each other. Subsequent research demonstrated similar inconsistencies among sexual attractions, behaviors, and identities. For example, psychologist Harry Stack Sullivan reported instances in which preadolescent close friends engaged in same-sex sexual behaviors, but this conduct had little impact on their observed current or future sexual identities as otherwise being heteronormative.

Contemporary researchers are often concerned that traditional research recruitment strategies of same-sex sexual orientation sample from self-identifying populations and therefore may not be appropriately representative of the much larger cohort of same-sex attracted individuals who may have more traditional or heteronormative erotic behaviors or sexual identities. For instance, one sex survey demonstrated that two times as many men as women self-identified as gay/lesbian or bisexual, but that the same proportion of men and women experienced same-sex erotic attractions, and more than twice as many men as women experienced any same-sex behaviors after puberty. Furthermore, in a 2000 survey of college students, participants reported approximately three times more same-sex attractions than same-sex identities or behaviors. Therefore, as scholars continue to strive to address the needs of the younger generation, they are ever-increasingly struggling to understand that today's youth—not just self-identified sexual-minority youth—may potentially doubt that their sexual orientation can be categorically isolated to homosexual or bisexual or heterosexual. In nearly every study conducted that allows young people a choice of responding to both same and opposite sex attractions, young people report varying degrees of homoerotic and heteroerotic attractions regardless of their sexual identities or sexual behaviors. For them, erotic attractions for others are not mutually exclusive, but rather fall along separate continuums.

Sexual orientation is traditionally considered an immutable quality that remains consistent over time and resistant to conscious control. Research demonstrates that it is sexual identity and behavior that are most subject to conscious choice and that are dynamic over time, not sexual arousal and attraction. Etiological theories of sexual orientation include genetic factors, intrauterine-environmental factors (i.e., hormones), and social-environmental factors. Although studies of hormone levels have yielded inconsistent results, neuroanatomic studies have found structural brain differences between homosexual and heterosexual individuals, but, with high sampling variation and inconsistent replication, these findings are subject to further verification. The current literature and a vast majority of scholars suggest that genetic factors are primarily responsible for sexual orientation as some studies report approximately 50 percent concordance for homosexuality in monozygotic males versus only 4 percent of homosexuality in brothers of nongay males.

Mammal research suggested that behavioral conditioning can induce same-sex mate preferences. However, research manipulating the environment found that same-sex conditioning persisted only in the laboratory setting. Nonhuman primate experiments utilizing unisex rearing demonstrated increased same-sex behaviors, but the behaviors significantly decreased when animals were returned to the co-ed enclosures. Isolated same-sex rearing rarely occurs in humans; therefore researchers must be careful when applying animal findings to human behavior. Moreover, many of these findings were unsuccessfully validated in later study replications.

Sigmund Freud's psychosexual stage of same-sex erotic attractions among males was arguably the earliest scientific explanation of same-sex erotic attractions resulting from an emotionally strong mother and/or the absence of a dominant, protective father. Thus, a sustained same-sex erotic attraction was either slowed normative psychosexual development or a fixation in the same-sex attraction stage. Subsequent social explanations for same-sex erotic attractions include imprinting theories and sex role theories. Imprinting theory states that strong emotional bonds formed early between same-sex individuals can lead to long-term same-sex preferences. Males demonstrating atypical sex-role behaviors may develop confused sex or gender identities and prefer female sex roles, thus increasing their chances of same-sex erotic preferences. However, none of these theories are scientifically validated.

In conclusion, sexual orientation may not derive from any one cause or theory, but may represent a set of biological and psychosocial interactions multiply determined by individual, interpersonal, and cultural experiences.

Further Reading: Kinsey, A.C., Pomeroy, W.B., & Martin, C.E. (1948). *Sexual behavior in the human male.* Philadelphia: W.B. Saunders. Laumann, E.O., Gagnon, J., Michael, R.T., & Michaels, S. (1994). *The social organization of sexuality: Sexual practices in the United States.* Chicago: University of Chicago Press. Lippa, R.A. (2000). Gender related traits in gay men, lesbian women, and heterosexual men and women: The virtual identity of homosexual-heterosexual diagnosticity and gender diagnosticity. *Journal of Personality, 68,* 899–926. Savin-Williams, R.C. (2005). *The new gay teenager.* Cambridge, MA: Harvard University Press. Savin-Williams, R.C., & Cohen, K.M. (1996). *The lives of lesbians, gays, and bisexuals: Children to adults.* United States: Wadsworth/Thomson Learning.

Tamara B. Pardo

Shweder, Richard Allan

Richard Allan Shweder (1945–) is at the vanguard of the Cultural Psychology movement, emphasizing multiplicity and cultural validity in social science theory and methods. Bringing a cultural perspective to moral psychology, he has proposed the Three Ethics Approach that encompasses diverse moral reasons. Shweder is also a leading public intellectual. He addresses moral and legal topics that arise when different cultures come into contact.

Shweder is the William Claude Reavis Distinguished Service Professor with the Department on Comparative Human Development at the University of Chicago. He received his Ph.D. in social anthropology from the Department of Social Relations at

Harvard University in 1972. His primary fieldwork site for more than three decades has been the temple town area of Bhubaneswar, India. Shweder has received numerous honors and awards, including being selected as Carnegie Scholar and Fellow of the American Academy of Arts and Sciences. He has also been an Invited Fellow with the Stanford Center for Advanced Study in Behavioral Sciences, the Institute for Advanced Study in Berlin, and the Russell Sage Foundation. Shweder was born in New York, New York. He is married to Candy Shweder, and they have two children.

Culture Theory

At the heart of Shweder's scholarship is the observation that human development across cultures is characterized by "universalism without uniformity." According to Shweder, all people share common concepts. For example, the justice concept of treating like cases alike and different cases differently is recognized universally. But cultural communities (both within and across countries) are not uniform in their elaboration and application of general concepts. For example, different peoples have different views of which cases are alike and different (e.g., animals, children, humans, fetuses, souls). They also differ as to when justice should supersede or be superseded by other concepts (e.g., communal harmony). Given the observation that universal concepts translate into culturally diverse ways of thinking, feeling, and living, Shweder has put forth two key guidelines for cultural psychology and psychology in general. (1) Psychology must give serious attention to cultural multiplicity in addition to the prevalent focus on universals. (2) Psychology must highlight the rationality characteristic of diverse peoples. From these guidelines also follow a need to be wary of overassimilation of indigenous concepts or classification of such concepts as developmentally inferior. Taking a cultural psychology perspective, Shweder has provided incisive analyses on topics such as moral reasoning, emotional functioning, gender roles, and conceptions of health and suffering.

Culture and Morality

Shweder has distinguished three Ethics of Autonomy, Community, and Divinity in order to encompass culturally diverse moral reasoning. Each ethic highlights different conceptions of the self and includes different moral reasons. Briefly, the Ethic of Autonomy presupposes a conception of the self as an individual with needs and preferences. Moral reasoning within this ethic addresses individuals' interests, well-being, and rights, and equality between individuals. The Ethic of Community rests on a presupposition of the self as a member of social groups. Here moral reasoning pertains to role-related duties and concern for the interests, customs, and welfare of groups. The Ethic of Divinity presupposes a self that is a spiritual or religious entity. Reasoning within this ethic addresses divine and natural law, lessons from sacred texts, and concerns with purity and pollution. Research has shown the presence of the three ethics in different cultural communities in countries such as Brazil, India, Finland, Japan, the Philippines, and the United States. Research has also indicated significant cultural variation in use of the ethics.

Culturally Valid Methods

In an effort to gain culturally valid understanding of peoples' moral psychology, Shweder and his colleagues have used innovative research methods. These methods include naturalistic observations of child-adult conversations about moral matters, recordings of everyday behaviors that convey moral meanings (e.g., sleeping arrangements), and interviews about locally salient issues (e.g., a Hindu Indian son engaging in the disrespectful and polluting practice of eating chicken shortly after his father's death). As a cultural psychologist, Shweder's concern has been to employ methods that both capture the breadth of moral concepts and uncover the reasoning and logic that undergird peoples' indigenous moral judgments and behaviors.

Public Policy and Law

In varied media, Shweder has addressed public policy implications of the meetings of different cultures. Among the issues addressed by Shweder are globalization, female circumcision, and the American government's handling of the Branch Davidians in Waco, Texas. Thus, Shweder has taken on what he regards as an essential role of the cultural psychologist, providing the public with insight into the rationality of other cultures.

Further Reading: Haidt, J., Koller, S.H., & Dias, M.G. (1993). Affect, culture, and morality, or, is it wrong to eat your dog? *Journal of Personality and Social Psychology, 65,* 613–28. Jensen, L.A. (2004). *Coding manual: Ethics of autonomy, community, and divinity (revised).* Unpublished manuscript, Clark University. Jensen, L.A. (1998). Moral divisions within countries between orthodoxy and progressivism: India and the United States. *Journal for the Scientific Study of Religion, 37,* 90–107. Miller, J.G. (2006). Insights into moral development from cultural psychology. In M. Killen, & J. Smetana (Eds.), *Handbook of moral development.* New York: Lawrence Erlbaum. Rozin, P., Lowery, L., Imada, S., & Haidt, J. (1999). The CAD triad hypothesis: A mapping between three moral emotions (contempt, anger, disgust) and three moral codes (community, autonomy, divinity). *Journal of Personality and Social Psychology, 76,* 574–86. Shweder, R.A., Goodnow, J., Hatano, G., LeVine, R., Markus, H.R., & Miller, P. (2006). The cultural psychology of development: One mind, many mentalities. In W. Damon & R. Lerner (Eds.), *Handbook of child psychology* (6th Ed.). New York: Wiley. Shweder, R.A. (2003). *Why do men barbecue? Recipes for cultural psychology.* Cambridge, MA: Harvard University Press. Shweder, R.A., Minow, M., & Markus, H.R. (2002). *Engaging cultural differences: The multicultural challenge in liberal democracies.* New York: Russell Sage Foundation. Shweder, R.A. (1991). *Thinking through cultures: Expeditions in cultural psychology.* Cambridge, MA: Harvard University Press.

Lene Arnett Jensen

Six Pillars of Character

The Six Pillars of Character are the foundation of the Josephson Institute of Ethics, Character Counts! education program. The Six Pillars are ethical values believed to develop character and transcend race, class, creed, and gender and include trustworthiness, respect, responsibility, fairness, caring, and citizenship. Each pillar is defined and summarized as delineated by the Josephson Institute of Ethics (2002).

Trustworthiness

A reliance on the integrity, ability, or character of an individual is essential to every relationship, whether a parent-child relationship or teacher-pupil relationship. The set of principles one should abide by to be trustworthy are as follows: demonstrate integrity, be honest, keep promises, and be loyal.

Respect

A regard for the worth of people, including self-worth, knowing one's safety and happiness matters to others, and understanding all people are important and worthy. The set of principles one should abide by to demonstrate respect are as follows: value all persons, live by the golden rule (do unto others as you would have them do unto you), respect other's dignity, privacy, and freedom, be courteous and polite, be tolerant and accepting of differences, and avoid violence in all forms.

Responsibility

Individual duty or obligation to make choices that are ethically right. The principles that frame the pillar of responsibility include: doing one's duty, being accountable, pursuing excellence, practicing self-control, planning and setting goals, choosing positive attitudes, being self-reliant, being proactive, being persistent, being reflective, setting a good example, and being morally autonomous. As free human beings it is our responsibility to make correct ethical decisions, thus developing stronger character.

Fairness

Following the standards of what is right without involving one's own feelings. To be completely fair a decision must be made without prejudice and impartiality. Fairness commonly goes hand in hand with the construct of justice. The principles of fairness include: consistency, listening, openness, refrainment from judging others, treating people equally and equitably, and following fair procedures.

Caring

Showing love, regard, or concern for the well-being of others. The set of principles outlined for the demonstration of caring are as follows: compassionate, kind, loving, considerate, empathic, charitable, and unselfish.

Citizenship

The duties, rights, and responsibilities of an individual to the community, state, and nation. Demonstration of citizenship includes a variety of activities including voting, volunteer work or military service. The principles of citizenship include: be a good citizen, do your share, help the community, play by the rules, and respect authority and the law.

Together, the Six Pillars of Character of the Character Counts! educational program—trustworthiness, respect, responsibility, fairness, caring, and citizenship—have the potential to build and promote character in America's youth.

Further Reading: Josephson Institute of Ethics. (2002). Character development seminars. In *Victory with honor: Summit on youth sports* (pp. 42–55). Los Angeles: Josephson Institute of Ethics.

Nicole M. LaVoi and Erin Becker

Skepticism and Amoralism

"Skepticism," which connotes an attitude of doubt over the possibility of attaining knowledge or justified belief, derives from a philosophical position associated with the

Skeptikoi (literally "enquirers" or "questioners") of Ancient Greece. Classically, skeptics were much exercised by the way that sense perception and the application of logic, human beings' best methods of inquiry into truth, tended to yield contradictory judgments or generate ever-greater uncertainty. Today, the sources of skepticism are more varied, but the term is still associated with epistemological doubt, either directed toward all forms of knowledge or used only in reference to a specific knowledge domain. A moral skeptic is one who denies or calls into question truth in ethics.

There are at least three broad varieties of moral skepticism that we label dogmatic moral skepticism, Pyrrhonian moral skepticism, and practical moral skepticism. Roughly speaking, dogmatic moral skepticism is the view that it is impossible to know whether any substantive moral belief is true. Pyrrhonian moral skepticism, named after the celebrated ancient Greek radical skeptic Pyrrho of Ellis, is at once weaker and more skeptical than dogmatic moral skepticism. Pyrrhonian moral skeptics share with dogmatic moral skeptics grave doubts about the possibility of ethical truth but they go beyond dogmatic moral skeptics in doubting even whether one can ever be certain that moral knowledge is impossible. So, while a dogmatic moral skeptic would claim, for example, that one can never say for sure whether spanking children is wrong, a Pyrrhonian moral skeptic would even doubt whether one can say for sure whether one can never say for sure whether spanking children is wrong. Pyrrhonian moral skepticism, then, is a kind of moral agnosticism. Practical moral skepticism stands apart from both dogmatic moral skepticism and Pyrrhonian moral skepticism in that it is concerned not with reasons to entertain moral beliefs but rather with reasons to be moral. The most familiar form of practical moral skepticism does not deny that there might be some good reasons to believe that some act in a set of circumstances—for example, disposing of a factory's toxic effluents into a source of local drinking water—might be morally wrong. It merely doubts or denies that moral reasons should sometimes or always motivationally override nonmoral reasons, such as narrow self-interest and the bottom line.

Skepticism is relevant to moral education because of its reputation as a source of moral degradation. In particular, skepticism is thought to lead to immorality and moral relativism. Both of these charges are highly dubious. Holding and acting on substantive moral beliefs is not inconsistent with skepticism. It is characteristic of skepticism to doubt that the truth about moral matters can be known with certainty not to reject morality out of hand. In point of fact, skepticism is compatible with theologically grounded moral beliefs. The Christian virtue of faith, for example, and faith's requirement to let go of ordinary standards of rational justification are nourished by doubt about the possibility of knowing God's will. As for moral relativism, skepticism is better considered as a means of avoiding moral relativism than as a source of moral relativism. Far from denying the possibility of moral knowledge, moral relativism positively asserts the contrary: moral claims are justifiable relative to an individual's moral perspective (i.e., individual moral relativism or moral subjectivism) or to some set of social values and norms (i.e., social or cultural relativism). What moral relativists do deny is that there is a universal standard of moral judgment. It is true, however, that a radical form of dogmatic skepticism which holds that all substantive moral beliefs are false can feed into amoralism.

Amoralism implies an absence of morality. While "amoral" and "immoral" are commonly treated as synonyms, it is more proper to speak of immorality as deviance from an accepted moral code (or the selective or inconsistent application of a moral code one accepts), whereas amorality is the explicit rejection of any moral code or a failure to acknowledge that one is bound by a moral code. Amoralism, in this sense, is a recognized trait of the severe social and emotional disorder known as psychopathy. Amoralism understood as a philosophical position—as opposed to a moral-psychological construct—is usually referred to as "nihilism." Friedrich Nietzsche (1911–1968), philosophy's best known advocate of nihilism, affirms the essential falsehood of all moral systems (and other sources of human purpose and value), deplores the ways in which morality governs people's lives, and regrets how moral constraints prevent what he considers to be the best and most able from realizing their full potential.

Further Reading: Empiricus, S. (2000). *Outlines of scepticism* (2nd ed.). (J. Annas & J. Barnes, Trans.). Cambridge, England: Cambridge University Press. (Original work from ca. 200 B.C.E.) Nietzsche. F. (1968). *The will to power.* (W. Kaufmann & R.J. Hollingdale, Trans.). New York: Vintage. (Original work published 1911.) Sinnott-Armstrong, W. (2006). *Moral skepticisms.* New York: Oxford University Press.

Bruce Maxwell

Skinner, B. F.

B.F. Skinner's view of human behavior is properly called operant behaviorism (or behavior analysis). Behavior itself, overt (public) and covert (private), is the basic subject matter of operant behaviorism. Unlike traditional psychology and social science, Skinner did not look at behavior as an indirect means of studying something else, such as mind or brain or cognition or personality.

Early in his career Skinner played a major role in distinguishing between respondent (or classical) conditioning and operant (or instrumental) conditioning. Respondents are elicited by events coming before behavior (sudden loud noises elicit pounding hearts; high temperatures elicit sweating), while operants are strengthened in reinforcement or weakened in punishment and extinction by what follows behavior. An operant is a class of responses, not a single response. One can open a door in a variety of ways, for example, each way resulting in an open door. Clarifying this difference represents a very important advance because earlier thought assumed that each response we make requires some compelling prior stimulus. By showing that the consequences of our actions affect subsequent behavior, Skinner took the lead in moving the study of behavior away from the mechanistic, stimulus-response psychology of the time.

An operant analysis can be expressed in terms of an A-B-C formulation, where A, B, and C stand for antecedent events, behavior, and consequences. Skinner referred to the subtle and complex relations among these three elements as the contingencies of reinforcement (or punishment). It would be difficult to exaggerate the fundamental importance of an A-B-C analysis. Some psychologists believe that any system of education that neglects any component of the analysis is bound to be weak. Consider, for example, the lecture method, a conspicuous method of instruction at most levels of education. Yet one cannot say that it is an especially effective method of teaching. Why? Perhaps because of the heavy emphasis on the lecture itself (A), the relative neglect of learner action during the lecture (B), and the failure to provide enough feedback for student responses when they do occur (C).

An A-B-C analysis has been effectively applied to a wide variety of behaviors. Consider an example of how attention to consequences made a big difference in one classroom where students were said to be unmotivated. Even though the students were not completing many assignments, they were given daily access to several highly motivating activities, such as free time and access to computers. Motivation to complete assignments increased markedly simply by making preferred activities contingent on task completion. The only major change in the classroom was when the activities were provided.

It is often very difficult to see the contingencies at work in everyday life, especially when one has learned to "look inside" a person for an explanation of behavior. The following episode exemplifies the problem. As an 18-year-old high school student, Jill on occasion bought clothes for herself and charged her parents' account. Her parents found out about her excursions when they saw Jill wearing something new or when a new balance statement arrived. Scolding Jill failed. When asked for an explanation of her daughter's behavior, her mother spoke of Jill's "uncaring attitude toward the family" and her "irresponsibility." This explanation focused on two assumed inner factors. A behavior analysis requires looking elsewhere for an explanation. As an indicator of the strength of Jill's habit, the analyst might try to determine how often Jill charged the account in the past. He might then look for pertinent relationships between Jill's shopping and situational factors, especially the antecedents and consequences that accompany the act of shopping. It might be found, for instance, that Jill is likely to buy clothes when she has a date with a new boyfriend and when she is accompanied by a girlfriend who encourages shopping. Consequences also influence buying. For instance, she gets attention and compliments when she wears new clothing. She also likes what she sees when she models purchases in front of a mirror. And, if she likes the way the new clothes feel, tactile consequences are in play. The fact that Jill's parents, complaints to the contrary, ultimately paid for her purchases is another consequence that might account for Jill's actions.

It can be seen that Jill's mother turned to inner factors to explain her daughter's clandestine shopping. In contrast, a behavior analysis focused on the contingencies of reinforcement, on clothes buying itself (its frequency), on antecedents (when it occurred and with whom), and on consequences following the purchases (attention, visual and tactile stimulation, and parents' payment). This analysis relied not on dubious explanations but on observable actions and their link with environmental events.

Skinner's message to educators and parents is that they can place themselves in a favorable position to analyze behavior by paying close attention to what people do and the conditions under which they do it. Although this is a very practical message, it is in conflict with the traditional belief that behavior is an expression of feelings and states of mind.

Unabridged dictionaries list thousands of words that refer to human personality and behavior. Skinner was alarmed at the large number of words that give rise to what he called explanatory fictions. An explanatory fiction is a statement that merely describes in different terms the behavior that is supposedly explained. For example, to say that a student who turns in assignments late, criticizes school, and plays truant has a negative attitude toward school can be appropriate and helpful if "negative attitude" is a summary description of the behaviors—late assignments, criticism, and truancy. But if one goes on to say that the student engages in these behaviors because of a negative attitude, a fictitious explanation has been given: negative attitude and the behaviors, although expressed differently, actually mean the same thing. Skinner's concern has less to do with explanatory fictions per se than with the general effect of their use: they tend to stop inquiry into the genetic and environmental origins of behavior and hence have hindered the development of a science of human behavior.

Skinner carried these ideas forward to an analysis of human values and morality. Values refer to reinforcement, to those behaviors, outcomes, and objects that are sought and favored (reinforced) by the practices, customs, and expectations of communities. It is, of course, true that individuals develop a sense of honesty, tolerance, kindness, and so on, but Skinner thinks the origin of behavior is to be traced to what directly happens to people, rather than to intervening states. Social contingencies (practices, customs, expectations) change behavior directly; they do not implant a trait or virtue. In response to the classic question, "Is a person moral because he behaves morally, or does he behave morally because he is moral?" Skinner answers, "Neither." The person behaves morally and is called moral because he lives in a particular kind of social environment.

Further Reading: Skinner, B.F. (1971). *Beyond freedom and dignity.* New York: Bantam Books. Skinner, B.F. (1974). *About behaviorism.* New York: Alfred A. Knopf. Skinner, B.F. (1989). The origins of cognitive thought. *American Psychologist, 44*(1), 13–18.

Frank J. Sparzo

Social and Emotional Learning

Social and emotional learning (SEL) involves processes through which children and adults develop fundamental emotional and social competencies to recognize and manage emotions, develop caring and concern for others, establish positive relationships, make responsible decisions, and handle challenging situations constructively. SEL takes place within the context of safe school, family, and community environments that support children's development and provide opportunities and recognition for successfully applying these competencies.

SEL is based on the knowledge that our emotions and relationships affect how and what we learn. It is grounded in research findings that social and emotional skills can be taught and that they promote positive development, reduce problem behaviors, and improve children's academic performance, citizenship, and health-related behaviors (Greenberg et al., 2003). Academic outcomes promoted by SEL include greater motivation to learn and commitment to school, increased time on schoolwork and mastery of subject matter, improved attendance and graduation rates, improved grades and test scores, and better prospects for constructive employment and work satisfaction (Zins et al., 2004).

Intrinsically, learning is a social process. Students do not learn alone but rather in collaboration with their teachers, in the company of their peers, and with the support of their families. Emotions can facilitate or hamper children's learning and ultimate success in school. Because social and emotional factors play such an important role, schools and families must attend to this aspect of the educational process for the benefit of all students.

The Collaborative for Academic, Social, and Emotional Learning (CASEL), a scientific group devoted to advancing the science and evidence-based practice of SEL, has identified five core groups of social and emotional competencies (CASEL, 2005):

- **Self-awareness**—accurately assessing one's feelings, interests, values, and strengths; maintaining a well-grounded sense of self-confidence
- **Self-management**—regulating one's emotions to handle stress, control impulses, and persevere in overcoming obstacles; setting and monitoring progress toward personal and academic goals; expressing emotions appropriately
- **Social awareness**—being able to take the perspective of and empathize with others; recognizing and appreciating individual and group similarities and differences; recognizing and using family, school, and community resources

- **Relationship skills**—establishing and maintaining healthy and rewarding relationships based on cooperation; resisting inappropriate social pressure; preventing, managing, and resolving interpersonal conflict; seeking help when needed
- **Responsible decision-making**—making decisions based on consideration of ethical standards, safety concerns, social norms, respect for others, and likely consequences of various actions; applying decision-making skills to academic and social situations; contributing to the well-being of one's school and community

Evidence-based SEL programs teach these competencies intentionally and sequentially, as well as in ways that are developmentally appropriate. They establish contexts where these skills can be expressed, practiced, and encouraged throughout the day. Optimally, programs are implemented in a coordinated manner throughout the school, from preschool through high school; lessons are reinforced in the classroom, during out-of-school activities, and at home; educators receive ongoing professional development in SEL; and families and schools work together to promote children's social, emotional, and academic success (Devaney et al., 2006).

Much of the educational power of SEL lies in its providing educators with a common language and framework for organizing a wide range of activities, for example, prevention and youth development programs, character and citizenship education, health promotion, service learning, and differentiated instruction. By addressing the shared social and emotional variables that mediate positive behavioral outcomes across these approaches, SEL provides a coordinated, integrating framework for promoting student success (Elias et al., 1997).

As an education movement, SEL has gained momentum with the growth of research findings connecting SEL interventions with improvements in academics, including standardized test scores. At the policy level, Illinois has provided leadership in recognizing SEL as essential to education, developing Social and Emotional Learning Standards that specify the skills all children should have before graduation. Other school districts, states, and countries are building from the Illinois standards to guide their SEL policies.

Further Reading: Collaborative for Academic, Social, and Emotional Learning. (2005). *Safe and sound: An educational leader's guide to evidence-based social and emotional learning (SEL) programs.* (Illinois ed.). Chicago: Author. Devaney, E., Utne O'Brien, M., Resnik, H., Keister, S., & Weissberg, R.P. (2006). *Sustainable schoolwide social and emotional learning (SEL): Implementation guide and toolkit.* Chicago: CASEL. Elias, M.J., Zins, J.E., Weissberg, R.P., Frey, K.S., Greenberg, M.T., Haynes, N.M., et al. (1997). *Promoting social and emotional learning: Guidelines for educators.* Alexandria, VA: Association for Supervision and Curriculum Development. Greenberg, M.T., Weissberg, R.P., Utne O'Brien, M., Zins, J.E., Fredericks, L., Resnik, H., et al. (2003). Enhancing school-based prevention and youth development through coordinated social, emotional, and academic learning. *American Psychologist, 58*(6/7), 466–74. Zins, J.E., Weissberg, R.P., Wang, M.C., & Walberg, H.J. (Eds.). (2004). *Building academic success on social and emotional learning: What does the research say?* New York: Teachers College Press.

Roger P. Weissberg, John W. Payton, Mary Utne O'Brien, and Susan Munro

Social Development

Social development is the emergence and continuing growth of an individual's capacity for social interaction and interpersonal relationships. Anyone who has held a young baby knows that social development begins among the very young. Infants exhibit the rudimentary underpinnings for social interaction. Their perceptual abilities allow them to be socially active by opening and closing their mouths, smiling, vocalizing, and imitating faces. When distressed or needy, infants convey their desire for food, contact, warmth, or comfort. This early emergence of signals is a normative developmental precursor to more elaborate sociability.

Social development is shaped through the medium of parent-child attachment. Attachment, an affectionate emotional bond, is a biologically rooted desire of infants to draw themselves closely and securely to a protective adult. Babies become attached to caregivers who are predictable, are consistent, and respond appropriately to their signals and other physical needs. Bowlby (1982) outlined four phases of parent-infant attachment, beginning with a preattachment phase in which the infant does not distinguish the caregiver from other people. Between three and six months of age, a unique bond forms between parent and child in phase two. The infant exhibits a more diverse array of attachment behaviors—separation anxiety, locomotor skills, and stranger anxiety—in phase three, about six months to three years of age. In the final stage (third year and on), child and parent progress to a more complex, interactional relationship, largely defined by the child's growing awareness that other people (i.e., the caregiver) have needs of their own and that the child's wishes may not always come first. The three identified patterns of attachment are secure, insecure-avoidant, and insecure-resistant (Ainsworth et al., 1978). The attachment relationship forms a foundation for healthy personality development and for later social relationships and throughout the life span.

Social play is an important context for the ongoing development of children's social competence. Moreover, through play, children develop their sensorimotor and cognitive skills. Early observational studies of play identified five types of play: (a) solitary—playing alone with toys but near a caregiver; (b) onlooker—watching other children engaged in play but not themselves involved; (c) parallel—playing in close proximity to another child but with his/her own toy; (d) associative—playing with other children with the same toy or equipment but each child in his/her own way, and (e) cooperative play—playing in concert with other children around a common game or shared object. By the end stage of that progression, children are able to respond to the actions and ideas of other children. Research on children's social participation activities reveals that sociodramatic play (e.g., role play) and playing games with rules increase from ages two through six.

Social development continues through child and adolescent peer relations and friendships (Berndt, 1982). A major psychosocial task of childhood and adolescence is the creation and maintenance of peer relationships and friendships. For children, peers and friends are sources of amusement and excitement. They are the play partners of choice and provide easily accessible relationships for shared activities and companionship. Developmental growth is fostered through these social relationships: children learn about behavioral norms and knowledge, create and view their own self-impression, contribute to their own sense of self-worth, and have opportunities for self-disclosure. As children mature cognitively and emotionally, adolescence sets the stage for more complex and intimate social relations. With a more defined sense of identity and autonomy, early adolescents band together in same-sex groups known as cliques. A same-sex clique is often informally associated with an opposite-sex clique. The association between the two groups creates a setting for more intimate relationships and possibly individual dating. Close, stable friendships emerge in adolescence, relationships in which the individuals continue to enhance their social skills, the process of self-revelation, and the exploration and expression of their sexual selves. The mutual role taking of intimate adolescent relationships is foundational to a successful social passage from adolescence into adulthood.

The early adulthood period often crystallizes patterns of social development. The intimate relationships of adulthood are qualitatively different from those of adolescence in that each person has clearly established a self-identity and freely chooses to share that self with another. As intimate relationships deepen, many are carried forward throughout the life span. Many adults continue the processes of dating, cohabitation, mate selection, and courtship. Some intimate relationships are formally acknowledged through marriage and the creation of new families. The consistent hallmark of stable, adult social relationships is mutuality, a state in which one person cares for the other as much as oneself, and these relationships may be sexual or nonsexual.

Further Reading: Ainsworth, M., Blehar, M.C., Waters, E., & Wall, S. (1978). *Patterns of attachment.* Hillsdale, NJ: Erlbaum. Berndt, T.J. (1982). The features and effects of friendships in early adolescence. *Child Development, 53,* 1447–1460. Bowlby, J. (1982). *Attachment and loss: Vol. 1. Attachment.* New York: Basic Books. Hartup, W.W. (1992). *Having friends, making friends, and keeping friends: Relationships as educational contexts.* Urbana, IL: ERIC Clearinghouse on Elementary and Early Childhood Education.

James M. Frabutt

Social Justice

Social justice represents an ideal quality or condition of human equality, respect, and right relationships. It is a rich yet complex concept. While concerns about justice are long-standing, the term social justice developed in the nineteenth century, and highlights both social ends and means. It can be a goal as well as a personal virtue. What constitutes social justice may be understood in cultural, philosophical, religious, and social science contexts.

What is normal and just in one culture—for example, the exclusion of women or minority groups from voting, or punishment by the state for violating a religious tradition—may be considered morally unacceptable or even abhorrent in another. Discussion of social justice thus raises issues of power and access. Long-established cultural patterns that have facilitated acceptance of differential treatment may be resistant to change. Yet many views of social justice include respect for cultural differences as well as hope that inherent tensions can be overcome through dialogue and cooperation.

An examination of justice is central to philosophy. John Rawls (1999) suggests that principles of justice are those that rational, free persons would come to without regard for personal gain. Other philosophers have focused on distributive justice (how fairly socioeconomic resources are shared across social groups) and procedural justice (whether decision making and organizational processes are fair and equitable). Other paradigms are also instructive: restorative justice examines how relationships or equality can be restored after injustice, while a more recent focus on the justice of recognition emphasizes the need to include and respect those of all identities despite differences from the status quo. All such conceptions of justice are germane to social justice, though justice terms are often held up as ideals with limited attention to definitions.

Religious and theological views also frame understanding of social justice. World religions present overlapping (though sometimes divergent) conceptions of justice and how to achieve it. Catholic Social Teaching, for example, highlights the principles of human solidarity and the common good. In the Jewish tradition the notion of "tikkun" encourages social action and reparation, and the Islamic Qur'an emphasizes justice and human equality.

Various lines of research relevant to understanding social justice have emerged within the social sciences. One focuses on theories of equity, procedural fairness, and the role of beliefs about justice (e.g., is the world a just place?) in human motivation. Another builds upon the work of Lawrence Kohlberg, whose theory of moral reasoning emphasizes principles of justice at higher (postconventional) levels of development. Kohlberg maintained, and presented cross-cultural data to support, that individuals cognitively construct personal frames of morality, and at advanced stages incorporate more universal principles of justice (versus a focus on social conventions or personal interest). While more recent conceptualizations in the cognitive-developmental tradition focus less on justice per se, research by Wendorf, Alexander, and Firestone (2002) using a measure of moral reasoning known as the Defining Issues Test confirms the role that justice concerns play in moral development. Related developments in positive psychology promote a vision of human flourishing that includes work for the common good.

Given the importance of both understanding and promoting social justice, many proponents emphasize the role of education (see Griffiths, 2003). One of the primary challenges in work for social justice is overcoming historically pervasive beliefs in human inequality. Even the sciences are not immune to such: from Darwin to current controversies about intelligence, assumptions of differing human capacities have been supported in scientific circles then later refuted.

Those seeking to promote social justice must also foster understanding of social systems that may promote or inhibit inequalities. Indeed, it is often those who are critical of such systems that use the term "social justice." Yet, as Friedrich Hayek (see Novak, 2000) emphasized, no democracy can control all the factors that may yield injustices, while systems that attempt to command individual actions or economies are also problematic. The challenge is to promote a vision of social justice that activates the imagination of those of differing political and cultural persuasions. Indeed, it may be argued that social justice is dependent on human imagination, on our ability to envision social equality, and on the means to promote it. Then we may be energized to foster habits of mind and relevant skills to build new and just social systems.

Further Reading: Griffiths, M. (2003). *Action for social justice in education: Fairly different.* Philadelphia: Open University Press. Novak, M. (2000, December). Defining social justice. *First Things: A Journal of Religion, Culture, and Public Life 108,* 11–13. Rawls, J. (1999). *A theory of justice.* Cambridge, MA: Belknap Press of Harvard University Press. Wendorf, C. A., Alexander, S., & Firestone, I. J. (2002). Social justice and moral reasoning: An empirical integration of two paradigms in psychological research. *Social Justice Research, 15*(1), 19–39.

Jay W. Brandenberger

Social Responsibility

Social responsibility is the perceived obligation or sense of commitment to the common good exhibited by an individual, group, or institution. While it may begin with direct connection to and caring for others, social responsibility is often characterized by a broader frame of reference to complex human concerns mandating sustained collaboration and social change. Social responsibility includes personal behavior—what one should do or avoid in moral contexts—but, for many, also involves proactive attention to systemic challenges. Similarly, it is not limited to professional codes or boundaries, but is aspirational.

Individual responsibilities are often framed in contrast with the rights of citizenship. While the language of rights is quite well developed, especially in America, notions of concurrent responsibilities are often left vague. Since obligations and roles develop in context, cultural factors are salient in framing expectations of responsibility. The motivation or capacity for responsibility may be influenced by the political state, laws, customs, and religious dynamics.

Formal study of responsibility begins well in philosophy. Deontology emphasizes the role of duties: note especially the moral imperatives outlined by Immanuel Kant. Another philosophical tradition, virtue ethics, focuses attention on matters of character and the shaping of the person. William Schweiker emphasizes that responsibility extends both traditions and is central to the overall study of ethics. Our ability to respond to others—to both understand their needs and consider positive actions—is fundamental to moral thought and behavior. Social responsibility has also been associated with psychological well-being, and with what it means to lead a good life (Markus et al., 2001).

Social responsibility also extends to groups and institutions. In recent decades various professional organizations have outlined conceptions of responsibility in relation to broad social challenges. Medical doctors have formed Physicians for Social Responsibility to extend attention to issues of war, prevention, and environmental health (notably, their efforts were recognized with the Nobel Peace Prize). In business, corporate social responsibility (CSR) has emerged as an important factor for both consumers and producers. Whether corporations should or can be altruistic has been contested by those who emphasize the primacy of stockholders, but most agree that "strategic" CSR (actions taken to enhance the public image of companies) is a growing enterprise (see Lantos, 2002). Others argue that business is best developed as an intentional prosocial enterprise that serves public need.

Research in psychology by Markus, Ryff, Conner, Pudberry, and Barnett (2001) examines how conceptions of responsibility vary across domains such as family, work, and community, and documents differences by educational level. Research participants who had completed college demonstrated more individualistic and abstract notions of responsibility (with more frequent reference to the self and the balancing of demands) compared to participants with high-school educations (who more often framed responsibility in relation to keeping commitments and adapting to external demands). The authors also point out that, especially in America, responsibility to others is often weighted less than (and seldom exceeds) concern for personal needs in deliberation regarding responsibility, while in more collectivist cultures, interpersonal responsibilities are more frequently salient.

The Kohlberg tradition in moral psychology emphasizes responsibility to others (in terms of principles of justice), though in ways that also have been critiqued as individualistic. Yet a focus on the self is natural in responsibility considerations: a sense of responsibility is linked with a sense of personal agency—indeed, the concept of responsibility seems meaningless if no personal control is possible in a situation. Augusto Blasi suggests that individuals develop a sense of responsibility through experience, through seeing themselves as agents in the world and reflectively appropriating a sense of self as responsive. Others (see Freire, 2000; Berman, 1997; Brandenberger, 2005) echo that social responsibility is learned through experience, through reciprocal interaction and relationships.

Recent theory development suggests that the sense of self as responsible and committed to social concerns may serve as an important link between moral reasoning and moral action (responsibility focuses on one's moral role after something is judged right or wrong). Toward this end, Berman (1997) suggests that social responsibility has become a field of study (one can now earn a master's degree in social responsibility) that integrates beliefs and action, character and ethics, caring and political engagement. He also outlines a variety of educational strategies that have been shown to foster social responsibility. Given increasing human interdependence and the complexity of social challenges, our potential to enhance social responsibility—both in local communities and across boundaries—is critical.

Further Reading: Berman, S. (1997). *Children's social consciousness and the development of social responsibility.* Albany: State University of New York Press. Brandenberger, J.W. (2005). College, character, and social responsibility: Moral learning through experience. In D. Lapsley & F.C. Power (Eds.), *Character psychology and character education* (pp. 305–34). Notre Dame, IN: University of Notre Dame Press. Freire, P. (2000). *The pedagogy of freedom: Ethics, democracy, and civic courage.* Lanham, MD: Rowman & Littlefield Publishers, Inc. Lantos, G. (2002). The ethicality of corporate social responsibility. *Journal of Consumer Marketing, 19*(3), 205–30. Markus, H.R., Ryff, C.D., Conner, A.L., Pudberry, E.K., & Barnett, K.L. (2001). Themes and variations in American understandings of responsibility. In A.S. Rossi (Ed.), *Caring and doing for others: Social responsibility in the domains of family, work, and community* (pp. 349–99). Chicago: University of Chicago Press.

Jay W. Brandenberger

Socialization

Socialization is the process of learning—a process by which individuals learn the rules, norms, behaviors, and competencies needed to function competently in a given societal niche. Through the process of socialization, children learn the expected and appropriate behaviors common to most members (i.e., norms) of a given group. Socialization involves coming to an understanding of the culture (i.e., values, truths, rules, expectations, and goals) of one's group, whether that group is a family, school, religion, or nation.

In developmental terms, the process of socialization begins at birth. As children develop the capacity for language, they become even more active actors in the process of socialization. Daily, informal, and often repetitive developmental interactions and experiences are the building blocks of socialization. While much socialization does happen during childhood, socialization does continue throughout the life span. Even as adults age, they take on new roles or statuses—each requiring a new and more sophisticated level of socialization. As adults engage new learning opportunities, explore broader social networks, and integrate novel life experiences, the process of social learning continues.

Those who provide the socialization—known as agents of socialization—can be parents, close friends, peers, extended family members, the media, religious groups, and broad societal norms. Parents, however, serve as the earliest and most immediate teachers for their children, conveying through hundreds of parent-child interactions each day the adaptive skills and behaviors necessary for social well-being and functioning. Maccoby (1992) outlined four key teachings of parent-child socialization: (a) to avoid deviant behavior; (b) to contribute both to self and family economic support; (c) to develop and sustain close relationships; and (d) to be able to rear children of their own. Parents socialize their children in several ways. Parents use rewards and punishments. Parental authority figures model behavior that they hope their children will observe and imitate. Parents usually use direct teaching to try to impart values and lessons, especially those that they have found personally useful. Children, too, shape the socialization process, making it bidirectional. Their natural interests and inclinations contribute to the socialization context.

Other socialization agents are critical as well. Through the process of formal education, schools deliver a steady curriculum of specific capabilities, knowledge sets, and ways of thinking both logically and critically. Peers can exert a powerful socialization influence on other children, setting a tone of acceptance or disdain for a variety of behaviors, thoughts, and modes of expression. Religion functions as a socializing agent through its codified set of beliefs, values, and practices that lay a foundation for living adhered to by followers of that faith. Even within religions themselves, milestones (e.g., baptism, bar mitzvah) symbolize and commemorate one's growing socialization into the particular religious community of believers. The media is a pervasive agent of socialization, portraying through images, text, audio, and video formats that which is new, novel, unique, and acceptable.

At a very young age, children receive input from a variety of sources about what it means to be a girl or a boy in society. Since gender is a socially defined construct, children are socialized into gender-based attitudes, knowledge, and behaviors, a process known as gender role socialization (Ruble & Martin, 1998). Gender role socialization conveys an array of behaviors and attitudes that are deemed socially acceptable for a given sex. Through myriad encounters with parents, peers, teachers, and close friends, there are covert and overt directives that encourage wanted gender role behaviors and discourage unwanted gender role behaviors. Mechanisms to explain gender role socialization include identification theory, social learning theory, and cognitive development theory.

Another specific category of socialization centers on children's emerging awareness of and linkage to one's own ethnic group, referred to as ethnic or racial socialization. Ethnic and racial socialization refers to messages and practices that provide information concerning the nature of race status as it relates to: (a) personal and group identity; (b) intergroup and interindividual relationships; and (c) position in the social hierarchy (Thornton et al., 1990). Parents may provide both direct and indirect (i.e., nonverbal) messages to their children that focus on racial barriers, racial pride, discrimination and prejudice, and racial/ethnic identity.

Further Reading: Maccoby, E.E. (1992). The role of parents in the socialization of children: An historical overview. *Developmental Psychology, 28,* 1006–1017. Maccoby, E.E., & Martin, J.A. (1983). Socialization in the context of the family: Parent-child interaction. In E.M. Hetherington (Ed.), *Handbook of child psychology: Vol. 4. Socialization, personality, and social development* (pp. 1–101). New York: John Wiley and Sons. Ruble, D.M., & Martin, C.L. (1998). Gender development. In N. Eisenberg (Ed.), *Handbook of child psychology: Vol. 3. Social, emotional, and personality development* (5th ed., pp. 933–1016). New York: Wiley. Thornton, M.C., Chatters, L.M., Taylor, R.J., & Allen, W.R. (1990). Sociodemographic and environmental correlates of racial socialization by black parents. *Child Development, 61,* 401–409.

James M. Frabutt

Sociomoral Reflection Measure

Measures of sociomoral reflection, developed by John Gibbs and colleagues, assess one's maturity in moral judgment, which is one's justification of benevolent and fair behavior. Four different measures of sociomoral reflection exist: the 1982 Sociomoral Reflection

Measure, the 1984 Sociomoral Reflection Objective Measure, the 1987 Sociomoral Reflection Objective Measure—Short Form, and the 1992/1995 Sociomoral Reflection Measure—Short Form (SRM-SF). The most recent measure of sociomoral reflection, the SRM-SF, has been the more widely used measure, has a broader target age range, and also has stronger evidence for reliability and construct validation compared to the other three. Thus, the SRM-SF is the only measure of sociomoral reflection that is discussed hereafter.

The theoretical basis for the SRM-SF has a strong Kohlbergian foundation, in that one is posited to progress in moral judgment from a superficial level to a more mature level in which the individual has a more profound understanding of the meaning and basis of interpersonal relationships and society (Gibbs, Basinger, & Fuller, 1992). The progression is depicted as movement through two moral development levels, each comprising two stages. Each stage depicts qualitatively different justifications pertaining to benevolent and fair behavior. Stages 1 and 2 make up the immature level of moral reasoning. Both stages are concrete justifications, confusing morality with either physical power and authority (stage 1; e.g., "your friend will beat you up if you do not keep your promise to him") or pragmatic deals (stage 2; e.g., "your friend will keep a promise to you if you keep a promise for him now"). The mature level consists of stages 3 and 4. The mature moral reasoner justifies moral judgments by appealing to the bases of interpersonal relationships (stage 3; e.g., "you should keep a promise to your friend to keep his trust in you") or society (stage 4; e.g., "you should keep a promise to your friend because trust and respect is necessary for solid relationships and friendships"). It is important to note that sociomoral maturity, as measured by the SRM-SF, does not include Kohlberg's theoretical stages 5 and 6, the postconventional level. According to Gibbs et al. (1992), stages 5 and 6 are simply more verbally complex forms of stages 3 and 4—not theoretically distinct from them.

The SRM-SF is a production measure of moral maturity, meaning that participants are asked to describe or explain their moral justification rather than to choose which of several already-provided justifications they prefer. The unique aspect of the SRM-SF is that it does not include moral dilemmas. Rather, it uses 11 different moral behaviors, such as keeping promises, helping others, and obeying the law. Participants are asked to rate how important each behavior is (very important, important, or not important) and then write why they think it is important or not important. The written responses then must be scored to determine which moral reasoning stages (1 through 4) were used for each of the 11 questions. The highest stage is recorded for each question and then averaged across the 11 questions to produce an SRM-SF score that ranges from 1 to 4.

The SRM-SF is designed to measure moral maturity in participants ranging in ages from 9 to 100. Completion time ranges from 15 to 40 minutes (the latter being more common with younger participants). The SRM-SF can also be group or individually administered.

The psychometric properties of the SRM-SF are very good to excellent. Acceptable levels of reliability have been evidenced, with highly significant test-retest correlations, excellent indices of internal reliability, and very strong interrater correlations (Gibbs et al., 1992). Evidence for convergent validity includes high correlations between the SRM-SF and the Moral Judgment Interview, Kohlberg's measure of moral judgment. The SRM-SF also correlates with other theoretically relevant variables, such as social perspective taking and prosocial behavior (Gibbs, Basinger, & Grime, 2003). Regarding discriminant validity, the SRM-SF showed no correlation with social desirability and consistently classified delinquent adolescents as being developmentally delayed in moral maturity (Gibbs et al., 2003). In regards to gender differences, SRM-SF research has shown that females score higher than males at certain ages, specifically in early adolescence (Garmon, Basinger, Gregg, & Gibbs, 1996).

Further Reading: Garmon, L.C., Basinger, K.S., Gregg, V.R., & Gibbs, J.C. (1996). Gender differences in stage and expression of moral judgment. *Merrill-Palmer Quarterly, 42*(3), 418–37. Gibbs, J.C., Basinger, K.S., & Grime, R.L. (2003). Moral judgment maturity: From clinical to standard measures. In S.J. Lopez & C.R. Snyder (Eds.), *Positive psychological assessment: A handbook of models and measures* (pp. 361–73). Washington, D.C.: American Psychological Association. Gibbs, J.C., Basinger, K.S., & Fuller, D. (1992). *Moral maturity: Measuring the development of sociomoral reflection.* Hillsdale, NJ: Lawrence Erlbaum Associates.

Tonia Bock

Sports and Character

A common assumption is that sports develop character; however, few empirical studies support this contention. In reality sports can just as likely build character as they can undermine positive character. Generally most scholars agree that sports have the potential to build character, as they provide a ready-made context in which to test and develop social, emotional, and cognitive as well as physical skills, but sports alone do not automatically build character (Bredemeier & Shields, 2006).

Coakley (2007) refutes key assumptions regarding the relationship between sports and character including: sports do not possess unique qualities in which character develops; sports may not develop character, but select-in and filter-out individuals with character traits valued by coaches; and individuals can have positive or negative experiences in sports and perceptions of those experiences. Sport experiences vary greatly, even among individuals on the same team or in the same family. A universal assumption that sport builds character is misinformed. Coakley asserts character is more likely to develop when the athlete is encouraged to critically think about sports, to develop all facets of his or her identity, and to be given a wide variety of experiences and responsibilities outside of competitive sports.

If the goal is to increase the likelihood that character will develop in and through sports, then awareness of the explicit processes and expertise needed to achieve the goal should be considered and employed deliberately and consistently. While little empirical evidence exists to support efficacy of the following suggested strategies, based on research in the classroom—also an achievement climate—these may provide utility in sports contexts.

Character develops within a moral-motivational sport climate created by adults—coaches, parents, and administrators—who possess requisite skills and expertise. It takes deliberate and conscious effort and a high degree of expertise to create a moral-motivational climate in which character can develop. In essence, the coach-athlete relationship takes on an apprenticeship quality, where the expert coach provides experiences and creates a climate in which the novice athletes can learn, test, and refine character skills and virtues. The moral component of the sport climate rests not only on acting with fairness and care for everyone—including opponents, referees, and spectators—but on doing the right thing for the right reason. The moral component emerges out of Kohlberg's structural developmental theory of moral reasoning, as well as from the school of thought that a few virtues are universal—such as fairness/justice and care. An individual or team within a moral-motivational sport climate does the right things for the right reasons and intrinsically values the sport experience for its own sake, above and beyond competitive advantage or personal satisfaction.

The second component to understanding and promoting character through sports, some believe (see Bredemeier & Shields, 2006; LaVoi & Power, 2006), is motivation. The motivational component provides rationale and impetus for why and how people act within sports. Two motivational theories are proving to be useful in understanding how the achievement context of sports and character development intersect—Achievement Goal Theory (Nicholls, 1983; Duda, Olson, & Templin, 1991) and the Self-Determination Theory (Deci & Ryan, 1987). Achievement Goal Theory facilitates understanding how individuals who possess a disposition to focus on mastery and self-referenced achievement compared to a focus on outcome, winning and outperforming others can lead to good/poor sport and adaptive/maladaptive behaviors. Sport climates also reflect a focus on mastery and outcome (Sefritz, Duda, & Chi, 1992). Research consistently demonstrates that a mastery goal orientation and a mastery motivational climate are linked to adaptive behaviors and positive character. The Self-Determination Theory posits that humans have three inherent needs—to feel a sense of belongingness, being cared about, and being known; to feel competent; and to feel autonomous and in control of one's own destiny. The degree to which these three needs are met determines the quality of one's motivation, ranging from amotivation to intrinsic. When all needs are satisfied, intrinsic motivation is more likely that which can lead to human flourishing, development, and optimal performance.

Bredemeier and Shields (2006) suggest coaches can develop character through teaching athletes perspective taking, empathy, and role taking, in addition to providing opportunities for dialogue about team rules, sportsmanship, fair play, right and wrong, and team values. Character may also develop through team norms, shared expectations for specific actions, based on moral ideals where members of the team hold each other accountable to act in certain ways. A team in which character is likely to develop is characterized by a high degree of caring for and responsibility to the good of each individual member, for the team as a whole, and for those outside the team. Alternatively, character is more likely to develop when coaches, parents, and sport administrators are in agreement regarding the focus on sport, are taught explicitly how to create a mastery motivational climate, and meet athletes' needs (LaVoi & Power, 2006). However, research-based sport character educational interventions are scarce, and there is a need to develop effectiveness testing. Character Counts! Sports: Pursuing Victory with Honor is one of the more well-known transmittal-based sport character educational programs.

Further Reading: Bredemeier, B.L., & Shields, D.L. (2006, March). *Sports and character development,* Series 7 (1). President's Council on Physical Fitness and Sports. Coakley, J. (2007). *Sport in society* (9th ed.). New York: McGraw-Hill. Deci, E.L., & Ryan, R.M. (1987). The support of autonomy and the control of behavior. *Journal of Personality and Social Psychology, 53,* 1024–1037. Duda, J.L., Olson, L., & Templin, T. (1991). The relationship of task and ego orientation to sportsmanship attitudes and the perceived legitimacy of injurious acts. *Research Quarterly for Exercise and Sport, 62,* 79–87. LaVoi, N.M., & Power, C.F. (2006). Pathways to fostering civic engagement in collegiate female athletes: An exploratory study. *Journal of College and Character, 7*(3). Nicholls, J.G. (1983). Conceptions of ability and achievement motivation: A theory and its implications for education. In S.G. Paris, G.M. Olson, & H.W. Stevenson (Eds.), *Learning and motivation in the classroom.* Hillsdale, NJ: Erlbaum. Sefritz, J.L., Duda, J.L., & Chi, L. (1992).

The relationship of perceived motivational climate to intrinsic motivation and beliefs about success in basketball. *Journal of Sport and Exercise Psychology, 14,* 375–91.

Nicole M. LaVoi and Erin Becker

Stage Theory

Stage theory is a type of conceptual tool used to model human growth and development. In a stage theory, developmental achievement is viewed not as a continuous line moving ever upward through time but more like the steps of a staircase, where developmental plateaus are reached after significant and qualitative change in thought structures have occurred.

Jean Piaget established the stage theory approach to human development during his original research on stages of cognitive growth (sensiomotor intelligence, preoperational thought, concrete operational thought, and formal-operational thought). The Piagetian conceptual and empirical criteria for a theory of development to be considered a "stage theory" include the following:

a. *Qualitative differences.* Stages are qualitatively different from each other in terms of cognitive structures or ways of thinking; each stage is qualitatively different from other stages in terms of approaching the same type of task, such as moral judgment.

b. *Structured wholes.* Each stage is a structured whole, a patterned process of thinking, a worldview or perspective. Such a structured whole consists of an integrated set of mental operations that account for how the person makes sense of, or performs operations on, the contents of his or her world, including moral issues.

c. *Invariant sequence.* Each stage develops out of the previous one, and a person must progress up the hierarchy one step at a time without skipping or reversing any of the stages. An individual can become fixated at a particular stage, regress, or even proceed rapidly, but all people go through the same stage sequence.

d. *Hierarchically integrated.* A higher stage is constructed on the foundation of the previous stage, reintegrating it into a more highly differentiated, flexible, and complex stage, which is more adequate than the previous stage to resolve problems, such as moral dilemmas.

e. *Cultural universality.* All persons, regardless of their sociocultural setting, can be expected to go through the same stages. Nevertheless, different cultural ecologies may promote, moderate, or hinder progress through stages.

According to Piagetian stage theory, stages are not simply the result of internal factors (nature) or external factors (nurture) but are forms of equilibrium constructed out of an interactive exchange of thought structures and the structure of the environment. Stage theory stresses the activity of the internal thought structures on the external environment through a process of accommodation (changing thought structures to fit the environment) or assimilation (fitting the environment into existing thought structures). When thought structures no longer adequately explain and can no longer assimilate an experience, a person is said to be in a state of disequilibrium and will achieve equilibrium when new thought structures are developed to satisfactorily fit experience. Stages do not match particular ages, although modal age ranges exist for each stage.

Beyond Piaget's stage theory of cognitive development, Lawrence Kohlberg's stage theory of moral judgment is the clearest example of a Piagetian stage theory. Kohlberg claimed that Piagetian criteria listed above are satisfied by at least the first five of his six stages (i.e., obedience and punishment orientation, instrumental purpose and exchange, mutual interpersonal expectations, good relations, social systems and conscience mainte-nance, prior rights and social contract). Robert Selman's related developmental model of social cognition is also a Piagetian stage theory.

Kohlberg, with Cheryl Armon and other colleagues, made a distinction between hard and soft stage theories. The distinction is based primarily on the satisfaction of Piagetian criteria and the role of conscious reflection in the acquisition of a stage. In a hard stage theory, the structure of cognitive-neural behavior is transformed largely unconsciously and, as noted above, such changes satisfy Piagetian criteria. In contrast, soft stages are quasi-structural stage theories that do not satisfy fully Piagetian criteria, and the affective and self-reflective characteristics of a person play a role in soft stage advancement. Exam-ples of soft stage theories, in Kohlberg's view, included his model of moral types, Piaget's model of heteronomous and autonomous morality, as well as life-span stage models pro-posed by Jane Loevinger, Robert Kegan, James Fowler, and William Perry.

Kohlberg and colleague John Snarey also distinguished two other forms of stage theory that are not based directly on Piagetian criteria: the functional and the cultural-age stage models of development. Functional stages differ from hard structural stages in several ways, but the most critical is that functional stages do not represent simply cognitive structures, but also evolving levels of ego functioning responding to culturally scheduled developmental crisis or tasks. Functional changes are psychosocial, rather than simply cognitive or moral-philosophical ones; they represent a psychology of biologically rooted ontogenetic growth interacting with culturally rooted social requirements, which produce functional stages of psychosocial growth. Erik H. Erikson's model of psychosocial stages exemplifies a functional stage model. Cultural age models view the life cycle as divided into successive age periods as defined by a particular cultural group, delineated primarily by shifts in culturally defined roles or milestones (e.g., ascent to adulthood).

Snarey and David Bell integrate all four types of stage theories on a continuum with Piagetian-structural stage and cultural-age models defining the extremes and functional stage models in the middle of the continuum. Soft stage models are placed between hard structural stage models and functional stage models. Stage theory, while not without con-troversy, provides a useful method of conceptualizing human development and continues to guide fruitful research and effective programming for enhancing cognitive, social, and moral development.

Further Reading: Kohlberg, L. (1984). *Essays on moral development: Volume II. The psychology of moral development: The nature and validity of moral stages.* San Francisco: Harper & Row. Piaget, J. (1977). The stages of intellectual development in childhood and adolescence. In H. Gruber & J. Voneche (Eds.), *The essential Piaget* (pp. 814–19). New York: Basic Books. (Original work pub-lished 1955.) Snarey, J., Kohlberg, L., & Noam, G. (1983). Ego development in perspective: Struc-tural stage, functional phase, and cultural age-period models. *Developmental Review 3,* 303–38. Snarey, J., & Bell, D. (2003). Distinguishing structural and functional models of human develop-ment: A response to "What transits in identity status transition?" *Identity: An International Journal of Theory and Research, 3*(3), 221–30.

Peter L. Samuelson and John Snarey

Stages of Religious Judgment

Fritz Oser's theory of the development of religious judgment profoundly influenced the psychology study of religion, particularly in Europe. Oser began to develop his theory just after James Fowler had begun his study of faith development. Both Oser and Fowler relied heavily on Lawrence Kohlberg's cognitive developmental theory of moral development for their theories but did so in very different ways. While Fowler used a narrative approach for interviewing and relied heavily on Erik Erikson for his stage descriptions as well as for his understanding of how development itself takes place, Oser adopted a rigorously Piagetian structuralist approach. Unlike Fowler's Stages of Faith, which focused broadly on epistemological and identity development, Oser's stage of religious judgment centered explicitly on religious understanding. Oser was interested in how people thought about God not in some abstract and distant way but as a moral constant in their lives and in the world.

Building on the moral dilemma interview method of investigating moral development, Oser devised a set of dilemmas for exploring the development of religious judgment. Oser's dilemmas involve both moral and religious content. For example, the Paul Dilemma tells the story of a medical school student who makes a vow to God that he will devote his life to serve the poor if his life is spared in an impending plane crash. The Paul Dilemma and other dilemmas evoke thinking about the nature of God and God's relationship to human beings and to the world more generally. What does it mean to make a promise to God? Is it possible to communicate with God? If so, does God communicate with us, and if so how? Is it possible to influence God's will through good deeds or through prayer? How can we explain events like a plane crash in relationship to God's will? How do we explain human freedom in terms of God's will? These are but a few of the questions that Oser's interviews provoke.

Through careful cross-sectional analysis, Oser identified a sequence of six stages of religious judgment. Oser claimed that these stages are not derivative of Piaget's logical stages or Kohlberg's moral stages. Appealing to theology as well as to empirical data, Oser held that religious judgment is an autonomous cognitive domain and, therefore, that religious stages are "mother-structures" constituting their own domain.

According to Oser, religious judgment development starts from stage 0 in which children do have the conceptual framework for differentiating and coordinating different kinds of external forces including God. At stage 1, children believe that God acts in the world and in their lives but that God is a blind external force beyond human comprehension or influence. Oser refers to this notion of God as "*deus ex machina*" and calls stage 1 heteronomous insofar as God's power is completely beyond human comprehension and influence. All that humans can do in response to God's power is to react. At stage 2, children believe that God and humans have what Oser calls a "*do ut des*" relationship. God rewards and punishes and can be influenced through prayer, worship, and promises, such as Paul's. Stage 2 is characterized by bargaining with God and by the expectation that God's actions are within human control. Stage 3 begins in early adolescence and is characterized by a strict differentiation between God and the human realm. Unlike at stage 3 in which God is conceptualized like the Greek gods, as a "superhuman," God at stage 3 is ontologically distinct from the human. This sharp differentiation between God and the world leads to a chasm between the human and the divine in which the world proceeds according to its own laws without God's involvement. Oser refers to this as a stage of absolute autonomy. Although humans are not compelled to acknowledge God, one can choose to have a relationship with God on a personal level. At stage 4, which Oser finds in late adolescence and early adulthood, individuals begin to see God as the "ground" of human freedom of action. Often individuals think of God as having a plan for human history and seek to define their role within God's infinitely vast and complex cosmic order. At stage 5, which is the highest stage for which Oser has clear empirical evidence, the relationship between the human and the divine is expressed as intersubjectivity. Loving social engagement becomes a way of expressing God's love. God's immanence and transcendence, and human freedom and dependence, are coordinated and experienced in a way that Oser describes as "strange and marvelous" (Oser, 1991a, p. 12). Oser sometimes describes a stage 6 in which the individual experiences the "fulfillment of absolute meaning" as a "highest possible structure of...religious consciousness" (Oser & Gmünder, 1991, p. 81).

Further Reading: Oser, F. K. (1980). Stages of religious judgement. In C. C. Brusselmans (Ed.), *Toward moral and religious maturity* (pp. 277–315). Morristown, NJ: Silver Burdett. Oser, F. K. (1985). Religious dilemmas: The development of religious judgement. In C. G. Harding (Ed.), *Moral dilemmas, philosophical and psychological issues in the development of moral reasoning* (pp. 275–90). Chicago: Precedent Publishing. Oser, F. K. (1991a). The development of religious judgement. In F. K. Oser & W. G. Scarlett (Eds.), *Religious development in childhood and adolescence* (pp. 5–25). San Francisco: Jossey-Bass, Inc. Oser, F. K. (1991b). A logic of religious development. In K. E. Nipkow, J. W. Fowler, & F. Schweitzer (Eds.), *Stages of faith and religious development: Implications for church, education, and society* (pp. 37–64). New York: Crossroad. Oser, F., & Gmünder, P. (1991). *Religious judgement: A developmental approach.* Birmingham, AL: Religious Education Press.

F. Clark Power

Stages, Nature of

Stage theories of development assume that change is patterned and sequenced. It has a direction and goal, a *telos* or endpoint, a final stage whose vision of mature functioning is critical to developmental explanation. Developmental progression is explained by noting how closely it approximates the normative endpoint represented by the final stage.

Stage theories come in many varieties. Stages of motor and physical development chart patterns of change that are largely under maturational control. Sigmund Freud's psychosexual stage theory describes how libido is invested successively in the (oral, anal, phallic, genital) erotogenic zones. In Freud's theory, fixation could occur at any stage, resulting in possible neuroses and dysfunction. Erik Erikson's "epigenetic" sequence of ego development stages describes eight psychosocial challenges that are encountered across the life course from infancy to senescence.

Stage theory in the cognitive developmental tradition is perhaps the classic usage of the concept. Jean Piaget famously proposed a sequence of four broad stages that describe the development of logico-mathematical and scientific reasoning from infancy to adolescence. The common view received is that Piaget took a "hard" line on what counts as stage development. Each stage is characterized by a general cognitive structure that unifies reasoning across a broad range of content. The sequence of stages unfolds in a constant order of succession without skipping or regression. Stages do not merely replace one another but rather each successive stage subsumes the capacities of early stages in a dynamic process of hierarchical integration. Movement from stage-to-stage represents discontinuous, saltatory change in the quality of reasoning. Children at different stages see the world in different ways, representing differences in kind of intelligence, not differences in amount.

This ostensible Piagetian stage theory was elaborated further by Lawrence Kohlberg's moral stage theory. Kohlberg insisted that true developmental stages describe structured totalities that are transformed in qualitatively distinct ways across an invariant sequence that is observed universally. Holistic consistency and invariant sequence are the two most important features of stages, according to this view.

However, several decades of research has not unequivocally vindicated the received view of Piagetian stage theory. Research has shown, for example, that Piagetian tasks that share the same underlying logical structure are nonetheless solved at very different ages—a phenomenon that Piaget called horizontal decalage. Moral reasoning has shown evidence of regression and variation relative to the dilemma type, casting doubt on the two core assumptions of "hard" stage criteria: invariant sequence and holistic consistency of responding across different contents.

It is now better understood that this evidence is contrary only to the received view of Piagetian stage theory, but not Piaget's own view of the matter. Piaget did not propose hard stages. Rather, stages should be viewed as taxonomic classifications much the way biologists classify species on the basis of their structural characteristics, although in this case it is species of intelligence that are stage-typed. Moreover, Piaget's view of stages is entirely consistent with evidence of stage variations by content (horizontal decalage) given his view that cognitive structures are organized around specific actions and therefore always retain an element of domain specificity.

During the 1970s and 1980s two prominent "neo-Piagetian" stage theories were developed, mostly with the aim of better explaining horizontal decalage while keeping faith with the broader tenets of Piaget's theory. According to Robbie Case, cognitive development is driven by increased automaticity of cognitive operations that frees up more attentional resources for working memory. For Juan Pascual-Leone, cognitive development is driven by increases in the size of mental capacity, or M-space, that increases one unit every two years. These theories were attractive because the language of attention and mental capacity promised a tighter integration with the information-processing paradigm that was ascendant in the field of cognitive development. Moreover, these theories offered an explanation for horizontal decalage: tasks that share the same underlying logical structure are solved nonetheless at different ages because such tasks place different demands upon working memory.

There are additional stage models in the moral domain that are some distance from the strict notions of invariant sequence, hierarchical integration, and structural unity laid down by Kohlberg. Nancy Eisenberg has proposed an age-developmental account of prosocial reasoning that makes no assumptions about invariant sequence. The "partial structures" model of distributive justice reasoning has soft notions of structural unity that allows for "content" differences in reasoning about fair sharing. Reasoning about social conventions is an evolving dialectical struggle between affirmation and negation of social conventions that builds cognitive disequilibria into the very core of the stage theory. Although the stage-and-sequence tradition in developmental psychology has waned in influence, and few new stage theories have been proposed in recent years, stage theory is valuable as a powerful heuristic to describe developmental change, although the search for explanatory mechanisms must be sought elsewhere.

Further Reading: Campbell, R.L., & Richie, D.M. (1983). Problems in the theory of developmental sequences: Prerequisites and precursors. *Human Development, 26,* 156–76. Feldman, D.A. (2004). Piaget's stages: The unfinished symphony of cognitive development. *New Ideas in Psychology, 222,* 175–231. Flavell, J. (1971). Stage-related properties of cognitive development. *Cognitive Development, 2,* 421–53. Lapsley, D. (2005). Moral stage theory. In M. Killen & J. Smetana (Eds.), *Handbook of moral development* (pp. 37–66). Mahwah, NJ: Lawrence Erlbaum Associates. Snarey,

J., Kohlberg, L., & Noam, G. (1983). Ego development in perspective: Structural stage, functional phase and cultural age-period models. *Developmental Review, 3,* 303–38.

Patrick L. Hill and Daniel K. Lapsley

Steadfastness

Steadfastness is a disposition of choice to embrace and pursue a worthy goal despite obstacles. As a moral virtue, steadfastness is not to be confused with obstinacy or the tenacious pursuit of an ignoble or evil goal. Moral virtues, Aristotle explains in his *Nicomachean Ethics,* guide and direct our choices toward living worthily and well. Steadfastness characterizes our being faithful to those commitments and promises that are good for us as human beings, those pursuits that enable us to live excellently. According to Aristotle, moral virtue involves habitually choosing "what is best and right," the mean between two vices, one of excess and one of deficiency. If steadfastness is about committing oneself resolutely toward a worthy goal, a vice of deficiency is laziness, giving up too easily or giving in to temptations that distract us from pursuing such goals. Vices of excess include zealotry or a slavish allegiance to an ignoble goal such as Nazism or bigotry.

To be steadfast is not simply to be gutsy or tough. It requires an intentional tenacity and endurance acquired through habit, practice, and deliberate choice, which enable us to achieve something honorable, to hold fast to our ideals, and to cross the finish line, no matter how difficult the course. We have seen exemplary steadfastness in individuals such as Viktor Frankl, author and psychotherapist who endured the tribulations of a concentration camp and remained focused on the love of his wife and the power of the human spirit to transcend suffering. He subsequently dedicated his professional life to helping victims of trauma find meaning in the midst of their pain. Steadfastness is required to break an addiction and acquire good habits, as well as to rebuild a life for oneself and one's family after surviving the loss of a job or falling victim to a natural disaster. It is also required to raise children well, to take care of the sick, or to learn a difficult subject. It is essential to good leadership.

Steadfastness is a mark of moral maturity. It becomes evident both in stressful circumstances (the "stress test" that tests our will) and in contexts where we are free to do anything we want (the "leisure test" that tests our character). Steven S. Tigner, "Signs of the Soul" (1995), offers an eloquent account of these two tests. We are met with stress tests all the time in our personal and professional lives. A student's will is tested, for example, when she has to deal with a demanding family situation and maintain a certain grade point average to retain an academic scholarship. Leisure tests of character include all of those occasions when people find themselves in a position to do as they please, to make choices when no one else is watching and there is little risk of getting caught. People exemplify steadfastness when they choose honorably under all circumstances.

Steadfastness is related to the virtues of courage (*andreia*) or fortitude and self-mastery (*sophrosune*) or temperance. Courage, knowing what is to be feared and what is not to be feared, relates to external challenges of character. It disposes us to choose the right course of action in accordance with the counsels of wisdom (*phronesis*) or prudence. As Ludwig van Beethoven once observed, "This is the mark of a really admirable man: steadfastness in the face of trouble." Job is the quintessential model of steadfastness in the Bible. Steadfastness is invoked numerous times throughout the Old and New Testaments as it pertains to fidelity and heroic virtue. "For you know that the testing of your faith produces steadfastness" (James 1:3). "For this very reason, make every effort to supplement your faith with virtue, and virtue with knowledge, and knowledge with self-control, and self-control with steadfastness, and steadfastness with godliness, and godliness with brotherly affection, and brotherly affection with love" (2 Peter 1:6).

Temperance or self-mastery deals with internal challenges to character, such as moderating the desire for money, power, and pleasure. Steadfastness, like self-mastery, characterizes people who direct or orient their appetites toward their overall well-being. This proper channeling of desire strengthens people's resolve and enables them to remain steadfast and not succumb to temptations that would hinder them in the pursuit of noble goals.

On the occasion of the queen of England's 50-year jubilee, June 4, 2002, the Archbishop of Canterbury spoke of her "abiding constancy" and offered this tribute: "Today at the height of another Elizabethan reign, we may speak again of love and glory, and of the steadfastness of a faithful sovereign." Steadfastness involves unwavering commitment, a determination to embrace noble ideals regardless of the stresses or temptations an individual meets along the way.

Further Reading: Aristotle. (1992). *Nicomachean ethics* (D. Ross, Trans.). New York: Oxford University Press. Frankl, V. E. (1984). *Man's search for meaning.* New York: Simon & Schuster. *Holy Bible* (English Standard Version). Carey, G. (2002). *The steadfastness of a faithful sovereign.* (Sermon by Archbishop of Canterbury; http//news.bbc.co.uk/1/hi/uk/2024568.stm.) Tigner, S. S. (1995). *Signs of the soul.* In G. S. Fain (Ed.), *Leisure and ethics: Reflections on the philosophy of leisure* (Vol. II, pp. 9–24). Reston, VA: American Association for Leisure and Recreation.

Karen Bohlin

Stereotyping

Children form stereotypes about one another early in life, as young as 4 and 5 years of age, and these attitudes change and evolve into adulthood. Generally, stereotypes are defined as the attribution of labels to individuals based solely on group membership, without consideration of intragroup variability. Stereotypes are a form of social categorization, and often lead to prejudicial attitudes and, less often, discriminatory behavior. Stereotypes can become deeply entrenched by adulthood, making it very difficult to change these types of cognitions (Dovidio, Brigham, Johnson, & Gaertner, 1996). In light of the effects stereotypes can have on prejudice and discriminatory reactions to groups, reducing children's tendency to form stereotypes about others is an important goal for moral education.

Gender stereotypes emerge during the preschool period, whereas racial, ethnic, religious, and cultural stereotypes form during the elementary and middle school years (Ruble & Martin, 1998). At the same time, children are forming and developing concepts of justice, equality, and fairness (Killen, Margie, & Sinno, 2006). Children often have to make difficult decisions involving both stereotypes and fairness judgments, and this often emerges in situations involving inclusion and exclusion. For example, children often define group play activities in terms of gender stereotypic expectations (girls play with dolls, boys play with trucks). Yet, when situations arise in which someone of the opposite gender wants to join a group playing a gendered activity, decisions about exclusion are juxtaposed with stereotypic expectations. Children give priority to moral values such as fairness in straightforward exclusion situations. In complex situations (for example, choosing between either letting a girl or a boy play with a group of boys playing with trucks), children often give priority to stereotypes. Yet, it has also been shown that discussions about fairness can influence children to focus on fairness rather than stereotypes (Killen, Pisacane, Lee-Kim, & Ardila-Rey, 2001).

In this vein, introducing children to the concept of stereotype threat has the potential to be yet another tactic to reduce the harmful effects of stereotyping. Broadly defined, stereotype threat is the finding that when negative stereotypes are present in a certain domain (e.g., low academic expectations based on group membership, such as ethnicity) they operate to reduce performance in that domain (Steele, 1997). For example, when ethnic minority students are told that their group performs poorly on a math test, then minority students are more likely to score lower than minority students who are told that there is no relationship between ethnic background and math performance. It is theorized that overcoming cognitively distracting thoughts about stereotype fulfillment lowers performance on standardized tests. This is proposed to be a negative outcome of stereotyping. Introducing children to the indirect negative effects of stereotypes may help to underscore the moral implications of stereotyping others. The fact that stereotypes can affect anyone makes the problem highly salient for everyone and makes the need for a reduction in stereotyping a top priority.

Moral education can facilitate children's awareness about using stereotypes by fostering discussions about the inherent lack of fairness that assignment of labels based on group membership puts on individuals of stereotyped groups. The consequences of stereotyping have to be spelled out clearly for children as these outcomes are often subtle and indirect. Creating morally relevant curriculum, designed to educate children and adolescents about the direct and indirect negative consequences of stereotyping, is both timely and developmentally important for reducing prejudice.

Further Reading: Aronson, J., & Steele, C.M. (2005). Stereotypes and the fragility of academic competence, motivation, and self-concept. In A.J. Elliot & C.S. Dweck (Eds.), *Handbook of competence and motivation* (pp. 436–56). New York: Guilford Publications. Horn, S.S. (2003). Adolescents' reasoning about exclusion from social groups. *Developmental Psychology, 39,* 71–84. Killen, M., Stangor, C., Price, B.S., Horn, S., & Sechrist, G.B. (2004). Social reasoning about racial exclusion in intimate and nonintimate relationships. *Youth & Society, 35,* 293–322.

References: Dovidio, J.F., Brigham, J.C., Johnson, B.T., & Gaertner, S.L. (1996). Stereotyping, prejudice, and discrimination: Another look. In C.N. Macrae, C. Stangor, & M. Hewstone (Eds.), *Stereotypes and stereotyping* (pp. 275–322). New York: Guilford Press. Killen, M., Margie, N.G., & Sinno, S.S. (2006). Morality in the context of intergroup relationships. In M. Killen & J.G. Smetana (Eds.), *Handbook of moral development* (pp. 155–183). Mahwah, NJ: Lawrence Erlbaum Associates. Killen, M., Pisacane, K., Lee-Kim, J., & Ardila-Rey, A. (2001). Fairness or stereotypes? Young children's priorities when evaluating group exclusion and inclusion. *Developmental Psychology, 37,* 587–96. Ruble, D.N., & Martin, C.L. (1998). Gender development. In W. Damon & N. Eisenberg (Eds.), *Handbook of child psychology* (pp. 933–1016). New York: John Wiley & Sons, Inc. Steele, C.M. (1997). A threat in the air: How stereotypes shape intellectual identity and performance. *American Psychologist, 52,* 613–29.

Cameron Richardson and Melanie Killen

Stewardship

Stewardship is the virtue of exercising the proper care for resources—human, material, and fiscal—that one has been given. Stewardship is a form of responsible management where an individual or a group thoughtfully and carefully administers the various assets in their possession for the common good.

Stewardship takes on many forms in the life of families, schools, communities, and nations. Individuals are often challenged to be good stewards of their natural gifts and talents. This means that there is a responsibility that accompanies one's natural abilities. Stewardship calls for the cultivation of those gifts in a way that enriches the lives of others. Families are called to exercise good stewardship of their resources. Parents are especially responsible for seeing to the appropriate disposition of the family's resources so that all are fed, housed, educated, and cared for. Such stewardship necessitates a sense of balance and justice.

Civic communities also function as stewards of the common good, collecting taxes, building roads, providing for public services, and protecting the environment. Such stewardship involves the oversight of goods held in common by the community and the disposition of those resources for the good of all. Nations similarly exercise stewardship in managing, protecting, and advancing the common good of all citizens.

Stewardship includes more than the effective management of goods. Stewardship has an outward orientation for the good of others, so that the ultimate purpose of the call to stewardship is not merely the multiplication of resources, or the presence of a superabundance of resources even after needs are met. Rather, stewardship has as its focus an altruistic understanding that resources are best disposed in the pursuit of the well-being of others.

The principle of stewardship is broadly applied in many sectors. One can exercise stewardship for children, for money, for the environment, or for an historic building. In each case, the stewardship depends on the careful disposition of resources for the good of another.

In theological parlance, stewardship has taken on a uniquely fiscal understanding as a way to describe the way in which believers in a particular church offer financial support to operate the church. In this instance, stewardship refers to a philosophy of giving in which believers are challenged to give a monetary gift to the church as a generous response to the gifts that God has already given them. Stewardship so understood is more than a way of giving; it is a way of giving back, returning to God and to the church some of the material blessings that have been received.

Stewardship is an important element in moral education. Because stewardship includes the management of resources and the good of others, moral values come into play and into conflict. In order to exercise good stewardship of resources, competing demands often need to be balanced and careful discernment conducted regarding what constitutes the best use of particular resources. The demands of stewardship are particularly complicated when the resources in question are human resources, that is, people, whose skills, talents, and limitations all come into play in complex situations. Stewardship decisions can be made with reference to the good of the community, to the welfare of individuals, or in relationship to God who is often understood as the origin of all that is good.

In religious understandings, stewardship asserts that caring for what God has provided is a primary responsibility shared by all. This includes the earth, our bodies, other people, and everything that makes up our universe. Stewardship is not a social agenda, but rather has an inherently moral character. Private property and personal ownership are social conventions for good order. In God's eyes, no one owns anything absolutely; everything we possess we hold in trust for everyone, including future generations. Problems of sickness, poverty, hunger, global scarcity, war, and pollution are examples of a dire need for better stewardship. Such issues call for an understanding of stewardship that condemns the use of technology and human talent for global trade and profit through environmentally unsustainable development. Stewardship calls for preserving the dignity of the human person, the common good, and the gifts of creation.

Further Reading: Block, P. (1993). *Stewardship: Choosing service over self interest.* San Francisco: Berrett-Koehler. Canadian Conference of Catholic Bishops. (2004). "You love all that exists…all things are yours, god, lover of life…" A pastoral letter on the Christian ecological imperative. *Catholic Education: A Journal of Inquiry & Practice, 8*(1), 34–43. John Paul II. (1990). *The ecological crisis: A common responsibility.* Washington, D.C.: United States Catholic Conference. Thompson, T.K. (Ed.). (1960). *Stewardship in contemporary theology.* New York: Association Press. United States Catholic Conference. (1991). *Renewing the earth: An invitation to reflection and action on environment in light of catholic social teaching.* Washington, D.C.: Author.

Ronald J. Nuzzi

Structure-Content Distinction

In analyzing the moral reasoning and judgment, cognitive developmentalists, such as Lawrence Kohlberg, make a fundamental distinction between structure—the underlying rational organization of a judgment—and content—the surface elements of a judgment. Cognitive developmental stage theories describe sequences of structural development, marked by increasing differentiation and integration of reasoning. Each moral stage is a structure with its own internal moral logic. As the stages develop, each new stage integrates the logic of the previous one to form a hierarchical sequence.

The structure-content distinction is central to Lawrence Kohlberg's theory of moral stages and to the moral judgment scoring manual (Colby, Kohlberg, et al., 1987). At the most superficial level, individuals choose one or the other action alternative in the dilemma. Thus, for example, in the Heinz Dilemma the interviewee is forced to decide whether or not Heinz should steal a drug that would save his wife's life after having exhausted all other legal means of procuring the drug. The choice, to steal or not to steal, is considered moral content. The choice in and of itself does not reveal the reasoning that led to the choice. After the respondent has made a choice, the interviewer asks her or him to explain that choice. Why should Heinz steal the drug or why should Heinz not steal the drug? Respondents initially mention the values that influenced their choice. So, for example, a respondent may say that Heinz should not steal because stealing is against the law, or another respondent may say that Heinz should steal the drug because he should care for his wife. Obeying the law and caring for one's wife are important moral values, and they tell us something about the way in which the respondents are reasoning; yet they are still very general moral considerations. We still do not know how obedience to the law or the duty to care is understood. Should laws be obeyed because their violations will be punished or should they be obeyed because this is necessary for order in society? Is caring important because it is a strong feeling or because care is due to all human beings in need?

Choices and the values that support those choices make up the content of a moral judgment. Justifications of the decisions and explanations of the values appealed to in those decisions make up the structure of a moral judgment. The statement that Heinz should not steal the drug because stealing is against the law could be scored at any stage from one to five. The statement that Heinz should not steal the drug because if individuals were to decide for themselves whether or not to break the law the social order would be shattered would be scored at the fourth stage of moral judgment. In the second statement the decision to not steal is sufficiently justified so that we can determine how the law is understood and how this understanding is used to resolve the dilemma.

Moral structures are often implicit in moral decision making and in everyday discourse about moral problems. We typically make decisions about what is right or wrong without articulating the reasoning that led up to the judgment. This does not mean that this reasoning is unimportant or is simply a rationalization of our judgment. Moral structures give meaning to moral actions. They frame our moral intentions.

Making a distinction between structure and content is of fundamental importance to coding the stage of moral judgment. Yet we should note that the distinction is not absolute. In a sense, the structure of a moral judgment is inferred from the content of an interview. Moral judgment scoring involves interpretation. Value words taken in isolation from each other have little meaning. However, value words considered in the context of arguments that justify a course of actions have meaning as parts within a whole. Debate over whether Kohlberg's stages are real structures largely revolves around the extent to which the consistency among individuals' moral reasoning and judgment is an artifact of the scoring system, which interprets individual statements in light of the whole or the reality of individuals' moral reasoning. The more content-oriented the scoring system, the more individuals' responses will be seen to vary by stage. The more structurally oriented, the more individuals' responses will be seen to be consistent. Kohlberg attempted to make his structural scoring system more open to variation by identifying "criterion judgments" as the units of analyses. These criterion judgments are the different arguments that individuals make in resolving moral dilemmas and are based on discrete values.

The structure content distinction is key to understanding what Kohlberg and other cognitive developmental psychologists meant by moral stages. It is also key to understanding the problem that moral stage theory has had in explaining the relationship between moral judgment and moral action. As structures, moral stages represent only formal ways of reasoning, which can be used to justify very different moral decisions. Moral psychologists, however, are interested in bridging the structure content gap to understand how reasoning leads to action.

Further Reading: Colby, A., Kohlberg, L., Speicher, B., Hewer, A., Gibbs, J., & Power, C. (1987). *The measurement of moral judgment, Vol 1: Theoretical Foundations and research validation.* New York: Cambridge University Press. Kohlberg, L. (1984). *Essays on moral development. Vol. 2: The psychology of moral development.* San Francisco: Harper & Row.

F. Clark Power

Superego Formation

According to Sigmund Freud, the cornerstones of psychoanalysis include the discovery of unconscious mental processes, the theory of repression and transference, and the importance of infantile sexuality and the Oedipus complex for development of the personality and of neuroses. It is the Oedipal drama of the toddler years that sets the stage for the emergence of the superego as the third structure of the personality, joining the id and ego in Freud's tripartite division of mental life.

The id is the most primitive psychic structure and one that represents the biological foundations of the personality. It surges with atavistic instinctual sexual and aggressive impulses that demand gratification, which is experienced as "pleasure." But within the id are elements that lie close to perceptual systems and "reality." The region of the id that is in close proximity to perception and consciousness is modified into the ego. The ego, then, is a modification of the id that emerges as a direct result of the influence of external reality. The ego is the executive of the personality. It regulates sexual drive energy ("libido"), marshals defense mechanisms, and otherwise ensures that primitive impulses are satisfied in a way that accords with reality, if at all.

Hence, the id is a cauldron of libidinal desire that seeks pleasure and tension release, while the ego is oriented toward reason, common sense, and the reality principle. Nevertheless, the ego and the id are not differentiated completely. Moreover, the ego is not entirely an agent. The ego operates as an impersonal apparatus or mechanical device for regulating drive energies. It is a control system and not a personal self. It is not even entirely conscious. After all, many of Freud's patients were unaware of using defense mechanisms, a fact that led Freud to conclude that much of the work of the ego is also unconscious.

The superego emerges not from the id-ego matrix but from the sexually charged complex of Oedipal strivings that characterize early psychosexual development. The boy, for example, develops libidinal attachment ("cathexis") to mother. The erotic investment in mother intensifies, but father looms as an obstacle and jealous rival. Although the boy wishes to possess mother and displace father, this engenders considerable ("castration") anxiety insofar as the jealous rival is capable of significant retaliation. The surge of castration anxiety makes the Oedipal situation untenable for the boy. As a result, the boy must abandon his libidinal desire for mother by means of repression, yet the immature ego is too feeble. One way to build up the ego so that it can carry out the required act of repression is to borrow the resources of the father. The boy incorporates the father within the ego through identification so that the boy can now borrow the resources of the introjected parent to repress dangerous libidinal desire. The incorporation of father through identification is so momentous that a new psychic structure emerges from within the ego, the superego.

The superego is the conscience of the personality. It demands perfection of the ego, and holds it accountable to ideal standards. It retaliates against the ego by imposing guilt for its pragmatic compromises with the id's demands for libidinal satisfaction. Freud argued that because the origin of the superego is linked to the Oedipus complex, which is unconscious, the experience of guilt is also unconscious. This leads to an interesting paradox. Because one is unconscious of having irrational libidinal desires, one is far more "immoral" than one believes. Yet because the superego (and the guilt it imposes as punishment) is also unconscious, one is also more moral than one knows.

Freud's tripartite theory of id-ego-superego is criticized for its inability to give an account of early conscience development in girls; for its emphasis on energy dynamics as the foundation of personality; and for its "Centaur" model of the human person. Most neo-Freudian theories deny that the human person is at first bestial and asocial, beset by instinctual impulses, and only later becomes social and socialized. The Freudian vision of the ego as an impersonal apparatus for channeling drive energy is also rejected in favor of a personal self who is involved in motivated relationships from the beginning. Moreover, to link the origin of conscience to incestuous libidinal desires is a fantastic notion to many critics. Yet, although the Oedipus complex is unpalatable as a scientific account of the emergence of conscience, it is the one aspect of Freud's theory that captures a keen insight of great value—that the origin of personality is grounded in the nexus of family relationships. The superego is the only psychic structure that emerges as an outcome of interpersonal relationships. This relational perspective, already evident in Freud's account of superego formation, would inspire many theoretical innovations in subsequent accounts of psychoanalysis, such as the object relations school.

Further Reading: Freud, S. (1962). *The ego and the id.* New York: Norton. Greenberg, J.R., & Mitchell, S.A. (1983). *Object relations in psychoanalytic theory.* Cambridge, MA: Harvard University Press. Grunbaum, A. (1984). *The foundations of psychoanalysis: A philosophical critique.* Berkeley, CA: University of California Press. Guntrip, H. (1985). *Psychoanalytic theory, therapy and the self.* New York: Karnac Books. Mitchell, S., & Black, M.J. (1995). *Freud and beyond: A history of modern psychoanalytic thought.* New York: Basic Books.

Daniel K. Lapsley

T

Teacher's Role in Moral Education

In a New York City subway station, January 2007, a 19-year-old had a seizure and fell onto the subway tracks with the train coming. Within a split second, and while the young man was still having his seizure, a man leaped from the platform, pulled the young man onto the center of the tracks, and laid on top of him, allowing the train to pass over them. Why would this person act in such a way for a total stranger, putting his own life at risk? It is likely that he felt a sense of obligation to act, that for him, to not act would have created a sense of guilt stemming from a disconnect with his guiding belief system—his morality, or moral sense (Damon, 1988; Hoffman, 2000; Kant, 1797/1991; Kohlberg, 1970; Nucci, 2001; Piaget, 1948/1965).

The development of a moral sense or moral compass, as some may refer to it, is the result of a lifetime of experiences that help an individual come to understand, care about, and act upon situations that have social, emotional, and moral implications. Most importantly, the literature on this subject agrees that the components of reflection and critical thinking contribute as much to a moral compass as does recognition that, as with the case of the hero in the subway story, there is an internalized pattern of behavior allowing the individual to do what is right with little time to think about it (Aristotle, 1984; Berkowitz & Fekula, 1999; Berkowitz & Grych, 1998; Dewey, 1909; Lickona, 1991; Vessels, 1998). As with learning to play an instrument or becoming a top performer in sports or academics, there is, in the process of developing this moral sense, a need for the role models to observe, to obtain explicit teaching and guidance, and to practice, practice, practice. The teacher's role in moral education rests within all three of these needs.

Students spend over 12,000 hours at school from kindergarten through high school graduation. As teaching itself is a moral endeavor, deciding on issues of fairness, relationships, care, and understanding of others (DeVries & Zan, 1994; Fenstermacher, 1990; Hansen, 1995; Sockett, 1993), teachers have an obligation to be thoughtful and knowledgeable about moral education; they simply cannot rely only on the home and religious institutions to provide experiences necessary for positive moral development. Teachers model for moral education when they explicitly demonstrate and teach about empathy and perspective taking, social problem solving, and respect for others. They do this by creating a classroom climate with opportunities to discuss moral issues, choosing teaching strategies that challenge students academically at the same time that they learn to work cooperatively, integrate ethical themes into their academic subjects, and choose class management and discipline strategies that are intentional in helping young people develop internal guiding belief systems that support the kind of moral compass demonstrated by the subway hero (Beland, 2003; Schwartz, 2007; Watson, 2003).

Further Reading: Aristotle. (1984). *Nicomachean ethics.* Princeton, NJ: Princeton University Press. Beland, K. (Ed.). (2003). *The eleven principles sourcebook.* Washington, D.C.: Character Education Partnership. Berkowitz, M.W., & Fekula, M.J. (1999). Educating for character. *About Campus, 4*(5), 17–22. Berkowitz, M.W., & Grych, J.H. (1998). Fostering goodness: Teaching parents to facilitate children's moral development. *Journal of Moral Education Ltd., 27*(3), 371–91. Damon, W. (1988). *The moral child.* New York: The Free Press. DeVries, R., & Zan, B. (1994). *Moral classrooms, moral children.* New York: Teachers College Press. Dewey, J. (1909). *Moral principles in education.* Carbondale, IL: Southern Illinois University Press. Fenstermacher, G.D. (1990). Some moral considerations on teaching as a profession. In J. Goodlad, R. Soder, & K.A. Sirotnik (Eds.), *The moral dimensions of teaching* (pp. 130–54). San Francisco: Jossey-Bass. Hansen, D. (1995). Teaching and the moral life of classrooms. *Journal for a Just and Caring Education, 2,* 59–74. Hoffman, M.L. (2000). *Empathy and moral development: Implications for caring and justice.* Cambridge, England: Cambridge University Press. Kant, I. (1991). *The metaphysics of morals.* Cambridge, England: Cambridge University Press. (Original work published 1797.) Kohlberg, L. (1970). *Education for justice: A modern statement of the Platonic view.* Cambridge, MA: Harvard University Press. Lickona, T. (1991). *Educating for character.* New York: Bantam Books. Nucci, L. (2001). *Education in the moral domain.* Cambridge, England: Cambridge University Press. Piaget, J. (1948/1965). *The moral judgment of the child.* Glencoe, IL: The Free Press. Schwartz, M.J. (Ed.). (2007). *Effective character education: A guidebook for future teachers.* New York: McGraw-Hill. Sockett, H. (1993). *The moral base for teacher professionalism.* New York: Teachers College. Vessels, G.G. (1998). *Character and community development: A school planning and teacher training handbook.* Westport, CT: Greenwood Publishing Group. Watson, M. (2003). *Learning to trust: Transforming difficult elementary classrooms through developmental discipline.* San Francisco: Jossey-Bass.

Merle J. Schwartz

Tolerance

Children's development of tolerance manifests in many forms. Tolerance is usually defined as appreciating different perspectives and respecting diversity regarding group membership, culture, and social values. Typically, there is an assumption that tolerance is positive in that this means being inclusive and open-minded. There may be times, however, when tolerance is negative, particularly when it connotes an acceptance of cultural norms that may be wrong from a moral viewpoint. Thus, the value placed on tolerance has to be understood in the context of the moral consequences to others in terms of fairness, justice, and others' rights.

According to modern theories of development of prejudice in children and adolescents, being tolerant means accepting others who are members of out-groups, and those who have different social identities. How children group others is viewed as a necessary part of social life, and tolerance of differences is viewed as important for social harmony. For example, Wainryb et al. (2001) has shown that children's disagreements depend on the content of the message, and this is an important aspect of relating tolerance to morality. Her research has shown that diversity is the least acceptable when it involves dissimilarity of beliefs about moral transgressions (e.g., what is considered a violation of fairness or equality), followed by the differences in personal psychological beliefs (e.g., how to be a good friend), social conventions (e.g., how to behave in a restaurant), and last, differences in abstract metaphysical beliefs (e.g., how many gods there are), which are deemed to be the most tolerable of all (Wainryb, Shaw, Laupa, & Smith, 2001). In general, tolerance for dissimilar beliefs is higher when such beliefs do not involve direct harm to others or are based on personal preferences or individual differences in perception (e.g., taste), misinformation, or cultural traditions. Moreover, dissenting individuals may still be tolerated even if their values are not. Additionally, simply holding dissimilar beliefs is more acceptable than expressing these beliefs or acting on them, with adolescents and young adults expressing more tolerance of holding and expressing divergent beliefs than children.

Starting at a very young age, children categorize individuals into groups based on external characteristics and realize that there are stereotypes associated with different groups. By applying cognitive categorization processes to themselves, children develop a sense of their own group membership as well. This process of learning about group differences and determining one's own group membership is an essential part of social identity development, such as gender and ethnic identity.

At the same time, according to the social identity theory, the need for positive self-identity often results in attributing more positive characteristics to the members of one's own group, or in-group favoritism. This positive in-group image may or may not be associated with a negative view of the out-group, depending on the specific nature of the intergroup attitudes and the degree to which an individual identifies with beliefs and values of his/her group.

Fortunately, research has also shown that children's decisions regarding peer groups and friendships are not always guided by in-group preference; children are often inclusive when evaluating whether it is all right to exclude others, even in situations in which their own group may be displaying exclusive attitudes (Killen, Henning, & McGlothlin, in press). Interviewing children about complex situations reveals stereotypes and biases that reflect a lack of tolerance for others who are different from the self, especially in peer situations. Thus, helping children to understand the relationship between inclusion and tolerance is important.

The implications for moral education are that teachers and educators have to be very concrete and content-based when promoting the concept of tolerance. Tolerance is not an absolute value as there are times when it is wrong to be tolerant (for example, tolerance of hate groups is not desirable). Yet, tolerance in the context of moral values, such as fairness and equality, is very important, given the multicultural nature of most communities and the many different categories that most people identify with and believe to be part of their social existence.

Further Reading: Aboud, F., & Levy, S. (2000). Interventions to reduce prejudice and discrimination in children and adolescents. In S. Oskamp (Ed.), *Reducing prejudice and discrimination* (pp. 269–93). Mahwah, NJ: LEA. Gaertner, S., & Dovidio, J.F. (2000). *Reducing intergroup bias: The common ingroup identity model.* Philadelphia, PA: Psychology Press. Killen, M., & McKown, C. (2005). How integrative approaches to intergroup attitudes advance the field. *Journal of Applied Developmental Psychology, 26,* 616–22.

References: Killen, M., Henning, A., & McGlothin, H. (in press). Implicit biases and explicit judgments: A developmental perspective. In S.R. Levy & M. Killen (Eds.), *Intergroup relationships:*

An integrative developmental and social psychology perspective. Oxford, England: Oxford University Press. Wainryb, C., Shaw, L.A., Laupa, M.L., & Smith, K.R. (2001). Children's, adolescents', and young adults' thinking about different types of disagreements. *Developmental Psychology, 37,* 373–86. Wainryb, C., Shaw, L.A., & Maianu, C. (1998). Tolerance and intolerance: Children's and adolescents' judgments of dissenting beliefs, speech, persons, and conduct. *Child Development, 69*(6), 1541–1555.

Alexandra Henning and Melanie Killen

Transition

A transition is a change in life that can be viewed as positive or negative depending on how a person participates in or views the transition. Transitions can be major events such as a job change, marriage, divorce, geographical move, or graduating college. Or, transitions can be fairly minor such as how a life role is played. Whether major or minor events, the person either initiates or responds to the transition.

There are typically three parts to a transition: the content; the process of working through the transition; and the outcome. Content refers to the events or changes in one's life. These can be either voluntary or involuntary changes. Voluntary transitions represent those changes in which a person freely participates and views as necessary. Examples might include moving away to college or accepting a job for better pay. Involuntary transitions, however, are changes forced upon a person such as being laid off by an employer or his/her child getting married and relocating. Unlike voluntary transitions, involuntary change can catch a person off guard in terms of being prepared for dealing with the transition or what the transition will mean to his/her future.

The process of transition is influenced by how a person copes with change. Because transitions represent an ending and a beginning, there is usually a sense of loss to the prior way of being and some uncertainty as to how things will be. The degree to which a person successfully works through a transition has much to do with his/her attitude toward the transition. There is no mandatory time limit for experiencing transitions. However, there is a responsibility for reflecting on the change in relation to one's sense of wellness and choices.

The outcome of a transition marks the beginning of the new way of being. If expectations are met, then there is minimal coping strategies needed. If expectations are exceeded, then satisfaction with the transition occurs. If, however, the outcome of the transition falls below one's expectations, then a typical reaction might be to blame others or blame oneself. This style of coping may lead to a person basing his or her worth on the outcome of the transition, which may not always be in his/her control.

Recognizing transitions helps in disciplines such as counseling and business to better understand how persons and groups experience change. As such, there are many models used as frameworks to understand transitions. William Bridges (1980) views the transition process as a series of phases that are fairly predictable. The first phase consists of an ending that has four substages: disengagement, disidentification, disillusionment, and disorientation. Disengagement is the end of the content, such as a job or relationship. Disidentification is experienced as an inner loss while disillusionment is the challenge to our belief of how things would always be. Disorientation as to how things were or will be is the culminating experience of the ending part of a transition.

The second phase of the transition process, according to Bridges, is the neutral zone, which is simply a time to reevaluate and possibly reprioritize one's goals. The challenge during this phase is to pay attention to one's own inner voice instead of being dependent on others to make the decision. The third phase is marked by beginning a new life role or activity. The risk at this point is to forge ahead into unknown territory. The tendency for some is to resort to a former, safer way of being as opposed to beginning a new path with uncertainty yet more promise.

Schlossberg's (1984) social interaction model of transition focuses on the type of transition, the context, and the impact of the transition. How a person views the transition and his/her coping strategies is a major determinant as to the outcome of the transition. According to Schlossberg, there are several aspects to a transition that must be considered. Fundamental is the manner in which a person evaluates the transition based upon his or her personal, developmental, and environmental characteristics. These might include personality, age and maturity level, and social supports. Additionally, perceived coping resources can influence the degree of stress in dealing with a transition.

With any transition there is a loss and a beginning. Kubler-Ross's (1969) model of the grieving process provides a framework for understanding how persons cope with involuntary loss. The process begins with confusion and possible shock over the loss, followed by rationalization and denial as defense mechanisms. Former or newly developed coping strategies are used, which might include external support systems. Coping strategies, however, do not eliminate anger toward the unwanted transition or fear of the future as to how things will be.

Transitions are a part of everyday life and serve as a challenge to how persons initiate, react, or respond to change in their lives. This is true for simple decisions or major life events.

Further Reading: Brammer, L., & Abrego, P. (1981). Intervention strategies for coping with transitions. *The Counseling Psychologist, 9,* 19–36. Bridges, W. (1980). *Transitions: Making sense out of life changes.* Reading, MA: Addison-Wesley. Kubler-Ross, E. (1969). *On death and dying.* New York: Macmillan. Schlossberg, N. (1984). *Counseling adults in transition.* New York: Springer.

Scott E. Hall

Tufts, James H.

James Hayden Tufts was born in Monson, Massachusetts, on July 9, 1862. He entered Amherst College in the fall of 1880, and continued his studies at Yale Divinity School where he earned his B.D. degree in 1889. Upon graduation, he was invited to accept a faculty position in philosophy at the University of Michigan. Under the supervision of John Dewey, Tufts taught a variety of courses during the next two years at Michigan (1889–1891) but then left for study abroad to complete his doctorate in 1892. After returning from Berlin with his Ph.D., Tuft was hired by the University of Chicago. Persuaded by Tufts to leave the University of Michigan, both John Dewey and George H. Mead joined their former colleague at the University of Chicago in 1894. Over the next decade, the collaboration of these three philosophers would come to be renowned as the Chicago School of Pragmatism. Although Dewey would leave for a position at Columbia in 1904, Tufts remained at the University of Chicago until his retirement in 1930. He then moved to California, where he taught occasionally at UCLA until his death on August 5, 1942.

Tufts was the most prolific writer of the Chicago pragmatists, publishing ten books, more than 100 articles, and over 200 book reviews during his academic tenure. Additionally, he served as editor of the *School Review* for three years and the editor of *International Journal of Ethics* for 17 years. Together with Jane Addams, George Meade, and John Dewey, Tufts was instrumental in creating greater opportunities for Chicago's urban immigrants and the public schools. As an active member of the famous Chicago City Club, he and his colleagues worked tirelessly to improve social and economic conditions for those suffering from the hardships of poverty and unfair labor practices (Feffer, 1993). Besides serving on the board of directors of Jane Addams's University Settlement House, Tufts also chaired an arbitration board for the garment industry and was president of the Illinois Association for Labor Legislation and chairman of the Illinois Committee on Social Legislation. His enthusiasm for serving the public was also matched by his willingness to serve among his academic colleagues in philosophy, and he was elected president of the Western Philosophy Association in 1906 and 1914, president of the American Philosophical Association in 1914, and president of the Pacific Philosophical Association in 1934.

Tufts was among the strongest supporters of the progressive movement in American education, and his early work in social and political philosophy demonstrated his commitment to promote the common good through the framework of liberal democracy. During most of Tufts's tenure at the University of Chicago, labor relations were an important factor contributing to local educational and political issues in Chicago. He was instrumental in helping to facilitate contract negotiations between labor unions and management, and he also often mediated labor disputes. Tufts pressured business owners to resolve labor disputes through open arbitration with the labor unions, and he encouraged public disclosure regarding labor law and health code violations (Feffer, 1993).

In Tufts's later writings, his commitment to the principles of liberal democracy is reiterated by his pragmatic theory of justice and cooperative civic obligations. For example, his approach to pedagogical issues in education was in many ways close to a modern constructivist approach, particularly regarding the need to develop moral character in the context of interacting with the community of knowers. Justice was not an abstract principle best served by blindly impartial standards of measurement; to the contrary, he believed that the principle of justice should be based on standards of equity. This pragmatic sense of justice, if practically applied, would embrace normative judgments of moral and legal culpability based on consideration of the context and culture of community standards of justice. According to Tufts, civic responsibility in a democratic society would need to be seen as a commitment to fully participate in all aspects of community life (Bernstein, 1998). Tufts thought that self-control and responsibility were excellent traits of moral character that needed to be acquired and practiced as social skills through association with others (Shook, 2000).

Because of his commitment to pragmatism, Tufts viewed moral character as being derived through an educational process that made pedagogical use of social collaboration and continuous revision. Unlike Kant, who believed that morality is primarily a function of obeying an absolute moral rule, Tufts saw morality as involving some commitment to community standards of conduct. In Tufts's view, our moral obligations as citizens in a democratic society must always be understood in the context of our practical need to cooperate and collaborate with fellow citizens in order to successfully impact public policy. Therefore, Tufts's ethical theory extended moral obligation beyond the matter of negotiating relationships between individual parties. In his pivotal work "The Social Standpoint" he suggested that moral obligations should be extended to all realms of our social existence, including the home, the workplace, and political and religious activities (Shook, 2000). Although much of Tufts's philosophical writings have been overshadowed by the greater influence of John Dewey's works, James Campbell has credited Tufts with having developed an influential body of work not only on social pragmatism but also on educational policy and pedagogical issues that still reflect his significant contributions.

Further Reading: Bernstein, R.J. (1998). Community in the pragmatic tradition. In M. Dickstein (Ed.), *The revival of pragmatism: New essays on social thought, law, and culture.* Chapel Hill, NC: Duke University Press. Campbell, J. (Ed.). (1992). *Selected writings of James Hayden Tufts.* Carbondale, IL: Southern Illinois University Press. Feffer, A. (1993). *The Chicago pragmatists and American progressivism.* Ithaca, NY: Cornell University Press. Tufts, J.T. (2000). The social standpoint. In J.R. Shook (Ed.), *The Chicago school of pragmatism, volume 2.* Bristol, England: Thoemmes Press. (Original work published in *Journal of Philosophy, Psychology, and Scientific Methods,* 1904.)

Monalisa M. Mullins

Turiel, Elliot

Elliot Turiel is Chancellor's Professor and Associate Dean of the Graduate School of Education at the University of California, Berkeley. He was born on September 23, 1938, on the Island of Rhodes. At that time Rhodes was part of Italy, an ally of Nazi Germany during World War II. In the latter stages of the war, the Italian government complied with German requests to send Italian Jews to Germany. In 1944, Turiel's father along with other Jewish men living in Rhodes were rounded up and held in preparation for transfer to Germany. His mother, who was a Turkish citizen, prevailed upon a Turkish diplomat to get her husband released on the grounds that Turkey was an ally of Germany. The diplomat accepted her argument and achieved the release of Turiel's father along with several other men the diplomat claimed to be Turkish citizens. Turiel, along with his parents and older brother, escaped to Turkey from Rhodes in a row boat.

Turiel and his family lived in Turkey until 1946 when they moved to New York. He attended City College of New York and received his B.A. in 1960. He went on to Yale University where he studied with Edward Zigler and Lawrence Kohlberg and received his Ph.D. in Psychology in 1965. His dissertation was an experimental study of the effectiveness of arguments in raising moral reasoning levels. He reported that arguments placed one stage above the individual's modal stage resulted in moral growth, while arguments below the individual's modal level or more than one stage above were ineffective in producing moral growth. This study led to subsequent research on the uses of moral argumentation in moral education.

Following graduate school, Turiel was an Assistant Professor of Psychology at Columbia University until 1969 when he joined the faculty at Harvard University with Lawrence Kohlberg. In 1975 he left Harvard to join the faculty in psychology at the University of California at Santa Cruz, where he stayed until joining the faculty at the University of California at Berkeley in 1980.

While at Harvard, Turiel worked with Kohlberg and other colleagues on Kolhberg's stage theory of moral growth. In the process of that work, it was discovered that, contrary to theory, there was a period of apparent "moral regression" in the thinking of college-age adolescents and young adults. These young people exhibited moral reasoning that appeared to be relativistic and instrumental, and in some ways similar to the "stage 2" thinking of younger children. Turiel's analysis of this problem led him to conclude that the apparent moral relativism resulted from a temporary conflation of morality with the conventions of society. This led to a systematic investigation of the origins of children's differential concepts of morality and convention, and progressively led Turiel to propose what has become known as the "domain theory" of social cognitive development.

Upon joining the faculty of the University of California at Santa Cruz in 1975, Turiel and his students conducted research on his proposition that social cognition is constructed within distinct conceptual and developmental frameworks. This early work provided considerable evidence for the distinction between concepts of morality and social convention, and it identified a third domain of personal privacy and prerogative.

In the mid-1980s, Turiel shifted his attention from work on specific domains to how individuals employ their knowledge within multiple domains to reason about complex issues in social context. He proposed a multifaceted process of contextualized social reasoning in which individuals isolate or coordinate the moral and nonmoral dimensions of social events. Turiel employed this analysis of social decision making to account for the inconsistencies observed in the reasoning and actions of individuals across contexts. It also led to a series of articles and book chapters on reasoning and action. From the 1990s to the present Turiel's work has focused upon the ways in which hierarchical social structures impact the social judgments of persons holding different positions within the social system. This has included analyses of opposition and resistance offered by individuals living within hierarchical systems, such as women living in traditional male dominated societies.

Turiel has vigorously argued against social critics who have employed claims that American youth are in moral crisis as a way to bolster their arguments in favor of a return to traditional forms of character education. In his view, the emphasis on presumed moral decay is a misrepresentation of transitions in social structure reflecting resistance to social conventions that had unjustly privileged White males within American society. Moral education, rather than stifling such resistance on the part of the young, should acknowledge that conflict and questioning is integral to moral and social growth.

Further Reading: Turiel, E. (1983). *The development of social knowledge: Morality and convention.* Cambridge, England: Cambridge University Press. Turiel, E. (2002). *The culture of morality: Social development, context, and conflict.* Cambridge, England: Cambridge University Press.

Larry Nucci

U

United Nations

The United Nations (UN) was founded at the conclusion of the United Nations Conference on International Organization through the signing of its charter in San Francisco, California, on June 26, 1945, and came into force on October 24, 1945. The United Nations was originally intended to be a collective security organization to help ensure that the horrors of the First and Second World Wars would not be repeated. The League of Nations, founded following World War I, was expected to achieve a system of "collective security"; however, it failed in part due to the United States not becoming a member and to the unwillingness of member nations to invoke its covenant to challenge pre–World War II military expansion. The United Nations was to remedy the weaknesses and failings of the League of Nations. When President Harry Truman, on July 2, 1945, presented the Charter of the United Nations to the U.S. Senate for review leading to ratification, he stated, "This Charter points down the only road to enduring peace. There is no other."

The Charter of the United Nations clarifies its collective security intentions and its support for human rights. The Preamble states it is to "save succeeding generations from the scourge of war" and "reaffirm faith in fundamental human rights, in the dignity and worth of the human person, in the equal rights of men and women and of nations large." The first article of Chapter One delineates purposes that include: to maintain international peace and security through collective measures; to develop friendly relations among nations based on respect for the principle of equal rights and self-determination of peoples; to achieve international cooperation in solving international problems of an economic, social, cultural, or humanitarian character; and to be a center for harmonizing the actions of nations in the attainment of these common ends. The second article, presenting the UN's principles, states that "All Members shall settle their international disputes by peaceful means in such a manner that international peace and security, and justice, are not endangered" and that they are to refrain from "threat or use of force against the territorial integrity or political independence of any state." The Charter clearly establishes that the sovereign nature of states is to be respected and that intervention is not to occur "in matters which are essentially within the domestic jurisdiction of any state."

The United Nations had 51 member nations at its birth, and this number had grown to 191 by 2002. Six principal organs of the United Nations carry out its responsibilities: the General Assembly, Security Council, Economic and Social Council, Trustee Council, International Court of Justice, and Secretariat. The General Assembly is a forum made up of the member states where consideration is given to issues of international peace and security, economic, social, cultural, educational, health, and human rights. The Security Council, the primary mechanism meant to establish peace and prevent war, includes five permanent members (i.e., Britain, China, France, the Russian Federation, and the United States) and ten temporary members elected from five regions of the world by the General Assembly for two-year terms, and requires a nine-vote majority on procedural matters and support of each of the five permanent members on substantive matters. The Economic and Social Council has 54 members elected by the General Assembly. It promotes advances in standards of living, employment, economic and social well-being, health, and respect for human rights and fundamental freedoms. The Trustee Council administers territories under the trusteeship system. It suspended operations on November 1, 1994, and has been dormant and awaiting requests for activation since then. The International Court of Justice, based in The Hague, Netherlands, with 15 judges elected to nine-year terms by the General Assembly and Security Council, is responsible for applying international law in settling legal disputes submitted by states and in advising on legal questions. The Secretariat works under and supports the UN Secretary General in dealing with operational issues.

Human rights, based on ethical-moral principles, have been promoted by the United Nations through numerous entities and mechanisms. They have been championed by the General Assembly, the Economic and Social Council, and the Commission on Human Rights. The Commission on Human Rights, the main policy-making body dealing with human rights issues, ended its 60-year history of work on March 27, 2006, when it was replaced by the Council on Human Rights that was created on March 15, 2006, to overcome complaints of influence through political cronyism and by human rights violating nations. To advance human rights, the United Nations has adopted nonbinding but influential declarations and legally binding human rights agreements. The Universal Declaration of Human Rights (1948), the Declaration on the Right to Development (1986), and the Declaration on Protection of All Persons from Enforced Disappearance (1992) are examples of the first. Examples of the second include the International Covenant on Economic, Social and Cultural Rights and the International Covenant on Civil and Political Rights (entered into force in 1976), the Convention on Prevention and Punishment of the Crime of Genocide (1951), the International Convention on the Elimination of All Forms of Racial Discrimination (1969), the Convention on the Elimination of All Forms of Discrimination against Women (1981), the Convention Against Torture and Other Cruel, Inhuman or Degrading Treatment or Punishment (1987), and the International Convention on the Protection of the Rights of All Migrant Workers and Members of their Families (not yet in force). The most comprehensive and influential human rights treaty focused specifically on children is the Convention on the Rights of the Child (entered into force in 1990), which includes strong support for education and for moral and spiritual development. The United Nations incorporates treaty bodies, special rapporteurs, representatives, experts, and working groups to monitor compliance with human rights standards and to investigate alleged human rights abuses. It has provided human rights advisory services since 1951, with technical assistance added in 1987. UNICEF, the United Nations Children's Fund, works to promote child survival, protection, and development worldwide through education, advocacy, and fund-raising.

The United Nations promotes education for children through the Convention on the Rights of the Child (see particularly Articles 28 and 29 on the right to and aims of education, respectively) and through its bodies and their initiatives. UNESCO, the United Nations Education, Scientific, and Cultural Organization, has education as one of its primary responsibilities. UNESCO's central education initiative is Education for All (EFA), based on the fundamental premise that education is central to the promotion of human rights, social equality, democracy, and economic growth. UNESCO works with nations throughout the world to achieve EFA's six goals to achieve sustainable human development: to early learning, universal primary education, life skills, literacy, girls' education, and quality education. UNESCO's International Bureau of Education specializes in contents, methods, and the structure of education, and works closely with national ministries of education. UNESCO and the Living Values Educational Program launched the Early Childhood and Values Education international initiative in 2000.

Further Reading: Bowles, N. (2004). *The diplomacy of hope: The United Nations since the cold war.* London: I.B. Tauris. Muravchik, J. (2005). *The future of the United Nations: Understanding the past to chart a way forward.* Lanham, MD: AEI Press. United Nations. (2004). *Basic facts about the United Nations.* Lanham, MD: Bernan Press. United Nations General Assembly. (1945, June 26). *The charter of the United Nations.* New York: Author. Weiss, T.G., Forsythe, D.P., & Coate, R.A. (2004). *United Nations and changing world politics* (4th ed.). Boulder, CO: Westview Press.

Stuart N. Hart

Utilitarianism

Utilitarianism is a moral theory based on the principle that moral obligation is determined by the consequences of action. According to John Stuart Mill's 1863 expression of utilitarianism, an action is morally obligatory if it produces the greatest happiness for the greatest number of people. In his general introduction to utilitarianism, Mill argues that all moral theory is approached either intuitively or inductively. While both approaches are distinct in significant ways, they nonetheless share the view that moral theory yields some definitive normative principle regarding the moral worth of actions. The place of departure between intuitive moral theory and inductive moral theory is their disagreement about how such normative principles are discerned. The intuitive approach assumes that we have knowledge of moral worth (that is, the rightness of an action) without appeal to sensory experience; Kantian moral theory is an example of this intuitive approach. By contrast, the inductive approach to moral theory assumes that the moral worth of actions can only be known based on sensory experience and observation. Mill is considered to have offered the clearest defense of the inductive method of moral reasoning, which is best known as utilitarianism but also is referred to as consequentialism. His treatise on moral theory first appeared in *Fraser's Magazine* in 1861 and was reprinted in the small volume *Utilitarianism* in 1863.

Following his predecessor and mentor Jeremy Bentham, Mill argued that actions are right if they tend to increase happiness, and wrong if they tend to decrease happiness.

He referred to this as the principle of utility (hence the name "utilitarianism"). However, Mill's theory differed from Bentham's with respect to the definition of happiness. Bentham suggested that we should tabulate all the pleasures and all the pains that would result as the consequence of some action, and then simply calculate the net pleasure and net gain attached to that consequence. Bentham's mathematical calculus included consideration of the likely results to all persons affected by the action and required an impartial counting of all pleasures and pains as equal for each person. Thus, this quantitative measurement of happiness would provide direction for following the course of action that weighed in with the largest net pleasure and the smallest net pain. By contrast, Mill argued that, although happiness is produced by both intellectual and sensual pleasures, our sense of human dignity would have us choose intellectual pleasures over sensual ones. This departure from Bentham's purely quantitative calculus for measuring happiness made utilitarianism more palatable to some moral theorists, particularly since Mill introduced a qualitative measure of happiness by attributing greater importance to intellectual pleasures than sensual pleasures (as did Aristotle, in his *Nicomachean Ethics*).

According to Mill, our motivations to follow the utilitarian standard of morality come from two different sources. First, we have external motivations to promote general happiness; these external motivations are driven by our concern to please God and to please other persons. More importantly, though, is an internal motivation to promote general happiness that arises from within each person. This internal motivation is driven by an internal sense of duty, which sounds very much like Immanuel Kant's principle of the good will. However, unlike Kant, Mill argues that this moral sense of duty is a subjective feeling that develops over the course of one's lifetime and is based on one's own experiences (Singer, 1993). Nonetheless, for Mill, the principle that guides all these various subjective internal motivations is the principle of promoting general happiness for the greatest number of people. Mill offered an inductive proof of the principle to promote general happiness that took as its major premise the assumption that only happiness is desired.

This commitment to the ultimate valuation of happiness remains the most controversial aspect of utilitarianism, with many critics arguing that there are other things we desire besides happiness, such as honor, respect, and virtue. Indeed, critics of utilitarianism suggest that morality is not based on the consideration of consequences of our actions, but is instead based on such universal concepts as justice and virtue. Mill anticipated at least some of this criticism, arguing that even the principle of justice depended on social utility, or the consideration of rights that all persons have to pursue happiness (Hinman, 1998).

Central to utilitarian moral theory is the idea that our actions are best measured by the amount of happiness they generate in society. Because of this central claim, critics charge that utilitarian moral theory would permit conduct that violates the rights of minorities and the interests of persons who do not speak from the perspective of the majority opinion. Thus, unfettered utilitarianism is viewed as having the potential to lead to tyranny in the achievement of majority satisfaction of most of the population. Such concepts as human dignity and worth of individual liberty would stand in jeopardy if the application of pure utilitarian principles were embraced by a democratic form of government, without regard for the interests of minority members of the society. Modern utilitarians continue to attempt to reconcile the general happiness principle with the democratic principles of equal representation and equal rights for everyone, especially with respect to the law.

Further Reading: Hinman, L.M. (Ed.). (1998). *Ethics: A pluralistic approach to moral theory.* Fort Worth, TX: Harcourt Brace. Mill, J.S. (2002). *Utilitarianism* (George Sher, Ed.). New York: Hackett. Sen, A. (1982). *Utilitarianism and beyond.* Cambridge: Cambridge University Press. Shaw, W. (1999). *Contemporary ethics: Taking account of utilitarianism.* Cambridge, MA: Blackwell Publishers. Singer, P. (1993). *Practical ethics* (2nd ed.). Cambridge: Cambridge University Press.

Monalisa M. Mullins

V

Values

Like "ego," "unconscious," "wellness," and "role," the word "values" has trickled down from the formal language of the social sciences to become an all but indispensable item in the popular lexicon of folk psychology. "Value" means worth, and it is in this broad sense that one speaks of such things as artistic value, cash value, and land value. The pluralized "values" as it is used in ordinary language, however, typically refers to ethical or moral values: an ensemble of principles, standards, or fundamental beliefs that inform a person or a society's conception of a meaningful, flourishing, or well-lived human life and what constitutes proper self-regard and treatment of others.

Five features of the use of "values" in this everyday use may be observed. First, values are generally regarded as being inherited from one generation to the next; values transmission, it is thought, occurs primarily during childhood and is mediated by the family or the broader cultural milieu (e.g., "I got my values from my parents"). People are not, therefore, entirely free to choose their values. To the extent one's values are contingent upon a set of historically unique circumstances, values are unique to the individuals or cultures that possess them. This might be one reason why values are, second, held to be central to identity. Values are not just as important as a personal narrative, the identification of social roles, and a sense of community membership in the construction of a mature self-conception. People, in fact, commonly interpret their roles and their collective identity and structure their life narratives through the lens of their perceived values (for example, "I chose to become a doctor and to sacrifice a fulfilling family life because I value helping those who are most in need" or "What it means to be Canadian is to value peace, order, and good government"). Although it is openly acknowledged that the content of one's values is largely a matter of chance and circumstance and that it is the values that a person or culture ascribes to that make it unique, values are nevertheless commonly considered to be, third, universalist. That is to say, the set of basically true ideas that individuals and cultures tend to perceive their values as depicting apply not just to themselves but to all human beings, including those who do not share those values. Because of this, values can be a point of pride, but they can also be a source of conflict and, as the long history of European colonialism attests, can be appealed to as a sinister pretext for the domination of one community by another in the name of the dominated group's own good. That values are inherited does not, furthermore, prevent them from being, fourth, susceptible to revision. In light of rational reflection, life experiences, or self-discovery, or by some other means, values can change. Values transformation in this psychological sense is the stuff of literature. More particularly, the literary device of dynamic character development wherein the events of a story elicit seemingly inevitable changes in a protagonist's character trades on values' commutative nature. Fifth and finally, values are dispositional. Values, like moral judgments, are action guiding. They do not just describe inert cognitive states but have a practical implication: the belief that stealing is wrong, say, ordinarily entails the belief that one should not steal. Values, however, are distinguishable from moral judgments in that, while values inform discrete action choices, they are also supposed to be able to account for and predict long-term and relatively stable patterns of evaluative response and action.

The notion that moral education should be concerned with promoting a set of collective values is both perennially attractive and yet fraught with problems. In liberal democracies, disagreement on important moral questions is accepted as a social reality, and space is made for the pursuit of a wide range of sometimes controversial conceptions of the good life. Here, an articulated set of core values, adopted and promoted by schools with confidence and authority, might seem apt to function as a counterweight to the individualism and social disunity to which liberal democracies are notoriously inclined and help to create a sense of collective belonging and common purpose. Against the notion that society's values can be meaningfully codified and passed on to the next generation in a straightforward didactic way, two considerations recur. The first is that the proposal is based on the false assumption that people disagree about fundamental values. On the contrary, it is claimed, people are remarkably of one mind as regards what is most important and meaningful in life, at least when such core values are stated in very broad, general, and abstract terms. What divides them, rather, is the question of the precise interpretation and application of those values in particular circumstances. To illustrate, the matter is not, of course, that, say, Catholic Christians oppose legalized abortion, whereas liberal humanists are in support of it because Catholic Christians value life and liberal humanists do not. The two moral camps just have completely different conceptions of what it means to value life in the case of abortion. The second objection is that even if there were widespread agreement on questions of interpretation and application, community values would still be a questionable basis for moral education. Of course, merely being endorsed by a community does not *ipso facto* make a set of values correct. This being the case, moral education conceived of as the promotion of a set of common values seems to fix itself on the horns of a dilemma. If young people are encouraged to stand outside society's values system and to criticize it, then collective values lose much of their force as a vehicle of moral certainty and social cohesion. However, if young people are taught that society's values system is beyond reproach, then one is at risk of stifling their capacity for moral reflection and promoting a set of values that might under closer scrutiny and further experience turn out to be mistaken.

Further Reading: Talbot, M., & Tate, N. (1997). Shared values in a pluralistic society. In R. Smith & P. Standish (Eds.), *Teaching right and wrong* (pp. 1–14). Stoke-on-Trent: Trentham Books. Warnock, M. (1996). Moral values. In J.M. Halstead & M. Taylor (Eds.), *Values in* *education and education in values* (pp. 45–53). London: Falmer. Wringe, C. (2006). *Moral education: Beyond the teaching of right and wrong.* Dordrecht: Springer.

Bruce Maxwell

Values Clarification

Historically embedded in and influenced by the human potential and affective educational movement of the late 1960s, Values Clarification (VC) is claimed first as a theory of valuation and second as a means by which individuals come to a deeper understanding of the values they espouse. Drawing on John Dewey's conceptualization of value, Louis Raths is credited with providing for VC's theoretical justification based on his own work with children's thinking and empowerment. Other major proponents include Sidney Simon, Howard Kirschenbaum, Merrill Harmin, and Leland Howe. Goodman (1976) cites four essential readings that give an adequate understanding of the development of the field. In *Values and Teaching: Working with Values in the Classroom* (1966), Raths, Harmin, and Simon provide the basic foundation that "gave birth to the field." The second book, *Values Clarification: A Handbook of Practical Strategies for Teachers and Students* (1972), was acclaimed as the "most useful collection of values-clarification strategies yet published." Written as a response to growing criticism of the initial *Values and Teaching,* in *Values Clarification,* Simon, Howe, and Kirschenbaum offer 79 specific process strategies designed to engage elementary through adult populations whereby all become "value-able individuals." Further refinement for integrating VC with classroom content is found next in Harmin, Kirschenbaum, and Simon's *Clarifying Values through Subject Matter* (1973), written "for the teacher who likes the value-clarification approach, but wonders where to fit it in." The fourth work, *Readings in Values Clarification* (1973) with Kirschenbaum and Simon, is a "comprehensive collection of thought-provoking readings" that, in part, "draws on the expertise of others involved in values education (including Kohlberg, Rogers, and Rokeach)." Ironically, both Kohlberg and Rokeach became two of the most forceful critics of the VC approach.

The theoretical grounding within each of these works is not aimed at the content of one's values but rather at the process used to arrive at a value position. VC theory rejects any direct inculcation or transmission of preexisting adult values to the young. There is no ultimate authority, no correct values.

VC initially experienced rapid growth and strong popularity. Kirschenbaum, in *Advanced Value Clarification* (1977), indicates some 12 books on VC have been published with a combined circulation of 1,000,000 copies and over 500,000 copies of *Values Clarification: A Handbook of Strategies for Teachers and Students* having been sold. Additionally, by 1978, a network of over 100 trainers had conducted workshops attended by more than 200,000 teachers, counselors, and helping professionals (Kurtz, 1978). Practitioners were attracted by VCs simple implementation techniques and engaging, fun characteristics. It motivated students, it was intriguing, and "it made classrooms come alive." VC also assumed a position of mediating relevance whereby connections between subject matter material and student lives could be made. An additional benefit was its supposed value neutrality. Educators could declare themselves free from inculcating morality and thus not be accused of foisting their own values upon students.

Criticism of VC has been equally strong in that it:

1. Confuses philosophically by claiming value neutrality within a process that in itself meets its own criteria of value and thus is self-contradictory.
2. Makes no distinction between values of trivia and values of social consequence, thereby avoiding moral deliberation and dialogue.
3. Leads to the superficial and highly individualistic moral relativism.
4. Misreads Dewey's theory of value, which rejects individual value neutrality in favor of community and social benefit.
5. Emphasizes process at the expense of outcomes that may lead to moral quandaries. For example, what is one to do when a clarified value denies the Holocaust?

By the 1990s VC had declined in popularity. While direct cause is impossible to establish, its influence waned perhaps due to the decline of the humanistic education movement of which it was a major player and the subsequent rise of the "nation at risk" mentality. The criticisms also seem to have had a strong impact with particular reference to the expanding fields of cognitive moral development and character education.

There has not been a similar growth pattern in VC. In 1995, Kirshenbaum, Simon, and Howe published *Values Clarification: A Practical, Action-Directed Workbook* as a "new and revised edition" of the 1972 *Values Clarification: A Handbook*. However, this later work is essentially the same as the original with only minor changes.

Should VC be classified as moral education, or if not, what is its role? Clearly, it has focused attention on the relationship between values and education. Its motivating characteristics should not be ignored but used only as a starting point from which substantive moral deliberation can occur. VC can be adjunctive, but it is hardly sufficient as the means for moral education.

Further Reading: Goodman, J. (1976). Values clarification: A review of major books. In J. Pfeiffer & J. Jones (Eds.), *The 1976 annual handbook for group facilitators* (pp. 274–79). La Jolla, CA: University Associates. Harmin, M., Kirschenbaum, H., & Simon, S. (1973). *Clarifying values through subject matter: Applications for the classroom.* Minneapolis, MN: Winston. Kirschenbaum, H. (1977). *Advanced values clarification.* La Jolla, CA: University Associates. Kirschenbaum, H., & Simon, S. (1973). *Readings in values clarification.* Minneapolis, MN: Winston. Kirschenbaum, H., Simon, S., & Howe, L. (1995). *Values clarification.* New York: Warner. Kurtz, P. (1978, November/December). Moral education and secular humanism. *The Humanist, 38,* 17. Raths, L., Harmin, M., & Simon, S. (1966). *Values and teaching: Working with values in the classroom.* Columbus, OH: Merrill. Simon, S., Howe, L., & Kirschenbaum, H. (1972). *Values clarification: A handbook of practical strategies for teachers and students.* New York: Hart.

Tom Wilson

Values Education

A person could hardly claim to be educated who had no understanding of the fundamental values of the society in which he or she lived, who was ignorant of the diversity of values that exist in the world, or who was unaware of the way that values (whether acknowledged or simply taken for granted) influence personal and political decision making. The processes by which schools and other institutions make children aware of the importance of values in human society are sometimes known collectively as "values education." The term is a comparatively new one, more popular in Australia, the Far East, and the United Kingdom than in the United States. Nevertheless, its general meaning is clear and its usage is growing both in popular discourse and in academic writing. In the United

Kingdom the Values Education Council was established in 1995, and in Australia values education is a growing area of academic research and development since the publication of the *National Framework for Values Education in Australian Schools* in 2005.

Two factors in particular have contributed to an increasing awareness of the importance of values education in recent years. The first is a recognition of the role that schools have in responding to the growing cultural diversity (and hence diversity of values) within all Western societies. Schools are responsible for upholding core human values and the shared values of society and encouraging children to develop a commitment to these. At the same time they have a responsibility to encourage respect for distinctive personal and community values that are not shared by society at large, so long as these are not in conflict with the public interest.

The second factor is a recognition that at a time of heightened concern about young people's values schools are uniquely placed to exert a positive influence on the continuing development of their values. This influence may be seen in three often overlapping but not always compatible ways. First, while recognizing that values education always begins in the home, schools can fill in the gaps in children's understanding of values and take that understanding further. Second, in upholding the shared values of society, especially where these have emerged through open, democratic debate, schools can help to counterbalance any extreme opinions and values that children may have picked up elsewhere. Third, and perhaps most important, schools can help children to make sense of the diversity of values they encounter in everyday life, so that through critical reflection children can begin to shape, construct, and develop their own values. Critical reflection in this sense involves sifting, evaluation, synthesizing, appraising, and judging, and, while this is a lifelong process, schools are uniquely placed to begin to develop these essential skills through values education.

Although the central goals of values education are clear, there is less agreement over what precisely the term covers. For some, it is virtually synonymous with moral education. For others, there are different types of values (including intellectual, aesthetic, or spiritual values) and values that relate to different departments of life (political, economic, health-related, or environmental values) or worldviews (liberal, Islamic, or democratic values), and values education is potentially concerned with all of these, even if moral values remain central. For some, values education may be an umbrella term that includes all major approaches to moral education, including character education, values clarification, moral reasoning, and caring. For others, it may be a distinctive approach to moral education, differing from character education because of its strong emphasis on critical reflection and on public social, political, and economic values, differing from values clarification because it is prepared to promote society's shared values explicitly, and differing from moral reasoning because value-based decision making is seen as involving much more than rational reflection and debate.

Values education may be explicit and overt or implicit and covert. Implicit values education occurs through many school practices, such as seating arrangements, disciplinary procedures, praise and blame, insistence on neatness and accuracy, putting one's hand up, queuing, and learning to wait one's turn. Children may learn—consciously or unconsciously—from all of these practices. But if values are simply picked up by children ("caught rather than taught"), this may be a haphazard process with uncertain outcomes. On the other hand, when values education is part of the overt curriculum, other questions arise: Should schools ever encourage children to challenge the values of the home? Whose values should schools teach? Can schools teach values that apply only within certain cultures or traditions? Should schools teach both public and private values? Can religion ever provide a justifiable foundation for values education in the common school? Values education is rarely a subject on the curriculum, since most subjects contribute to it, but it has been particularly linked to two subjects in particular—religious education and citizenship education/civic education.

Values education is a small but growing area of educational research. Major topics include: how children learn values; the contribution of school subjects to values education; children's values and the way these harmonize or clash with the values taught in schools; comparative approaches to values education; and values education in the hidden curriculum.

Further Reading: Australian Department of Education, Science and Training. (2005). *National framework for values education in Australian schools.* Canberra: Author. Cheng, R.H.M., Lee, J.C.K., & Lo, L.N.K. (Eds.). (2006). *Values education for citizens in the new century.* Hong Kong: Chinese University Press. Halstead, J.M., & Taylor, M.J. (Eds.). (1996). *Values in education and education in values.* London: Falmer Press. Taylor, M.J. (Ed.). (1994). *Values education in Europe: A comparative overview of a survey of 26 countries in 1993.* Slough: NFER/CIDREE/UNESCO.

J. Mark Halstead

Veil of Ignorance

Statues of "Lady Justice" in many Western nations show a powerful robed woman holding a weighing scale, with a blindfold over her eyes. This is to symbolize that the law does not discriminate against citizens who are poor versus rich, Black or Hispanic (versus Caucasian), or female versus male. Neutrality or equal treatment is portrayed as a kind of blindness to biasing differences among people.

Here lies the basis of the veil of ignorance, a conceptual device designed to decrease bias in our judgment and ensure neutrality. It works this magic by depriving our deliberations of biasing information. Or it rules out the use of such information in the process by which we reach conclusions. The "veil" was made prominent in Western ethical and legal history by the philosopher Immanuel Kant. More recently it was used in John Rawls's (1972) classic theory of justice to create a negotiation arrangement in which people create a fair, democratic contract with each other, not rigging the outcome to favor some groups or individuals arbitrarily.

Even in childhood many of us find this image of justice unsettling. We expect those who are judging the fairness of someone's case to be knowledgeable, indeed wise in their judgments. We expect them to use all the life experience and information at their command. We choose judges and legislators on this very basis, wishing them to be of a somewhat advanced age so that their experience will be as broad and extensive as possible. To think of them blindfolded and ignorant when rendering decisions is a political nightmare. It is one thing to be blind to bias, after all, but quite another to be blinded in order to avoid bias.

Here we face the main problem—the inherent problem—with any veil-of-ignorance approach. Critics make much of it. Even as the logic of decision making under uncertainty develops, it cannot compensate for this basic flaw in the veil's design. Neutrality at the expense of knowledge is simply not a good trade.

Not that there is not a psychological basis for this approach, crucial to education. Some prejudices are evoked at subliminal levels of consciousness. Primitive portions of the brain likely play a crucial part. (This is one reason why acting out of social prejudice, to the detriment of a victim, is often termed a hate crime.) Thus, if we allow someone to have information that is likely to be prejudicial, then simply exposing them to it can skew their thinking. No effort to avoid the influence of this knowledge, through reflective self-criticism—no amount of judge's instructions to a jury to "ignore the previous remark"—can offset the prejudicial damage done. In fact, many of us find such instructions laughable, if not counterproductive—akin to the direction "Do not think of pink elephants," which often causes people to do so.

Education can help here by creating prejudice-safe environments for students. This is especially so when students are first forming certain opinions or engaging in crucial classroom negotiations with classmates. It can also help students foresee the types of information sources they may wish to stay away from.

In small doses the planned ignorance approach to nonbias is helpful. Teachers are often surprised by the results of evaluating classroom work without knowing the names of its authors. A teacher's expectations are high that certain students who participate excellently in class will write extensive, high-quality papers. This often is not so. And the tendency to grade via these expectations, the tendency toward self-fulfilling prophecy, is effectively quashed by anonymity. The reverse expectations are predictable regarding students who seem in a daze in class. Their papers often show the opposite, exposing a mind that was at work the whole time and hyperattentive behind those seemingly dead eyes. Fairer assessment results from self-imposed ignorance here.

In many school systems social prejudices have created self-fulfilling preferences that lead to the undergrading of racial minorities, women, and children with working class backgrounds, speech patterns, and dress. More children of socially refined, white-collar, or professional backgrounds appear smarter to socialized eyes. Kant adopted the veil of ignorance to ensure equal treatment of people overall. Thus, at least in social application, the veil of ignorance should be designed to offset these kinds of prejudices and their detrimental prophecies.

The problem is that in just those situations where we must guard most against bias—where biasing influences are most numerous and powerful—the greatest amount of ignorance must be imposed, and that most reduces the insightfulness and reliability of judgment involved. Often, because these decisions fight social prejudice, these are the most ethically important decisions we must make. And we least wish to be casting about in the dark on such decisions.

Uncertainty may not even be the worst problem here. The key to ethical decisions is that they are self-determined. They are made on the ethical merits involved and on the merits of the people involved, attempting to render each their just due. The form of imposed ignorance that undermines our prejudices in making judgments often occludes precisely the same information we need to determine merit—to determine justice in a way that respects each individual as he/she deserves. It strikes at individual differences. And just deserts is often based on individual differences in effort, work, productivity rate, or accomplishment.

These meritorious differences are often tied to an individual's motivational proclivities —his/her natural get up and go. An individual's upbringing also affects his/her work effort and self-discipline, other natural talents, social positions or status, and sometimes the resulting educational advantages. Hosts of social and productive accidents come into play as well—even reflective accidents where an individual happens on an opportunity that he/she then seizes, moving in a fortunate social direction. Some of these influences seem unfairly distributed in society or any life, while others seem simply accidental. And, while it is clear that a robust sense of justice wishes to avoid letting injustices figure into otherwise fair decisions, it is unclear to what degree they should compensate for accident. Human justice, social justice, is not quite the same as cosmic justice, which may compensate for the indifference of nature or fate toward our systems of ethics.

Conflicts over the role justice should play here, relative to arbitrary or accidental factors, pits traditional religious ethics against more secular ethics. It also pits moral and ideological liberals against conservatives or libertarians regarding what the veil of ignorance should cover. A version of this conflict defined the popular Rawls-Nozick dispute, which has important implications for moral education. Lessons from this dispute, applied to the illustration of fair grading above, provide final illumination into the veil's features here.

Rawls argued that the most potentially or demonstrably talented members of our socio-economy should be allowed larger shares of wealth. Strict equality of wealth was most just, but it might not be unjust for people to allow certain inequalities. But such chosen inequality had to be viewed as a fair exception. And it was fair only if larger shares were accorded as necessary incentives to the most productive aimed at boosting economic production and overall social benefit. But this trade of equal welfare for higher quality welfare had to be approved of, because of advantage of the poor—or those whose status would be most reduced by the inequality.

Rawls acknowledged that on the face of it, this "Difference Principle exception would suffer from a fatal flaw of Utilitarian ethics." That is, it would basically use the more talented or productive members of society as a means to benefit the least—thinking good ends could justify intolerable means. Adam Smith was a noted utilitarian, and his view of capitalism promoted this ethic of using some for the benefit of all.

By contrast, Rawls's view of justice (shared by his critic Nozick) is that we could not use anyone in this way—that doing so was the mark of disrespect for persons. And the Kantian ethic of respecting persons as equally self-determining individuals was sacrosanct for justice. Even those at the bottom rung of a society could not legitimately choose to lower their status in order to up their wealth by using (exploiting) those who would be given the incentives in this way.

But Rawls argued that what was really being used here was not the moral essence of the person—our free choice. It was instead the contingent natural talents and their support by socialization that certain individuals were blessed with good fortune that was being harnessed by society for overall social benefit and help of the needy, and that this good fortune was not deserved by those who possessed it in the first place, nor could it be called part of their personhood. (We could lose these talents or fall behind in educational benefits and still be the same basic person, worthy of respect.)

Nozick argued that to split an individual's identity in this way—separating out his/her natural talents—was itself disrespectful. Doing this allowed society to reach inside his/her psychology, the very personal traits of his/her personal being, treating him/her as a commodity or natural resource. Personal talents should not be regarded in the same way as minerals or timber. The veil of ignorance should not rule out information about people's talents and social legacy. These are morally relevant, not arbitrary or biasing factors.

At least on Kantian grounds, Nozick seems simply wrong here. Kant's view of what was to be respected in people was essentialistic—it dealt with the necessary features of personhood that defined who we were, not contingent features like our degrees of talent or motivation, much less our social legacy. Rawls wished only to treat the expressions or productive results of these traits as resources in any case, not the traits themselves. (This is how he believed we should regard traits as social resources.) And he noted that what makes the traits positive, what makes them talents versus liabilities, is the value people happen to place on their expression or products, based often on mere whims. One group's valuable shaman is another's disadvantaged epileptic. There is no inherent value or goodness to most talents in the way virtues often have inherent value.

Noting above, then, how the veil of ignorance was meant to ensure equality by nullifying social prejudices hardly gets at its depth. The veil was to hide information about any features that were not part of our core identity as persons—indeed as moral persons. And this was so whether or not they were different among us, more and less, better or worse. These were not to count not only because of the inequalities they could create but because they were not part of that personal essence in us that was considered equal by definition—our personhood.

Anyone with personhood—not by degree of, but categorically—is equal as a person. Simply not being an animal or thing, but a person of any sort, makes one equal. This is so regardless of good qualities or character to any degree and bad ones as well. Even if we all grew our hair and fingernails equally long, this information is not to figure into how we treated each other at all. Much less could it figure as a basis for preference should someone's hair or fingernails start growing longer (perhaps through a person's choice to take somewhat dangerous, growth-producing drugs or through the extraordinary paranormal exertion of meditative concentration).

Now let us trace the practical implications of this theoretical debate. Suppose we define the veil of ignorance, and of morally relevant versus biasing features in this Rawlsian way. How should we construct a fair grade for our students, or determine fair treatment of each relative to each other? Should we try to compensate or at least neutralize the effects of their backgrounds, social advantages, and disadvantages? (Do some of our kids have a library of books in their homes, with parents reading at night as role models, or do they spend much of their evening being physically or psychologically abused in some way?) If some kids have mild attention deficit disorder, and others a high natural propensity toward concentration, should we compensate for this in determining how much and how well they learn, relative to these advantages and obstacles, which are outside their control?

In college, students come to class with very different high school backgrounds and with very different IQs. Some work extra jobs in between taking classes, and others use that time to study or for parent-paid extra tutoring. Some students have taken college courses that cover some of the material in the present course. Others never took a course of the sort. Would it be fair to let these influences determine much of their grades by just grading the quality of their resulting work? Or should we try to ferret out merely how much effort they seem to have put into this particular course, and what they have learned at the end, relative to what they knew when they started? Can we possibly estimate amount of effort or work relative to accomplishment, given our current measures of learning?

These are difficult ethical issues. But now imagine trying to handle them by making ourselves ignorant about all these background conditions. Just what we need to know would be ruled out. We can be helped, as most supporters of the veil of ignorance advocate, by being informed about general facts, general trends, while having particular pieces of information hidden from us. This could capture some of the disadvantages that students with certain racial backgrounds might have suffered, especially if we are in a dangerous urban or extremely rural environment. These general features can tell us that females in the class may have some disadvantages relative to males regarding class participation or taking initiative in class debates.

But such general information often will be completely inaccurate in individual cases. And some general information contradicts it—such as the fact that poverty often requires some children to develop high motivation just to survive—street savvy and street hustle. And so some poor Blacks or Hispanics in urban areas may have an advantage in some respects.

Imagine the alternative ignorance approach of trying to impose a learning and testing framework that made ignorance a watchword for nonbias. Imagine, that is, designing the class so that students could find no way to use their prior advantages to do well in the course. This is fairer to some students in some respects, as a measure of their actual learning. But this measure then misleadingly conveys to them and the world that they have certain overall levels of ability—ability that transfers into qualifications that likely predict their (job) performance upon graduation. This is highly unlikely to be the case. How much they learn in a particular course is unlikely to correlate with how much they know in that area of study.

Here, as elsewhere, it is often because our sense of morality and justice is asked to do too many jobs that trying to rule out injustice and its requisites in blanket fashion goes wrong. Justice measures merit, and also somehow unsystematically "balances" the importance of effort, work hours, productivity rate, and final accomplishment in doing so, then distributes "rewards" for that contribution in a system that distributes far more than rewards. That is, socioeconomic justice is trying to ensure equality of opportunity, the mitigation of undeserved and to some extent recklessly self-engendered deprivation, the encouragement of greater productivity, industry, and trade, the promotion of general or widespread welfare, and so forth.

A well-designed veil should be able to blind us selectively as well as in turn to different considerations at different times when making certain sets of these calculations. It should then restore the same information it has filtered out, for other required tasks.

Further Reading: Kohlberg, L. (1973). The claim to moral adequacy of a highest stage of moral. *Journal of Philosophy, 70,* 630–646. Rawls, J. (1972). *A theory of justice.* Oxford: Clarendon Press.

Bill Puka

Vice

Generally speaking, virtues are excellences of character and intelligence, qualities that typically enable one to achieve a good human life, and vices are their opposites. They are not all or none but matters of degree.

On Aristotle's account of the virtues and vices of character, virtues are dispositions to act in appropriate ways, and vices are dispositions to err on the side of excess or deficiency. For instance, a courageous person dares to risk in an appropriate manner and for good purposes. A cowardly person dares too little, and a rash person too much, relative to what is at stake.

As vice has been understood in the Aristotelian tradition, there is a difference between acting from a vice and doing something wrong. One acts from a vice only when the action is in character. Someone may steal, for instance, shoplifting once as a teenager, acting in a way that is out of character. One such incident does not make one a thieving person.

On the other hand, one may have a disposition to act badly without doing so for some period of time because of an absence of the conditions that set the context for the characteristic action. An obsequious person may refrain from excessive fawning and flattery, and yet have the tendency to fawn and flatter, or, at the other extreme, a cantankerous person may have a tendency to be crabby and bad tempered in certain circumstances, but not be so, the two just not finding themselves in those circumstances. Or the absence of flattery or crabbiness on some occasion may simply be out of character.

A bad or wrongful act may be bad in two ways: by violating a standard of moral conduct or by falling short of an ethical ideal. In the former, one falls below a minimum standard of conduct required for the very possibility of achieving a good human life. In the latter, one falls short of an ideal though perhaps well above the minimum. The difference is sometimes a matter of degree and knowing where to draw the line. In other cases, there is an explicit, publicly stated minimum standard, such as the civil law.

By extension, vice may be exhibited either in a tendency to violate minimum standards of conduct or in a tendency to fall short of an ideal though well above the minimum with respect to that ideal. Patience with one's children or one's rivals at work, for instance, can sometimes require holding one's anger, or not even getting angry, in circumstances in which many might get upset. If one is easily angered, or at the other extreme is never angered, one may violate minimum standards of sociability or parenting. On the other hand, one may typically fall short of an ideal patience, where one would get angry in the proper amount in appropriate circumstances, and yet still exhibit more patience than may be normal for most others.

In this sense, we might say that there are degrees of vice just as there are degrees of perfection. One might be more or less licentious and self-indulgent, say, in matters of food, drink, and sexual activity, or might be insensible to the proper pleasures of food, drink, and sex, without being fatally or very harmfully so in either case. That is, one may tend to fall more or less short of the ideal of moderation and temperance, where one would tend to experience just the right desire for pleasures, at the right time, in the right amount.

There is no need to suppose, therefore, that vice and virtue are all or none. There are degrees, relative to an ethical ideal, above a minimum we think of as the requirement of morality. A person who possesses many virtues may meaningfully think of his/her tendency to enjoy and partake in dessert more than would be ideal as a vice, in the context of his/her other attributes, even if it is a relatively minor one.

How does vice become characteristic? "Getting into the habit," or "habituation," according to the traditional account, is caused by repetitive action that makes a certain type of conduct routine or automatic in certain circumstances. For instance, using a turn signal, or pressing the clutch before pressing the brake in a standard transmission automobile, becomes automatic, even unconscious, after repeated trials, in the circumstances in which one approaches a turn or recognizes the need to brake. Similarly, vainly claiming more honor than one is due, or with undue humility refusing honor when it is appropriate, can become characteristic—and unreflective and automatic—through repetition, according to the traditional account. The metaphors for this process are various, from carving a groove in one's character to establishing a sociocognitive schema or a complex pattern of neuron firing.

Further Reading: Foot, P. (1978). *Virtues and vices and other essays in moral philosophy.* Oxford: Blackwell. Lapsley, D. K., & Narvaez, D. (2006). Character education. In W. Damon & R. Lerner

(Series Eds.) & A. Renninger & I. Siegel (Vol. Eds.), *Handbook of child psychology: Vol. 4* (pp. 248–96). New York: Wiley. MacIntyre, A. (2007). *After virtue.* Notre Dame, IN: University of Notre Dame Press. McKinnon, C. (1999). *Character, virtue theories, and the vices.* Toronto: Broadview Press.

Don Collins Reed

Violence

Violence is a behavior leading to the harm and injury of a victim. Violence can be arbitrary, automatic, and conditioned. Violence may also grow out of calculations of self-interest with the purpose of inflicting specific harm on one or more individuals. Moral development is defined as the formation of a system for making decisions about what is right and wrong. Implied in this discussion is the notion that individuals vary, in comparison and over time, in their ability to reason and make appropriate judgments and decisions involving abstract concepts like fairness and justice. Definitions of morality can also overlap with definitions of violence in situations such as terrorism. Jenkins (1980) argues the label "terrorism" implies that a moral judgment has been made about an act of violence.

In terms of development, aggression is most often studied as a precursor to violence. Age of onset, severity, and persistence of aggression in childhood plays an important role in determining levels of future violence. Research indicates violence and victimization significantly increases in the second decade of life, peaking in late adolescence, and drops sharply during the early twenties. A similar pattern is found in other countries (Home Office, 2004), and it is believed that delinquent and sometimes violent lifestyles are left behind as adult responsibilities and roles develop. Not all youth "age out," however, and a significant number engage in higher levels of violence throughout adulthood. Moffitt (1993) refers to this group as "life-course persistent" and argues their behavior originates early and is exacerbated by high risk social environments and fewer opportunities to learn prosocial skills. Indeed, Kohlberg (1969) recognized the importance of reaching these aggressive children early via moral education and found the presentation and resolution of moral dilemmas in something like a discussion group context could advance moral reasoning (Blatt & Kohlberg, 1975).

While it is recognized that violence is mostly a young person's activity, there are important individual, biological, family, and neighborhood factors predictive of violence. According to the Youth Risk Behavior Surveillance System Survey, African Americans and Hispanics engage in physical fights at a higher rate than Whites, and males are twice as likely as females to have been in a physical fight in the previous year (Eaton, Kann, Kinchen, et al., 2006) though these gender differences are less pronounced when it comes to relational violence and females are more likely to kill a family member (Flannery, Hussey, Biebelhausen, & Wester, 2003; see Ellickson & McGuigan, 2000, for a review of early individual level predictors of adolescent violence).

Biological risk factors have also been identified. Most notably is the consistent finding that antisocial and violent people have lower resting heart rates (Raine, 1993). Other individual and biological factors include impulsivity, low IQ, and low school attainment. Farrington (2006) states that these factors are linked to deficits in the executive functions of the brain including concentration, reasoning, sequences of behavior, self-monitoring, and self-awareness of behavior. This is particularly concerning because morality, social conventions, and psychological knowledge formulate from differentiating social experiences and interactions (Smetana & Turiel, 2003).

Family factors and processes predictive of aggression and later violence as an adult include having antisocial parents, parents convicted of crime, poor parental supervision, harsh and punitive discipline including child abuse and neglect, and low socioeconomic status (Farrington, 2006). Research also suggests environmental factors at the neighborhood and cultural levels are predictive of violence. For example, living in a disadvantaged, high crime, high poverty, and disorganized neighborhood increases levels of violence (Shaw & McKay, 1969) but considerable debate exists on the direct and indirect effects of these factors on aggression and violence on individuals and families (Gottfredson, McNeil, & Gottfredson, 1991).

In sum, research suggests approaches that target social-cognitive processes such as moral reasoning and shifting normative beliefs about aggression can reduce aggression and violence (Blasi, 1980), but the multicomponent programs that also take into account family processes and the social ecology seem to hold the most promise (Henggeler, Melton, & Smith, 1992).

Further Reading: Eaton, D.K., Kann, L., Kinchen, S., Ross, J., Hawkins, J., Harris, W.A., et al. (2006). Youth risk behavior surveillance—United States, 2005. *Morbidity and Mortality Weekly Report, 55*(ss–05), 1–108. Farrington, D.P. (2007). Origins of violent behavior over the lifespan. In D.J. Flannery, A.T. Vaszonyi, & I. Waldman (Eds.), *The Cambridge handbook of violent behavior.* London: Cambridge University Press. Moffitt, T.E. (1993). Adolescence-limited and life-course-persistent antisocial behavior: A developmental taxonomy. *Psychological Review, 100,* 674–701.

Bibliography: Blasi, A. (1980). Bridging moral cognition and moral action: A critical review of the literature. *Psychological Bulletin, 88,* 1–45. Blatt, M., & Kohlberg, L. (1975). The effects of classroom moral discussion upon children's level of moral judgment. *Journal of Moral Education, 4,* 129–61. Eaton, D.K., Kann, L., Kinchen, S., Ross, J., Hawkins, J., Harris, W.A., et al. (2006). Youth risk behavior surveillance—United States, 2005. *Morbidity and Mortality Weekly Report, 55*(ss–05), 1–108. Ellickson, P., & McGuigan, K.A. (2000). Early predictors of adolescent violence. *American Journal of Public Health, 90*(4), 566–72. Farrington, D.P. (2007). Origins of violent behavior over the lifespan. In D.J. Flannery, A.T. Vaszonyi, & I. Waldman (Eds.), *The Cambridge handbook of violent behavior.* London: Cambridge University Press. Flannery, D.J., Hussey, D., Biebelhausen, L., & Wester, K. (2003). Crime, delinquency and youth gangs. In G.R. Adams & M.D. Berzonsky, (Eds.), *The Blackwell handbook of adolescence* (pp. 502–22). Oxford: Blackwell. Gottfredson, D.C., McNeil, R.J., & Gottfredson, G.D. (1991). Social area influences on delinquency: A multilevel analysis. *Journal of Research in Crime and Delinquency, 28,* 197–226. Henggeler, S., Melton, G., & Smith, L. (1992). Family preservation using multisystemic therapy: An effective alternative to incarcerating serious juvenile offenders. *Journal of Consulting Clinical Psychology, 60,* 953–61. Home Office. (2004). *Criminal statistics: England and Wales, 2003.* London: The Stationery Office. Jenkins, B.M. (1980). *The study of terrorism: Definitional problems.* P–6563. Santa Monica, CA: RAND Corporation. Moffitt, T.E. (1993). Adolescence-limited and life-course-persistent antisocial behavior: A developmental taxonomy. *Psychological Review, 100,* 674–701. Kohlberg, L. (1969). Stage and sequence: The cognitive-developmental approach to socialization. In D.A. Goslin (Ed.), *Handbook of socialization theory and research* (pp. 347–480). Chicago: Rand McNally. Raine, A. (1993). *The psychopathology of crime: Criminal behavior as a clinical disorder.* San Diego, CA: Academic Press. Shaw, C.R., & McKay, H.D. (1969). *Juvenile delinquency and urban areas* (Rev. ed.). Chicago: University of Chicago Press. Smetana, J.G., & Turiel, E. (2003). Moral development during adolescence. In G.R. Adams & M.D. Berzornsky (Eds.), *Blackwell handbook of adolescence* (pp. 247–68). Malden, MA: Blackwell Publishing Ltd.

Chris R. Stormann and Daniel J. Flannery

Virtue Ethics

Virtue ethics is a particular approach to understanding moral dispositions that is usually traced—though not exclusively—to the influence of Aristotle. One way to appreciate the distinctive theoretical character of virtue ethics is via a familiar distinction between so-called deontic and aretaic accounts of moral agency. Basically, deontic accounts are largely concerned with understanding the moral rightness or otherwise of prescriptions (the term "deontic" is derived from the Greek for duty) and with identifying the objective rational principles upon which these might be based. Kantian and other so-called deontological theories that attempt to ground morally right action in certain allegedly self-justifying universal prescriptions (such as the categorical imperative) represent one type of deontic account. Utilitarian and other so-called consequentialist theories that seek to measure the moral correctness of actions in terms of their beneficent outcomes represent another kind of deontic perspective.

However, as the term (from the Greek *arête* for virtue or excellence) suggests, interest in the aretaic dimension of agency focuses less on the objective rationality of actions and more on that wider range of action properties captured in descriptions of actions as noble, spiteful, well-meaning, admirable, dishonorable, vicious, reluctant, and so on. Indeed, in so far as such "aretaic" action descriptions refer as much to the psychological sources as to the overt expressions of agency, aretaic accounts generally attend no less to the characters, intentions, motives, and other "inner" states of agents than to the rectitude of their actions. Virtue ethics can be regarded as (for the most part) a variety of aretaic ethics that is not just interested in understanding virtues as one important class of moral character traits, but that also attempts to explain the moral status of action by reference to its sources in character. In short, for most mainstream virtue ethicists (some theoretical complications aside), any and all understanding of moral conduct and association needs to start with attention to moral character traits as properties of agents. Indeed, this approach is perhaps most succinctly captured in the answer that key figures in the mainstream virtue ethical tradition have been inclined to give to the basic ethical question of what a good action is: that a morally good or virtuous action is the kind of action that a virtuous agent would perform.

As already noted, Aristotle is normally acknowledged as the classical authority and source of mainstream virtue ethics, although St. Thomas Aquinas—whose ethical views are much shaped by Aristotle—is also usually cited as another seminal figure. However, the twentieth century revival of virtue ethics is often traced to the publication of Elizabeth Anscombe's 1958 essay "Modern moral philosophy." Although Anscombe did not herself write much specifically on the virtues, she immediately inspired the revival of a new virtue-focused moral naturalism of the 1960s and 1970s and may be credited with promoting wider analytical interest in the topic. Since Anscombe, interest in virtue ethics has escalated, the virtue ethical approach is commonly regarded as offering a viable alternative to its main ethical rivals, and there is now a very extensive literature in the field in which different approaches to virtue ethics are apparent.

We may conclude by distinguishing five contemporary varieties of virtue ethics. First, in Anscombe's wake, one tradition of virtue ethics begins with the 1960s and 1970s "neo-naturalists" and seems to have been continued in the more recent work of Rosalind Hursthouse: on this view, virtues are natural human dispositions conducive to objectively determinable goals of human flourishing. Second, the sociocultural virtue ethics of Alasdair MacIntyre rejects such naturalism in favor of a more "historicist" understanding of virtues as conditioned by "rival" if not incommensurable cultural traditions. Third, the "moral realist" virtue ethics of John McDowell resists the inclination to ground virtue and/or virtuous action in objective criteria of any "external" (natural or cultural) kinds. This view holds (in a way that may link it to the Platonically inspired moral realism of Iris Murdoch) that virtue is essentially a matter of the development of capacities to perceive the world (morally) rightly that also lie beyond the grasp of the nonvirtuous. Fourth, Michael Slote's agent-based ethics identifies virtue with certain intrinsically valuable states of benevolence and caring that are regarded as admirable in their own right (and therefore again without reference to any "external" criteria). Fifth, the more recent "pluralist" virtue ethics of Christine Swanton rejects the general idea—in the light of the diversity of virtuous fields of concern—that virtues need to be given any unitary justification. In drawing as much upon such philosophers as Hume and Nietzsche as Aristotle, moreover, Slote, Swanton, and others have sought the "coming of age" of modern virtue ethics as a broader field of normative concern.

Further Reading: Carr, D., & Steutel, J. (1999). *Virtue ethics and moral education.* London: Routledge.

David Carr

Virtue Theory

Until well into the twentieth century, much if not most ethical theory seems to have been concerned with moral epistemology, with the analysis of such key terms of ordinary moral usage as "good" and "ought" and with questions of the rational basis of "right" moral conduct. It is arguable, however, that the history of Western ethics takes off with a normative (Socratic) question about how one ought to live—to which most early Greek philosophers seem largely agreed in replying that one should live a life of (moral) virtue. The word "virtue" is itself directly derived from the Latin *virtus,* which is usually taken to be a more or less faithful rendition of the Greek *arete* meaning (moral or other) "excellence." However, despite some Socratic or Platonic inclination to identify virtue with knowledge of the good, possession of virtue or the virtues would seem to be a matter of more than (what would be ordinarily meant by) such knowledge. On the face of it, since someone could know what is morally right or good without being virtuous or even be virtuous without any explicit knowledge or understanding of the good, virtue is more than just mere knowledge. In short, the cultivation of virtue would appear to be a matter of explicit commitment to what is morally good or admirable, and to be as much if not more a matter of the cultivation of moral dispositions as of knowledge and understanding.

In ethical theory, the topic of virtue is normally taken to fall within the domain of moral psychology and to be concerned with the study of those qualities of human personality, character, and conduct that conduce to positive moral commitment and behavior. That said, it should be appreciated that these general concerns of virtue theory are wider than those of what has come to be known as "virtue ethics." Virtue ethics presents a more particular approach to the understanding of virtue, usually associated with the ethics of Aristotle and his modern moral heirs, which regards the characters of agents as having logical priority with respect to any evaluation of the moral status of their agency. Indeed, some versions of virtue ethics hold that we can have no grasp of right action apart from an appreciation of good or virtuous moral character: that, precisely, good or right actions are best understood as the sort of actions that an agent of virtuous character would perform.

It should be clear, all the same, that other approaches to understanding virtuous character might seek to explain moral character by establishing first what sorts of actions it would be appropriate for a virtuous agent to perform. In fact, although such influential modern ethical theories as Kantianism and utilitarianism have often been sharply contrasted with virtue ethics, they have been far from unmindful of questions of moral motivation in general or of the notion of virtue in particular, despite seeking to understand virtuous character in just such a more "deontic" way. Thus, for example, on Kant's highly developed account of virtue, virtues as empirically conditioned states or dispositions of character are of considerable if not indispensable executive value for reinforcing the commitment of agents to the requirements of the moral law. However, it is integral to Kant's view that the categorical imperative is not empirically grounded, and that virtuous character is defined as conformity to rational moral prescription rather than the other way about. Likewise, although the naturalist and teleological emphases of utilitarianism relate it more closely to Aristotelian virtue ethics than to Kantian deontology, its general assessment of the moral quality of actions in terms of utility is ultimately no less deontic than the deontology of Kant. In short, even in the case of trait utilitarianisn (arguably the closest utilitarian relative of virtue ethics), what makes an action virtuous is that it is right, and what makes it right is not that it is expressive of virtuous character, but that it has beneficial consequences.

What deontology, utilitarianism, and virtue ethics all have in common, of course, is that they are all ethical perspectives that attempt to find objective rational grounds for virtuous or moral conduct (and, despite a common misconception, mainstream virtue ethics does not necessarily repudiate moral principles). It may, however, be possible to develop accounts of virtue that are more subjectivist or emotivist and that eschew any such moral rationalism. For example, while denying that there can be any rationally objective grounds for moral and other values, David Hume clearly supposed that certain natural human and socially beneficial dispositions could be regarded as virtues. Likewise, some modern forms of care and relationship ethics, which are suspicious of, if not actually hostile to what they perceive as "ethics of principle," have been thought to have distinct affinities with modern varieties of virtue ethics, and might to this extent leave room for the development of "noncognitivist" (and nonvirtue ethical) concepts of virtue.

Further Reading: Carr, D., & Steutel, J. (1999). *Virtue ethics and moral education.* London: Routledge.

David Carr

W

Watson, Marilyn Sheehan

Marilyn Watson is the principal architect of the Child Development Project (CDP), one of the most theoretically coherent, comprehensive, and rigorously evaluated school-based approaches to promoting prosocial development in the United States. Born and raised in Connecticut, Watson earned her B.A. in philosophy from Connecticut College in 1959. While doing graduate work in philosophy at Cornell University, she became deeply interested in evolutionary theory, in part because of her husband John's research on evolutionary mechanisms in infant development. John also introduced her to Bowlby's seminal work on attachment, which was to play a central role in Watson's emerging perspective on the influence of schooling on sociomoral development. She subsequently abandoned work on her philosophy dissertation and enrolled in the Graduate School of Education at the University of California, Berkeley, where she studied developmental psychology and constructivist approaches to education and received her doctorate in 1975.

While at Berkeley, Watson began integrating theory and research on attachment and family socialization with the constructivist theories of Jean Piaget and Lev Vygotsky, and applying this perspective to understanding how teachers and schools influence students' sociomoral development. She joined the education faculty of Mills College in 1977 and began putting her theoretical views into practice as Head Teacher and, subsequently, Director of the Children's School. In 1981, she left Mills to work with several other educators and psychologists to develop the educational innovation that eventually became known as CDP, which was the impetus for the founding of the Developmental Studies Center (DSC) of Oakland, California.

Originally a member of the research team, Watson's strong theoretical views and deep understanding of socialization and child development brought much-needed coherence to CDP, and she quickly became the project's Program Director. Her focus on the centrality of relationships to human development, and of the teacher's role as caregiver, moral advocate, and "scaffolder" of students' sociomoral development became the core of CDP's approach to schooling. She was thus at the forefront of the emerging "care" perspective on morality, and CDP was the first systematic application of this perspective to educational practice.

The work of Watson and her colleagues on CDP not only provided strong empirical support for the care perspective in moral education, but CDP's depiction of schools as participatory, democratic communities in many ways paralleled, at the elementary level, the work of the Just Community in high schools. The project's theoretical model and supporting research also informed and contributed to emerging emphases in the field of prevention on promoting resilience and positive youth development, and the view of schools as social contexts that promote (or hinder) students' positive development. At the core of all of this work was Watson's emphasis on attachment and the quality of interpersonal relationships as critical determinants of developmental outcomes.

Watson's unique application of attachment theory to educational practice is most powerfully illustrated in her book (with Laura Ecken), *Learning to Trust* (2003). Here, Watson masterfully presents her theory and research-based approach to classroom management through rich description and insightful analysis of the experiences of one inner-city elementary teacher and her young students as they struggle to create a caring community of learners. This depiction convincingly demonstrates the power of a teacher to help even the most challenging students to learn not only how to succeed in school but how to be good people as well.

Watson's ideas and work on the Child Development Project have been widely disseminated through her scholarly publications and extensive work with teachers and teacher educators. Including *Learning to Trust*, she has co-authored three books, and published over 40 journal articles and book chapters. In addition to working directly with hundreds of practicing teachers, Watson also has worked extensively with preservice teachers and teacher educators, initially in conjunction with U.C. Berkeley's Developmental Teacher Education Program and subsequently as director of DSC's Preservice Initiative, which for five years provided summer institutes for education faculty from around the United States to infuse CDP principles and practices into teacher preparation programs.

Watson retired from DSC in 2000, but continues to work with educators, publish, and conduct research. She recently completed a follow-up study of students described in *Learning to Trust*, currently in high school, which provides further evidence of how caring and trusting relationships with teachers can dramatically improve the lives of disadvantaged children. Watson is one of the most original and insightful thinkers in moral education and school reform. Her work has not only contributed greatly to the scholarly arenas of theory and research but has directly improved the lives of countless educators and their students.

Further Reading: Watson, M., & Battistich, V. (2006). Building and sustaining caring communities. In C. Evertson & C. Weinstein (Eds.), *Handbook of classroom management: Research, practice, and contemporary issues* (pp. 253–79). Mahwah, NJ: Lawrence Erlbaum and Associates. Watson, M., & Ecken, L. (2003). *Learning to trust: Transforming difficult elementary classrooms through developmental discipline.* San Francisco: Jossey-Bass. Watson, M., Solomon, D., Battistich, V., Schaps, E., & Solomon, J. (1989). The child development project: Combining traditional and developmental approaches to values education. In L. Nucci (Ed.), *Moral development and character education: A dialogue* (pp. 51–92). Berkeley, CA: McCutchan.

Victor Battistich

Wellness

Wellness is typically referred to as the opposite of sickness and pertains to the balanced development of three categories of needs: personal, relational, and collective. Personal needs are health, having purpose and meaning, spirituality, opportunities for growth, autonomy, and so forth. In addition, wellness from an individual viewpoint is to develop healthy psychological perspectives, emotions, physical shape, and behavioral decisions in life.

The ability to meet personal needs is inherently united with the fulfillment of collective needs such as equal access to quality health care and education, economic opportunities, and environmental protection. Without societal programs and opportunities in place, many personal needs would be difficult to pursue or meet successfully. Because we are social beings, relational needs are important to consider and practice. Healthy relationships are fundamental components to one's psychological and emotional well-being yet require work to maintain. Two strategies for developing positive relationships are diversity appreciation and democratic participation. Respecting diversity of opinion and allowing for others to share their opinions promote a level of mutual consideration that is paramount to healthy relationships. Mutual consideration, however, does not mean mutual agreement. Persons can seek to understand one another, thereby showing respect, without the expectation that agreement will follow. Conversing with this attitude is fundamental to respectful and democratic relationships.

Finding balance in the three sets of needs presents a challenge to individuals and communities. There seems to be a natural inclination for personal needs to be the first priority, sometimes at the expense of forgoing community progress. Prilleltensky (2000) identified several implications to having an imbalance between personal and collective needs. Societies that encourage personal needs tend to neglect or minimize activity that ensures justice, equality, and fairness for all the citizens of the society. On the other hand, societies that promote community equality may run the risk of encouraging autonomy and individual needs of the community members.

What constitutes well-being is often predicated on one's subjective experience, expectations, and desires. Desires are often grounded in cultural expectations such as consumerism and individual accomplishment and are filtered through a level of influence experienced on a daily basis, namely, parents, schools, churches, and work settings. The wellness structure can be viewed as a pyramid with the larger economic and cultural needs at the base followed by the needs at the community and family level. The peak of the wellness pyramid is reserved for individual needs. By viewing the wellness structure in this manner, one can see that levels of need do not sit in isolation. They influence and are influenced by one another and therefore are important to consider.

Wellness decisions at all levels are not immune from having moral overtones. Ideas of what is good/bad, healthy/unhealthy, or productive/nonproductive influence decision makers and outcomes. Discussing decisions to be made in the context of wellness is, in fact, a move toward wellness. This approach extends beyond thoughts to activities, emotions, and relationships.

Personal wellness, often labeled as subjective well-being (Diener, 2000), is simply an individual's evaluation of the quality of his/her life from a cognitive and affective position. Wellness is related to having a higher positive affect and view that life is good. Individuals who view their life pessimistically will in turn be more prone to have negative emotions toward life experiences. The notion of happiness has become a popular idea along with the emergence of the positive psychology movement. Having positive emotions in turn leads to optimistic thoughts and the ability to be flexible and resilient with others. Becoming socially connected and participating in activities of interest are strong predictors of life satisfaction. Overall, wellness is about the choices we make and taking responsibility for those choices.

Wellness is a multifaceted concept that embraces an individual and societal responsibility. As such, discussions of wellness that benefit all levels are logical beginnings to wellness decisions.

Further Reading: Conrad, P. (1994). Wellness as virture: Morality and the pursuit of health. *Culture, Medicine, and Psychiatry, 18,* 385–401. Diener, E. (2000). Subjective well-being: The science of happiness and a proposal for a national index. *American Psychologist, 55,* 34–43. Keating, D., & Hertzman, C. (Eds.). (2000). *Developmental health and the wealth of nations.* New York: Guilford. Marmot, M., & Wilkinson, R. (Eds.). (1999). *Social determinants of health.* New York: Oxford University Press. Prilleltensky, I., & Nelson, G. (2000). Promoting child and family wellness: Priorities for psychological and social interventions. *Journal of Community and Applied Social Psychology, 10,* 85–105.

Scott E. Hall

Wilson, John

John B. Wilson (1928–2003) was a pioneer of the philosophy of moral education, acknowledged in the United Kingdom and across the world. He directed our attention to moral concepts and particularly to what would count as a morally educated person.

From his childhood experiences in the family, as a public school scholar, and later at Oxford, Wilson learned to attend to language and the skills of discussion and debate. A Christian religious framework, dialectic, conceptual, and linguistic analysis, and classical scholarship permeated his writing and teaching style. He often drew on his experience as a public school teacher and housemaster. Over his 40-year career he held posts and was visiting professor at several universities in the United Kingdom and North America, notably at the University of Oxford, Department of Educational Studies (Lecturer and Tutor, 1972–1994; Senior Research Associate, 1994–2003). While director of the Farmington Research Unit on Moral Education, Oxford (1965–1972), Wilson became the founding editor of a short-lived journal, *Moral Education* (1970–1971). He was a founder of its successor, the *Journal of Moral Education,* remaining an active Editorial Board member for 30 years. He was also co-editor of the *Oxford Review of Education* for nearly 20 years from 1979.

The scope of Wilson's prolific publications—over 40 books and 200 articles—included: sex education, religious education, educational research, philosophy of education, and the emotions, especially love. He wrote consistently about the nature of morality and the form and content of moral education, particularly concepts such as neutrality, discipline, and authority.

At the Farmington Research Unit Wilson and his interdisciplinary team (1967) made seminal contributions to contemporary Western thinking about moral education. He delineated a set of components to characterize the morally educated person. Wilson always started with conceptual questions, such as "What is to count as morality and moral education?" arguing that only then could progress in moral education be made. In his view, morality has distinctive concepts, aims, and logically necessary procedures. His conceptual analysis of morality required having the concept of "person" and being interpersonal—sharing with others and attachment of the self to others. He was also centrally concerned about the psychology of moral behavior, moral motivation, reason, emotion, will, alertness, determination, and courage. For Wilson, having appropriate feelings was as important as knowing what one should do and doing it for the right reasons.

Wilson tended to emphasize the form of moral education, with method and content as logically interconnected. This required the direct teaching of how to think morally, the establishment of ground rules, and an initiation into a critical liberal tradition. Practical methods of moral education needed to be connected consistently and coherently across teaching and learning contexts. This involved respecting and drawing out the distinctiveness of moral thinking, systematically and explicitly, possibly in a separate curriculum focus, and always in an appropriate social context. Wilson argued that specifying the aims and the components of moral education should enable moral education to be assessed. He attempted to show that the morally educated person will hold the right moral views, do the right thing morally, and also follow the right procedures of moral reasoning. However, 25 years later Wilson (1996) still claimed that, both conceptually and empirically, the "first steps" in "education in morality" had yet to be taken due to "psychological resistance." Contributors to the *Journal of Moral Education* special issue (Halstead & McLaughlin, 2000) show the complexities of Wilson's thinking, its subtle changes over time, and its strengths and weaknesses.

Wilson's distinctive style, in writing, lecturing, and teaching, was analytic, closely nuanced, illustrative, and provocative. He was cogent, questioning, and challenging on a huge range of philosophical and educational topics, and enjoyed fierce discussion and repartee. In later years, what he said and how he said it did not fit well with feminism, antiracism, and postmodernism, and some were irritated by his seeming lack of political correctness. As if in perpetual debate with himself, trying to work out his own thoughts and attitudes, Wilson was always thought provoking; he made his audience, readers, and students think again and argue for their own viewpoints. He demonstrated, through example in practice, a process-oriented Socratic style of philosophy of moral education. The volume, sustained quality, and consistency of Wilson's work are an unrivaled professional legacy to the philosophy of moral education. He remained controversial, never gaining full acceptance in philosophical or moral education circles, though he was inspirational to many students and colleagues around the world.

Further Reading: Halstead, J.M., & McLaughlin, T.H. (Eds.). (2000). Philosophy and moral education: The contribution of John Wilson [Special issue]. *Journal of Moral Education, 29*(3). Wilson, J.B. (1981). Motivation and methodology in moral education. *Journal of Moral Education, 10*(2), 85–94. Wilson, J.B. (1996). First steps in moral education. *Journal of Moral Education, 25* (1), 85–91. Wilson, J.B., Williams, N., & Sugarman, B. (1967). *Introduction to moral education.* Harmondsworth, UK: Penguin.

Monica J. Taylor

Wynne, Edward Aloysius, Jr.

Edward Aloysius Wynne Jr. (November 8, 1928–August 15, 1999), longtime professor of education at the University of Illinois, Chicago, was one of the most influential contributors to the resurgence of character education in the second half of the twentieth century, organizer and editor of a national statement on character education (1984), and the first recipient of the Lifetime Achievement Award in Character Education from the Character Education Partnership (1998). Wynne was a prolific writer, publishing 10 books and over 120 articles, monographs, and book chapters in an academic career that spanned 30 years.

Born in Brooklyn, New York, Wynne graduated from Brooklyn Technical High School and attended Brooklyn College. He received his legal education and the L.L.D. from Brooklyn Law School (1954) and practiced law till 1968, representing, among others, the National Labor Relations Board and the Textile Workers Union of America. In 1964 he began a four-year tenure with the federal government working for the Office of Economic Opportunity, the U.S. Office of Education and Follow Through. He received the Ed.D. in Educational Policy Studies in 1970 from the University of California, Berkeley, and subsequently moved to his academic position in Chicago where he remained until his death.

Wynne described himself as "a sociologist essentially concerned with how young people move toward wholesome adulthood" (1991, p. 276). His continuing interest in the power of education was propelled by two sources of information: the statistics on trends in youth disorder that demonstrated a dramatic rise among American youth in rates of illegitimate births, drug and alcohol abuse, and death by both suicide and homicide; and, for-character policies implemented by societies throughout history that he believed could stem the rise of those symptoms (1976).

Like Emile Durkheim before him, Wynne studied the statistical trends for insights into problems of youth alienation and how they were detrimental to American democracy. He believed the survival of any society depended on its ability to create successive cohorts committed to the continuity of its major traditions. The increasing trends in youth disorder he charted raised serious questions about the social stability and cohesion of the United States, justifying immediate attention regarding remediation in preparing children who would become resilient and diligent enough to perpetuate and enhance America's participatory, democratic society.

He saw as a remedy a constant, intense, constructive level of interaction between adult role models and youth. Wynne believed that youth alienation was the cause of many of the symptoms of the disorders he had studied, that America's youth were increasingly perceived as being needed only as consumers, and that society had removed from them any serious responsibilities. By contrast, he believed that people with simple, immediate obligations to others (for example, mothers, residents of farming communities, dedicated teachers) tended to choose social alternatives when faced with life's difficulties because of those obligations. They rejected, for example, suicide because such behavior betrayed those immediate commitments. The solution, according to Wynne, involved creating more structured and intense responsibilities for youth, the creation of age-appropriate, but significant, responsibilities for them to feel socially integrated and respected.

Wynne's subsequent career was an explication of these foundational constructs. From 1979 to 1981 he published monthly an interdisciplinary newsletter, *Character,* focusing on policies related to youth character and written by prominent academics from a variety of fields. On Thanksgiving Day 1984 he released the booklet, *Developing Character: Transmitting Knowledge,* that called attention to his analysis of the youth disorder data and to specific steps to be taken to deal with deficiencies in American schools' character policies. Twenty-seven prominent scholars, educators, and policy makers signed the statement. This was followed by the lead article in the December 1985/January 1986 issue of *Educational Leadership* in which he designated the transmission of moral values to school students as "the great tradition in education" (p. 4). He described that tradition in a historical context and defined it as transmitting such principles as good habits of conduct, day-to-day reinforcement of moral issues such as telling the truth, and suppression of wrong conduct. The journal's editor introduced Wynne by writing that he was "a persistent pioneer in the character education movement" (Brandt, 1985, p. 3).

Wynne also addressed practical, sometimes controversial, recommendations ensuring the promise of the "great tradition." He wrote extensively about school actions and called for both high academic and character standards. He was an early proponent of group (i.e., cooperative) learning, community service projects, high-level adult-to-student interactions, and meaningful school ceremonies (Wynne & Walberg, 1985/1986). In 1993 he and professor Kevin Ryan published *Reclaiming Our Schools,* a handbook for moral instruction in elementary and secondary schools. The book began with a checklist of observable acts and policies that readers could use to estimate the quality of their school's focus on character, academics, and discipline, followed by chapters giving context and specific suggestions on teaching for character and impacting the moral climate of the school. That same year he published *A Year in the Life of an Excellent Elementary School,* a book of photographs and interpretative narrative of one school over one year. In addition to his academic research, Wynne organized and managed the For Character School Recognition Program in the Chicago area, the first effort to recognize and award excellent schools of character.

He is survived by his wife Judith and three children.

Further Reading: Wynne, E.A. (1985, December/1986, January). The great tradition in education: Transmitting moral values. *Educational Leadership, 43*(4), 4–9. Wynne, E.A. (1995). The moral dimension of teaching. In A.C. Ornstein (Ed.), *Teaching: Theory into practice* (pp. 190–202). Boston: Allyn and Bacon. Wynne, E.A., & Ryan, K. (1993). *Reclaiming our schools: A handbook on teaching character, academics, and discipline.* New York: Macmillan.

References: Brandt, R. (1985, December/1986, January). Character and critical thinking. *Educational Leadership, 43*(4), 3. Wynne, E.A. (1976). Adolescent alienation and youth policy. *Teachers College Record, 78*(1), 23–40. Wynne, E.A. (Ed.). (1982). *Character policy: An emerging issue.* Washington, D.C.: University Press of America. Wynne, E.A. (Ed.). (1984). *Developing character: Transmitting knowledge.* Posen, IL: ARL. Wynne, E.A. (1985, December/1986, January). The great tradition in education: Transmitting moral values. *Educational Leadership, 43*(4), 4–9. Wynne, E. A. (1991). Edward A. Wynne. In J.S. Benninga (Ed.), *Moral, character, and civic education in the elementary school* (p. 279). New York: Teachers College. Wynne, E.A. (1993). *A year in the life of an excellent elementary school: Lessons derived from success.* Lancaster, PA: Tecnomic. Wynne, E.A., & Ryan, K. (1993). *Reclaiming our schools: A handbook on teaching character, academics, and discipline.* New York: Macmillan. Wynne, E.A., & Walberg, H.J. (1985, December/1986, January). The complementary goals of character development and academic excellence. *Educational Leadership 43*(4), 15–18.

Jacques S. Benninga

Bibliography

Aristotle. (1985). *Nicomachean ethics*. (T. Irwin, Trans.). Indianapolis, IN: Hackett.

Bebeau, M., Rest, J. R., & Narvaez, D. (1999). Beyond the promise: A framework for research in moral education. *Educational Researcher, 28*(4), 18–26.

Benninga, J. S. (Ed.). (1991). *Moral character and civic education in the elementary school*. New York: Teachers College Press.

Bergman, R. (2002). Why be moral? A conceptual model from a developmental psychology. *Human Development, 45,* 104–124.

Berkowitz, M. (1981). A critical appraisal of the educational and psychological perspectives on moral discussion. *Journal of Educational Thought, 15,* 20–33.

Berkowitz, M. W. (2002). The science of character education. In W. Damon (Ed.), *Bringing in a new era in character education* (pp. 43–63). Stanford, CA: Hoover Press.

Berkowitz, M. W., & Grych, J. H. (1999). Fostering goodness: Teaching parents to facilitate children's moral development. *Journal of Moral Education, 27*(3), 371–391.

Blasi, A. (1980). Bridging moral cognition and moral action: A critical review of the literature. *Psychological Bulletin, 88,* 1–45.

Blasi, A. (1983). Moral cognition and moral action: A theoretical perspective. *Developmental Review, 3,* 178–210.

Blatt, M., & Kohlberg, L. (1975). The effects of classroom moral discussion upon children's moral judgment. *Journal of Moral Education, 4,* 129–161.

Bryk, A. S., Lee, V. E., & Holland, P. B. (1993). *Catholic schools and the common good*. Cambridge, MA: Harvard University Press.

Carr, D. (1991). *Educating the virtues: An essay on the philosophical psychology of moral development and education*. London: Routledge.

Carr, D., & Steutel, J. (Eds.). (1999). *Virtue ethics and moral education*. London: Routledge.

Character Education Partnership. (2002). *2002 National schools of character: Practices to adopt and adapt*. Washington, D.C.: Author.

Colby, A., & Damon, W. (1993). *Some do care*. New York: Free Press.

Colby, A., & Kohlberg, L. (1987). *The measurement of moral judgment, Vol. 1: Theoretical foundations and research validation*. New York: Cambridge University.

Damon, W. (1988). *The moral child: Nurturing children's natural moral growth*. New York: Free Press.

Damon, W. (1995). *Greater expectations: Overcoming the culture of indulgence in our homes and schools*. New York: Free Press.

Damon, W. (Ed.). (2002). *Bringing in a new era in character education.* Stanford, CA: Hoover Institution Press.

DeVries, R., & Zan, B. (1994). *Moral classrooms, moral children: Creating a constructivist atmosphere in early education.* New York: Teachers College Press.

Dewey, J. (1966). *Democracy and education.* New York: MacMillan.

Doris, J. (2005). *Lack of character.* Cambridge, UK: Cambridge University Press.

Durkheim, E. (1973). *Moral education: A study in the theory and application of the sociology of education.* New York: Free Press. (Original work published 1925.)

Flanagan, O. (1991). *Varieties of moral personality: Ethics and psychological realism.* Cambridge, MA: Harvard University Press.

Foot, P. (2001). *Natural goodness.* Oxford, UK: Oxford University Press.

Fowler, J.W. (1981). *Stages of faith: The psychology of human development and the quest for meaning.* San Francisco: Harper and Row.

Fowler, J.W. (1984). *Becoming adult, becoming Christian: Adult development and Christian faith.* San Francisco: Harper and Row.

Fowler, J.W. (1987). *Faith development and pastoral care.* Philadelphia: Fortress Press.

Fowler, J.W. (2001). *Faithful change: The personal and public challenges of post-modern life.* Nashville, TN: Abington Press.

Frankfurt, H. (1988). *The importance of what we care about.* New York: Cambridge University Press.

French, P.A., Uehling, T.E., & Wettstein, H. (Eds.). (1988). *Ethical theory: Character and virtue.* Notre Dame, IN: University of Notre Dame Press.

Gilligan, C. (1982). *In a different voice: Psychological theory and women's development.* Cambridge, MA: Harvard University Press.

Goodlad, J. (1992). The moral dimensions of schooling and teacher education. *Journal of Moral Education, 21*(2), 87–98.

Goodman, J.F., & Lesnick, H. (2001). *The moral stake in education: Contested premises and practices.* New York: Longman.

Guttman, A. (1987). *Democratic education.* Princeton, NJ: Princeton University Press.

Hansen, D.T. (1993). From role to person: The moral layeredness of classroom teaching. *American Educational Research Journal, 30,* 651–674.

Hardy, S., & Carlo, G. (2005). Moral identity theory and research: An update with directions for the future. *Human Development, 48,* 232–256.

Hart, D. (2005). The development of moral identity. *Nebraska Symposium on Motivation, 51,* 165–196.

Hart, D., & Fegley, S. (1995). Prosocial behavior and caring in adolescence: Relations to self-understanding and social judgment. *Child Development, 66,* 1346–1359.

Hartshorne, H., & May, M.A. (1928). *Studies in the nature of character: Studies in self-control.* New York: Macmillan.

Hogarth, R.M. (2001). *Educating intuition.* Chicago: University of Chicago Press.

Hunt, T., Joseph, E., & Nuzzi, R. (Eds.). (2004). *Catholic schools still make a difference: Ten years of research 1991–2000.* Washington, D.C.: National Catholic Educational Association.

Hunt, T., & Mullins, M. (2005). *Moral education in America's schools: The continuing challenge.* Greenwich, CT: Information Age.

Hunter, J.D. (2000). *The death of character: Moral education in an age without good or evil.* New York: Basic Books.

Hursthouse, R. (1999). *On virtue ethics.* Oxford, UK: Oxford University Press.

Jackson, P.W., Boostrom, R.E., & Hansen, D.T. (1993). *The moral life of schools.* San Francisco: Jossey-Bass.

Keller, M., & Edelstein, M. (1993). The development of the moral self from childhood to adolescence. In G. Noam & T. Wren (Eds.), *The moral self* (pp. 310–336). Cambridge, MA: MIT Press.

Killen, M., & Smetana, J. (Eds.). (2006). *Handbook of moral development.* Mahwah, NJ: Lawrence Erlbaum.

Kochanska, G. (1993). Toward a synthesis of parental socialization and child temperament in early development of conscience. *Child Development, 64,* 325–347.

Kohlberg, L. (1969). Stage and sequence: The cognitive developmental approach to socialization. In D.A. Goslin (Ed.), *Handbook of socialization theory and research* (pp. 347–380). Chicago: Rand McNally.

Kohlberg, L. (1971). From is to ought: How to commit the naturalistic fallacy and get away with it in the study of moral development. In T. Michel (Ed.), *Cognitive development and epistemology* (pp. 151–235). Cambridge, MA: Harvard University Press.

Kohlberg, L. (1976a). The cognitive-developmental approach to moral education. In D. Purpel & K. Ryan (Eds.), *Moral education...It comes with the territory* (pp. 176–195). Berkeley, CA: Phi Delta Kappa.

Kohlberg, L. (1976b). Moral stages and moralization: The cognitive-developmental approach. In T. Lickona (Ed.). *Moral development and behavior: Theory, research and social issues* (pp. 31–53). New York: Holt, Rinehart, and Winston.

Kohlberg, L. (1981). *Essays on moral development: Vol. 1. The philosophy of moral development.* San Francisco: Harper & Row.

Kohlberg, L. (1984). *Essays on moral development: Vol. 2. The psychology of moral development.* San Francisco: Harper & Row.

Kohlberg, L., & Mayer, R. (1972). Development as the aim of education. *Harvard Educational Review, 42,* 449–496.

Kohn, A. (1997). How not to teach values: A critical look at character education. *Phi Delta Kappan, 78,* 429–439.

Kupperman, J.J. (1991). *Character.* New York: Oxford University Press.

Lapsley, D. (1996). *Moral psychology.* Boulder, CO: Westview.

Lapsley, D. (2005). Moral stage theory. In M. Killen & J. Smetana (Eds.), *Handbook of moral development* (pp. 37–66). Mahwah, NJ: Erlbaum.

Lapsley, D., & Narvaez, D. (Eds.). (2004). *Moral development: Self and identity.* Mahwah, NJ: Erlbaum.

Lapsley, D., & Narvaez, D. (2006). Character education. In A. Renninger, I. Sigel, W. Damon, & R. Lerner (Eds.), *Handbook of child psychology, Vol. 4* (pp. 248–296). New York: Wiley.

Lapsley, D., & Power, F.C. (Eds.). (2005). *Character psychology and character education.* Notre Dame, IN: University of Notre Dame Press.

Leming, J.S. (1993). In search of effective character education. *Educational Leadership, 51*(3), 63–71.

Lickona, T. (1983). *Raising good children: From birth through the teenage years.* New York: Bantam.

Lickona, T. (1991). *Educating for character: How our schools can teach respect and responsibility.* New York: Bantam.

Lickona, T. (2004). *Character matters: How to help our children develop good judgment, integrity, and other essential virtues.* New York: Simon & Schuster.

MacIntyre, A. (1984). *After virtue* (2nd ed.). Notre Dame, IN: University of Notre Dame Press.

Mann, H. (1848). *Twelfth annual report covering the year 1848.* Boston: Wentworth and Dutton, State Printers.

McClellan, B.E. (1999). *Moral education in America: Schools and the shaping of character from colonial times to the present.* New York: Teachers College Press.

McCluskey, N.G. (1958). *Public schools and moral education.* Westport, CT: Greenwood.

McKinnon, C. (1999). *Character, virtue theories, and the vices.* Toronto: Broadview Press.

Meilaender, G. (1984). *The theory and practice of virtue.* Notre Dame, IN: University of Notre Dame Press.

Michaelsen, R.S. (1970). *Piety in the public school.* New York: Macmillan.

Murphy, M.M. (1998). *Character education in America's blue ribbon schools: Best practices for meeting the challenge.* Lancaster, PA: Technomic.

Narvaez, D. (2005a). Integrative ethical education. In M. Killen & J. Smetana (Eds.), *Handbook of moral development* (pp. 703–733). Mahwah, NJ: Erlbaum.

Narvaez, D. (2005b). The neo-Kohlbergian tradition and beyond: Schemas, expertise and character. In G. Carlo & C. Pope-Edwards (Eds.), *Nebraska Symposium on Motivation* (Vol. 51; pp. 119–163) Lincoln: University of Nebraska Press.

Narvaez, D., Gleason, T., Mitchell, C., & Bentley, J. (1999). Moral theme comprehension in children. *Journal of Educational Psychology, 91*(3), 477–487.

Narvaez, D., & Rest, J. (1995). The four components of acting morally. In W. Kurtines & J. Gewirtz (Eds.), *Moral behavior and moral development: An introduction* (pp. 385–400). New York: McGraw-Hill.

Nash, R.J. (1996). *"Real world" ethics: Frameworks for educators and human service professionals.* New York: Teachers College Press.

Nash, R.J. (1997). *Answering the virtuecrats: A moral conversation on character education.* New York: Teachers College Press.

Noddings, N. (2002). *Educating moral people.* New York: Teachers College Press.

Nucci, L. (1982). Conceptual development in the moral and conventional domains: Implications for values education. *Review of Educational Research, 52,* 93–122.

Nucci, L. (Ed.). (1989). *Moral development and character education: A dialogue.* Berkeley, CA: McCutchan.

Nucci, L. (2001). *Education in the moral domain.* Cambridge, UK: Cambridge University Press.

Oakes, J., Quartz, K.H., Ryan, S., & Lipton, M. (2000). *Becoming good American schools: The struggle for civic virtue in education reform.* San Francisco: Jossey Bass.

Oser, F.K., Achtenhagen, F., & Renold, U. (Eds.). (2006). *Competence oriented teacher training: Old research demands and new pathways.* Rotterdam: Sense Publishers.

Oser, F.K., Dick, A., & Patry, J. (Eds.). (1992). *Effective and responsible teaching: The new synthesis.* San Francisco: Jossey-Bass.

Oser, F.K., & Gmünder, P. (1991). *Religious judgment: A developmental approach.* Birmingham, AL: Religious Education Press.

Osmer, R.R., & Schweitzer, F.L. (Eds.). (2003). *Developing a public faith: New directions in practical theology: Essays in honor of James W. Fowler.* St. Louis, MO: Chalice Press.

Osterman, K. (2000). Students' need for belonging in the school community. *Review of Educational Research, 70,* 323–367.

Perry, W.G. (1970). *Forms of intellectual and ethical development in the college years.* New York: Holt, Rinehart, & Winston.

Piaget, J. (1965). *The moral judgment of the child.* New York: Free Press. (Original work published 1932.)

Power, F.C., Higgins, A., & Kohlberg, L. (1989a). The habit of the common life: Building character through democratic community schools. In L. Nucci (Ed.), *Moral development and character education: A dialogue* (pp. 125–144). Berkeley, CA: McCutchan.

Power, F.C., Higgins, A., & Kohlberg, L. (1989b). *Lawrence Kohlberg's approach to moral education.* New York: Columbia University.

Pritchard, I. (1988). Character education: Research prospects and problems. *American Journal of Education, 96,* 469–495.

Raths, L.E., Harmin, M., & Simon, S. (1966). *Values and teaching: Working with values in the classroom* (2nd ed.). Columbus, OH: Charles E. Merrill.

Rest, J. (1979). *Development in judging moral issues.* Minneapolis: University of Minnesota Press.

Rest, J. (1983). Morality. In P. Mussen (Ed.), *Handbook of child psychology: Vol. 3. Cognitive development* (4th ed.; J. Flavel & E. Markman, Vol. Eds., pp. 556–628). New York: Wiley.

Rest, J.R., Narvaez, D., Bebeau, M.J., & Thoma, S.J. (1999). *Postconventional moral thinking: A neo-Kohlbergian approach.* Mahwah, NJ: Praeger.

Ryan, K., & Bohlin, K. E. (1999). *Building character in schools: Practical ways to bring moral instruction to life.* San Francisco: Jossey-Bass.

Ryan, K., & McLean, G. F. (Eds.). (1987). *Character development in schools and beyond.* New York: Praeger.

Ryle, G. (1972). Can virtue be taught? In R. F. Dearden, P. H. Hirst, & R. S. Peters (Eds.), *Education and the development of reason* (pp. 434–447). London: Routledge & Kegan Paul.

Scales, P. C., & Leffert, N. (1999). *Developmental assets: A synthesis of the scientific research on adolescent development.* Minneapolis, MN: Search Institute.

Simon, S., Howe, L., & Kirschenbaum, H. (1972). *Values clarification: A handbook of practical strategies for teachers and students.* New York: Hart.

Solomon, D., Watson, M., Battistich, V., Schaps, E., & Delucchi, K. (1996). Creating classrooms that students experience as communities. *American Journal of Community Psychology, 24,* 719–748.

Strike, K. (1996). The moral responsibilities of educators. In J. Sikula, T. Buttery, & E. Grifton (Eds.), *Handbook of research on teacher education* (2nd ed., pp. 869–882). New York: Macmillan.

Tappan, M. (1998). Moral education in the zone of proximal development. *Journal of Moral Education, 27*(2), 141–160.

Thompson, R. A. (1998). Early sociopersonality development. In W. Damon & N. Eisenberg (Eds.), *Handbook of child psychology: Vol. 3. Social, emotional and personality development* (pp. 25–104). New York: Wiley.

Turiel, E. (1983). *The development of social knowledge: Morality and convention.* Cambridge, UK: Cambridge University Press.

Turiel, E. (1998). The development of morality. In W. Damon (Ed.), *Handbook of child psychology: Vol. 3. Social, emotional and personality development* (5th ed.; pp. 863–932). New York: Wiley.

Turiel, E. (2002). *The culture of morality.* Cambridge, UK: Cambridge University Press.

Veugelers, W., & Oser, F. K. (Eds.). (2003). *Teaching in moral and democratic education.* New York: Peter Lang.

Watson, M. (2003). *Learning to trust: Transforming difficult elementary classrooms through developmental discipline.* San Francisco: Jossey-Bass.

Weissberg, R. P., & O'Brien, M. U. (2004). What works in school-based social and emotional learning programs for positive youth development. *Annals of the American Academy of Political and Social Science, 591,* 86–97.

Wentzel, K. R. (2002). Are effective teachers like good parents? Teaching styles and student adjustment in early adolescence. *Child Development, 73,* 287–301.

Williams, M. M., & Schaps, E. (1999). *Character education: The foundation for teacher education.* Washington, D.C.: Character Education Partnership.

Wynne, E., & Ryan, K. (1997). *Reclaiming our schools. A handbook on teaching character, academics and discipline.* New York: Merrill.

Youniss, J., & Convey, J. J. (Eds.). (2000). *Catholic schools at the crossroads.* New York: Teachers College Press.

Youniss, J., & Yates, M. (1997). *Community service and social responsibility in youth.* Chicago: University of Chicago Press.

Index

*Page numbers appearing in **bold** type refer to main entries.*

About the Editors and Contributors

The Editors

Thomas C. Hunt joined the faculty of Virginia Tech in 1971 after receiving his Ph.D. from the Educational Policy Studies Department at the University of Wisconsin (Madison). He remained at Tech, where he served in a number of leadership positions, receiving numerous awards in teaching, research, and service, until 1996, when he joined the faculty at the University of Dayton. At Dayton, Hunt received the Alumni Award for Scholarship in 2002 and has edited or authored ten books and has served as editor of *Catholic Education: A Journal of Inquiry and Practice,* the only refereed journal on Catholic schools in the nation, since 1998.

Daniel K. Lapsley is a Professor in the Department of Psychology and Fellow of the Institute for Educational Initiatives at the University of Notre Dame. He is the author or editor of five books and numerous articles and chapters on moral psychology, moral and character education, and adolescent development. He is on the Executive Board of the Association for Moral Education and serves on the editorial boards of the *Journal of Educational Psychology, Journal of Early Adolescence,* and *The Teacher Educator.*

Darcia Narvaez is an Associate Professor of Psychology and directs the Center for Ethical Education at the University of Notre Dame. She is co-author or co-editor of *Moral Development in the Professions: Psychology and Applied Ethics* (1994), and the award-winning books, *Postconventional Moral Thinking* (1999) and *Moral Development, Self and Identity* (2004). She has also published many journal articles and book chapters on moral development, character education, and moral information processing. She has published various curriculum materials and was the leader of the design team for the Minnesota Community Voices and Character Education Project, which she reported on at a White House Conference on Community and Character.

Ronald J. Nuzzi, a Catholic priest of the Diocese of Youngstown, Ohio, is the Director of the Alliance for Catholic Education's (ACE) Leadership Program at the University of

Notre Dame. Nuzzi has served as editor of *Catholic Education: A Journal of Inquiry & Practice* and has authored and edited major research publications in the field of Catholic education including: *Catholic Schools in the United States: An Encyclopedia, Handbook of Research on Catholic Education, Catholic Schools Still Make A Difference,* and *Handbook of Research on Catholic Higher Education.* The ACE program at Notre Dame is the single largest source for Catholic school teachers and administrators in the United States.

F. Clark Power is a Professor in the Program of Liberal Studies, a Concurrent Professor in the Department of Psychology, Associate Director of the Center for Ethical Education, and a member of the graduate faculty of the Alliance for Catholic Education. He received his Ed.D. in Human Development from Harvard University and his M.A. in Systematic Theology from the Washington Theological Union. He is a past President of the Association for Moral Education and a recipient of the Kuhmerker Award for his contributions to the field of moral education. His publications focus on moral development and education, civic engagement, and religious development. He is a co-author of *The Measurement of Moral Judgment, Vol. II: Standard Issue Scoring Manual; Lawrence Kohlberg's Approach to Moral Education; Self, Ego and Identity: Integrative Approaches; The Challenge of Pluralism: Education, Politics and Values;* and *Character Psychology and Education.*

The Contributors

Carol E. Akai is a doctoral candidate in Developmental Psychology at the University of Notre Dame and an NIH predoctoral fellow. Her research in parenting has concentrated on understanding children's maladaptive developmental trajectories and developing effective intervention programs for at-risk families.

Cheryl Armon is Professor of Human Development at Antioch University Los Angeles.

Mary Louise Arnold is Associate Professor in the Department of Human Development and Applied Psychology at the Ontario Institute for Studies in Education of the University of Toronto. Her research focuses on sociomoral development, with specific interests in moral identity and its role in the mediation of cognition and behavior, adolescents' conceptions of (and commitment to) social justice, value socialization in family and school contexts, and the ethical dimensions of teacher-student relations.

Victor Battistich is currently Associate Professor of Educational Psychology at the University of Missouri–St. Louis. He was a founder and, for over 20 years, principal researcher at the Developmental Studies Center of Oakland, California, the developer of the Child Development Project.

Erin Becker is a graduate student in sport psychology in the School of Kinesiology at the University of Minnesota.

Jacques S. Benninga is Professor of Education at California State University Fresno and director of its Bonner Center for Character Education and Citizenship. His recent work has focused on the relation of character education and academic achievement and on the development of ethical scenarios for professionals in education.

Marvin W. Berkowitz is the Sanford N. McDonnell Professor of Character Education and Co-Director of the Center for Character and Citizenship at the University of Missouri–St. Louis. A developmental psychologist, he specializes in character education and moral development. He is founding co-editor of the *Journal of Research in Character Education*.

Charles Blakeney is Research Associate at the University of Fribourg, Switzerland, studying the recovery of integrity after chronic addiction with a specific focus on resistance to learning from person-environment interaction. He has served for many years as a public policy consultant, including the Federal Office of Public Health in Switzerland and the White House Office of Domestic Policy in the United States.

Ronnie Frankel Blakeney teaches moral misbehavior and cross-cultural communication in the Hochschule für Sozial Arbeit in Switzerland. Her research focuses on discordance in cross-racial moral reasoning, developmental disturbances in adolescence, and processes of value continuity and change in three-generation Swiss families.

Augusto Blasi is Professor Emeritus of Psychology at the University of Massachusetts Boston. Within the field of personality development, his work mainly addressed questions concerning the development of identity, moral development, and the integration of morality in personality.

Tonia Bock is Assistant Professor in the Psychology Department at the University of St. Thomas in St. Paul, Minnesota. Her current research interests include moral theme comprehension, moral identity, and service-learning and moral development.

Karen E. Bohlin is Head of School at the Montrose School in Medfield, Massachusetts, and senior scholar at Boston University's Center for the Advancement of Ethics and Character. Bohlin is author of *Teaching Character Education through Literature: Awakening the Moral Imagination* (2005), *Building Character in Schools* (with Kevin Ryan, 1999), and its companion, *Building Character in Schools Resource Guide* (with Deborah Farmer and Kevin Ryan, 2001). In addition to writing numerous articles and speaking widely on teacher preparation and character education, she has also edited two books: *Great Lives, Vital Lessons* (with Bernice Lerner, 2005) and *Higher Education and Citizenship* (with James Arthur, 2005).

Jay W. Brandenberger is a faculty member at the University of Notre Dame. He directs academic and research initiatives at the Center for Social Concerns, and holds concurrent appointments in Psychology and the Institute for Educational Initiatives. Brandenberger's research focuses on ethical development and social responsibility in the contexts of higher education.

David E. Campbell is the John Cardinal O'Hara, C.S.C. Associate Professor of Political Science at the University of Notre Dame. He is the author of *Why We Vote: How Schools and Communities Shape Our Civic Life*, editor of *A Matter of Faith: Religion in the 2004 Presidential Election*, and co-author of *Democracy at Risk*. He has also published numerous articles in academic journals.

Gustavo Carlo is Professor of Developmental Psychology at the University of Nebraska–Lincoln. His main research interest is in prosocial and moral behaviors in children and adolescents. He is past Associate Editor for the *Journal of Research on Adolescence* and has several publications in distinguished research journals. He co-edited (with Carolyn Pope Edwards) the 51st Nebraska Symposium on Motivation volume on *Moral Development through the Life Span.*

David Carr is Professor of Philosophy of Education in the University of Edinburgh. He is author of *Educating the Virtues* (1991), *Professionalism and Ethics in Teaching* (2000), and *Making Sense of Education* (2003), as well as of many philosophical and educational papers. He is also editor of *Education, Knowledge and Truth* (1998), co-editor (with Jan Steutel) of *Virtue Ethics and Moral Education* (1999), and (with John Haldane) of *Spirituality, Philosophy and Education* (2003).

Danny Cevallos is the founding member of the Law Offices of Daniel L. Cevallos, P.C., in Philadelphia, Pennsylvania. He is a practicing attorney and an adjunct professor of Health Care Law at Drexel University.

James C. Conroy is Professor of Religious and Philosophical Education and Dean of the Faculty of Education at the University of Glasgow. He has taught and researched in the fields of moral education, religious education, and liberalism and education. His most recent monograph is entitled, *Betwixt and Between: The Liminal Imagination, Education and Democracy* (2004).

Alexandra F. Corning is a faculty member in the Department of Psychology at the University of Notre Dame. She publishes in the area of prejudice and discrimination. Her research is aimed at uncovering the social-psychological processes people use in ambiguously discriminatory situations to discern whether or not discrimination has taken place.

Brooke Crawford currently works for the Center for Ethical Education at the University of Notre Dame. A former Division I Lacrosse Coach, Brooke is assisting with the development of the Play Like A Champion Today™ Educational Series, a set of programs designed to educate youth sport coaches and parents and elevate the current climate of youth sports.

Craig A. Cunningham is Associate Professor and Program Director of technology in education at National-Louis University in Chicago. In addition to his interest in instructional technology, Cunningham writes about the history and philosophy of moral education, and is especially interested in ways that "character" is conceived in debates about the public purposes of education.

Matthew L. Davidson is President and Director of the Institute for Excellence & Ethics. He is co-author, with Thomas Lickona, of *Smart & Good Schools: Integrating Excellence & Ethics for Success in School, Work, and Beyond.* Previously he has been on staff at the Center for the 4th & 5th Rs at SUNY Cortland, the Mendelson Center for Sport, Character, and Culture at the University of Notre Dame, the Family Life Development Center at Cornell University, and the Values Program at LeMoyne College.

Maria Rosario T. de Guzman is an Adolescent Development Extension Specialist and Assistant Professor of Child, Youth and Family Studies at the University of Nebraska–Lincoln. Her research examines the socioecological factors that promote prosocial outcomes among youth from various cultural communities. She has conducted research on these issues among youth in Kenya, Brazil, Turkey, the Philippines, and the United States.

Daniel J. Flannery is Professor of Justice Studies and Director of the Institute for the Study and Prevention of Violence at Kent State University. His research interests are in aggression, delinquency, and youth violence with a focus on etiology, on prevention, and on the relationship between violence and mental health. He received his Ph.D. in Developmental and Clinical Child Psychology from The Ohio State University.

Michelle E. Flaum is a Professional Clinical Counselor and Adjunct Professor at the University of Dayton, and is finishing her doctorate in Counselor Education at the University of Cincinnati. She is a Partner in The Highlander Group, LLC, an innovative consulting group specializing in professional skills training and organizational development.

David R. Forman received his Ph.D. in psychology from the University of Iowa. He is currently Canada Research Chair in Human Development, as well as an Assistant Professor at the Centre for Research in Human Development, and in the Department of Psychology at Concordia University in Montreal.

James M. Frabutt is a faculty member in the ACE Leadership Program and a Concurrent Associate Professor of Psychology at the University of Notre Dame. He previously served as Deputy Director of the Center for Youth, Family, and Community Partnerships at the University of North Carolina at Greensboro. His professional interests are action research, juvenile justice, at-risk youth, and university-community partnerships.

Jeremy A. Frimer is a doctoral student in developmental psychology at the University of British Columbia. His research focuses on aspects of personality and identity relevant to issues of moral motivation.

Susana Patino Gonzalez is Professor in the Department of Ethics at the Instituto Tecnológico y de Estudios Superiores de Monterrey. Her research interests include dialogical ethics and moral education.

Joan F. Goodman, Professor of Education at the Graduate School of Education at the University of Pennsylvania, is the co-author (with Penn Law Professor Howard Lesnick) of *The Moral Stake in Education: Contested Premises and Practices* (2001) and *Moral Education: A Teacher-Centered Approach* (2004). With Usha Balamore, a kindergarten teacher turned principal, she co-authored *Teaching Goodness: Engaging the Moral and Academic Promise of Young Children* (2003). Recently she has published on the moral issues of discipline and the importance of mission in schools.

Andrew M. Guest is Assistant Professor in the Department of Social and Behavioral Sciences at the University of Portland. His research interests include cultural psychology, children's competence, and the role of recreational activities in development.

Scott E. Hall is a Professional Clinical Counselor and Associate Professor at the University of Dayton. He is a Partner in The Highlander Group, LLC, a counseling and advisory practice focusing on personal, professional, and character development.

J. Mark Halstead is currently Head of the Department of Community and International Education at the University of Huddersfield, United Kingdom, and was for many years Professor of Moral Education at the University of Plymouth. He has contributed widely to the *Journal of Moral Education,* and his publications include *Citizenship and Moral Education* (2006), *Education in Morality* (1999), and *Values in Education and Education in Values* (1996).

Sam A. Hardy is Assistant Professor of Psychology at Brigham Young University. His research focuses on moral personality development and dynamics—primarily in adolescence and young adulthood, with a particular emphasis on understanding the role of identity in moral functioning.

Stuart N. Hart is Deputy Director of the International Institute for Child Rights and Development, Centre for Global Studies, University of Victoria, British Columbia; Founding Director of the Office for the Study of the Psychological Rights of the Child; and Professor Emeritus of the School of Education, Indiana University Purdue University Indianapolis. He is a past president of the International School Psychology Association, the National Association of School Psychologists (USA), and the National Committee for the Rights of the Child (USA). He is a member of the Committees of the Interfaith Council on Ethics Education for Children (Arigatou Foundation and the Global Network of Religions for Children).

Edward T. Hastings is the Director of the Center for Sport, Spirituality and Character Development at Neumann College in Pennsylvania. He received his doctorate from Duquesne University in Formative Spirituality.

Ethan Haymovitz received his A.B. in psychology at Vassar College, his M.S.S.W. in Social Work at Columbia University, and was the recipient of the Ruth L. Kirshstein National Research Service Award from the National Institute of Health. He is a consultant, psychotherapist, and Vice President of the Ninth Street Center in New York City.

Alexandra Henning is a doctoral candidate in the Department of Human Development at the University of Maryland. Her research focuses on the relationship between ethnic identity and social reasoning about intergroup bias.

Patrick L. Hill is a fourth-year graduate student at the University of Notre Dame, Notre Dame, Indiana. His research interests include evaluating measures of explicit and implicit moral cognition, and investigating the processes underlying adolescent risk-taking behaviors.

Nicholas J. Houpt is a Program of Liberal Studies and German double major at the University of Notre Dame. His research interests include ethics, social justice, and the intersections of law and ethics. He plans to pursue further study in the fields of law and philosophy.

Robert W. Howard is Associate Professor at the University of Washington, Tacoma. His research interests include moral education and development, social capital, and education for polity.

Emery Hyslop-Margison is Associate Professor in the Faculty of Education at the University of New Brunswick, Fredericton, Canada. His research interests include work studies, character development, citizenship, and moral education.

Eric Jefferis is Assistant Professor in the Department of Justice Studies at Kent State University, and is also a Research Fellow at the Institute for the Study and Prevention of Violence (ISPV). Jefferis's research interests include the spatiotemporal analysis of crime and the effectiveness of policing strategies and technologies. Prior to joining the ISPV, he was a Social Science Analyst at the National Institute of Justice.

Lene Arnett Jensen is Associate Professor in the Department of Psychology at Clark University. Her work in moral development employs a "cultural-developmental" approach, addressing how morality is both culturally and developmentally situated. Jensen serves as Editor-in-Chief of *New Directions for Child and Adolescent Development.*

Eva Johansson is an Associate Professor of Education in the Department of Education, Childhood Studies, Göteborg University, Sweden. She is engaged in questions on moral learning in early childhood education, including studies on how children experience and develop morality and how teachers approach such issues in their work. Her research also includes studies on quality aspects in preschool as well as on the relation between play and learning.

Peter H. Kahn Jr. is Associate Professor in the Department of Psychology at the University of Washington. He received his Ph.D. from the University of California, Berkeley, in 1988. He is the author of two books with MIT Press: *The Human Relationship with Nature: Development and Culture,* and an edited volume (with S. Kellert) *Children and Nature: Psychological, Sociocultural, and Evolutionary Investigations.*

Dianne L. Kerr is Associate Professor and Program Coordinator of Health Education at Kent State University. Kerr has served as the Executive Editor of the *Journal of American College Health* and Chair of the Board of Associate Editors for the American Journal of Health Education. She was awarded the American School Health Association's Distinguished Service Award in 2005.

Melanie Killen is Professor of Human Development, the Director of the NIH Training Program in Social Development, and the Associate Director for the Center for Children, Relationships, and Culture at the University of Maryland. Killen's research interests are children's and adolescents' social and moral development, peer relationships, awareness of stereotype threat, children's conceptions of gender roles, inclusion and exclusion, intergroup relationships and attitudes, morality, and theory of mind.

Douglas Kirby is a Senior Research Scientist at ETR Associates. For almost 30 years, he has directed statewide or nationwide studies of adolescent sexual behavior, abstinence-only programs, sexuality and HIV education programs, school-based clinics, school condom-availability programs, and youth development programs. He co-authored research on several curricula that significantly reduced unprotected sex, either by delaying sex, reducing the number of partners, increasing condom use, or increasing contraceptive use. He has summarized the effects of programs designed to reduce adolescent sexual risk in more than 100 publications.

Peter Lang is a member of the Institute of Education at the University of Warwick, United Kingdom. He has written about and researched aspects of affective education in the United Kingdom, Europe, and internationally for more than 20 years. He set up the European Affective Education Network and remains its coordinator. He has also run circle time training in a number of countries.

Nicole M. LaVoi is currently the Associate Director of the Tucker Center for Research on Girls & Women in Sports, in the School of Kinesiology at the University of Minnesota, where she also teaches in the graduate sport psychology program. Through her research, she examines the influence of coach and parent behavior on youth psychosocial outcomes.

James M. Lies, C.S.C., is Assistant Professor in the Department of Social and Behavioral Sciences at the University of Portland. His current research focuses on the effectiveness of educational and service-learning interventions on the moral development of adolescents and emerging adults.

Josina Makau is Professor of Philosophy and Communication and Co-Coordinator of the Program in Practical and Professional Ethics at California State University, Monterey Bay. Makau has published widely in the areas of communication ethics, law, and moral reasoning. Her diverse leadership roles within the university and broader community have included service as Dean of Arts and Humanities, Chair of the Regional Media Literacy Alliance, Chair of the National Communication Ethics Commission, and Medical Ethics Advisor.

M. Kyle Matsuba is Assistant Professor of Psychology at the University of Northern British Columbia, Canada. His research incorporates different facets of the moral domain including reasoning, emotions, personality, and identity, and their development. He also studies the antecedents and consequences of prosocial (e.g., volunteering) and antisocial behaviors under different contexts.

Bruce Maxwell is a researcher and lecturer affiliated with the Institute of Educational Studies and the Institute for the Ethics, History and Theory of Medicine at the Westfälische-Wilhelms Universität Münster, Germany. His fields of research are the philosophy of moral education and professional ethics, and he is the author of the forthcoming book, *Professional Ethics Education: Studies in Compassionate Empathy.*

Winnie Mucherah teaches Developmental Psychology at Ball State University in the department of Educational Psychology. Her research interest is in classroom climate and student achievement as well as program evaluation.

Monalisa M. Mullins is currently at the University of Dayton where she lectures for the School of Education and the College of Arts and Sciences. Mullins has been actively involved with community education programs and has served on the Board of Trustees for Dayton's AmeriCorps Program. Her research is primarily focused on the philosophy of education and applied ethics in teacher education programs.

Susan Munro is President of SBM Solutions for Nonprofits, a consulting firm in the Chicago area. Previously she was director of communications and development for the Collaborative for Academic, Social, and Emotional Learning.

Robert J. Nash is an Official University of Vermont Scholar in the Social Sciences and Humanities. He is the author of over 100 articles and book chapters, and eight books, among them such bestsellers as *Answering the Virtuecrats* and *Real World Ethics*. His latest book, to be published in early 2008, is *Igniting the Fire of Conversation: How To Talk about Hot Topics on a College Campus without Getting Burned.*

Alven Neiman is a Professional Specialist in the Department of Philosophy, University of Notre Dame, Notre Dame, Indiana. His main areas of concern are philosophy of education, including spiritual education, and philosophy of religion.

Larry Nucci is Professor of Educational Psychology at the University of Illinois at Chicago where he is also Director of the Office for Studies in Moral Development and Education. He is the author of *Education in the Moral Domain* (2001), and is the Senior Editor of the journal *Human Development.*

Mary Utne O'Brien is Executive Director of CASEL and Research Professor of Psychology and Education at the University of Illinois at Chicago. Her career in behavioral and social sciences has spanned the boundaries of a number of disciplines and research methodologies, but with a consistent focus on issues of social justice.

Tamara B. Pardo is a doctoral student in developmental psychology in the Department of Human Development at Cornell University working with Dr. Ritch C. Savin-Williams. Her current research interests focus on psychosocial adolescent development, particularly identity development, sexual minorities, and gender nonconformity.

Sharon E. Paulson is Professor of Psychology-Educational Psychology at Ball State University. Dr. Paulson is a member of the Developmental Psychology faculty with an expertise in adolescent development. For over 15 years, her research has been focused on the family context, specifically on relations between parenting and adolescent school achievement. More recently, she has published several studies on the impact of family demographics on students' standardized test scores.

John W. Payton is Assistant Research Professor and Senior Research Scientist in the Collaborative for Academic, Social, and Emotional Learning Department (CASEL) at the University of Illinois at Chicago (UIC). In this role, he works on the development of school leadership programs, standards, and assessment tools for social and emotional learning (SEL).

Adán Pérez-Treviño is Lecturer in the Department of Ethics at the Instituto Tecnológico y de Estudios Superiores de Monterrey. His research interests include Spanish ethical approaches and metaphysics.

Ann Marie R. Power is the Director of Undergraduate Studies in the Department of Sociology at the University of Notre Dame. She is also a research fellow in the Center for Ethical Education. Power is a Sociologist of Education, who has published studies in the areas of moral education, service learning, and participation in extracurricular activities.

Bill Puka is Professor of Philosophy, Psychology and Cognitive Science at Rensselaer Polytechnic Institute. His work focuses on ethics, moral reasoning, and democratic process. He founded a character education program, Be Your Own Hero: Careers in Commitment, and a sister-city program in Umuluwe, Nigeria, and was the first APA Fellow in the U.S. Senate. In Washington, and later in the Capital District of New York State, he specialized in employee ownership and economic development tax policy.

Brandy A. Randall is Assistant Professor of Child Development and Family Science at North Dakota State University. Her research is on the development of positive and problem behaviors, including prosocial behaviors.

Don Collins Reed is Professor of Philosophy at Wittenberg University in Springfield, Ohio. His research focuses on the early intellectual debts and insights of Lawrence Kohlberg. Reed also serves on the five-member elected Board of Education of Springfield City Schools.

Alan Reiman is Associate Professor of Curriculum and Instruction at North Carolina State University where he also is the Executive Director of SUCCEED, an innovative university/school partnership that supports studies of new teacher induction and teachers' moral and epistemological development. He is the co-author of *Mentoring and Supervision for Teacher Development* (1998).

Cameron Richardson is a doctoral student studying Developmental Science in the Department of Human Development at the University of Maryland, College Park. He is co-author on a chapter for a book to be edited by John Dovidio and colleagues on prejudice with his thesis advisor, Melanie Killen. Cameron investigates social and moral reasoning, stereotype threat, and intergroup attitudes.

Júlio Rique is Associate Professor in the Department of Psychology at the Federal University of Paraíba, Brazil. He teaches and researches the psychology of interpersonal forgiveness and compassion in criminal justice in a center for studies in social and moral development. Júlio Rique received his Ph.D. from the University of Wisconsin–Madison, United States, doing cross-cultural work on Interpersonal Forgiveness.

Kathleen Roney is Associate Professor in the Department of Elementary, Middle Level, and Literacy Education at the University of North Carolina, Wilmington, where she also serves as program coordinator for the middle grades education undergraduate and graduate programs. In her publications and presentations she focuses on issues related to the middle level education research agenda. Roney is Past President of the Middle Level Education Research Special Interest Group of AERA.

Marilyn Martin Rossmann is Professor Emeritus of Family Education at the University of Minnesota, where her research, teaching, and service focused on parent education programs. Since her 2005 retirement, she has become the Coordinator of the Parent Warmline at the Children's Hospitals and Clinics of Minnesota.

Peter L. Samuelson serves as the Senior Pastor at Emmanuel Lutheran Church in Atlanta, Georgia. He recently completed his Ph.D. in Educational Psychology at Georgia State University. His research interests are in moral development, moral imagination, and empathy.

Ana Laura Santamaría is Lecturer in the Department of Ethics at the Instituto Tecnológico y de Estudios Superiores de Monterrey. Santamaría's research interests include narrative ethics and theatre and literature studies.

Julian Bruno Gonçalves Santos is a psychology student and research assistant in the Center for Studies in Social and Moral Development at the Federal University of Paraíba, João Pessoa, Brazil. His interests are in cognitive development, moral education, and justice.

Marta Sañudo is Professor and Coordinator of the Ethics Doctoral Program at the Instituto Tecnológico y de Estudios Superiores de Monterrey. Sañudo's research interests include business ethics, narrative ethics, modern philosophy, and theology.

Alice C. Schermerhorn is a postdoctoral scholar in the Department of Psychology at the University of Notre Dame. Her research interests involve socioemotional development, particularly in the context of family relationships. Her research focuses on mutual family influence processes over time.

Dawn E. Schrader is Associate Professor of Educational Psychology at Cornell University in the Learning, Teaching and Social Policy program. A graduate of Harvard University and student of the late Lawrence Kohlberg, Schrader conducts research on the relationship between moral development, moral judgment, moral action, and metacognition. Currently her work focuses on social, self and moral psychology of adolescent girls' social and relational aggression, and moral integrity.

Lynn Hickey Schultz is Professor of Psychology at the Massachusetts School of Professional Psychology and an Instructor in Psychology in the Department of Psychiatry at Harvard Medical School.

Merle J. Schwartz serves as Director of Education and Research at the Character Education Partnership, and is a content specialist and lead creator of adult learning formats for CEP *Sourcebook Institutes* and *Seminars*. She directs CEP's professional development offerings, including affiliate development and large-scale district and cross-district regional initiatives, working across the United States and in Canada. Schwartz conducts national institutes and seminars on CEP's *Eleven Principles of Effective Character Education*™, trains CEP trainers, and prepares CEP coaches to do systemic culture-changing work in schools. Schwartz is a published author in the field of character education.

Rachel L. Severson is a doctoral student in Developmental Psychology at the University of Washington. Her research investigates children's social-moral conceptions of natural and computational "others." Her publications have appeared in such journals as *Interaction Studies: Social Behavior and Communication in Biological and Artificial Systems* and *Human-Computer Interaction*.

Eva Skoe is Professor of Psychology, University of Oslo, Norway. She received her Ph.D. in Clinical Psychology from Simon Fraser University, Canada, and has been a visiting scholar at Harvard and Arizona State Universities. Her work on the ethic of care, identity, and gender is widely published.

John Snarey, Professor of Human Development and Ethics at Emory University, uses developmental, cross-cultural, and brain imaging methods to study the psychology of morality. He is also the President of the Association for Moral Education and the co-author of *Race-ing Moral Formation* (2004).

Frank J. Sparzo is Professor of Educational Psychology at Ball State University. He specializes in learning and applied behavior analysis.

Jason M. Stephens is Assistant Professor in the Department of Educational Psychology at the University of Connecticut, where he teaches classes on cognition, motivation, instruction, and research methods. His research interests include moral development, achievement motivation, and academic dishonesty among secondary and postsecondary students.

Chris R. Stormann is Project Director at the Institute for the Study and Prevention of Violence at Kent State University and evaluator for a SAMHSA-CMHS System of Care grant serving multisystem involved youth with serious emotional disturbances in Cleveland, Ohio. He is the co-founder of PeopleThatClick.com, a profiling and business networking site serving entrepreneurs from over 70 countries, and he served as the former Director of Research & Development at a corporate think tank called the Eureka! Ranch. His doctorate is in criminal justice with an emphasis in policing and systems theory.

Mark B. Tappan is Professor of Education and Human Development and Chair of the Education Program at Colby College in Waterville, Maine. His research and teaching interests focus on moral development and moral education, identity development, boys' development and education, risk and resilience in childhood and adolescence, and social justice. He is co-editor (with Martin Packer) of *Narrative and Storytelling: Implications for Understanding Moral Development* (1991) and *Cultural and Critical Perspectives on Human Development* (2001).

Monica J. Taylor has been Editor of the *Journal of Moral Education* for 30 years and is a Research Associate of the Institute of Education, University of London. Although her disciplinary background is in Philosophy, she subsequently had a career in Educational Research, specializing in values, personal and social, religious and citizenship education, and has published widely in these areas. She was a founding member and first president of the Values Education Council of the United Kingdom and a past president of the Association for Moral Education, the first from outside North America, and recently received the Association's Kuhmerker Award.

Stephen J. Thoma is Professor and Program Coordinator of Educational Psychology at The University of Alabama. He is also a member of the Center for the Study of Ethical Development, University of Minnesota. Thoma received his Ph.D. in Educational Psychology from the University of Minnesota.

Juan Gerardo Garza Treviño is the Dean of the Center of Values at the Instituto Tecnnológico y de Estudios Superiores de Monterrey. His research interests include business ethics and discourse ethics.

Paul Warren is Associate Professor of Philosophy at Florida International University. His main areas of interest are social and political philosophy, Marx and recent Marxism, and ancient Greek philosophy. He has published articles in the *Canadian Journal of Philosophy,* the *Journal of Political Philosophy, Clio, Archi fur Rechts- und Sozial Philosophie,* and other scholarly publications.

Marilyn Watson recently retired from the Developmental Studies Center, where she was the Program Director of the Child Development Project), and headed the center's work in preservice education. She is interested in the implications of attachment theory for classroom environments and learning and the role of classroom relationships in children's moral development. Her most recent book, *Learning to Trust: Transforming Difficult Elementary Classrooms Through Developmental Discipline,* documents one inner city teacher's efforts to build a classroom community supportive of all her students' moral as well as intellectual development.

Roger P. Weissberg is Professor of Psychology and Education at the University of Illinois at Chicago. He is also President of the Collaborative for Academic, Social, and Emotional Learning (CASEL), an international organization committed to making evidence-based social, emotional, and academic learning an essential part of preschool through high school education. For the past three decades, Weissberg has trained scholars and practitioners about innovative ways to design, implement, and evaluate family, school, and community interventions.

Tom Wilson currently directs the Paulo Freire Democratic Project in the School of Education, Chapman University, in Orange, California. His current interests include the development of school democratic culture, the relationship among civic and moral education, the work of Paulo Freire, and educational ethics.

Scott Wowra is a social psychologist who studies ethical decision making and behavior. Scott recently edited a special issue for the journal *Ethics and Behavior* on the problem of academic dishonesty in American schools.

Thomas Wren is Professor of Philosophy and Director of the Social Philosophy graduate program at Loyola University Chicago. He has written and edited several books in ethics and moral psychology, including *Agency and Urgency, The Personal Universe, Caring about Morality, The Moral Domain, The Moral Self, Philosophy of Development,* and *Moral Sensibilities and Education* (3 vols.). He is currently finishing a book on the philosophical foundations of multicultural education.